D0955209

"Aaronovitch displays great patience and intellectual curiosity in guiding the reader through a dozen conspiracies . . . *Voodoo Histories* is as concerned with understanding conspiracies as it is with rebutting them, and Aaronovitch's tone throughout is that of a sage psychologist, his method that of the forensic historian . . . Illuminating . . . *Voodoo Histories* is a welcome reminder that the sleep of reason breeds monsters, and an elegant attempt to rouse misguided souls from their slumber."

—*New Statesman*

"A guidebook to prepare readers for that party where they get cornered by someone who wants to tell them about the truth behind 9/11, or discuss any of more than a dozen major conspiracy theories of the last century. Aaronovitch starts each analysis by laying out a theory and discussing how it came about, some of its major advocates, and the seemingly reasonable people who bought it. He then meticulously breaks it down, showing the fantastical leaps of logic necessary, and often discrediting the players involved in lending the ideas authority in the first place."

—*The A.V. Club*

"Gloriously readable . . . Aaronovitch fillets conspiracy theories brilliantly."

—*The Independent*

"Sensible and absorbing . . . A rich and fascinating account, and the unpicking of conspiracy theories themselves is especially instructive—and entertaining, for even though Aaronovitch manages to restrain his exasperation with the confectors of the theories, his wry sense of humor gets the better of him at times, further leavening an already tasty loaf."

—*The Times*

VOODOO HISTORIES

THE ROLE OF THE CONSPIRACY THEORY IN SHAPING MODERN HISTORY

David Aaronovitch

RIVERHEAD BOOKS

New York

RIVERHEAD BOOKS
Published by the Penguin Group
Penguin Group (USA) Inc.
375 Hudson Street, New York, New York 10014, USA
Penguin Group (Canada), 90 Eglinton Avenue East, Suite 700, Toronto, Ontario M4P 2Y3, Canada
(a division of Pearson Penguin Canada Inc.)
Penguin Books Ltd., 80 Strand, London WC2R 0RL, England
Penguin Group Ireland, 25 St. Stephen's Green, Dublin 2, Ireland (a division of Penguin Books Ltd.)
Penguin Group (Australia), 250 Camberwell Road, Camberwell, Victoria 3124, Australia
(a division of Pearson Australia Group Pty. Ltd.)
Penguin Books India Pvt. Ltd., 11 Community Centre, Panchsheel Park, New Delhi—110 017, India
Penguin Group (NZ), 67 Apollo Drive, Rosedale, North Shore 0632, New Zealand
(a division of Pearson New Zealand Ltd.)
Penguin Books (South Africa) (Pty.) Ltd., 24 Sturdee Avenue, Rosebank, Johannesburg 2196,
South Africa

Penguin Books Ltd., Registered Offices: 80 Strand, London WC2R 0RL, England

The publisher does not have any control over and does not assume any responsibility for author or
third-party websites or their content.

First published in Great Britain in 2009 by Jonathan Cape.
First Riverhead hardcover edition: February 2010
First Riverhead trade paperback edition: January 2011
Riverhead trade paperback ISBN: 978-1-59448-498-8

The Library of Congress has catalogued the Riverhead hardcover edition as follows:

Aaronovitch, David.
Voodoo histories : the role of the conspiracy theory in shaping modern history /
David Aaronovitch.—1st American ed.
p.   cm.
Includes bibliographical references and index.
ISBN 978-1-59448-895-5
1. Conspiracies.   2. Conspiracies—History.   I. Title.
HV6275.A27   2010   2009037018
909.08—dc22

PRINTED IN THE UNITED STATES OF AMERICA

10   9   8   7   6   5   4   3   2   1

For Sarah, Rosa, Lily, Eve, and Ruby. My girls.

CONTENTS

LIST OF ILLUSTRATIONS

INTRODUCTION: BLAME KEVIN

This is the age of conspiracy, the age of connections, secret links, secret relationships.

—DON DELILLO, *RUNNING DOG* (1978)

This book is the fault of a fellow named Kevin Jarvis. Kevin was—is, though I haven't seen him since February 2002—a tall, youngish man with a wicked grin and a shaved head. We had been sent by the BBC to Tunisia to make a short film for a program on holiday destinations in places that, away from the beaches and tourist sights, abused their citizens. Kevin was the cameraman-producer and I was what used to be called the "lips."

All the filming had to be done secretly as Kevin and I moved between the mosaics of Carthage and the homes of tortured dissidents; otherwise we would have been arrested and quite possibly roughed up and deported. Several times we caught sight of the ubiquitous Tunisian secret police in their leather jackets and shades as—terribly bored—they staked out the lives of opponents of the government.

It was, I think, in a rental car on the road down from Tunis to the Roman amphitheater at El-Jem (where I was to deliver one of those "behind this attractive façade" pieces to the camera) that Kevin told me about how the 1969 *Apollo* moon landing had been faked by NASA and the American government. This was a shock for me; unlike Kevin, I was old enough to have watched the One Small Step for Man on television, and it was part of my personal history, like England's 1966 World Cup win. I wasn't anxious to lose it.

Kevin's argument rested on one essential proposition: all the picture coverage of the landing, moving and still, was demonstrably fraudulent. There were things happening in the pictures that were impossible, and things not happening in them that certainly should have been. These phenomena included a flag that seemed to flutter in the nonexistent lunar breeze, an unnatural absence of stars, and a certain staginess about the movement of the astronauts. All of this was attested to by an army of photographic experts and scientists who had done years of research and whose conclusions were practically irrefutable. If the pictures were fake, then, it followed, the moon landings themselves must have been counterfeited.

My immediate reaction was one of skepticism. It wasn't that I was forearmed with arguments to disprove his theory; it was just that it offended my sense of plausibility. My uncogitated objection ran something like this: a hoax on such a grand scale would necessarily involve hundreds if not thousands of participants. There would be those who had planned it all in some Washington office; those in NASA who had agreed; the astronauts themselves, who would have been required to continue with the hoax for their entire lives, afraid even of disclosing something to their most intimate friends at the most intimate moments; the set designers, the photographers, the props department, the security men, the navy people who pretended to fish the returning spacemen out of the ocean, and many, many more. It was pretty much impossible for such an operation to be mounted and kept secret, and inconceivable that anybody in power would actually take the risk that it might be blown. Given the imbalance in probabilities, I was therefore sure, without even scrutinizing it, that Kevin's evidence was wrong. Besides, probably unknown to him, the entire thesis was familiar to moviegoers of a certain age: in 1978, the film *Capricorn One* had been based on a similar premise, except that time the earthbound crew had to be eliminated lest they tell the world about the non-landing. In that respect, at least the movie was more credible than the theory.

But the ball was already rolling. I became obsessed by conspiracy theories and what it was that made people believe them. Kevin was not some credulous blotter, absorbing any old liquid that his mind settled upon. He was a bright, well-educated, and commonsensical man—you could trust him when the Tunisian secret police were around. What's more, he'd probably have characterized himself, like me, as a skeptic. So why did someone like Kevin choose to believe, and argue for, a theory that was so preposterous? I wanted to understand what was going on, not least because, at the beginning of 2002, it wasn't just the events of 1969 that were under particular scrutiny. All sorts of conspiracy theories were springing up around the attack on the World Trade Center and the subsequent coalition invasion of Afghanistan, theories that seemed to me potentially dangerous in the worldview they expounded. As I researched, these theories didn't evaporate or appear purely marginal. Instead they seemed to become more insidious, more pervasive.

Conspiracy in the Bookshops

We in the West are currently going through a period of fashionable conspiracism. Books alleging secret plots appear on the current affairs and history shelves as though they were as scholarly or reliable as works by major historians or noted academics. Little distinction is made between a painstakingly constructed biography of John F. Kennedy and an expensive new tome arguing—forty-three years after the event—that the president was killed by the Mafia. Meanwhile, in music and DVD chains across the United States and Britain, among the limited number of books on sale, the young browser is likely to come across oversize paperbacks with titles such as *Abuse Your Illusions, You Are Being Lied To,* and *Everything You Know Is Wrong: The Disinformation Guide to Secrets and Lies.*

Checking in at a rather substantial thirty dollars each, these books consist of a series of bite-size essays by different authors dealing with myriad (and, frankly, random) subjects, from the oil industry to crime, via geopolitics. Their avowed purpose is to "act as a battering ram against the distortions, myths and outright lies that have been shoved down our throats by the government, the media, corporations, organized religion, the scientific establishment and others who want to keep the truth from us."[1]

Browsing through one of the books in the Disinformation series (published by the countercultural tycoon Richard Metzger), I came across a chapter titled "The European Union Unmasked: Dictatorship Revealed." In it, a Lindsay Jenkins—formerly a civil servant in the British Ministry of Defense—details the Eurocratic plot to destroy nation-states. At one point, Jenkins suggests that the encouragement of regionalism is part of this complicated conspiracy, the idea being to weaken Europeans and render them unable to resist the imposition of the superstate. So, she writes, "insistence on the use of minority languages, especially in educating children, will ensure that the locality is isolated and will limit the opportunities for people in the wider world. It will make them second-class citizens and easier to control. All regional assemblies will have multiple translation services, which will further reduce their effectiveness." A theory that I suppose could be summed up as "How the Welsh Destroyed the United Kingdom."

One recent book published in the popular Rough Guides series, listing some of the most significant conspiracy theories and tacitly accepting quite a few of them, even goes so far as to situate itself at a turning point in the Great Historiographical Debate. "The idea," write the authors, "that long ago it was great men's deeds that drove world affairs gave place to the notion that much bigger historical and social forces were at stake. Now, once again, it is being recognized that plans, projects conspiracies and even conspiracy theories can change the world."[2]

Ideas like this may also be observed in television and, latterly, in factual movies. Documentaries are increasingly partisan and liable to include material that suggests conspiracy on the part of someone or other. One only has to think of sequences from Michael Moore's 2004 documentary *Fahrenheit 911* for examples. And such works are given the same treatment as major exercises in historical analysis or substantial pieces of investigative journalism. In fact, they are often given a better billing. Uncountered, their arguments enter popular culture.

So, What Is a Conspiracy?

If a conspiracy is defined as two or more people getting together to plot an illegal, secret, or immoral action, then we can all agree that there are plenty of conspiracies. Many criminal acts are the consequences of conspiracies; security agencies whose plans are necessarily confidential are continually conspiring; and companies who seek to preserve commercial confidentiality—while sometimes employing others to infiltrate the confidentiality of others—often act in a conspiratorial fashion. An agreement not to tell your mother that you are sleeping with your boyfriend would qualify. A conspiracy theory, however, is something rather different, and it is the aim of this book to try to characterize what makes it so.

An American scholar and author of two books about conspiracy theories, Daniel Pipes, argues that, in essence, a conspiracy theory is simply a conspiracy that never happened, that it is "the nonexistent version of a conspiracy." For the U.S. historian Richard Hofstadter, on the other hand, writing in the early 1960s, what distinguished the true "paranoid" conspiracy theory was its scale, not that "its exponents see conspiracies or plots here and there in history, but that they regard a 'vast' or 'gigantic' conspiracy as *the motive force* in historical events."[3]

These two definitions don't quite work for me. How, for example, can Pipes prove categorically that a conspiracy is "nonexistent"? Obviously, any conspiracy is a theory until it is substantiated; therefore, those supporting a conspiracy theory might be entitled to observe either that their own particular notion was simply awaiting definitive proof or, just as likely, that in their judgment such proof was already available. And I find it hard to accept Hofstadter's definition of conspiracy, which would, for example, include the idea—given play in Dan Brown's *The Da Vinci Code*—that the

Church has for two millennia systematically suppressed the truth about the bloodline of Jesus (a truly vast deception), but not the smaller-scale accusation that British (or French) intelligence agencies had Diana, Princess of Wales, brutally done away with in Paris in 1997. It is important not to overlook the smaller theories, since, if believed, it seems to me, they eventually add up to an idea of the world in which the authorities, including those whom we elect, are systematically corrupt and untruthful.

I think a better definition of a conspiracy theory might be "the attribution of deliberate agency to something that is more likely to be accidental or unintended." And, as a sophistication of this definition, one might add "the attribution of secret action to one party that might far more reasonably be explained as the less covert and less complicated action of another." So, a conspiracy theory is the unnecessary assumption of conspiracy where other explanations are more probable. It is, for example, far more likely that men did actually land on the moon in 1969 than that thousands of people were enlisted to fabricate a deception that they did.

Occam's Razor

In arriving at this definition, I was influenced by the precept known as Occam's razor long before I knew what this famous implement was. In Latin, this precept reads, *"Pluralitas non est ponenda sine neccesitate,"* translated as "Plurality should not be posited without necessity." This can be restated as "Other things being equal, one hypothesis is more plausible than another if it involves fewer numbers of new assumptions."[4] Or, far more vulgarly, "Keep it simple." The razor is given to William of Ockham (Occam), a fourteenth-century Franciscan monk and theologian, not because he invented it but because it was his favorite tool in a dispute.

What is also called the principle of parsimony may usefully be applied in other situations where credulity is demanded. Take the mind reader or the séance medium. We should accept only that the one has ESP and the other communes with the dead (things none of us have or can do) once we have exhausted the much simpler explanation that they have shills communicating information to them by some agreed-upon system. It is strange that we understand that magic tricks aren't really magic at all, but are willing to be convinced that our minds can be read by a man on a stage.

The eighteenth-century radical and skeptic Tom Paine applied exactly this thinking to religious doctrine in his book *The Age of Reason*. "If we are to suppose," wrote Paine, "a miracle to be something so entirely out of the course of what is called nature, that she must go out of that course to accomplish it, and we see an account given of such miracle by the person who said he saw it, it raises a question in the mind very easily decided, which is, is it more probable that nature should go out of her course, or that a man should tell a lie?"

Of course, definitions of historical likelihood and unlikelihood can be argued about. So it was possibly inevitable that any strenuous argument against conspiracy theories should come to be described—by certain academics—as being as flawed as the theories themselves. Writers like Daniel Pipes, argues Peter Knight in his book *Conspiracy Culture*, seem to see a belief in conspiracy theories as a "mysterious force with a hidden agenda that takes over individual minds and even whole societies." This is a neat inversion, but Pipes's systematic attempt to show how conspiracist thinking can contaminate political argument seems hardly to merit this rather lurid description.

In a similar way, it has been argued that a coherent argument against conspiracism constitutes its own, and equally questionable, ideology. "Contingency theory," as this way of thinking is called, essentially seeks to defuse where conspiracy theory seeks to inflame. Instead of trying to find an explanation, as conspiracism does, of why power is concentrated in the hands of a few, and why society is riven by unresolved antagonisms, contingency theory pacifies its clients by telling them that there are no such antagonisms and that everything is fundamentally all right. It "salvages the American status quo by turning a blind eye to the social relations underlying 'large events' and spinning these often traumatic moments as the product of 'addled individuals.'"[5] Contingency theory, then, is supposed to be the ruling-class response to insurrectionary conspiracism. It is a way of thinking that has, say its critics, an "equally ideological vision of historical causality."[6]

My response is this: fraught though the understanding of history is, and although there can be no science of historical probability, those who understand history develop an intuitive sense of likelihood and unlikelihood. This does not mean they are endorsing the status quo. As the great British historian Lewis Namier wrote, "The crowning attainment of historical study is a historical sense—an intuitive understanding of how things do not happen."[7] Conspiracy theories are theories that, among other things, offend my understanding of how things happen by positing as a norm how they do not happen.

Plots Throughout History

In his very entertaining little book on conspiracies, the doyen of British theorists Robin Ramsay takes a very different approach to historical causality. "By far the most significant factor in the recent rise of conspiracy theories is the existence of real conspiracies," he writes. "People believe conspiracy theories because they see the world full of conspiracies."[8] Ramsay goes on to cite the following as offering prima facie evidence of a string of political conspiracies: the assassination of President John F. Kennedy, of his brother Robert, of Martin Luther King, Jr., of Malcolm X, of the corrupt leader of the Teamsters union Jimmy Hoffa, and the shooting and wounding of former Alabama governor and presidential candidate George Wallace "when he appeared to threaten Richard Nixon's chances of winning the 1968 presidential election."*

Since each one of these conspiracies is, to say the least, questionable, Ramsay is saying no more in effect than that conspiracist ideas beget more conspiracist ideas. Perhaps if he were to be talking about the conspiracy theories

---

*The shooting, in fact, took place in the run-up to the 1972 presidential election.

of the Middle East rather than those of the Western and English-speaking worlds, he might have a point. Daniel Pipes argues that one reason why the Middle East is awash with conspiracy theories is because that region, almost more than any other, "has indeed hosted a great number of actual conspiracies in the past two centuries. Time and again, Western governments relied on covert collusion or devious means to influence Middle Eastern politics," from the secret 1916 Sykes-Picot agreement between France and Britain to carve up the Arab territories of the former Ottoman empire to U.S. and British involvement in the 1953 coup against the Persian prime minister Mossadeq.[9] And it would be surprising if many Latin Americans, subject for fifty years to a sequence of military takeovers, were not of the same mind. However, in the last hundred years there have been very few major conspiracies in Britain and America that any two serious historians have agreed upon.

Not counting Watergate, which was a rather pitiful botched conspiracy to cover up an attempt at political espionage, the Iran-contra affair of 1985–1986 is the closest the United States has come to a full-blown conspiracy. Here, senior members of the Reagan administration sought to thwart a congressional prohibition on financial support to anti-Communist Nicaraguan insurgents (the contras) by procuring weapons and selling them to America's sworn enemy Iran. The entire business unraveled; there were two inquiries; and two National Security Council employees were found guilty of minor felonies, their convictions being overturned on appeal on the grounds that they had been promised immunity from prosecution through testifying to Congress.

The great British conspiracy is the Zinoviev letter of 1924. The conventional story for years was that British security, wanting to remove the first-ever Labour government, led by Ramsay MacDonald, forged a letter ostensibly written by the head of the Communist International, Grigory Zinoviev. This letter, apparently approving of the pro-Bolshevik stance of Labour, was leaked to the *Daily Mail*, which—four days before the date for the October 1924 general election—ran it under the headline "Civil War Plot by Socialists' Masters: Moscow Orders to Our Reds; Great Plot Disclosed." Labour lost the election by a landslide.

In January 1999, at the behest of the new Labour government of Tony Blair, the chief historian at the Foreign Office, Gill Bennett, conducted an investigation into the affair. She concluded that the letter had originally been forged by anti-Communist White Russians in Latvia so as to derail new treaties concluded between Britain and the young Soviet Union. The letter was then passed to MI6, certain members of which leaked it to the *Daily Mail*. Bennett found that, while the Foreign Office probably regarded the letter as genuine, the officers at MI6, themselves mostly Conservatives, may have had doubts, doubts that it was in their interests to suppress. She also concluded that high-level intelligence responsibility for forging and disseminating the letter was "inherently unlikely," because such a responsibility would suggest "a degree of cohesion and control, not to mention political will, which simply did not exist."

Writing in the *Guardian* newspaper, the Labour foreign secretary, the late Robin Cook, allowed that "there is no evidence that MI6 forged the letter. There is no evidence of an organized conspiracy against Labour by the intelligence agencies."[10] Nor, as Bennett also pointed out in her report, did the letter lose Labour the election. Labour's problem was that it depended upon the dwindling Liberal Party for support. In fact, in October 1924 the Labour vote actually increased.

The Ties That Bind

What is evident from these examples is that true conspiracies are either elevated in their significance through exaggeration, or are in reality seemingly dogged by failure and discovery. That Richard Nixon, the leader of the most powerful nation on earth, could not even manage to get a few incriminating tapes wiped clean exemplifies most real conspiracies. Conspiracy theories, on the other hand, are often more successful at achieving their aims. As I researched the dozen major conspiracy theories that form the body of this book, I began to see that they shared certain characteristics that ensured their widespread propagation.

1. HISTORICAL PRECEDENT

As has already been noted, conspiracists work hard to convince people that conspiracy is everywhere. An individual theory will seem less improbable if an entire history of similar cases can be cited. These can be as ancient as the Gunpowder Plot of 1605, and today may include references to Pearl Harbor, the Reichstag fire, and the 1965 Gulf of Tonkin incident. The plot to murder JFK is first base if you want to convince people that RFK and MLK were also murdered by arms of the American state.

When examining some of the biographies of those involved in the 9/11 Truth movement, I was struck by how this normalization works over time. One energetic woman in her forties, who had become an indefatigable activist in the Californian branch of the lobby, described how she had become convinced of the 9/11 conspiracy. In her youth, she told her sympathizers, she had sailed around the world, but her "political activism" had only begun in 1992, when she saw a film "which disturbed her" and as a consequence of which she began to do her own research on the government and media. The film was Oliver Stone's *JFK*.

2. SKEPTICS AND SHEEPLE

A conspiracy theory is likely to be politically populist, in that it usually claims to lay bare an action taken by a small power elite against the people. Or, as a Californian professor of theology could tell an audience at the Copenhagen central library with regard to 9/11: "Members of the elite of our society may not think that the truth should be revealed." By contrast, belief in the conspiracy makes you part of a genuinely heroic elite group who can see past the official version duplicated for the benefit of the lazy or inert mass of people by the powers that be. There will usually be an emphasis on the special quality of thought required to appreciate the existence of the conspiracy. The conspiracists have cracked the code, not least because of their possession of an unusual and perceptive way of looking at things. Those who cannot or will not see the truth are variously described as robots or, latterly, as sheeple—citizens who shuffle half awake through their conventional lives.

3. JUST ASKING QUESTIONS

Since 2001, a primary technique employed by more respectable conspiracists has been the advocation of the "It's not a theory" theory. The theorist is just asking certain disturbing questions because of a desire to seek out truth, and the reader is supposedly left to make up his or her mind. The questions asked, of course, only make sense if the questioner really believes that there is indeed a secret conspiracy.

4. EXPERT WITNESSES

The conspiracists draw upon the endorsement of celebrities and "experts" to validate their theories, and yet a constant feature of modern conspiracy theories is the exaggeration of the status of experts. The former UK environment minister Michael Meacher, a leading "disturbing question" figure on the edges of the 9/11 Truth movement, was never a member of the British Cabinet, but in a radio interview on the U.S. syndicated *Alex Jones Show* was referred to as the "former number three in the Blair government." The theologist academic David Ray Griffin, perhaps the most respected of all the 9/11 conspiracists, feels able to lay claim to a large and rapidly acquired capacity to evaluate arguments made in the areas of physics, aerodynamics, and engineering. How dubious this claim is may be gauged by imagining his reaction were, say, the editor of the science journal *Popular Mechanics* to claim competence to comment upon Griffin's own work of theological scholarship, *A Critique of John K. Roth's Theodicy*.

If necessary, theorists become interestingly opaque about the qualifications of their experts. One of the two films made about the London bombings of July 7, 2005, included evidence from a Nick Kollerstrom, who was billed as a "lecturer and researcher." But a lecturer on what, and a researcher in which fields? Kollerstrom, it turned out, lectured on the effect of planetary motions on alchemy, and was the author of a book on crop circles.* Another aspect of this fudging is the tendency among conspiracists to quote each other so as to suggest a wide spread of expertise lending support to the argument. Thus, over the events of 9/11, the French conspiracy author Thierry Meyssan cites American conspiracy author Webster Tarpley; Tarpley cites David Ray Griffin; and David Ray Griffin cites Thierry Meyssan. It is a rather charming form of solidarity.

5. ACADEMIC CREDIBILITY

The conspiracists work hard to give their written evidence the veneer of scholarship. The approach has been described as death by footnote. Accompanying the exposition of the theory is a dense mass of detailed and often undifferentiated information, but laid out as an academic text. Often the theory is also supported by quotations from non-conspiracist sources that almost invariably turn out to be misleading and selective. To give one characteristic example, David Ray Griffin's book about 9/11, *The New Pearl Harbor*, describes Thierry Meyssan as the head of an organization "which the *Guardian* in April 2002 described as 'a respected independent think-tank whose left-leaning research projects have until now been considered models of reasonableness and objectivity.'"[11] This is a masterpiece in disingenuousness, given the full *Guardian* quote: "The French media has been quick to dismiss [Meyssan's] book's claims, despite the fact that Mr. Meyssan is president of the Voltaire Network, a respected independent think-tank whose left-leaning research projects have until now been considered models of reasonableness and objectivity. 'This theory suits everyone—there are no Islamic extremists and everyone is happy. It

---

*In 2008, Kollerstrom was removed from his position as a research fellow at University College London for having written a number of articles suggesting that there had been no gas chambers at Auschwitz, and drawing attention to the number of orchestras at the concentration camp, as well as the existence of a swimming pool for the use of the inmates.

eliminates reality,' said *Le Nouvel Observateur*, while *Libération* called the book 'The Frightening Confidence Trick . . . a tissue of wild and irresponsible allegations, entirely without foundation.'" Not the same thing at all.

Another example of this misuse of the mainstream media is the ascription of final, almost biblical authority to immediate and necessarily provisional news reports of an incident if they happen to demonstrate the inconsistencies that the conspiracists are seeking. Reporters in the West usually do the best they can in frightening and confused circumstances, but early explanations of major disasters will contain much that turns out to be mistaken or speculative. Similarly, the passing opinions of journalists are given the status of indisputable truth. In *The New Pearl Harbor*, Griffin questions the survival of evidence from the planes that crashed into the World Trade Center, using an article in the *Guardian* as support: "As a story in the *Guardian* said, 'the idea that [this] passport had escaped from that inferno unsinged would [test] the credulity of the staunchest supporter of the FBI's crackdown on terrorism.'" In fact, this was not a report but the passing opinion of a columnist, Anne Karpf, who had no more knowledge about what might or might not have emerged from the Twin Towers than had any other columnist in north London.

A final polish is given to the conspiracists' illusion of authority by the use of what is imagined to be secret service or technical jargon, as though the authors had been in recent communication with spies or scientists. Interesting words and phrases include "psyops" (short for "psychological operations"), "false flag," and more recently "wet disposal," meaning assassination.

6. CONVENIENT INCONVENIENT TRUTHS

Conspiracists are always winners. Their arguments have a determined flexibility whereby any new and inconvenient truth can be accommodated within the theory itself. So, embarrassing and obvious problems in the theory may be ascribed to deliberate disinformation originating with the imagined plotters designed to throw activists off the scent. One believer in a conspiracy to assassinate the Princess of Wales claimed that it was the very proliferation of absurd theories concerning Diana that first convinced her that this was MI6 at work seeking to cover up its real role in the killing. Few, however, match the schoolboy ingenuity of Korey Rowe, the producer of *Loose Change*, a highly popular documentary about 9/11, who, when challenged about the glaring factual mistakes in his film, replied, "We know there are errors in the documentary, and we've actually left them in there so that people discredit us and do the research for themselves."[12]

7. UNDER SURVEILLANCE

Conspiracists are inclined to suggest that those involved in spreading the theory are, even in the "safest" of countries, somehow endangered. During a February 2007 BBC program looking into the death of Dr. David Kelly, the Liberal Democrat MP Norman Baker, who had been contesting the verdict of suicide on the former weapons inspector, referred to his suspicions that his e-mails were being intercepted by persons unknown. Some e-mails sent to him, he told his interviewer, had been only partly received by his computer, and he thought this most ominous. Similarly, one of the physicians who began the Kelly conspiracy story by writing a letter to the *Guardian* disputing the forensic evidence—retired West Country orthopedic surgeon David Halpin—worried that his e-mails were being interfered with. In March 2005, Mr. Halpin sent this letter to the *Morning Star* newspaper:

> *Dear Sir,*
> *The firewall on my computer became inactive five weeks ago. Therefore I opened the email system for very brief periods only. However, in those few days every one of my 6000 plus email files was erased or removed. This will have been done by a state sponsored agency and not by an amateur acting singly.*
> *Who might wish to cause me great difficulty? I speak and act firmly for justice in Palestine and against an occupation of indescribable brutality. I have asked, with other specialists, for the law to be upheld in the case of the late Dr. David Kelly; that there*

should be a full inquest and not the half one that has taken place. I have spoken, marched and written to stop the war crimes committed against Afghans and Iraqis by our government and its odious leader.

So which agency is the most likely culprit? Only one other associate has lost a mass of email files and that is the lay chairperson of our "Kelly Investigation Group"—last Autumn. I have made a formal complaint to my MP and also about delayed email transmission. My right to privacy, association and free speech are ostensibly inviolate in this country—pro tempore.

Yours faithfully David S. Halpin, MB BS FRCS[13]

Fun or Frightening?

Part of my motivation for writing this book was the lighthearted aim of providing a useful resource to the millions of men and women who have found themselves on the wrong side of a bar or dinner-party conversation that begins, "I'll tell you the real reason . . ." and have sat there, knowing it was all likely to be nonsense but rarely having the necessary arguments to hand. It is designed to offer users of the Internet something that can act as a counterpoint to the tens of thousands of websites that argue, post-in post-out, that *They* are most certainly out to get you.

I also wanted to understand just why it was that the counterintuitive, the unlikely, and the implausible would so often have a better purchase on our imagination and beliefs than the real. In other words, I wanted to understand the psychology of the conspiracy theory.

But there is a more sinister aspect to jovial arguments about whether or not the moon landings actually took place, and to speculation about why we enjoy such arguments. The belief in conspiracy theories is, I hope to show, harmful in itself. It distorts our view of history and therefore of the present, and—if widespread enough—leads to disastrous decisions.

1. "THE UNCANNY NOTE OF PROPHECY"

1919

Now days are dragon-ridden, the nightmare
Rides upon sleep: a drunken soldiery
Can leave the mother, murdered at her door,
To crawl in her own blood, and go scot-free;
The night can sweat with terror as before
We pieced our thoughts into philosophy,
And planned to bring the world under a rule,
Who are but weasels fighting in a hole.

—W. B. YEATS, "NINETEEN HUNDRED AND NINETEEN"

In 1919, the European citizen—who five years earlier had perhaps, like the young Hitler, celebrated the outbreak of war—now surveyed a world that was utterly changed. For the victors, the alteration was great enough: millions of young men dead or wounded, women widowed and children left fatherless, mountains of debt, economies turned wholesale to the production of armaments, and colonies newly aware, through their own sacrifice, of their right and potential to become independent nations. But for the defeated, the change had been cataclysmic. The ancient empire of the Habsburgs had flown apart and was reconstituting itself as a series of small nations, with the flags of Hungary, Czechoslovakia, Yugoslavia, and Austria about to be added to the *Children's Illustrated Encyclopedia*. In Istanbul, though the sultan hung on, the Ottoman

Empire itself—which had lasted half a thousand years—was finally being dismembered by foreign forces and native independence movements, but not before the killing of a million Armenians in the hills of Anatolia and the plains of Syria. And then there was Russia, which had entered the war as a vast, creaking monarchy and exited—following an audacious coup d'état led by men with strange noms de guerre such as Lenin, Trotsky, Stalin—as an experiment in an entirely new type of government, one completely unrooted in history or experience. In 1918, the entire Russian royal family had been murdered in Yekaterinburg, the Orthodox Church suppressed, the lands of the nobility sequestered, and the factories of the magnates nationalized. An organization was set up, the Communist International, or Comintern, dedicated to spreading the revolution to all the nations of the world. In Europe the sound of strange marching songs could be heard coming from the East.

Everywhere peoples stared out of the abyss, their certainties and traditions replaced by extreme anxiety and dangerous novelty. The experience of war, so totally brutalizing and massive in its industrial scale, had shaken their faith in progress itself. The technologies that were supposed to bring comfort and prosperity had instead brought death and unbelievable destruction. No one, save a few eccentric doomsayers, had entered the war imagining its catastrophic consequences. Not the intellectuals, not the generals, not the leaders, the philosophers, or the clerics. How, then, should they now make sense of the world?

People could have blamed themselves. Many had tolerated or encouraged their governments in arms races, in belligerent patriotism, in imperial ambitions, in bellicose diplomacy and egoism. Journalists and writers had embraced the prospect of conflict—conflict in which one's own side was inevitably victorious and one's troops would be home by Christmas. Those who had argued loudest against war had been the most reviled. The people of 1919, however, were no more likely to point the finger of blame at themselves than we are today, we who enjoy universal adult franchise, a free press, and the free exchange of information. Instead, they looked elsewhere. They had, it seemed, been badly led, politically and militarily.

Some went as far as to believe they had been actively duped, fooled, lied to, and, where defeated, betrayed.

For the socialist and Marxist left, the culprit was obvious. Imperialism was to blame, an imperialism fostered by the insatiable demand by business interests for cheap raw materials, new markets, and vast profits. Who, after all, had gained from the four years of warfare? Men in top hats with currency signs on them, men from Krupp, Vickers, and Nobel, men with access to the highest reaches of government. The industrialists had effectively encouraged the carnage to begin and had then kept it going, making fortunes from the slaughter. You had to look no further than them and their agents; monopoly capitalism was the hidden hand.

For many people, however, capitalism was an abstraction. They needed to find a group that appeared to have benefited from the war and the revolutions that followed it. For if they had benefited (and were still benefiting), might they not also have helped bring this situation about?

The Jews

It did not seem ludicrous to the conservative man or woman of 1919 to suspect the Jews. Unlike most peoples, the Jews were international, living in every country and apparently holding positions of influence and wealth in almost all of them. But though they were omnipresent, they were also aloof, and though ubiquitous in public life, they were separate in the private domain. With their archaic language of worship, their aversion to mixed marriages, their extreme attachment to education, they gave the impression of being heirs to a great secret.

What was more, throughout history the Jews could be found standing next to—or just behind—the agents of radical change. It was pointed out by many right-wing writers and amateur historians that one of Oliver Cromwell's earliest acts, after executing Charles I, was to readmit Jews into England, whence they had been banished nearly four hundred years earlier, and that both the American and French Revolutions, with their advocacy of the rights of man, had released Jews from previous restrictions. Napoleon's conquests had been followed by Jewish emancipation, and in 1806, the Corsican tyrant had even convened the Grand Sanhedrin, a gathering of notable European Jews. Jews had been prominent in the bourgeois and nationalist revolutions of 1848, in the Paris Commune of 1871, and in the 1905 revolution in Russia.

But it was not just a matter of political radicalism. Jewish banks had financed the Industrial Revolution; Jewish entrepreneurs were at the forefront of the revolution in retailing, their names to be found on the fronts of great department stores. During the second half of the nineteenth century, public Jews like Disraeli and fictional Jews like Trollope's adventurer Melmotte in *The Way We Live Now* excited public opinion with their political and economic activities. The large populations of ordinary, poor, or illiterate Jews mostly failed to register. In proportion to their numbers, it was said, the Jews did incredibly well.

For the most part, this was seen as a product of the character of the Jewish community—family-oriented, cosmopolitan, and ambitious. There had always been that strain in European conservatism, however, which, observing that the natural order of things was being subverted by progress and radicalism, preferred a more organized explanation. They suggested that secret societies had been behind the major upheavals of the past century or so: the Freemasons had been the organizing force behind undermining the eighteenth-century *ancien régime*; a secret body called the Illuminati had been involved in French Jacobinism and the revolution; and the Jews and Freemasons working together were responsible for the Year of Revolutions in 1848. There was some historical basis for these beliefs. In the early stages of the movement for Italian unity, for example, secret societies known as the Carbonari (charcoal burners) had indeed met in dark forests, sworn horrible oaths, and conspired against foreign occupiers and petty kings. As the century ended, real anarchists with bombs and guns hatched plots to kill prime ministers and blow up emperors, sometimes with real success. So the idea of a more ambitious conspiracy seemed not so very far-fetched, and the possibility that the Jews might act in concert to achieve particular objectives not so very eccentric.

What brought the two ideas together was the Russian Revolution of October 1917. From the beginning, it was evident that a large number of those most active in the building of the new Soviet Russia were Jews. Persecuted under the tsars and subject to occasional massacres, known as pogroms, whenever there was political unrest in the empire, Jews had tended, naturally enough, to side with the reforming or revolutionary left, which promised an end to repression. In fact, the Bolsheviks had relatively few Jews in senior positions, in contrast to their allies the Mensheviks and Social Revolutionaries, who were led by men and women from Jewish families. These few, however, caught the eye. There was Trotsky (Lev Bronstein) at the head of the Red Army; Grigory Zinoviev (Apfelbaum), boss of the revolution-spreading Comintern; and Lev Kamenev (Rosenfeld) at Lenin's right hand.

The supposed prominence of the Jews in Soviet Russia was remarked upon by the professional diplomats working for the British Foreign Office. In 1919, the British ambassador in Copenhagen, Lord Kilmarnock, wrote to Foreign Secretary Lord Curzon that most Bolsheviks, as far as he could see, were either Germans or Jews. In the same year, an official report published by the Foreign Office contained observations made in a dispatch by the Reverend B. S. Lombard, a naval chaplain serving in Russia. The revolutionary movement, Lombard claimed, "originated in German propaganda and was, and is being carried out by international Jews." Lombard had also been ashore in Russia and seen the consequences of Red control over certain towns. "All business becomes paralyzed," he wrote, "shops were closed, Jews became possessors of most of the business houses."[1]

American diplomats were telling their bosses much the same thing. Documents from the State Department archives include a file dealing with the relationship between Jewish financial interests and the Russian Revolution. The main document, "Bolshevism and Judaism," dated

November 13, 1918, is a report stating that a Bolshevik takeover had been planned in early 1916, and listing ten or so Jewish companies whom the report's author, an employee of the U.S. War Trade Board, believed to have been involved. Also in the file are a number of cables sent between the State Department and the American embassy in London. One, which illustrates how this perception was commonplace among Western diplomats, is worth quoting in full.

> October 16, 1919 In Confidential File. Secret for Winslow from Wright. Financial aid to Bolshevism & Bolshevik Revolution in Russia from prominent Am. Jews: Jacob Schiff, Felix Warburg, Otto Kahn, Mendell Schiff, Jerome Hanauer, Max Breitung & one of the Guggenheims. Document re—in possession of Brit. police authorities from French sources.[2]

The perception that the Jews were behind the Russian Revolution informed the opinions of some of the most illustrious political figures of the time, even in phlegmatic Britain. On February 8, 1920, Winston Churchill contributed an article to the *Illustrated Sunday Herald*. In it he addressed the threat from Bolshevism. "This worldwide conspiracy for the overthrow of civilisation and for the reconstruction of society on the basis of arrested development, of envious malevolence, and impossible equality has been steadily growing," he warned readers. And as to who was behind it: "There is no need to exaggerate the part played in the creation of Bolshevism and in the bringing about of the Russian revolution by these international and for the most part atheistical Jews. It is certainly a very great one; it probably outweighs all others."[3]

In the minds of some, then, including a certain former corporal in the German army who, a thousand kilometers away in Munich, was saying similar things but with rather more venom, the notion that the Jews were behind the war and revolutions that had traumatized Europe began to take root. But this suspicion was as nothing compared to the conspiracy that others were suggesting might be at the heart of things.

Enter the *Protocols*

"Since the autumn of 1919," wrote a commentator seven years later, "a remarkable book has been circulating in Germany, the civilized countries of Europe and America."[4] This book was titled *Die Geheimnisse der Weisen von Zion*—in English, *The Protocols of the Elders of Zion*—and it contained within it the missing link between the events that had turned the world upside down and the Jews who seemed so prominent in upending it. It was what would now be called the smoking gun.

What were the *Protocols*? They consisted of eighty pages or so of instructions and observations with the amibitious goal of destroying all existing powers—empires, kingdoms, churches—and establishing a new world empire ruled by a supreme Jewish autocrat from the House of David. Getting to this hyperexalted point required the fomenting of class hatred, the provoking of wars, the incitement of revolutions, the discrediting of national institutions, and the promotion of liberalism to undermine traditional values and loyalties. This would lead to socialism, then Bolshevism; states would die and eventually the world would cry out for order. And when it did, guess who (with the help of the Freemasons) would be ready? The true, supreme—and Jewish—government of the world.

Set out under twenty-four headings, the *Protocols* now read like a series of lectures given to a senior management team by a very determined CEO, and much of what is said is couched in lofty abstraction. Toward the beginning of Protocol One, for example, we are told, "It must be noted that men with bad instincts are more in number than the good, and therefore the best results in governing them are attained by violence and terrorisation than by academic discussions." You can almost imagine a number of the supposed plotters nodding along, and some of the more conscientious or junior elders noting it all down on the paper provided.

Taken together, the *Protocols of the Elders of Zion* amounts to the ultimate election manifesto. There are sections on foreign policy, security, armaments, monopolies, the press, tax policy, and education. But this is a manifesto expressly designed to be hidden from the electorate. It is relentlessly Machiavellian in tone, calculating how to use the weakness of men for the ends of the would-be rulers. Take Protocol Twelve, on the control of the press. As the speaker says, "Literature and journalism are two of the most important educative forces, and therefore our government [the Jews] will become proprietor of the majority of the journals . . . This, however, must in nowise be suspected by the public." But how do you divert such suspicions?

> All journals published by us will be of the most opposite in appearance, tendencies and opinions, thereby creating confidence in us and bringing over to us our quite unsuspicious opponents, who will thus fall into our trap and be rendered harmless . . . All our newspapers will be of all possible complexions—aristocratic, republican, revolutionary, even anarchical . . . Like the Indian pagan god Vishnu, they will have one hundred hands and in each shall beat the pulse of a different intellectual tendency.[5]

There is also a call, not made even by the most liberal Swedish or Dutch party today, for more pornography. "Senseless, filthy, abominable literature" should be disseminated by the conspirators, so as "to provide a telling relief by contrast to the speeches and party programs, which will be distributed from exalted quarters of ours." So the pill of seriousness will be sweetened by the honey of smut, a kind of infernal Reithianism.

But if the *Protocols* were indeed born out of a meeting or a series of lectures, who exactly delivered them, when, and where? The German editor of the edition in circulation in 1919 was one Gottfried zur Beek—the pen name of a seventy-year-old former army officer, Captain Ludwig Müller von Hausen, who had dedicated the work "To the Princes of Europe." In the introduction to his edition, zur Beek explains how he came by the text. History records that in August 1897, in the Swiss city of Basel, the First Zionist Congress was held. What wasn't recorded, he says, was that alongside the official plenaries, which were open to all and which discussed the question of a homeland for the dispersed Jewish people, there were twenty-four secret sessions. At these sessions, Dr. Theodor Herzl, the father of Zionism, presided, and it was he who delivered the *Protocols*—a distillation of the wisdom of ages—much as Moses delivered the Commandments.

Of course, the very last thing that such a clandestine meeting would have wanted was the publication of a record of its deliberations. Unfortunately, some men have a price. After the congress finished, an emissary of the elders, en route to God knows where, took a manuscript of the lectures to a Masonic lodge in Frankfurt am Main. Waiting at the lodge was an agent of the Russian secret police and a crack team of transcribers. In return for payment, the emissary gave the agent one night to copy the *Protocols* in their original language, presumably Hebrew. In the morning, he collected his sensational cargo and disappeared from history. The copied manuscript itself was taken back to Russia, where it was recopied and given to scholars for translation and study.

For some reason—and oddly, given the extraordinary contents of the manuscript—this process took an inordinate amount of time. It was only in 1905, according to zur Beek, that a certain Sergei Nilus, described as a scholar from Moscow, published a book, *The Great in the Small*, that consisted mostly of the views of a pious Orthodox conservative on the imminence of the coming of the Antichrist. The *Protocols* were to be found as one of its appendices. As the book went through subsequent editions in 1911, 1912, and 1917, the protocols became more prominent. Zur Beek's book claimed to be based on the 1911 Nilus edition, brought to Germany after the Russian Revolution by anti-Bolshevik exiles.

One reason for the slow burn before the book came to widespread attention might be that it wasn't until after the Russian Revolution that it could be seen as prophetic. Nilus himself, though, had always understood the connection between the writings and real life. In the introduction to the 1911 edition, he anticipated: "The educated non-Jewish reader will see in his daily life and in the lightning-like events that have struck Russia and all of Europe a fullness of evidence for the authenticity of the *Protocols*." By 1919, he was right. Zur Beek's edition was followed by the publication of a Polish version in Warsaw, three French translations, an English version, three separate publications in America, and more in Scandinavia, Italy, and Japan. In 1925, following the publication of an Arabic version, the Latin patriarch in Jerusalem praised the work and called upon Christians to buy it.* What had been discovered appeared to be, in the words of the American academic Richard S. Levy, who has made a study of the *Protocols*, "the veritable Rosetta Stone of history."[6] It suddenly explained everything.

The *Protocols* on the Move

Nowhere had they been more anxious for that explanation than in Germany. Within weeks of zur Beek's publication, the *Protocols of the Elders of Zion* was circulating in the highest echelons of the old Reich. Prince Otto zu Salm-Horstmar, who in July 1918 had already called attention to the links between the Jews and the Freemasons in the German parliament, was an influential sponsor, as was the chairman of the Conservative Party in the Prussian upper house, Count Behr. Prince Joachim Albrecht of Prussia, youngest son of the abdicated kaiser, would strew the restaurants and luxury hotels that he visited with copies of zur Beek's book. And when Lady Norah Bentinck visited Wilhelm II in exile in Doorn in the Netherlands, she found the former emperor recommending it to his guests and reading individual chapters out loud after dinner.[7] It must have been a relief to the kaiser to discover that, contrary to Allied propaganda, it was not he who had started the First World War but somebody else.

---

*This was too much for some colonial authorities: the book, legal in France, was banned by the French high commissioner in Syria, presumably on the grounds that it was likely to inflame local hatreds.

If Wilhelm had reasons for wanting the blame shifted, the same could hardly be said of General Ludendorff, widely trusted in Germany and seen as one of its finest and most intelligent generals. Yet when Ludendorff—who had emerged from a lost war with his reputation enhanced—was shown the *Protocols*, he too leaped upon the exculpatory opportunity. "Several publications have recently appeared which throw more light on the position of the Jewish people," he wrote. When these documents had been studied properly, he predicted, "One suspects that, in many instances, we shall arrive at another version of world history."[8]

Among young Germans, the text had a receptive audience. To them it was doubly believable because it fitted with what other people were saying and what they were already inclined to think. The year 1919 had also seen the publication of Friedrich Wichtl's book *The World War, World Freemasonry, World Revolution*, which similarly advanced the notion that Jews and Freemasons had brought about the disastrous conflict. This book, a nineteen-year-old boy wrote in his diary, explained "all and tells us against whom we must fight."[9] The young man was Heinrich Himmler.

But even in the countries that had—officially, at least—won the war, the *Protocols* were not dismissed. Serious newspapers cogitated on the meaning of the revelations. In France, *L'Opinion* analyzed the content of the book as it would any other serious publication. In Italy, the Milan newspaper *Perseverenza* and the Roman *Vita Italiana* did the same.

What seems most surprising now, however, was what happened in Britain. In 1920, the first English edition of the *Protocols* was published, a private commission from Eyre and Spottiswoode, who bore the distinction (and the imprint) of being His Majesty's Printers. The British version was called *The Jewish Peril* and was soon being reviewed in some of Britain's most prestigious journals. On May 8, *The Times*, newspaper of the Establishment, published an editorial, quite possibly the work of its celebrated editor Mr. Henry Wickham Steed. This leading article was titled "A Disturbing Pamphlet: A Call for Inquiry." Its tone was urgent. "What are these *Protocols*?" it asked. "Are they authentic? If so, what malevolent assembly concocted these plans and gloated over their exposition?"

Then *The Times* asked, and seemed to answer, the key question. "Are they a forgery? If so whence comes the uncanny note of prophecy, prophecy in parts fulfilled, in parts far gone in the way of fulfillment?" Then the peroration. "Have we," *The Times* demanded, "been struggling these tragic years to blow up and extirpate the secret organization of German world dominion only to find beneath it another, more dangerous because more secret? Have we, by straining every fiber of our national body, escaped a 'Pax Germanica' only to fall into a 'Pax Judaeica'?"

A week later, it was the turn of the *Spectator* magazine. The edition of May 15 contained a long and respectful review of *The Jewish Peril*, accompanied by an editorial. The *Protocols* were described as being "of very great ability . . . brilliant in moral perversity and intellectual depravity . . . One of the most remarkable productions of their kind."[10] Both the *Spectator* and *The Times* were rapidly inundated by letters from horrified Jewish readers, an occurrence that for those who read the *Protocols* and believed them merely acted as corroboration.

Worse was to come. The Tory *Morning Post* commenced a series of twenty-three long leading articles backing the *Protocols*, and bound them together in another pamphlet, which was sold under the title of *The Cause of World Unrest*. Here was revealed how "a formidable sect" had brought about the First World War by manipulating the Germans, with the ultimate objective being "the destruction of Christianity and all religion except the Jewish." The *Morning Post* was doubtless influenced in this by its employee and former correspondent in Russia, Victor Marsden.[11]

In the autumn, the *Spectator* praised the *Morning Post* for its stance. "The evidence that the paper brings to support its plea of conspiracy is clearly of enough substance and enough importance to justify its action," argued the magazine. "We most sincerely wish that some body of the nature of a Royal Commission could be appointed to inquire into the whole subject."[12] One wonders now what such a royal commission would have been called, but the *Spectator* was in no doubt as to what ought to happen if such a body were to find the case against the Jews proved. In that situation, it demanded, "We must drag the conspirators into the open, tear off their ugly masks and show the world how ridiculous as well as how evil and dangerous are such pests of society." *Blackwood's Magazine*, unwilling to wait, advocated that Jews be excluded from public office and influence.

The *Protocols* crossed the Atlantic. In October 1919, they were published in the *Philadelphia Public Ledger* but with the Jewish references omitted. Soon afterward, an editorial in the *Christian Science Monitor* linked the *Protocols* to world events and argued, "It could be a tremendous mistake to conclude that the Jewish peril . . . does not exist . . . That a secret political organization exists, working unremittingly . . . is, to the man who can read the signs of the times, a thing unquestionable." On June 19, 1920, the *Chicago Tribune* carried an article headlined "Trotsky Leads Jew-Radicals to World Rule. Bolshevism Only a Tool for His Scheme." There was, the author claimed, a world revolutionary movement, part of which aimed "for the establishment of a new racial domination of the world. So far as the British, French and our own department's inquiry have been able to trace, the moving spirits in this second scheme are Jewish radicals."

Ford and the *Protocols*

The man who more than any other popularized the *Protocols* in America—and, as a result, abroad—was the industrialist Henry Ford. The Flivver King was the Bill Gates of his day. He had taken a modern product that few could afford and many wanted—the motor car—and turned it from a luxury into an everyday household item. He had liberated millions of Americans in that vast land from dependence on irregular public transport or horse-drawn conveyances. He had grown his business from a small workshop into one of the largest and most truly industrial in the whole of America.

However, the successful capitalist also had a social conscience and a political and social philosophy. Ford was one of those enlightened bosses who believed that screwing as much work for as little pay as possible out of your workforce was counterproductive. It was better to hire good folks and keep them happy, and to that end the Ford Company's Sociological Department employed fifty people to vet new employees. Those who were sober and didn't take in boarders (considered inimical to family life) were eligible for substantial bonuses. One irony of Ford's political philosophy was that despite its emphasis on traditional American values, his industrial techniques—and the machine that they produced—were altering America forever.

Ford hated war, describing it as "murder, desolation and destruction." From 1915, when America's involvement in the First World War began to be discussed, Ford argued vehemently against it. Parasites and absentee owners, he told a press conference that summer, wanted to get involved in an unnecessary venture. "New York wants war," he claimed, referring presumably to Wall Street. "The United States doesn't."[13] In the autumn of 1915, a woman antiwar activist met Ford at his Highland Park factory in Michigan. During the course of their meeting, Ford paused, slapped his breast pocket, and exclaimed, "I know who caused the war—the German-Jewish bankers! I have the evidence here! Facts!" It was a statement that he repeated at least once more during the discussion.[14]

America never found out exactly what Ford's facts were, and despite his campaigning the country did go to war in 1917, following the sinking by a German U-boat of the passenger liner *Lusitania*. By the time the U.S. doughboys were on their way home from Europe, there were new enemies for the celebrated industrialist to fight. There was, above all, Bolshevism, the negation of everything Ford believed in.

Ford, though a diffident man, did not believe in the quiet use of financial muscle. One lesson that he took from his antiwar campaign was that he could not rely upon the existing press to get his message over. Indeed, he was locked in a multimillion-dollar libel suit with one of the most powerful, the *Chicago Tribune*. Ford had also won the Michigan primary for the Republican presidential nomination in 1916 without ever agreeing to stand. It seemed to him that if he reached the people directly then he was likely to achieve political success. He was ever the innovator, and the solution seemed clear to him: he would become his own press, start his own newspaper. So in January 1919, the *Dearborn Independent* (Dearborn was the location of the first Ford plant) was launched, featuring, among the usual things, "Mr. Ford's Own Page." Promoted by Ford dealers throughout America, the *Dearborn Independent* soon had a print run of 300,000.

Initially, the newspaper manifested interest in the concerns of its readers, whom it took to be the hardworking folks of America and their families. But it wasn't long before "Mr. Ford's Own Page" was fulminating against the specter of Bolshevism and its threat to the American way of life. In April 1919, the paper printed an article about Russian Bolshevism, commissioned from a Russian exile, Boris Brasol, who had made an acquaintance of Henry Ford's personal secretary, Ernest Liebold.[15] Four weeks later, Liebold had his own article published, pointing out the "deep and sinister" role played in creating the conditions for the First World War by "financial interests." Like a Ford car, the components were being assembled by different people. Soon they would be put together, and the thing would begin to move.

It took a year or so for the various themes—the Americanization of immigrants (120,000 Jews arrived in the United States in 1920), the greed of the great bankers (with special mention of the Rothschilds), and the threat of alien Bolshevism—to coalesce. When they did, the impact was huge. On May 22, 1920, and for ninety-one successive weeks after that, the *Dearborn Independent* devoted itself to campaigning on what it called "The International Jew: The World's Foremost Problem."

The starting point of this sustained campaign was a folksy "just askin'" stance. The observable fact was, as the paper put it, "a sparse Jewish ingredient of three per cent in a population of 110 million—attaining in fifty years a degree of control that would be impossible to a ten times larger group of any other race."[16] How, the *Dearborn Independent* wanted to know, had such a remarkable state of affairs come about? What special and specific qualities did the Jewish people have? What did such minority power mean for the majority of Gentiles? Week by week, the paper went through various aspects of life and politics, naming the chosen people wherever it found them and becoming a veritable *Jew's Jew in America*. Sometimes the tone was plaintive. In an article about the music business, for example, the author lamented that once upon a time, "composers like Victor Hebery and Gustav Kerker" had been popular, "but now the Irving Berlins have forced themselves into places hewn out and established by Gentiles who had a regard for art." A regard that Mr. Berlin, we may deduce, did not have. Sometimes the tone was cross, as when noting that Jewish control of the movie industry had made it impossible to show a film called *The Life of the Saviour* because it "might offend the Hebrews."

We don't know exactly when Boris Brasol told Liebold that he had a copy of the Nilus version of the *Protocols*. We do know that around the end of May 1920, a stenographer in Washington, D.C., made a copy of the Brasol text of the *Protocols* on behalf of the Ford Motor Company, and had it sent to Liebold.[17] Then, on June 26, the *Independent* began to publish the *Protocols* as part of its series "The International Jew." The serialization began with a complaint about the fuss that the publication was likely to cause. "The chief difficulty in writing about the Jewish Question," the editor wrote, "is the supersensitiveness of Jews and non-Jews concerning the whole matter." It was an early complaint about what today might be described as political correctness. In August, the *Independent* claimed to show exactly the "connection between the written program of the documents and the actual program as it can be traced in real life."

When the series was finished, it was collected together by Ford's publishing house and sold in four volumes as *The International Jew*. Subsidized by Ford to the tune of $5 million, the books cost twenty-five cents per volume and sold half a million copies in the United States alone. But if Ford was a selling point in America, he was revered abroad. That such an endorsement of the *Protocols* should be made by someone so successful, so modern, and (presumably) so wise, added significant credibility to a document which had previously seemed rather outlandish. It is hardly surprising that versions of the *Protocols* published right up to today often quote the words of Henry Ford when interviewed by the *New York World* in February 1921: "They fit with what is going on," said Ford. "They are sixteen years old and they have fitted the world situation up to this time. They fit it now."

Enter Sir John

But even as Ford spoke, the *Protocols* were unraveling. Ten months earlier, in an article in the Berlin monthly journal *Im Deutschen Reich*, a German academic, Dr. J. Stanjek, had revealed that a secret meeting of Jewish elders, very much like the one supposed to be the source of the *Protocols*, had been described in a book published some time before. In fact, said Dr. Stanjek, it had been published more than thirty years before the First Zionist Congress had even met in Basel. And this earlier book was not a work of history or fact, but of fiction. A novel.

The book in question appeared in German in 1868, and had been supposedly authored by a certain Sir John Retcliffe. But Retcliffe was actually the nom de plume of a German journalist Hermann Goedsche. Goedsche had been convicted of political forgery back in 1848, when he had used fabricated letters to try to discredit the leader of the Prussian liberals Benedikt Waldeck. Sacked from his job in the post office, he had become a journalist on a right-wing Berlin newspaper, and supplemented his income by writing lurid novels under a romantic pseudonym. And it was in one of these, *Biarritz*, that a remarkable gathering takes place in a central European graveyard.

The scene is the Jewish cemetery in Prague, the oldest in Europe, during the Feast of Tabernacles. It is night and all is silent. Then the tower clock of the town hall strikes eleven. A key clicks in the lock of the cemetery gates. A rustling of long coats is heard; a white, shadowy figure appears, and then twelve more. These thirteen are the representatives of the twelve tribes of Israel plus the exiles, and they are greeted by someone who is addressed as "Son of the accursed." It is evident they are up to no good.

One by one, they report on what they've been doing for the last hundred years and their current thinking. Levi has got gold; Reuben has been setting up stock exchanges; Simeon has been getting his hands on all the best agricultural land, Judah on the factories. Manasseh from Budapest meanwhile is capturing the press, Benjamin the professions; Asher (from London) wants free marriage between Jews and Christians, and has been enjoying "the forbidden pleasure with the women of our enemies." Naphtali wants to seize government bureaucracies; Dan is after monopolies on bread, butter, liquor, and wool. Zebulon argues for siding with liberals to foment revolution, while Issachar is interested in discrediting the military classes in the eyes of the people and Aaron sees the advantages in undermining the Church. The board meeting of Evil Jews Inc. over, they depart with the words "Let us renew our oath, sons of the golden calf, and go out to all the lands of the earth!"

After *Biarritz*'s forgotten publication, the chapter titled "In the Jewish Cemetery at Prague" underwent some curious metamorphoses. In 1872, it turned up as a pamphlet in Russia, with a foreword arguing that, though the meeting was fiction, it nevertheless revealed a truth. In 1881, it was published in France in the magazine *Le Contemporain*. This time, however, it was called the "Rabbi's Speech," and consolidated all the various wicked claims into one address, whose speaker talked of "Our sole aim—world domination, as was promised to our father Abraham." By now it had mutated from fiction to fact, a speech supposedly delivered at a real gathering around the tomb of the "Grand Master Caleb." Furthermore, it was held to have been recounted by an observer—that most irreproachable of characters, an English diplomat by the name of Sir John Readclif![18]

In 1891, in Odessa on the Russian Black Sea, the "Rabbi's Speech" was published in a local newspaper but was said to have been given at a secret Sanhedrin eight years earlier—there had been a congress of Reform Judaism that year, held in Leipzig. It was reprinted again in France in 1896, in a book by François Bournand, *Les Juifs et Nos Contemporains*, and now the sinister speechifier was named as Chief Rabbi John Readclif. And so it went, with the rabbi subsequently becoming Rabbi Eichorn or Reichhorn, and sometimes speaking to a congress of Jews in Lemberg in Austria in 1912. In October 1920, *La Vieille France* published a Russian document recognizing the similarity between the Reichhorn speech and the *Protocols* but seeing this as evidence of the authenticity of both, the one backing up the other. In any case, hadn't the speech been vouched for by that valiant English diplomat Sir John Readcliffe, "who paid with his life for the divulgation"?[19] So fiction had become fact, and a German forger and author of pfennig dreadfuls had gradually turned into a power-hungry rabbi and a martyred English nobleman.

Enter Machiavelli

Dr. J. Stanjek's hypothesis of a fictional source for the *Protocols* wasn't enough, however, to discredit them. Even if there was a structural and philosophical similarity with the "Rabbi's Speech," this could have been coincidental. Just because Goedsche had imagined a ghastly get-together in which the world was subverted, that didn't mean that no such gatherings had ever happened. And the *Protocols* were, after all, a record, word for word, of what was said at a very particular time and place: Basel 1897. It took another journalist to unearth another strange similarity before people began to sit up and listen.

When the *Times* editorial worrying about a "Pax Judaeica" was written in May 1920, the newspaper's correspondent in Constantinople, Philip Graves, had worked for the paper for well over a decade. Sometime probably in the summer of 1921, he was approached by a Russian exile whom he calls "Mr. X"—"a landowner with English connections. Orthodox by religion, by political opinion, a Constitutional Monarchist."

Mr. X, Graves later wrote, had long been interested in the Jewish question and in Freemasonry, and had studied the *Protocols*. He was therefore intrigued when he was offered a number of old books for purchase by a former officer of the tsar's secret police, the Okhrana. "Among these books," Graves wrote, "was a small volume in French, lacking the title page, with dimensions of 5½ by 3½ inches. On the leather back was printed in Latin capitals the word Joli." The book appeared to have been published in the 1860s or 1870s, and the preface was placed and dated to "Geneva, 15 October 1864."

What was in this small book was sensational. For Mr. X, leafing through it idly one day, was suddenly struck by the resemblance between the passage he was reading and something he'd seen in the *Protocols*. He began a line-by-line textual comparison, and the truth rapidly became clear: the *Protocols* were a substantial paraphrase of this book. And in many places not even a paraphrase, but a direct copy, a plagiarism. Whoever had composed them had done so after first reading this very publication. And if that were true, the *Protocols* couldn't possibly be an account of an event that had happened thirty years after the "Joli" book was published.

The French book was not about Jews at all; in fact, it didn't even mention them. Its subject was French politics in the 1860s, the period of the corrupt Second Empire of Napoleon's nephew, Louis Napoleon or Napoleon III. The emperor was no liberal—direct printed criticism of him was banned—and the small book bought by Mr. X was an allegorical satire of him written in the form of an encounter in Hell between two historical figures—Machiavelli and the French philosopher Montesquieu. The author was a Parisian lawyer, Maurice Joly, and the book had probably been published in Brussels and then smuggled into France. The fact that it was allegorical did not prevent the courageous Joly from being tried for sedition, fined, and imprisoned for fifteen months.

In the book, *Dialogues in Hell Between Machiavelli and Montesquieu*, the best, wickedest lines belong to Napoleon III in the shape of Machiavelli. He explains to the sidelined Montesquieu the need for the ruthless use of power, the control of business and the media, and how to set rivals against each other—all things the emperor's enemies accused him of at the time. His is a language of total cynicism.

Scholars suggest that Protocols One to Nineteen correspond to Dialogues One to Seventeen.[20] According to the historian Norman Cohn, a total of 160 passages, or two-fifths of the total text of the *Protocols*, is lifted directly from Joly. Readers will recall the excerpt from Protocol Twelve quoted earlier, concerning control of the press (see page 23). They can now compare it with this, from Machiavelli in the *Dialogues*:

> I shall count on devoted journals in each party. I shall have an aristocratic one in the aristocratic party, a republican one in the republican party, a revolutionary one in the revolutionary party, an anarchist one, if necessary, in the anarchist party. Like the God Vishnu, my press will have a hundred arms, each hand of which will feel the nuances of public opinion.

Whoever transformed the *Dialogues* into the *Protocols* couldn't even be bothered to change the categories or the order in which they appeared.

The Times refutation, written by Graves and titled "The End of the *Protocols*," appeared over three days in August 1921, and should, one might imagine, have brought the curtain down on the matter. Even the *Spectator* was now calling the *Protocols* a "malignant lunacy." There were, however, a couple of questions remaining, of which the most interesting was, who had done it? Who had forged the *Protocols*, when, and why?

From Nilus to Rachkovsky

Zur Beek had claimed that the *Protocols* had been secretly transcribed by the *Okhrana* in 1897, taken back to Russia, and translated and studied by certain scholars, among them Sergei Nilus, who had published them in 1905. Nilus himself, it turned out, had another view. Or, rather, several other views. In the epilogue to the 1905 edition of his book, he had claimed that the *Protocols* were an extract from a longer document, removed from the "Zionist executive archives" somewhere in France. Six years later, however, the picture had become more complex. In the 1911 edition, Nilus gave the following account:

> In 1901 a now deceased acquaintance, Court Marshal Alexei Sukhotin of Tchernigov, gave into my possession a handwritten manuscript that detailed completely and clearly the secret Jewish-Freemason conspiracy that will surely lead to the end of our vile world. The person who gave me this manuscript assured me that it was a faithful translation of the original document. It had been stolen by a lady from one of the highest and most influential leaders of the Freemasons following a secret meeting in France . . . He mentioned her by name, but I have forgotten it.[21]

No Basel Congress, no crack team of scribes in Frankfurt, but a postcoital robbery by a brave lady.

Other publishers had variations on the theme. A French translator, Roger Lambelin, claimed the *Protocols* were stolen from an iron chest in a town in Alsace (then part of Germany) by the mistress of a top Freemason. A Polish translator averred that they were stolen from the home of the father of Zionism, Dr. Theodor Herzl himself. Theodor Fritsch, a German, told readers that the text had been confiscated during a house search by the Saint Petersburg police, who gave it to Nilus for translation.

Hermann Bernstein was an American journalist and diplomat who, on his return from an assignment in the Far East in January 1919, was asked by his editor at the *New York Herald* to take a look at the *Protocols*. They had been brought in to the newspaper by a Dr. Harris Houghton, who was connected with the army intelligence department. Houghton was enthusiastic, saying the documents were his "prized possession" and had been given to him by his assistant, a young woman named Natalie de Bogory, who, in turn, had acquired them from Russian exile Boris Brasol. Hermann Bernstein took a look and, unlike Henry Ford and Ernest Liebold, saw at once that they were a crude hoax, bearing no relationship to Jewish custom or life.

Bernstein also understood how dangerous the *Protocols* were.

Instead of verifying them, he set about exposing them. In February 1921, as a result of his researches, Bernstein published a book called *The History of a Lie*. This detailed the transfiguration of the cemetery scene in Goedsche's potboiler, but it also referred to a meeting in 1909 between Sergei Nilus and a French-Russian nobleman, Count Alexandre du Chayla. Although Nilus lived in a villa outside Moscow in a rather irreligious ménage with his wife and mistress, this encounter had taken place under the auspices of Archimandrite Xenophont at the monastery of Optina Pustyn in the district of Kaluga. After dinner, as du Chayla recounted later, the conversation turned to the *Protocols*. And here Nilus elaborated upon his earlier explanations. His mistress, said Nilus, was the woman who had brought him the manuscript, but she had acquired it in Paris from a "General Ratchkovsky," who had given her a manuscript removed, he said, from the secret archives of the Freemasons in France.

Piotr Ivanovich Rachkovsky was no invention. A former student radical turned secret policeman, he was, from 1884 to 1903, the head of the external branch of the Okhrana, based in Paris. Rachkovsky was not a bureaucrat by nature. He was a speculator, a politician, an author, a provocateur, an employer of assassins and, most notably, a forger. In 1892, he forged a newspaper letter from the Russian radical exile Plekhanov, and the following week some letters supposedly from other radicals attacking Plekhanov. And in the same year, under the pseudonym Jehan-Préval, he published a book, *Anarchism and Nihilism*, which argued, among other things, that following the French Revolution the Jews had become the masters of the continent, "governing by discreet means both monarchies and republics." This understanding, wrote Rachkovsky/Préval "provides the key to a host of disturbing and seemingly insoluble riddles."[22]

Subsequently, at least two colleagues of Rachkovsky were to testify that he had caused the *Protocols* to be concocted, creating evidence for the assertion he'd already made in the forged *Anarchism and Nihilism*. If this is true (and these people were, after all, police agents), it would seem that the forgers went about the business of creating their text by borrowing material that was already to hand but a bit obscure: a whole lot of Joly here, a dollop of Goedsche there.

The Rachkovsky *Protocols* were originally designed for the domestic Russian market—a weapon in the battle between those who wanted the absolutist regime to stay much the same and those who wished to reform it. As ever, the reform party was identified with the Jews, and Jews indeed supported it. The reactionaries, therefore, used the Jewish connection as part of their crusade against change, adding a religious and mystical dimension to an argument about power. And early appearances of the *Protocols* had a way of coinciding with anti-Jewish and anti-reform campaigns. A pre-Nilus version was published in southern Russia in 1903, around the time an anti-Jewish pogrom took place in the area. Nilus's own first effort appeared as the tsar was being forced into his October Manifesto of reforms, which created a constitution and a parliament. The leading absolutist politician was also the chief of police, D. F. Trepov, who responded by encouraging a series of pogroms in the Jewish Pale of Settlement, local peasants being told that the Jews had coerced the tsar into this devilish work. His deputy chief of police was one Piotr Ivanovich Rachkovsky.

Nicholas II himself received one of the first copies of Nilus's book and was delighted, scribbling exclamations in the margins: "What depth of thought!" "How prophetic!" "How perfectly they have fulfilled their plan!" "This year of 1905 has truly been dominated by the Jewish Elders!" "All of it is undoubtedly genuine! The destructive hand of Jewry is everywhere!" And more.[23] The sovereign's pleasure took a practical turn: in the years 1905–1906, he personally contributed 12 million rubles to disseminating anti-Semitic tracts.

And then, abruptly, the tsar withdrew his support from the *Protocols* and forbade their dissemination. Sixteen years before Bernstein, Graves, and Stanjek, Nicholas had become convinced that the book was tainted. "It is impossible," said the tsar honorably, "to defend something sacred by dirty methods."[24] Few partisans of the *Protocols*, however, shared his scruples.

"Reality Provides
the Best Commentary"

Salvaging the *Protocols* was not going to be an easy task. Anybody comparing the text with that of the much earlier *Dialogues* could see that the first was a plagiarism of the second, and anyone looking at the weird evolution of the "Rabbi's Speech" could trace the notion of the assembly of super-manipulative Jews back to the excited prose of "Sir John Retcliffe." The section of respectable Establishment opinion that had, like *The Times*, flirted with the notion of Jews sitting around and plotting the takeover of the world, was now lost to the Protocoliers.

But there were many other people outside the Establishment left to convince, and the conspiracy's partisans could not be accused of a lack of invention. At some point in his turbulent life, Lord Alfred Douglas, the "Bosie" whose caresses had helped earn Oscar Wilde his place in Reading jail, had become Britain's leading anti-Semite. Now in middle age, Douglas was the proprietor and editor of his own literary magazine, *Plain English*. Within a week of the Graves articles in *The Times*, Bosie had the answer: Maurice Joly was not Maurice Joly at all. In the edition of *Plain English* of August 27, 1921, it was revealed that he was, in fact, Moses Joel, a circumcised Jew.[25]

The implication of this racial identification was spelled out a little later by Gottfried zur Beek in the preface to his 1923 edition. Joly/Joel "is in fact a precursor of the Elders of Zion," he wrote, "and affords us an excellent look into the art of Jewish conspiracy."[26] In other words, though the *Dialogues* might have seemed to be about Napoleon III, coming from a Jew they were actually a revelation of Jewish thinking—thinking that would later become the *Protocols*. Another German *Protocols* supporter, Count Ernst zu Reventlow, added the twist that it was perhaps the elders who were plagiarists, with Herzl himself raiding the *Dialogues* for his speeches to the First Zionist Congress—though it has to be said that this theory does rather reduce the demonic potency of the *Protocols*, with the image of the supreme rulers of the world borrowing entire phrases from obscure French books.

In 1924, even the Moses Joel theory was exploded when, by chance, a Parisian legal journal published shortened biographies of past members of the profession. Included were excerpts from a lost autobiography of Maurice Joly himself, written in the 1870s. This showed that Joly, far from being Jewish, came from a strict Catholic family with links to the rural nobility. It even included a copy of his baptismal certificate from the church register, complete with the name of the presiding priest.

This discovery, however, did nothing to change the opinion of the man who was to become the most important and active supporter of the *Protocols*. After the abortive Nazi putsch in Munich in 1923, Adolf Hitler was imprisoned in the Landsberg fortress to serve an absurdly short sentence for armed insurrection. There he wrote his apocalyptic manifesto *Mein Kampf*. His attitude toward the *Protocols* is worth quoting at length.

The extent to which the whole existence of the people is based on a continual lie is shown in an incomparable manner in *The Protocols of the Elders of Zion*, which the Jews hate so tremendously. The *Frankfurter Zeitung* is forever moaning to the people that they are supposed to be a forgery; which is the surest proof that they are genuine. What many Jews do perhaps unconsciously is here consciously exposed. But that is not what matters . . . What matters is that they uncover, with really horrifying reliability, the nature and activity of the Jewish people, and expose them in their inner logic and their final aims. But reality provides the best commentary. Whoever examines the historical development of the last hundred years from the standpoint of the book will at once understand why the Jewish press makes such an uproar. For once this book becomes generally familiar to a people, the Jewish menace can be regarded as already vanquished.[27]

The argument is undefeatable: the *Protocols* confirm what I believe and what I think I see around me, therefore they are true in the most important sense, even if they themselves are forgeries. Furthermore, whether they are forgeries or not does not matter; because they confirm what we see around us, they will help people better understand what is going on. As Henry Ford had suggested, they fitted in the past, they fitted now.

Ford himself recanted in 1927. As early as January 1921, there had been loud voices raised in Christian communities against rising anti-Semitism. The writer John Spargo got up a petition urging Americans to "strike at this un-American and un-Christian agitation." Former presidents Woodrow Wilson and William Howard Taft signed, as did luminaries such as W. E. B. Du Bois, William Jennings Bryan, Clarence Darrow, and the poet Robert Frost. Under pressure, Ford issued a statement saying he was deeply mortified that his newspaper should have been used for the propagation of "gross forgeries." He asked forgiveness of the Jewish community "for the harm I have unintentionally committed." And he demanded of those people abroad who were reprinting *The International Jew*—particularly the German Nazi Theodor Fritsch—that they desist. They ignored him. Hadn't Ford been pressured into his change of heart? Wasn't he too a victim of the Jews? To Hitler, Heinrich Ford the anti-Semite was always to be a hero.

After 1933, the rise to power of the Nazis saw Germany ruled by people for whom the *Protocols* were literally and not just figuratively true. Two of Hitler's earliest *Parteigenossen* and friends, Dietrich Eckart and Rudolf Hess, were members of the Thule Society, a group of Germanic occultists and racial mystics who had funded the first zur Beek version of the *Protocols*. Alfred Rosenberg, who was to become responsible during the war for the occupied East, carried the *Protocols* in his luggage when he fled from Estonia to Munich in 1918. In 1929, the Nazi Party itself bought the rights to the zur Beek *Protocols*.

The "Rabbi's Speech" prospered too under the new regime. Johann von Leers, promoted to professor at the University of Jena by the Nazis, produced another version after 1933, as part of a longer work detailing various stories about the Jews and their devious (and sometimes disgusting) customs and habits. We will meet von Leers again, later in this chapter. And Theodor Fritsch's *Handbook of the Jewish Question*, which included the "Rabbi's Speech," became a compulsory school text in Nazi Germany. A fictional potboiler had been transformed for millions of schoolchildren into higher historical truth.

Who Would Have Believed It?

There were those, of course, who had no difficulty dismissing the *Protocols*. In 1934, their Swiss publishers were put on trial for producing "smut literature." At the end of the case, during which all the material about Joly, Nilus, Goedsche, and Rachkovsky emerged, Presiding Judge Meyer expressed his incredulity. "I hope to see the day," he said, "when nobody will be able to understand why otherwise sane and reasonable men should have had to torment their brains for fourteen days over the authenticity or fabrication of the *Protocols of Zion* . . . I regard the *Protocols* as ridiculous nonsense."[28]

Ridiculous nonsense, maybe, but also dangerous nonsense. For years the assumption has been that the *Protocols* were the kind of stuff served up by unscrupulous propagandists and absorbed by the ignorant.[29] We are used to seeing gross prejudices as the product of peasant credulity, lumpen ignorance, or provincial small-mindedness. People like us, this implies, would not be fooled.

But belief in the *Protocols* was not just a prejudice; it was a fully worked-out view of how, as the American author Stephen Bronner puts it, "history operates behind our backs." It was, in fact, a conspiracy theory, and one which took deep root in the youth movements, universities, professional bodies, and cultural associations of Germany—in other words, in organs of middle-class civil society. The German academic Binjamin Segel, for instance, was shocked by a speech given by the historian Professor Hans Kania in Potsdam in the spring of 1924. The occasion was the jubilee of the philosopher Immanuel Kant, but Kania "held forth about how wonderful it was that this remarkable historical and political document of 1897 had predicted events that were borne out a generation later. It was only logical to assume that those who foresaw these events were the very same people who caused them, that the Elders of Zion therefore constituted the secret supreme government of the world."[30] "If one reads objectively," Kania added, "one can espy the prophecy of the world war."[31]

This was a full three years after the public unmasking of the *Protocols*, and Kania was no country peasant, yet there isn't even a hint of qualification in his words. During the same period, a Jewish writer attempted to comprehend what was going on in the minds of his fellow countrymen. "In Berlin," he reported, "I attended several meetings which were entirely devoted to the *Protocols*. The speaker was usually a professor, a teacher, an editor, a lawyer or someone of that kind. The audience consisted of members of the educated class, civil servants, tradesmen, former officers, ladies, above all students, students of all faculties and years of seniority ... I observed the students. A few hours earlier they had perhaps been exerting all their mental energy in a seminar under the guidance of a world-famous scholar in an effort to solve some legal or philosophical problem." Now, the writer observed, they were angry, irrational, and bloodthirsty. He concluded sadly, "German scholarship [has] allowed belief in the genuineness of the *Protocols* and in the existence of a Jewish world conspiracy to penetrate ever more deeply into all the educated sections of the German population, so that now it is simply ineradicable."[32]

We can speculate that the educated classes were partly seduced by the neo-romanticism of the *Protocols* and their pseudo-intellectual content. But time and again we return to that phrase of Ford's: "They fit." And what these absurd forgeries appeared to fit was a world in which the middle classes, the salaried, the educated, the people who had something to lose, found themselves under threat—from communism, from industrialization, from uncertainty. These were the social classes who had exercised power and influence, and they were seeking some explanation for why everything was all now at hazard.

What Happened Next

However ridiculous the *Protocols* might have seemed to a Swiss judge, their propagation led to acts that ranged from the appalling to the unspeakable. In 1918, during the Russian Civil War, thousands of copies of the Nilus version were printed under the auspices of the White general Denikin in the Ukrainian city of Rostov and handed out to his troops, presumably to motivate them. Between 1918 and 1920, these same forces were responsible for the executing or massacre of up to 120,000 Jews before Denikin's eventual defeat. In Germany, there was the Holocaust.

Norman Cohn, in his book *Warrant for Genocide*, quotes the postwar testimony of SS captain Dieter Wisliceny, who was tried and executed in 1947 for his part in killing Hungarian, Greek, and Slovak Jews. A straight line, said Wisliceny, ran from *The Protocols of the Elders of Zion* to the precepts of the Nazis, and from there to the attempted murder of a race. The straightness of this line is evident from the activities of the Nazi academic Professor von Leers, last seen propagating the "Rabbi's Speech" at the University of Jena, but by 1942 publishing *The Criminal Nature of the Jews*. As the Holocaust moved from improvisation to industrial organization, von Leers wrote, "Not only is each people morally justified in exterminating the hereditary criminals—but any people that still keeps and protects Jews is just as guilty of an offense against public safety as someone who cultivates cholera germs."

Von Leers, with whom we haven't finished yet, was an extreme case. Most Germans were not involved in extermination and, even before the war, would not have described themselves as anti-Semitic. Can it be argued that, had there been no zur Beek and no Nilus to disseminate the *Protocols*, people would have behaved differently? At the very least, argues historian Richard S. Levy, they created a gulf between Jews and other Germans, so that when disaster struck, "the *Protocols* helped render Jews ineligible for rescue by the great majority of their fellowmen."[33] They also helped Adolf Hitler to believe that the war he himself had caused was

actually the fault of the Jews, and that this justified the attempt to liqui-
date them.

Carmen Callil's 2007 book *Bad Faith* shows how the fabulist and
spendthrift boulevardier Louis Darquier de Pellepoix (de Pellepoix being
yet another of Darquier's inventions) was helped into becoming Vichy's
commissioner for Jewish affairs and playing an active part in the deliv-
ery of French Jews to their wartime deaths by his complete belief in the
authenticity of the *Protocols*. No wonder that after the war and the Holocaust, the philosopher Hannah Arendt, in a reflexive echo of *Mein Kampf*,
argued that the provenance of the *Protocols* was not its main significance.
"The chief political and historical fact of the matter is that the forgery is
being believed. This fact is more important than the (historically speaking, secondary) circumstance that it is a forgery."[34]

Nor did the *Protocols* entirely die as a consequence of the Second World
War. Idi Amin promoted them in his mad Ugandan fiefdom. New translations were produced in Pakistan, Malaysia, and Croatia. No less than twelve
editions of the *Protocols* were published after 1945 in Argentina, which had
(and has) both sizable Jewish and German populations. In the 1970s, there
was a sudden rash of conspiracy stories in the Argentinian popular press,
in which it was claimed that a "Chief Rabbi Gordon" of New York City was
involved in a plot to create a second Jewish state, this time in Patagonia, to be
called Andinia. The tale sparked a dozen books elaborating on this conspiracy, many carrying direct excerpts from the *Protocols*. Needless to say, there
was no Rabbi Gordon and no plot.[35] In 1994, a car bomb went off outside
the Jewish Argentine Mutual Association in Buenos Aires, killing eighty-five
people. It was not only the worst terrorist outrage in Latin American history,
it was the worst act of anti-Semitic terrorism since the death of Hitler.

The *Protocols* and the Middle East

Gaza City, when I visited it in May 2003, was a terrible place: its beach
a parody with smashed concrete and rusting iron, the city a warren of

unfinished houses and tangled electric cables. On three sides, and over-head, were the Israelis, penning a population of more than a million Pal-estinians into a narrow strip of dust. The strongest political and social association among the Palestinians had come to be the group known as the Islamic Resistance Movement, or Hamas. That spring, I was there to see one of the leaders of Hamas, and to ask him about a most extraordi-nary aspect of his group's program.

The Hamas *Covenant* is about twenty pages long and made up of thirty-six articles. It is a mixture of political manifesto, historical obser-vation, and exaltation to the faithful. It begins with a quotation from the 1920s founder of the Muslim Brotherhood in Egypt, Hassan al-Banna—"Israel will rise and will remain erect until Islam eliminates it as it has eliminated its predecessors"—and sets out the nature and duties of the membership, who must be good and pious Muslims.

Article Seventeen is about "the role of Muslim women" but contains a digression concerning the enemies of Hamas, who will use every effort to further their cause, including education curricula, movies, and culture, "using as their intermediaries their craftsmen who are part of the various Zionist organizations which take all sorts of names and shapes such as: the Free Masons, Rotary Clubs . . . and the like . . . Those Zionist organi-zations control vast material resources, which enable them to fulfill their mission amidst societies, with a view of implementing Zionist goals."

By the time the reader reaches Article Twenty-two, "On the Powers That Support the Enemy," the scale of this malign mission has expanded.

> This wealth [allowed the Zionists to] take over control of the world media . . . They used this wealth to stir revolutions in parts of the globe . . . They stood behind the French and Communist Revolutions . . . They stood behind World War I so as to wipe out the Islamic Caliphate . . . They obtained the Balfour Declaration and established the League of Nations . . . They also stood behind World War II . . . and inspired the establishment of the United Nations . . . There's no war that broke out anywhere without their fingerprints on it.

And if you think you have heard all this somewhere before, Article Thirty-Two, "The Attempts to Isolate Palestinian People," confirms it. "Zionist scheming," the *Covenant* claims, "has no end, and after Palestine they will covet expansion from the Nile to the Euphrates . . . Their scheme has been laid out in *The Protocols of the Elders of Zion* and their present conduct is the best proof of what is said there."

It is like one of those novels in which the hero encounters an archaic or ancient legend which has somehow managed to survive, still potent, to the modern day. So, a Palestinian child in a Gazan class at the beginning of the twenty-first century may well be hearing things written by a Parisian lawyer about Napoleon III 140 years earlier, falsified by a Russian spy three decades later, and used as a pretext for racial mass murder in Germany.

Inside one of these concrete houses in Gaza, its walls and stairs bare, I met the man who was then Hamas's number two. Abdel-Aziz Rantisi wore tan slacks and one of those ubiquitous checkered shirts that are the new uniform for men in the Middle East. A serious-looking man with dark eyebrows, he had once been a pediatrician, his radicalization dating from a period he spent exiled to a no-man's-land on the Lebanese-Israeli border with four hundred others. Here in Gaza, in a room with curtains closed against spying eyes, containing a child's model of the Dome of the Rock in Jerusalem and a picture of al-Banna, we conducted a short interview. He spoke partly in English and partly in Arabic.

Toward the end, I asked him directly about the *Protocols* and what they were doing in the Hamas *Covenant*. Rantisi frowned. "You know," he said, "when I first heard about this document, I didn't want to believe it. But then I saw what was happening in Palestine and I could see that it was genuine." It fitted then, it fits now. Reality provides the best commentary. Hamas was then the second-largest organization among all Palestinians, and was growing fast as hope for peace receded. Rantisi, however, was dead within a few months. The second attempt on his life by a helicopter gunship succeeded. He was by that time the leader of Hamas, having replaced the assassinated blind Sheikh Yassin some weeks previously.

What I learned on that journey was that invocations of the *Protocols* and other manifestations of European anti-Semitism were rife in the Arab and wider Muslim world. Take just one example, from the "Political National Education" page of the Palestinian Authority daily newspaper *Al-Hayat al-Jadida* (January 25, 2001). There it claimed that "disinformation has been one of the bases of moral and psychological manipulation among the Israelis . . . *The Protocols of the Elders of Zion* did not ignore the importance of using propaganda to promote the Zionist goals." And it directly quoted our old friend Protocol Twelve, though leaving out any archaic references to the god Vishnu.

The Palestinians are few in number and the nature of their grievance against some Jews is well understood. The tensions in the Middle East also exemplify the danger that the *Protocols* still represent. At the time of this writing, there is considerable concern that the Islamic Republic of Iran might be developing a nuclear weapon. As the prime target for such a weapon, Israel might seek to take preemptive action—action which could lead to a wider war—as it did in 1981, when it bombed the first Osirak nuclear reactor in Iraq.

In April 2004, an Iranian TV station broadcast a documentary series titled *Al-Sameri wa al-Saher.* The series' purpose was to explain to Iranians how the Jews control Hollywood. For example, *Funny Girl*—starring "the ugly Jewish actress Barbra Streisand"—was one of a number of movies designed to depict the Jews favorably. *Tootsie* was another. *Yentl* "dealt with the Zionists' wish to benefit from feminism." *The Matrix* was a "meeting point between Hollywood and Jewish Zionist fundamentalism"; *Lawrence of Arabia* was an attempt to "infantilize the Arabs"; and *Alien* was designed to demonize non-Westerners. All of this, a narrator claimed, was "in total compliance with *The Protocols of the Elders of Zion.*"

But just in case the Iranian viewer of the early twenty-first century was not fully versed in the story of the *Protocols*, the documentary carefully outlined the story of the Basel Congress of 1897, with its own new twist. In this version, some Russian policemen set fire to the congress hall while the delegates were inside. Terrified, "the Jews fled, and the policemen went inside and gathered up all the documents and sent them to Moscow." Among these writings they found what was later called *The Protocols of the Elders of Zion*. "The *Protocols* were divided into twenty-four parts," the narrator claimed, "and included the Satanic Jewish ideas of taking over the world using a Jewish government, after destroying all of Orthodox Russia, Catholic Europe, the pope's reign, and Islam."

In May and June 2008, the Iranian television news channel IRINN showed a series titled *The Secret of Armageddon*, in which various academics and "researchers" testified to the truth of the *Protocols*. The narrator concluded the series by tying the old conspiracy to new ones:

> Today, there are many indications that the "hidden hands" of world Zionism were involved in the 9/11 terrorist attack. According to a large group of Western intellectuals, the Zionists are the real rulers of the United States. According to irrefutable documents published by independent American media outlets, the Zionists used intelligence agents and spies, with the full cooperation of agencies with[in] the country, to carry out this terrorist operation in full view of the world, in order to prepare the ground for taking over Afghanistan and Iraq, and to realize the dream of a greater Israel.

The thread from Goedsche to the present day has never properly been snapped. Johann von Leers died in 1965, incidentally, but not in prison or in Germany or even in a South American hideaway. Somehow he had fled to the Middle East, lain low, converted to Islam under the name of Omar Amin, and then resurfaced in Egypt as an adviser on propaganda to the Arab nationalist government of President Nasser. One of Nasser's practices, while von Leers was with him, was to hand out, to those who wanted them and those who didn't, copies of *The Protocols of the Elders of Zion*.

2. DARK MIRACLES

The Communist Party is based on the principle of coercion which doesn't recognize any limitations or inhibitions. And the central idea of this principle of boundless coercion is not coercion by itself but the absence of any limitation whatsoever—moral, political, and even physical. Such a party is capable of achieving miracles.

—GEORGY PYATAKOV, CONVERSATION WITH NIKOLAI VALENTINOV[1]

On January 23, 1937, a trial began in central Moscow, the second of three great Soviet judicial events that were to shock the world. Under the high ceiling of a room that had been, in prerevolutionary days, part of the fashionable Nobles' Club, seventeen senior members of the Communist Party confessed to having done everything they could to undermine the new Soviet Union and to bring about its collapse. For a week, during morning, afternoon, and evening sessions, an audience composed of party members, selected "workers," representatives of the diplomatic corps, and foreign journalists listened with growing consternation and bewilderment as the seventeen confessed to a secret campaign of deliberately sabotaging Soviet industry. And as if this weren't diabolical enough, the conspirators agreed that they had done this in collaboration with the Soviet Union's greatest enemies, the German National Socialists—all at the behest of the renegade exile, Leon Trotsky. The story that came out at the trial went like this.

In August 1931, Georgy (Yuri) Leonidovich Pyatakov, chairman of the Central Administration of Chemical Industries of the USSR, traveled to Germany on an official visit for discussions with local civil servants and industrialists. However, these legitimate contacts were not the only people he met. He also had a meeting that was well outside the official itinerary. In fact, the encounter was top secret, even from the Soviet security apparatus.

This clandestine rendezvous, arranged through intermediaries, took place at the restaurant Am Zoo just off Berlin's fashionable Kurfürsten-damm. Waiting for Pyatakov at a small table was a young, dark-haired man whom Pyatakov would have known immediately—though he hadn't seen him for a number of years—as Leon Trotsky's son, Leon Sedov.

Now Pyatakov, who in the 1920s had been one of Trotsky's most fervent supporters, was no longer an ally of the exiled leader, having on a number of occasions made clear his later allegiance to Trotsky's successful nemesis, Stalin. Nevertheless, he sat down with Sedov and listened to what the young man had to say. Apparently, Sedov had come at his father's urgent behest.[2] There may have been a recent lull in Trotsky's never-ending campaign against Stalin, but according to Sedov, the struggle was now being resumed. Except this time Trotsky had allies, big allies, at the heart of the Communist Party itself. The followers of two other major leaders, Grigory Zinoviev and Lev Kamenev, were going to join with Trotsky's acolytes in an all-out attempt to remove Stalin from power. "Trotsky asks," said Sedov, "do you, Pyatakov, intend to take a hand in this fight?"

As the waiters cleared away the dishes around the two Russians and as other customers sipped their coffees, Pyatakov gave his consent: he was in. Sedov was delighted. His father, he said, had never had any doubt that, despite their earlier falling-out, Comrade Pyatakov would step up to the plate when he was needed. Then the son outlined the plan. It was Trotsky's view that there was no way to get rid of Stalin by anything as noble as a mass movement of the workers and peasants. Only a strategy of "wrecking" was likely to work, in which the achievements of the rapidly industrializing socialist state were systematically undermined through sabotage and terrorism. But it had also been concluded that such wreck-ing was insufficient on its own. The plotters would require the help of countries antagonistic toward the still youthful Soviet Union. A betrayal of all Bolshevik values though this might seem, it was necessary to get the job done. "Whoever tries to brush these questions aside," said Sedov, passing on what Trotsky had told him, "signs his own *testimonium pau-peratis.*"³ Pyatakov didn't demur.

Party Quarrels

Let us stop a moment and consider this man Pyatakov, who has just given himself over to a plot to destroy almost everything that he and his com-rades have been building for nearly fifteen years.

Georgy Leonidovich Pyatakov (party names: Kyivsky, Lyalin, Petro, or Yaponets) was born in the Cherkassy district of Ukraine and had probably just celebrated his forty-first birthday at the time of his trip to Berlin. Into those forty-one years he had stuffed several lifetimes of agitating, revolu-tionizing, fighting, organizing, administering, and finally state-building. His proletarian record was exemplary. He joined the Bolsheviks in 1912, and in the civil war following the 1917 revolution helped organize the Red Army in Ukraine, which was then largely occupied by White Russian forces under General Denikin. On one occasion, he, along with his brother, was taken by the enemy. As Trotsky's biographer Isaac Deutscher heard it, the two Pyatakov brothers, along with a number of other Bolsheviks, were led out to be dispatched. "The execution was in progress and the brother had already been shot when the firing squad had to flee before the Reds who had captured the town and were converging on the site where the massacre took place. Straight from the corpses of his brother and of his nearest com-rades, Pyatakov went to assume command over the Red Guards."⁴

So this was no armchair revolutionary. Photographs taken at the time show a thin man in a leather jacket, with a thick blondish beard, an explo-sion of hair, and steel-rimmed spectacles. When the war was over and the

Bolsheviks had won, Pyatakov threw himself into the business of helping to construct the new economy of the world's first socialist state. He was to become, in Deutscher's words, the "moving spirit and chief organizer of the Soviet drive for industrialization."[5]

Pyatakov evolved into what some other Bolshevik leaders—believing in the primacy of revolutionary politics over mere administration and government—condescendingly called a *spetz*, or specialist. In 1921 he took over the vast coal-mining industry in the Donbas area, and in 1922 became a deputy head of the State Planning Committee (known as Gosplan) and deputy chairman of the Supreme Council of the National Economy of the USSR. By then he was in his early thirties, and his devotion to building the nation's economy earned him a strange double accolade from the living prophet of the Russian Revolution, Lenin himself. In his famous testament written over Christmas and New Year of 1922–1923 and designed to be read out at the Twelfth Party Congress later that spring, Lenin advised his colleagues to remove Stalin from the general secretaryship of the party and warned of the possibility of a serious future schism between the Georgian roughneck and Trotsky. But Lenin also singled out four other leading cadres for special mention: Zinoviev, Kamenev, and two of their more junior colleagues, Bukharin and Pyatakov. "Of the younger members of the Central Committee," Lenin wrote, "I want to say a few words about Bukharin and Pyatakov. They are, in my opinion, the most able forces among the younger ones." He added, "Pyatakov is a man undoubtedly distinguished in will and ability, but too much devoted to administration and the administrative side of things to be relied on in a serious political question."[6] Lenin hoped, however, that Pyatakov would be able to evolve.

Two months later, the father of Russian communism suffered a nearly fatal stroke that put an end to his effective leadership. He died at the beginning of 1924. His testament, too critical of almost all his potential successors, was never read to the congress, and the very battle he'd warned about was gradually joined.

Over the next five years, and in various permutations, Stalin, Trotsky, Zinoviev, Kamenev, and Bukharin made alliances against one another, now combining as a "left," now as a "right" strand. The two constants were that Trotsky and Stalin were always opposed to each other, and that Stalin—a master of such maneuvers—always won. Crudely, the right, led by Bukharin, Tomsky, and Rykov, believed in a more gradual transformation of society in alliance with the peasants, alongside some level of private enterprise. The left, antagonistic toward the peasants, opposed to any trace of capitalism and in favor of rapid industrialization, was headed by the Leningrad (as Saint Petersburg was called from 1924 to 1991) party boss Zinoviev, the Moscow boss Kamenev, and Trotsky himself.[7] Stalin held the ring, making and unmaking alliances as was convenient, using the personal jealousies and anxieties of the other leaders for his own ends. Trotsky, cast as the dangerous Bonaparte figure, waiting in the wings for the moment to end the Revolution and assert his own power, was deserted at the critical moment by Zinoviev and Kamenev. Together with Stalin, these two formed a temporary triumvirate at the head of the party.

It was in October 1926, at a meeting of the Politburo, that Trotsky finally lost his temper and in front of the astounded members denounced Stalin as "the gravedigger of the Revolution." Shocked and by now frightened, his supporters made their way to Trotsky's flat in the Kremlin. Among them was Pyatakov. In Trotsky's absence, he flopped down into a chair and muttered, "You know, I have smelled gunpowder, but I have never seen anything like this. Why did Lev Davidovich say it? Stalin will never forgive him until the third and fourth generation!"[8]

Stalin's inevitable revenge came a year later. Strengthened by the outraged reaction of many party members to Trotsky's displays of out-and-out factionalism, the Stalinists and their allies voted to send the recalcitrant prophet into internal exile. In January 1928, Trotsky took the train to Alma-Ata in Kazakhstan, where he was to languish for the next eleven months.

Back in Moscow, some of his erstwhile friends made their peace with the majority. Pyatakov was one of these, now emerging in public to describe Trotsky's views as "self-contradictory." The sound of harrumphing came all the way from central Asia. "All contradictions," snorted Trotsky, "disappear in a man who like Pyatakov makes a suicide jump into a river." Supporters of Trotsky who had accompanied him into exile were just as indignant, treating news of Pyatakov's desertion with "the contempt and derision reserved for renegades." Trotsky excommunicated Pyatakov and the other stay-at-homes from the opposition: "They have denied their own convictions and have lied to the working class," he wrote.[9] In January 1929, Trotsky was banished from the Soviet Union altogether and put on a boat, arriving in Constantinople on February 13, 1930.

One reason why Pyatakov may have found it possible to reach an accommodation with Stalin was that the general secretary had begun a great shift from what, in Soviet terms, was the pragmatic right to the radical left. Severe economic problems had led to a slowdown in industrialization. Falling out with Bukharin, Stalin blamed the peasantry and in particular the kulaks, the wealthier peasants. Moving the Bukharinites out of positions of influence, Stalin commenced what has been called the Second Russian Revolution, a combination of China's Great Leap Forward and Cultural Revolution. Private property was abolished; peasants' landholdings were appropriated in the process of collectivizing agriculture; there was an almost reckless drive to create heavy industry. A great army of rapidly trained engineers was commanded into being. As one writer put it, "Scientific industrial 'norms' and rational calculations were cast aside in favor of impassioned mobilization."[10]

One consequence of this was the almost incredible success of the first five-year plan, whose quotas were famously achieved a year early.* Another was a resulting period of chaos, hunger, and disease. Inevitably, someone had to be blamed for the suffering, and equally inevitably, the authors of the plan were not going to blame themselves. The good—the

---

*In the socialist version of "Green Grow the Rushes, O," five was for the "years of the five-year plan," and four "for the four years taken."

products of the Soviet economic miracle—was their doing. The bad was the fault of the enemies of the revolution—the kulaks, the backsliders, the saboteurs, and the oppositionists.

Back to the Plot

In February 1931, a few months before the meeting with Pyatakov that was to become so notorious at the 1937 trial, Leon Sedov, working as an outrider for his exiled father, arrived in Germany and rented an apartment in Berlin. His role in the city was described later by Trotsky: "Leon was always on the look-out, avidly searching for connecting threads with Russia, hunting up returning tourists, Soviet students assigned abroad, or sympathetic functionaries in the foreign representations."

Sedov's task was complicated by the presence of Soviet security agents, whose surveillance followed him as he chased "for hours through the streets of Berlin . . . to avoid compromising his informant."[11] This must have made his discussions with Pyatakov somewhat risky, since the red-haired, whiskery old Bolshevik was notable for his appearance. Even so, as Pyatakov testified at the trial, the two men agreed to meet again just a few days later, and in the same restaurant. This second conversation was very brief, lasting no more than ten or fifteen minutes. The subject under discussion was funding the conspiracy. "Sedov said, 'You realize, [Yuri] Leonidovich, that inasmuch as the fight has been resumed, money is needed. You can provide the necessary funds for waging the fight.'"[12] The funding mechanism Sedov specified was for Pyatakov to place as many Soviet government orders as possible at favorable prices with two German companies, Borsig and Demag. Sedov had presumably arranged to get a kickback from the Germans.[13] Now fully part of the great plot to bring down Stalin, Pyatakov went back to Russia.

A few months later, in December 1931, while Pyatakov was in his office at the Supreme Council of National Economy in Moscow, he received an unusual letter. It was brought by a coconspirator, A. A. Shestov, who had fabricated a pretext to come to the capital to discuss "the organization of Trotskyite work in the Kuznetsk basin."[14]

As Shestov told the judges at the same trial, he had been given the letter in Berlin by Sedov, who carried it concealed in a pair of shoes. The transcript of the 1937 proceedings contains the following *Boy's Own* exchange between Shestov and the state prosecutor Vyshinsky:

> **V:** In which shoe were the letters—in the right or the left?
> **SH:** A letter was secreted in each shoe. He said that there were marks on the envelopes of the letters. On one there was the letter P—that was meant for Pyatakov. And on the other was the letter M—that meant it was for Muralov.
> **V:** You gave a letter to Pyatakov?
> **SH:** I gave him the letter marked P.
> **V:** From which shoe, from the right or the left?
> **SH:** I cannot say exactly.[15]

The letter marked P was from Trotsky himself, written for some reason in German and signed LT. It thanked Pyatakov for his efforts so far, and reminded him of the three major tasks of the conspiracy: to use "every means" to remove Stalin and his "immediate assistants," to unite all anti-Stalin forces and to engage in economic sabotage.

It seems, however, that Pyatakov's efforts were not considered sufficient. In the autumn of 1932, there was yet another meeting with Sedov in Berlin, where the young man now showed impatience. "You are engaged all the time in organizational preparations and conversations," he chided Pyatakov, "but you have nothing concrete to show. You know the sort of man Lev Davidovich [Trotsky] is, he is roaring and raving, burning with impatience to have his instructions carried out as quickly as possible, and nothing concrete is visible from your report."[16] Sedov's exhortations were effective. Over the next two years, according to confessions from various accused, Pyatakov and his associates assiduously went about the business of sabotaging Soviet industry. In 1933 in Ukraine, for example, Pyatakov's protégé Loginov did his subtle bit by operating coke ovens deliberately inefficiently, "without utilizing valuable by-products."[17] The railways were damaged in the same year by Comrade Serebryakov, who, following a discussion with the energetic Pyatakov, disrupted freight traffic by "increasing the runs of empty cars, by refraining from making full use of the traction power and capacity of engines and so forth."[18]

A visit to the Central Urals Copper Works in 1935 worried Pyatakov. "I saw that the wrecking work was being carried out so unscrupulously crudely that even the most superficial observer could see that all was not right on the job." The sabotage clearly had to be conducted more cleverly, so that no one would notice. Pyatakov "was obliged to tell the chief of construction to be more cautious, to show at least some energy on the construction job."[19] On another occasion, Pyatakov made the decision to build a workers' housing settlement two kilometers closer to a major industrial plant than was recommended, in order to compromise the health and safety of the workforce. He delayed the building of new soda plants. He was the fiendish Fabian of industrial destruction, a gradualist deindustrializer.

But there was an ongoing problem with the Pyatakov approach—it was still too slow. Months were passing, Trotsky was still in exile and Stalin remained in power. Trotsky insisted something more daring had to be done.

The Oslo Accords

At 4:27 p.m. on December 1, 1934, the party boss of Leningrad, Sergei Kirov, was shot and killed in the Smolny Institute, where he had his office. His assassin, one Nikolayev, was captured immediately. Though scurrilous gossip had it that the priapic Kirov had been murdered for conducting one extramarital affair too many, official suspicion soon fell on various anti-Stalin politicians, and in particular his erstwhile allies Zinoviev and Kamenev. A month later, both men were tried for complicity in the assassination. Although found not guilty of the main charge, the two old Bolsheviks were convicted of anti-Soviet activities. Zinoviev was sentenced to ten years' imprisonment, Kamenev to five. All over Russia, followers of the two men were denounced and interrogated. Meetings called for punishment for those who were not wholly loyal to Stalin and the party line.

It was in this dangerous atmosphere that the Pyatakov conspirators decided that Trotsky's demands upon them were too exacting. As one of the codefendants at the trial, Karl Radek, testified, the exiled leader "had lost all sense of reality and was setting us tasks which we were unable to carry out." In December 1935, it was resolved that Pyatakov should take the risk of meeting, face to face, the great man himself, and putting him straight.[20]

At his trial, Pyatakov described how the meeting was arranged. He went to Berlin, where "Trotsky sent me a messenger whom I met in the Tiergarten, in one of the lanes, literally for a couple of minutes. He showed me a brief note from Trotsky, which contained a few words, 'Y. L., the bearer of this note can be fully trusted.' The word 'fully' was underlined." The messenger, whose name was "either Heinrich or Gustav, asked me if I would be prepared to travel by airplane." It was risky, but the situation was acute, so Pyatakov agreed. They arranged to meet next day at Berlin's Tempelhof airport. Early next morning, Pyatakov found Gustav or Heinrich at the entrance to the airport, with a false German passport for him. He boarded the airplane and took off into the winter skies. As he recalled at the trial, he was taken to Oslo, where a car drove him to a small house in a country suburb. "There I saw Trotsky, whom I had not seen since."[21] The old comrades spoke for two hours. Trotsky was apparently very animated, constantly interrupting Pyatakov with recriminations. "You are living in the same old way," he told his associate. "You can't break away from Stalin's umbilical cord: you take Stalin's construction for socialist construction." Trotsky treated Pyatakov to a thorough recapitulation of his analysis and strategy. Socialism couldn't be built in one country alone, so the collapse of Stalin's state was inevitable. Capitalism was recovering and wouldn't tolerate the Soviet Union much longer. There'd be a war, probably sometime in 1937, and if the Russian opposition was passive, then it would be consumed in the wreckage of the Stalinist state. Cadres had to be trained, saboteurs primed, the coup d'état prepared. But there was something else. The thing couldn't be done by Russians acting alone; allies were needed. "The real forces in the international situation," Trotsky explained, "are the fascists, and with these forces we must establish contact."[22]

Trotsky already had. In Pyatakov's words, "Trotsky told me that he had come to an absolutely definite agreement with the fascist German government and with the Japanese government . . . He then told me that he had conducted rather lengthy negotiations with the vice chairman of the German National Socialist Party—Hess." The arrangement was that, following a war in which the Germans used military force and the Trotskyites mobilized sabotage and assassination, the opposition would be helped to come to power, and in return a Trotsky-run Soviet Union would give Ukraine to the Germans. Naturally, the Germans had wanted, and got, an agreement that Trotskyite operations would be coordinated with the German general staff.[23] "In essence," Pyatakov told the court, "the Trotskyite organization was being transformed into an appendage of fascism."

His instructions received, Pyatakov now returned to Russia to get on with betraying the state, except this time in the knowledge that he was in alliance with communism's most mortal enemy. The next month, he met a man named Loginov, a co-conspirator. Loginov told the court that in January 1936 "the impression I got was that Pyatakov was no less stunned than I was, but he nevertheless transmitted it as a clear directive which had to be carried out. To retreat now was impossible because that would mean annihilation."[24]

In addition to acts of sabotage, such as deliberately overheating the coking ovens at a plant in Krivoy Rog and planning to set fire to the Kemerevo Combined Chemical Works, a list was now prepared of public figures to be assassinated. Kossior and Postyshev were to be murdered in Ukraine, while a group was set up in Moscow to see to Stalin, Molotov,

Kaganovich, Voroshilov, Ordzhonikidze, and Yezhov. But before this could happen, Pyatakov was unmasked. On September 11, 1936, he was expelled from the Communist Party, and the next day he was arrested.

Pyatakov Repents

What had supposedly happened was this. Sometime during July, secret police from the People's Commissariat for Internal Affairs (NKVD) had raided the apartment of Pyatakov's ex-wife. There they had turned up incriminating documents concerning his activities in the 1920s, when he had been one of Trotsky's closest allies. During August, Pyatakov was interviewed by the head of the NKVD, Yezhov. He protested his innocence and even wrote to the papers condemning Trotsky and Zinoviev. The August 21 edition of *Pravda* carried a letter from Pyatakov insisting that anti-Soviet plotters should be exterminated. "One cannot find words fully to express one's indignation and disgust. These people have lost the last semblance of humanity. They must be destroyed like carrion that is polluting the pure, bracing air of the land of Soviets, dangerous carrion that may cause the death of our leaders."[25] Privately, Pyatakov offered to testify against Zinoviev and Kamenev at their forthcoming second trial, and volunteered to execute them himself should they be found guilty. He was, he told the authorities, sufficiently zealous even to execute his ex-wife. He also wrote to his immediate boss, Sergei Ordzhonikidze, to declare his innocence, and repeated this protestation in a letter to Stalin himself.

In September, however, he told a different story. When Ordzhonikidze went to see Stalin to argue for Pyatakov's release, the general secretary handed him transcripts of confessions made by Pyatakov during interrogation. In these, Pyatakov admitted his continuing secret attachment to Trotsky since the latter's exile, and his participation in planning acts of sabotage. When Ordzhonikidze was allowed to see his deputy in prison, Pyatakov confirmed that his confessions were voluntary. From this moment on, Pyatakov didn't waver from his story. The 1931 meeting with Sedov had, he said at his trial, "only served as a fresh impetus" in his fight against the party and the Soviet Union. "Unquestionably, the old Trotskyite views survived in me, and they subsequently grew more and more."

On the face of it, the trial proved that Pyatakov and his codefendants had been involved in treason. Day after day, they agreed with the prosecutors that they were indeed Trotskyites, saboteurs, assassins, and collaborators with foreign fascist and militarist regimes. They affirmed the details of their guilt, adding small embellishments of their own along the way. At only one point did Pyatakov demur from the charges against him, and that was during the morning session of January 29, in his final plea to the court in mitigation of sentence: "I cannot reconcile myself to one assertion made by the state prosecutor, namely that even now I remain a Trotskyite . . . The only motive that prompted me to make the statements that I have made was the desire, even now, even at too late a date, to get rid of my loathsome Trotskyite past."²⁶ He continued: "I have landed in the very heart, in the very center of the counterrevolution— counterrevolution of the most vile, loathsome, fascist type, Trotskyite counterrevolution." The criminal mastermind deeply regretted, he said, that Trotsky was not in the dock beside him. And concluded: "In a few hours you will pass your sentence. And here I stand before you in filth, crushed by my own crimes, bereft of everything through my own fault, a man who has lost his party, who has lost his family, who has lost his very self."²⁷

His codefendant, the former journalist Karl Radek, spelled out the political significance of the trial. There were in the Soviet Union, he told the court, "semi-Trotskyites, quarter-Trotskyites, one-eighth Trotskyites, people who helped us, not knowing of the terrorist organization but sympathizing with us, people who from liberalism . . . gave us this help. . . . Before this court and in this hour of retribution, we say to these elements: whoever has the slightest rift with the party, let him realize that tomorrow he may be a diversionist, tomorrow he may be a traitor if he does not thoroughly heal that rift by complete and utter frankness to the party."²⁸

A more comprehensive warning against setting foot on the slippery slope of dissent could not have been given.

The court resumed at the appalling hour of three a.m. on the morning of January 30. Eleven of the defendants, including Pyatakov, were sentenced to be shot, and four others, including Radek, were given prison sentences. According to Lion Feuchtwanger, a celebrated German novelist present at the trial, as the prisoners were led out, the reprieved Radek "turned around, raised a hand in greeting, shrugged his shoulders very slightly, nodded to the others, his friends who were condemned to death, and smiled. Yes, he smiled."[29]

Within days, sixty hours at the most, Georgy Leonidovich Pyatakov, who had so fortuitously escaped the White firing squad during the civil war, received a bullet in the base of his skull from a comrade GPU (secret police) officer who was just doing his duty on behalf of the Soviet state.

Home Truths

In many Russian minds, it was easy enough to believe that Pyatakov and company were guilty. Fueled by the latent antagonism of workers toward the privileged *spetz* and the bureaucrats, the idea of a conspiracy seemed somehow plausible. And the people must have been impressed that the accusations and confessions came from within the heart of Bolshevism itself. Within the party, the very making of such accusations had become a kind of loyalty test. In July 1936, at around the time that Pyatakov's ex-wife's apartment was raided, the Central Committee of the Communist Party issued a resolution stating, "The indelible mark of every Bolshevik in the current situation ought to be his ability to recognize and identify enemies of the party no matter how well they may have camouflaged their identity."[30]

There was only one way in which such a sentiment could be interpreted: the enemy is all around us and will often be the person you least suspect; not only that, but it is your duty to unmask him. In such a situation it could only make sense to issue as many denunciations as you could, lest you were thought to be soft on Trotskyism and therefore a secret Trotskyite yourself, ripe to be denounced by someone else. It was also wise to see in every accident and every act of incompetence something more deliberate and sinister. And not just accidents happening today, but those that happened five years ago. So rail crashes or disappointing production figures from the past had now to be scrutinized for the possibility that they had been caused by conspiracy.

An insight into the psychology of this process is gained from an incident that took place a few days after Pyatakov's execution. The dead man's boss was the popular Communist and friend of Stalin, Sergei Ordzhonikidze, who had refused at first to believe in his subordinate's guilt. But on February 5, 1937, Ordzhonikidze met the heads of Soviet heavy industry. A transcript survived in the Soviet archives and was retrieved in the 1990s. Ordzhonikidze begins with a blast of total exasperation.

> You think that if I had as my first deputy a man like Pyatakov, who had worked in industry for the past fifteen years, who had tremendous connections with all sorts of people. You think that this person couldn't possibly sneak one or two of his people in. But sneak them in he did! Some of them were found out, others not. . . . You think a saboteur is someone who walks around with a revolver in his pocket, someone who waits in a dark corner for his victim? Who could think that Pyatakov could be a saboteur, and yet he turned out to be a saboteur and more still, a fine talker. He told the investigators how he did it. . . . Glebov was running the show at Borisov's. Did you bother to examine what was going on there, did you tell me how to rectify the disgraceful situation there? The hell you did! . . . How could this have happened? . . . How could it have been that Pyatakov was on our staff and yet no one, by God, saw through him? You'll say to me, "He was your deputy, but you didn't see through him. So what do you want from us?" It's not right. . . . This damned Pyatakov, this damned Rataichak and others! They have played such filthy tricks on us. . . . Now we must answer for it.[31]

Meanwhile, the security services and party apparatuses were now given specific targets for how many Trotskyites and assorted terrorist-saboteurs they were to uncover, prosecute, imprison, and execute in each region and city. It stood to reason, as Ordzhonikidze—who committed suicide shortly afterward—had said, that they must be out there. During what came to be known as the Great Terror, the quotas were surpassed.

The Reaction Abroad

In the rest of the world, a large and influential slice of opinion also believed that a great Trotskyite conspiracy had existed, with people investing a great deal of effort, and not a little authority, in attempting to show that Pyatakov and his codefendants were guilty as charged. These people, in turn, influenced significant parts of Western liberal and labor movements. It helped that not only the expected Stalin-worshippers and Communists were convinced the Pyatakov trial was genuine. There were also people such as the U.S. ambassador to Russia, Joseph Davies. In his diary of the time, later written up into a book, *Mission to Moscow*, and published during the Second World War, when the United States and Russia were allies, Davies reflected that, based on the best advice available to him, the seventeen codefendants were indeed traitors of some kind. "I have talked to many, if not all, of the members of the Diplomatic Corps here," he wrote, "and, with possibly one exception, they are all of the opinion that the proceedings established clearly the existence of a political plot and conspiracy to overthrow the government."[32] Of course, Davies may have been guilty of selective listening, seeking out and obtaining confirmation of his own impressions; it was already his view that the accused were telling something close to the truth. In his contemporary account, he described Pyatakov's statement as "dispassionate, logical [and] detailed." Furthermore, said Davies almost axiomatically, "the impression of despairing candor, with which he gave it, carried conviction." Davies, for one, could not conceive that Pyatakov was somehow playing a role.[33]

Others present at the trial were also swayed by Pyatakov's manner. The exiled German novelist Lion Feuchtwanger believed that there was a difference of view between those who watched the proceedings from afar—and believed them to be bogus—and those who attended in person. He himself had had grave doubts about the trial, in August 1936, of Zinoviev and Kamenev on similar charges. The accusations had then seemed "utterly incredible," the confessions fraudulent and obtained by some obscure but dubious method. Witnessing the proceedings themselves, however, had changed the novelist's mind. "When I attended the second trial in Moscow, when I saw and heard Pyatakov, Radek, and their friends and heard what they said and how they said it," confessed Feuchtwanger, "I was forced to accept the evidence of my senses and my doubts melted away as naturally as salt dissolves in water. If that was lying, then I do not know what truth is."[34] Feuchtwanger particularly noted the conduct of the leading conspirator:

> I shall never forget how this [Georgy] Pyatakov stood in front of the microphone, a middle-aged man of average build, rather bald, with a reddish, old-fashioned, sparse, pointed beard and how he lectured. Calmly and at the same time sedulously . . . he expounded, pointed his finger, gave the impression of a schoolteacher, a historian giving a lecture on the life and deeds of a man who had been dead for many years, named Pyatakov.[35]

Then there was the evidence provided by a memoir from an American engineer, John Littlepage, who worked as a foreign expert in the Soviet mining industry from 1927 to 1937. When the Pyatakov trial opened, Littlepage became convinced that the confessions made there explained some of his own experiences in Russia.

Littlepage had been in Berlin at the same time as the purchasing commission headed by Pyatakov. He noted that the commission had issued contracts to several companies for equipment to be supplied on what appeared to be more favorable terms than those of their competitors, but which turned out, on examination, to be more expensive. "I reported my findings to the Russian members of the commission with considerable self-satisfaction," wrote Littlepage. "To my astonishment the Russians were not at all pleased. They even brought considerable pressure upon me to approve the deal, telling me I had misunderstood what was wanted." Littlepage's immediate thought was that someone, somewhere was taking kickbacks. But "Pyatakov's confession is a plausible explanation, in my opinion, of what was going on in Berlin in 1931. I had found it hard to believe that these men were ordinary grafters . . . But they had been seasoned political conspirators before the Revolution, and had taken risks of the same degree for the sake of their so-called cause."[36]

And revelations about sabotage also chimed with things that Littlepage had encountered within the Soviet Union: sand in diesel engines, mining methods "so obviously wrong that a first-year engineering student could have pointed out most of their faults," the ignoring of good advice, the ensnaring in red tape of any proposal for improvement. All of these disastrous and wasteful phenomena "became clearer, so far as I was concerned, after the conspiracy trial in January 1937." "I am firmly convinced," concluded Littlepage, "that Stalin and his collaborators took a long time to discover that discontented revolutionary Communists were his worst enemies."

Britons, meanwhile, and in particular those of a progressive inclination, could turn to a two-hundred-page book, published by the Left Book Club within weeks of Pyatakov's execution, laying out a detailed case for believing both that the trial was entirely fair and criticisms of it entirely unfair. The author was Dudley Collard, a barrister at the famous law offices at the Temple in London, whose *Soviet Justice and the Trial of Radek and Others* was completed in February 1937.[*]

---

*Collard subsequently acted as counsel for the British Communist spy Percy Glading, who in 1938 was tried and convicted of acting as the messenger between informants in the Woolwich Arsenal and a Soviet intelligence officer, Theodore Maly. Glading and his fellow defendants were sentenced to prison for six years.

Attacking what he described as "distorted" accounts in the British press, Collard, like Davies, felt that his reading of the events in the courtroom was vindicated by the reaction of other observers, including "all those British and American correspondents present at the trial with whom I had an opportunity of discussing the case."[37] He confidently concluded that "the trial was conducted fairly and regularly according to the rules of procedure, that the defendants were fully guilty of the crimes charged against them and that in the circumstances the sentence was a proper one."

One by one, Collard took on and disposed of the arguments of those who saw the trial as a put-up job. Were, for instance, the confessions fabricated? Collard was incredulous. For that to be the case, "Someone other than the defendants must have written a seven-day play (to play eight hours a day) and assigned appropriate roles to the seventeen defendants, the five witnesses, the judges and the public prosecutor." It just wasn't possible. The accused would have needed to spend the entire period between their arrest and the trial rehearsing together what they were going to say "in such a way as to deceive all those who were present into thinking the play was real."[38] Besides, there was corroborative evidence from expert witnesses and documentary evidence including a diary with the phone numbers of German secret agents in it, names which checked off against the appropriate German telephone directory.

Might torture or some form of duress have been used to procure the confessions? No. "The defendants bore no visible signs of ill treatment . . . They behaved freely, spoke coherently and gave long and complicated accounts of their activity over several years with dates, names and places."[39] And wouldn't the dock of a trial conducted in front of international observers and the world's press have been the perfect place to complain of torture, had any been used? Yet none of the defendants made such a complaint.

Wasn't it beyond strange, though, that not one of the defendants pleaded not guilty and that all of them confessed fully? If they had been such steadfast foes of the new Russia, wasn't it improbable that they would not only have confessed, but also have described themselves as treacherous? One possibility, said Collard, was that they had simply changed their minds. A few years earlier, when they started the plotting, it "was easier to discover plausible reasons for maintaining that Stalin's policy was wrong than it is today when the success of his policy has been visibly demonstrated in the greater prosperity and comfort of life in the Soviet Union . . . The rising standard of living," concluded Collard, "must have had at any rate an unconscious effect upon most of them." And if that hadn't worked, then it was "likely too, that the opportunity for reflection which prison afforded them gave form to their subconscious doubts about the correctness of their own policy."[40]

The thing that many found truly unbelievable—that so many old Bolsheviks who had sacrificed so much for the cause should betray their country and principles in such an excessive fashion—Collard found all too credible. The list of crimes might seem shocking to people in peaceful England, he argued, but the context of the Russian struggle was very different. Here it was easy to imagine that political opposition might harden into enmity, and that enmity could mutate into treachery. In this way, Collard speculated, the former Communists "were logically and inexorably driven into the position of allies of all those forces hostile to the Soviet Union. Why should not they, wrecking railways because they disapproved of Stalin's policy, cooperate with the Japanese, wrecking railways in preparation for an armed attack on the Soviet Union? Nothing could be more natural."[41]

The Temple barrister reserved his most inventive shot for last. He acknowledged that much of world opinion was skeptical about the trial and consequently doubtful about the Soviet Union's claim to represent a new pinnacle in the achievement of human justice. But didn't the very fact of holding a public tribunal that was bound to be extremely embarrassing and lead to criticism suggest strongly that the crimes must be genuine?[42]

Collard's lawyerly ingenuity was matched by the dexterity with which the novelist Feuchtwanger deployed classical history and great literature in support of his argument about the integrity of the process. "If

Alcibiades [a leader of the Athenian Greeks] went to the Persians why not Trotsky to the Fascists?" he asked. And had not the piqued Roman general Coriolanus gone over to the Volscians? " 'Now this extremity hath brought me to this hearth,'" Feuchtwanger quoted. " 'But in mere spite, to be full quit of those my banishers, stand I before thee here.'" He then added, "This is Shakespeare's opinion on the likelihood of Trotsky's having come to an arrangement with the Fascists."[43]

Shakespeare's prescient view of Stalin's great rival was supplemented by Feuchtwanger's own rule that in any case all those who had been Bolsheviks were by nature and history plotters. Courageous, brave, and adventurous, they were born to create change by dramatic means. But when the defendants changed their minds and all simultaneously decided that Trotsky was wrong, then they strained every sinew to confess, to assist the authorities and thereby render one final service to the Revolution.

And Feuchtwanger had a final psychological ace in the hole. He was one of the relatively few outsiders who had managed to obtain an audience with Stalin, and he rested his final judgment on his assessment of the personality of the Soviet leader. "It at once becomes as clear as daylight," he concluded, "that this modest, impersonal man cannot have committed the colossal indiscretion of producing, with the assistance of countless performers, so coarse a comedy, merely for the purpose of holding a sort of festival of revenge." It was unimaginable. Why would anyone, let alone a modest, impersonal sort of man, do it?[44] Trotsky, it seemed, could be a conspirator by virtue of his revolutionary past, but Stalin couldn't.

The Truth

Whether Stalin himself "did it" will be discussed later, but the fact is that it was indeed done. Today only a few eccentric Stalinist diehards can be found to argue that the confessions were in any way true. Davies, Feuchtwanger, Collard, and the many, many more who accepted the show trials at something like face value—who thought that there had indeed been a gigantic conspiracy to destroy Stalin and his Soviet Union—are now seen as dupes, fools, or fellow travelers.

At the time, however, arguments raged within socialist and labor movements throughout the world. In America, Trotsky sympathizers even felt the need to set up a parallel tribunal, presided over by the famous philosopher John Dewey, to investigate the charges made against their hero and his supposed secret supporters. It was during the course of this inquiry that evidence was first heard that no planes had flown into Oslo airport at the time that Pyatakov was supposed to have landed there from Berlin, and a letter from Leon Sedov from the autumn of 1931 was cited in which he was supposed to have written, "Do you know whom I saw on Unter den Linden? The redhead. I looked him squarely in the eye, but he turned his face away as though he didn't recognize me. What a miserable fellow!"

This account was substantiated when, after 1990, Soviet secret police files were opened up. Among the reports was one from Agent B-187, variously code-named Max, Mack, Kant, and Tulip, who had infiltrated Sedov's immediate circle in the summer of 1934. Known to Sedov as Etienne (Sedov's secret-police code name was Sonny), Max had become an intimate of Sedov's wife, among others. Max reported to his bosses in Moscow that he understood from conversations with Sedov that Pyatakov had never met Trotsky after the latter's exile. He had therefore not been to Oslo.[45] Furthermore, Sedov had also told him that he had seen Pyatakov briefly in Unter den Linden on May 1, 1931. "Pyatakov had recognized him," reported Max, "but turned away and did not want to speak to him. Pyatakov then went off with someone else, apparently Shestov."[46]

If Pyatakov didn't meet Sedov and didn't meet Trotsky, then the entire conceit collapses. There was no moment of decision, no explanation to Pyatakov of the need to betray his country, no revelation of dealings with Nazi Germany, no conversations, nothing. And if that wasn't true, then the notes in shoes, the sabotage, the assassination plots, these too must all be seen as part of an extraordinarily elaborate and lethal fantasy.

A fantasy with the faintest glimmer of truth. That there were secret discussions between people who wanted Stalin's defeat cannot be denied—such meetings, after all, could not have been held in the open. According to American historian J. Arch Getty, the evidence shows that by 1932 Trotsky was indeed "actively trying to forge a new coalition in which former oppositionists from both Left and Right would partici- pate." In one letter, Trotsky acknowledged that under the circumstances, "One struggles against repression by anonymity and conspiracy, not by silence."[47] There were probably illicit gatherings and the smuggling of pro- hibited literature. But there is an immense gap between agitating against a dictator and a conspiracy on the scale claimed at the show trials.

How then do we explain the weird complexity of the confessions and the sangfroid of the accused? Feuchtwanger described them as "well- groomed, well-dressed men of a careless, natural bearing. They drank tea, had newspapers in their pockets and often looked toward the public. The whole thing was less like a criminal trial than a debate carried on in a conversational tone by educated men." Why didn't those old Bolsheviks, standing in front of the world, take the opportunity to indict the process itself? Surely, by January 1937, having seen Zinoviev and Kamenev sen- tenced to death, they couldn't have been hoping for clemency?

As we shall see, the famous Moscow Trials, of which Pyatakov's was the middle one of three, were actually the end of a process, not the begin- ning. Before senior party leaders were put on trial, others less exalted had been through the same ordeal. In the early spring of 1931, there had been a trial of alleged leaders of the Menshevik Party in Moscow—the so-called Union Bureau. As an exiled official of the party, Rafael Abramovich Rein, told a Berlin rally in March of that year, the defendants had confessed to all kinds of impossible meetings and contacts. For example, contacts had been cited that he knew—given that many of them were supposed to have involved him—had simply never happened.

Then Rein asked rhetorically, "How is it that experienced and honor- able people can make such ridiculous confessions and admissions?"

The answer lies in the methods used by the GPU [secret police] in such trials. The accused are subjected to continuous interrogation for up to 24 and 48 hours, during which time the investigators change, while the accused is made to wait for hours or even days, often in a corridor without food or rest. Prisoners are kept in strict isolation, frequently in windowless rooms, in which they lose all sense of time. They are given no information, they can send no messages, and are given no newspapers or books, nor pencils and paper. They are continually threatened with shooting, and put up against the wall. And if they continue to resist, they are put into a system of stone cubicles, alternately hot and cold, without the most elementary sanitation, which has a murderous effect not just on the health of the defendant, but also on his sanity. [Cries of indignation.] The accused is presented with the false testimony of his friends and comrades, threats are made against his family, provocateurs are placed in the room, and he is given false information about the well-being of his family, about the death of small children . . . And all this continues until the accused, finally, gives in. And then a cynical process of bargaining begins between the accused and the investigator as to what "admissions" he should make. This ends with the defendant simply signing and then obediently repeating in court everything that has been dictated or suggested to him by Soviet justice.[48]

Defectors from the Soviet security apparatus, such as Alexander Orlov, detailed how prisoners were subjected to intense physical and psychological abuse, including—crucially—promises that confessions would lead to safety for the victim's family, promises which were often not kept. Unsurprisingly, such testimony was often regarded as suspect in the West, as propaganda confected by "anti-Soviet" forces. But many years later, long after Stalin's death and Pyatakov's rehabilitation, the old dictator's right-hand man, Vyacheslav Molotov, was interviewed by the writer Felix Chuyev. Yes, he agreed, those who had been accused of crimes were often worked over during interrogation.[49]

After all the threats, the beatings, the use of prisoners' families as bargaining chips, there was also that weird loyalty to the party and the Revolution that forms the psychological core of Arthur Koestler's famous novel *Darkness at Noon*. It is possible, at the end, that some of the confessors may have come to believe that in toeing one last party line, they were somehow doing the right thing.

Why the Lie Was Believed

More important than the question of how the confessions were elicited is the issue of how Soviet society could accept such outlandish propositions. And how could men as intelligent as Ambassador Davies, a good portion of the diplomatic corps, a job lot of foreign correspondents, many independent intellectuals, and courageous labor leaders the world over not see through the dark farce of the proceedings in Moscow?

Clearly, Russians had private doubts about the veracity of the confessions. From 1935 to 1939, Lyubov Shaporina, wife of the composer Yuri Shaporin, kept a diary, which is now in a library in Saint Petersburg. Her entry for January 30, 1937, the day Pyatakov was sentenced, reads:

Each People's Commissariat has in its leadership a traitor and a spy . . . They are all party members who have made it through all the purges . . . For the last fifteen years, there's been a continual process of decay, treachery and betrayal going on, and all of it in full sight of the Chekists [secret police]. And what about the things that are not being said at the trial? Think how much more terrible they must be. And worst of all is the very openness of the defendants. Even Lafontaine's lambs tried to justify themselves before the wolf, but our wolves and foxes—people like Radek, Shestov, Zinoviev, old hands at this business—lay their heads down on the block like lambs, say "mea culpa" and tell everything; they might as well be at confession. Feuchtwanger [whose impressions of the trial must have been covered in the Soviet press] wondered why everyone is so forthcoming—how naive can you get! What's hypnosis for, anyway?[50]

Obviously worried lest her writings were discovered, Shaporina employed a tone that was a mixture of irony and contempt. She seems to be beyond belief or disbelief. But Shaporina was a member of the intelligentsia, an elite that had been an earlier target of the Stalinists. Many of her compatriots were more credulous.

In early 1937, Russia was just emerging from extraordinary and appalling social upheavals. An essentially agricultural nation badly damaged by war and civil war had been transformed from a peasant economy into a heavily industrialized and urban society. The peasants had been reorganized into collective farms or else had left the land to find work in new plants and mines. Central control had at first been weak: there had been substantial movements of population, dislocating and destroying ancient communities and creating entirely new ones. Millions had starved; millions had moved; millions had joined the Communist Party, mostly for practical rather than ideological reasons. At certain points during the Great Experiment, packs of feral children were to be found living wild in the cities and towns.

Hardly surprisingly, all kinds of strange things had happened. People had acquired positions of expertise or leadership despite their lack of qualifications for either. Raw engineers had been turned out from new institutes and immediately assumed complete responsibility for machinery they barely understood. Managers whose knowledge of running large enterprises was rudimentary were appointed nonetheless. And enormous discussions raged among senior Bolsheviks about whether and when to apply the brakes on the runaway train. But many of the difficulties encountered during what came to be known as the Soviet miracle—the human cost and the terrible errors committed along the way—had never been discussed overtly or even acknowledged. And somehow, from quite early on, the alteration of disastrous policies or the placing of blame for the hardships suffered by the Soviet people became entwined with a series of trials in which scapegoat figures were arraigned for deliberately creating the problems that society faced. One by one, starting in 1928, these trials first created and then elaborated on the idea that everything was the fault not of the Communist Party, nor of "scientific socialism," but of plotters. In other words, evil was not a consequence of something endemic in the system but of external, conscious decisions by ruthless enemies.

To understand this better, it's worth looking at what some have called the warm-up trials, which began by seeking explanations for a series of catastrophic accidents in fledgling Soviet industry. In the year that Trotsky was exiled, 1928, more than fifty Russian and foreign engineers were accused of blowing up mines in the Donbas region, close to the town of Shakhty. Eleven were given the death sentence, which was carried out on five of them. Two years after the Shakhty Trial came what was known as the Industrial Party Trial. During these proceedings, the prosecution alleged the existence of a clandestine Industrial Party two thousand strong, which, in collaboration with anti-Communist Russians based in Paris and with the assistance of French intelligence, planned to overthrow communism. Five were sentenced to death, but their sentences were later commuted.

Within three months, as we have seen, the Union Bureau of the Menshevik Party was on trial, accused of attempting to sabotage the Soviet Union's economic program and of planning an armed revolt. All of the accused "confessed," receiving long terms of imprisonment. In April 1933, in the Metropolitan Vickers Trial, six British electrical engineers were accused, alongside a large number of Russians, of "wrecking" and sabotage. Two of the British engineers confessed.

So, by the time of the murder of Kirov in December 1934, there was a long history of trials and confessions, of elaborate plots and complex conspiracies, all adding up to the idea that there was a constantly shifting but ever-present group in Soviet society determined to wreck progress by any means necessary. It was after the Kirov assassination, however, that this process became identified with leaders and former leaders of the Communist Party itself, and that old Bolsheviks found themselves in the dock.

First, Nikolayev—the assassin of Kirov—asserted at his trial, just before New Year 1935, that Trotsky may have contributed five thousand rubles to the plotters. Two weeks later, at the Moscow Center Trial, Zinoviev, Kamenev, and others were given prison sentences for having organized counterrevolutionary activities, and thus having incited the assassins of Kirov. By the end of July of the same year, Kamenev and thirty-seven others had been tried for plotting against Stalin. Two were shot and Kamenev received yet another long prison sentence. By August 1936, a doubtless exhausted Kamenev was back in the dock for the first of the great show trials, this time with his longtime ideological soulmate Zinoviev and a number of others, in what the authorities called the Case of the Trotskyite-Zinovievite Terrorist Center or, more colloquially, the Main Center. This time every single one of the defendants, including Kamenev, was shot—not before, however, implicating Pyatakov and others yet to be tried in their testimonies. One trial led to another.

And each added a new element. Pyatakov's trial partly focused on alleged complicity with fascist governments. Later in 1937, the secret trial of Marshal Tukhachevsky and some of his fellow officers suggested the possibility of a military coup d'état. Finally, the 1938 Trial of the Twenty-one, including Nikolai Bukharin, once known as the darling of the party, established a supposed connection between anyone who had belonged to the right opposition to Stalin and those on the Trotskyite left.

As one bestselling apologia for Stalinism, printed in the United States during the Second World War, had it, there had been three layers of Trotskyism uncovered. They had been separate, so that "if one of the layers was exposed, the others would carry on."[51] The taxonomy was something like this: layer one was the Trotskyite-Zinovievite Center, headed by Zinoviev and responsible for directing terrorism and assassination. Layer two, the Trotskyite Parallel Center, led by Pyatakov, was charged with sabotage. And finally, the most important and secret layer was the Bloc of Rights and Trotskyites, with Bukharin as its organizing genius. "The entire apparatus," said the author of *The Great Conspiracy Against Russia*, "consisted of not more than a few thousand members and twenty or thirty leaders."

And the separation of the layers helped explain why it was that the devious Pyatakov, despite his very full confession, failed to reveal the others, and why the Soviet authorities, as a consequence, had been able to cut into one layer at a time without messily slicing through the whole infernal conspiracy.

This possibility had been alluded to by at least one foreign observer in the period after Pyatakov's trial. Dennis Nowell Pritt KC, Labour MP for the constituency of Hammersmith, had noted that the statements from the dock in the Zinoviev Trial had, remarkably, failed to mention the extraordinary campaign of sabotage uncovered in court just five months later. In his preface to Dudley Collard's book, Pritt—who had been in Moscow for the Zinoviev Trial—acknowledged that the very testimony he had heard there might well be part of the conspiracy itself. Was it not possible, he asked his British readers, that "the real motive for the apparent complete abjectness of the confessions of some of the accused . . . was to lead the authorities to the belief that they had got to the bottom of the conspiracy, in order that the second or parallel center might escape detection?"[52] Thus was a possible question mark over the veracity of these proceedings turned instead into a confirmation of the next trial.

Similar thoughts must have impressed themselves on the minds of millions of ordinary Russians. Had Zinoviev not, after all, endorsed the reality behind the Shakhty Trial? Had Pyatakov not given his assent and backing to the prosecution of the Industrial Party? Had Bukharin not stayed in his Politburo seat during the arraignment of both? And if the Mensheviks had been guilty of such strange and complex plots—as everyone agreed they were—then why should not Pyatakov be guilty too?

As early as December 1930, the leading Communist V. V. Kuibyshev could address a plenum of the Central Committee with this dire warning of the dangers and treacheries ahead:

> The enemy has been dislodged, but the enemy has not given up. He has become hardened. He will resist and oppose us fiercely. Sabotage within the country, the resistance of the kulaks who are in the process of being liquidated—all of this expresses a bitter class struggle. The threats of an

intervention—this is the other side of the same coin . . . We demand of a leader of the party and of a leader of the Soviet state a relentless struggle against all attempts at concealing ideologically class-alien tasks from us.[53]

If you took a prophecy like this seriously, then little that happened subsequently would surprise you.

The Stalinist Buttress

To some extent, foreign sympathizers with the Soviet Union and the cause of the international proletariat had been subjected to the same indoctrination process as those inside the country. They had seen the young socialist state as being under external and internal attack from the very outset. During the civil war of 1918–1920, armies from the United States, Britain, France, and Japan had all intervened to lend assistance to a variety of anti-Soviet Russian generals and admirals. Not only were Soviet sympathizers inclined to believe that hostile forces would use any opening they could to destroy communism in the future, but many of them also routinely disbelieved everything their own governments or newspapers said about anything, let alone about Russia.

Many more were simply desperate for Russia to succeed in creating something new. They were sick of the capitalist system, which they blamed for war, colonialism, and the immiseration of millions, and the Soviet Union, flawed though it might be, remained their best hope. "The air which one breathes in the West," wrote Feuchtwanger, "is stale and foul. In the Western civilization there is no longer clarity and resolution." Whereas in Russia, "There is still everywhere debris and dirty scaffolding, but already the framework of the mighty building is rising up, pure and clear-cut . . . It is good, after all the compromise of the West, to see an achievement like this, to which a man can say, 'Yes,' 'Yes,' 'Yes,' with all his heart; and," concluded the novelist, "because it seemed ungrateful to keep this 'Yes' within me, I wrote this book."[54] Such idealists clung to the pronouncements of sympathetic and more moderate experts, like the socialist writers Sidney and Beatrice Webb and the liberal economist John Maynard Keynes, that Stalin and his colleagues were indeed building a better society, or, in Keynes's words, were "engaged in a vast administrative task of making a completely new set of social and economic institutions work smoothly and successfully."[55]

Some liberals and social democrats were actually happier with Stalin's apparently more practical (if brutal) attempts to build Socialism in One Country than with Trotsky's more radical and utopian demand that the revolution be spread all over the world. Their pragmatism led them to endorse the tough but concrete efforts made by the Stalinists to create their new society, as opposed to the windy posturing of the Trotskyists. It was, according to the late François Furet, a "revenge of the experts on revolutionary Marxism. . . . They believed their universe was taking shape in Russia."[56] So even those who were not Communist dogmatists or party members were already halfway to believing that Stalin was essentially good and Trotsky essentially bad.

A heavy investment had been made, emotionally and politically, in the success of the new civilization. And that was even before the rise of fascism. Hitler's coming to power, the threat from fascist movements throughout Europe and, in 1936, the beginning of the Spanish Civil War, seemed to force a choice on millions. With the capitalist West appearing to accommodate Nazi Germany and only Russia active in resistance, it had to be Hitler or Stalin. To those who sided with Stalin, the question of sticking with the Soviet government through the trauma of the trials could be presented as one of true commitment. As Pritt put it, "The more faint-hearted socialists are beset with doubts and anxieties . . . [but] we can feel confident that when the smoke has rolled away from the battlefield of controversy it will be realized that the charge was true, the confessions correct and the prosecution fairly conducted." Were you hardy enough, tough enough, to see it through? And the trouble was that if you lost faith in the process, then all was lost. If the trials were false, then the confessions were false, the accusations were false, the arguments of the anti-Soviet press were right, and the state and its leader were shown to be impossibly flawed. This gave every incentive for people to opt into Pritt's circular world, where every fact, no matter how awkward, could be construed as confirming the existence of the conspiracy.

What about men like Ambassador Davies, then? What could he possibly have to gain from being credulous about the Pyatakov trial? Five months after Pyatakov's demise, Davies wrote a dispatch to the U.S. secretary of state, Sumner Welles. It was his opinion, he said, that "The strength of the Red Army and the avowed and well-recognized adherence of the USSR to peace is regarded as a distinct factor in maintaining peace in Europe. It definitely could contribute to the balance of power and buttress the Democratic 'bloc.'"[57] And you don't, if you can help it, undermine a buttress.

A Paranoid Belief

The most intriguing question of all is how far Stalin and his surviving colleagues—men like Molotov, Kaganovich, and Voroshilov—believed in the conspiracy. Was the fabricated evidence at the trials merely an exaggeration of what they presumed actually to be taking place, or was it—as has often been suggested in the years since—a cynical ploy to frame and execute anyone who might constitute a rival or opponent to Stalin's supreme power within the USSR?

The escalation of internal repression after the Kirov murder led to a number of theories that it was Stalin himself who had had the Leningrad boss killed, thus simultaneously removing a potential rival and providing a pretext for getting rid of others. The defector Orlov made this claim, and in the post-Stalin era, when Khrushchev was leading the campaign to loosen the grip that the dead dictator still had on large sections of the population, the hint was dropped that Orlov might have been right. There were, said Khrushchev, "many things which are inexplicable and mysterious" about the assassination, including some convenient accidents and some timely executions. Two separate commissions were subsequently charged with investigating the events of 1934, but their conclusions were never published. The assumption grew that the Kirov case was Stalin's Reichstag fire—an event that was just too propitious. Then, in 1989, the last leader of the Soviet Union, the reformer Mikhail Gorbachev, commissioned his colleague Alexander Yakovlev to examine the case again. After working for two years, the Yakovlev team decided that there was no objective material to support either Stalin's or the NKVD's participation in the organization and carrying out of Kirov's murder. The killer, Nikolayev, was apparently a lone gunman with psychological and medical problems, a desire to make history, and a grudge against the party.

But, like Hitler, Stalin had grasped the opportunity when it was presented to him. Knowing from secret police surveillance that there had been clandestine meetings involving supporters of Zinoviev in Leningrad—indeed Stalin had been given a dossier relating to their activities on the day before the murder—the general secretary made Zinovievites the villains of the piece. Torture and duress did the rest.

Stalin, then, was turning what he *feared* might be the case into fact. Two contemporary pieces of evidence, one published long after Stalin's death, testify to the dictator's genuine paranoia. The French writer Romain Rolland, like Feuchtwanger, was granted an audience with the Soviet leader. Rolland agreed that he would not publish an account of their private conversation unless Stalin gave his permission, and Stalin never did. Understandably, because at one point the talk turned to plots. "There are women librarians in the Kremlin," Stalin said, "who visit the apartments of our comrades in the Kremlin to help maintain their libraries. It so happens that some of these librarians were recruited by our enemies to commit acts of terror. We found that these women carried poison, intending to kill some of our senior officials. Naturally, we arrested them but we are not going to execute them—we'll just isolate them."[58] Someone who can fear being poisoned by a librarian can easily see in any manifestation of opposition the possibility of treachery and murder. And Stalin certainly spoke as though he was convinced of the guilt of the Pyatakov trial defendants. To

Feuchtwanger, he expressed his anger with Radek, who had recently written a letter protesting his innocence followed the next day by his confession. "You Jews," the former seminarian told Feuchtwanger, "have created one eternally true legend—that of Judas."[59]

That same year, 1937, in November, Stalin hosted a reception at the Kremlin, and stunned his guests by telling them that the Soviet leadership would annihilate every enemy, even if they were old Bolsheviks. He went on, "We will annihilate his entire clan, his family! We will mercilessly annihilate everyone who by his actions and thoughts—yes, thoughts too—assails the unity of the socialist state. For the total annihilation of all enemies, both themselves and their clan!"[60] Stalin's idea was applied retrospectively. In the hunt for saboteurs and wreckers, it was most natural to start with those who were currently in opposition, and then equally natural to move on to those who once had been in opposition. Their past objective position revealed their current subjective intention. As Getty and his coauthor Naumov put it, "Virtually the entire elite (and even its victims) shared ideas about what constituted treason and conspiracy that differed sharply from ours . . . Their 'truth' was different from ours."[61]

Long after Stalin's death, the writer and poet Felix Chuyev interviewed the dictator's old comrade Lazar Kaganovich. Chuyev asked about the trials and the purges, and asked whether it was true that Pyatakov and friends had been shot because of their ideas. "Not for ideas," retorted Kaganovich. "Why for ideas at all? But who would believe that these old, experienced conspirators, using the experience of Bolshevik conspiracy and cooperation, underground organization, would not get together to form an organization . . . They did form an organization. Tomsky and Zinoviev did get together. They met at their dacha." Kaganovich outlined his own—and, presumably, Stalin's—fears: "The entire method of Lenin's struggle against the bourgeoisie could have been used against us. They had their people everywhere, in the army and elsewhere. They had formed organizations spread out in chains. Bukharin used to meet Kamenev and others and talk over the matters of the Central Committee. How could one let this happen freely?"

These men had, he reminded Chuyev, been unreliable in the past. Rykov, Kamenev, and Zinoviev had been against the October Revolution; Trotsky had once been a Menshevik; Bukharin had disagreed with Lenin in 1920. As he explained it: "With such people around him, Stalin could not have possibly waited for such a time when these people would have caught him by the neck and, as they did to Robespierre, annihilated him . . . Stalin acted decisively and strongly. Stalin was a man of great historical will." And then, in what seems to come off the page with a sigh, Kaganovich concluded: "Not everybody can understand this revolution where you have to destroy your own comrades and relatives. Each revolution, they say, devours its own children. Nothing of the sort!"[62] Which meant, of course, everything of the sort.

The Trotskyite plot in which Kaganovich's closest comrades were supposed to have been involved was the product of a very specific kind of conspiracy theory. Most modern theories have been conceived as a kind of historical revolt against the official version of events, but for authoritarian regimes in transitional periods, the idea of conspiracy becomes convenient for the authorities themselves, and also offers a painless explanation for massive failure. In Stalinist Russia, the revelation that a dedicated band of plotters had been at work sabotaging the first socialist state's otherwise inexorable march toward nirvana was—if anything—a relief. Because, if it were true, then the great problems of state socialism could be solved by rooting out the plotters. As *Time* magazine put it in the case of Pyatakov, his execution "leaves Dictator Stalin's 'Dear Friend Sergei' Ordzhonikidze Commissar for Heavy Industry, vindicated in the Soviet press for Heavy Industry's having fallen behind the Five-Year Plan. Other confessions and executions of the week vindicated virtually all Russia's thousands of recent wrecks and breakdowns."[63]

In more recent times, the failure of Arab states to democratize, modernize, or, in many ways, satisfy their citizenry has led to official toleration and propagation of conspiracy theories involving Israel. It would be reassuring to believe that these theories originated in pure cynicism. Reassuring but, as in the case of Comrade Pyatakov, probably wrong.

3. CONSPIRACIES TO THE LEFT

He didn't create this situation of fear; he merely exploited it, and rather successfully. Cassius was right, "The fault, dear Brutus, is not in our stars, but in ourselves."

—EDWARD R. MURROW ON SENATOR JOE MCCARTHY[1]

This is the story of how the idea of conspiracy at the very heart of government took root in the American psyche. It takes us from the U.S. Midwest to Pearl Harbor and on to Hollywood, but it begins in the early 1930s, with the activities of one John T. Flynn, a muckraking financial journalist with a specialty in attacking government links to big business.

In the 1930s, the term "muckraker" wasn't necessarily pejorative. It was used first in 1906 by President Theodore Roosevelt to describe the new breed of reporter that had risen with the expansion of newspapers at the end of the nineteenth century, the breed that performed valuable work in exposing and attacking abuses of power by unregulated corporations and corrupt politicians. Roosevelt did, however, have certain reservations about the role. "The men with the muck-rakes," he said, "are often indispensable to the well-being of society; but only if they know when to stop raking the muck, and to look upward to the celestial crown above them, to the crown of worthy endeavor. There are beautiful things above and round about them; and if they gradually grow to feel that the whole world is nothing but muck, their power of usefulness is gone."[2]

Muckraking journalism appealed hugely to the ever-growing number of newspaper and magazine readers in America, boosting the profits of the newspaper magnates and turning many of its exponents—people like Upton Sinclair, Lincoln Steffens, and Ida Tarbell—into quasi-celebrities. Initially, these investigative journalists, as we would call them now, tended to be men and women of the political left. Lincoln Steffens famously went to Soviet Russia and said, "I have seen the future, and it works"; Upton Sinclair stood in elections as a socialist candidate. But their appeal was not limited to the left. They were seen as taking on the likes of Standard Oil and J. P. Morgan on behalf of the little guy, and therefore dovetailed into an aspect of American political life that was almost as psychological as it was ideological—populism.

At this time, America was a frontier and an immigrant nation. Its foundation had been based on rebellion against oppression, its development upon pioneering, and its essential myth on the fulfillment of individual dreams. Its people tended to see themselves as having escaped persecution or poverty to make a new life for themselves almost entirely through their own efforts. Their successes, therefore, were their own; their failures were another matter altogether. When things went wrong or when times were difficult, it was natural to look around for an external culprit. Or culprits, because populism typically imagined a loose and infernal alliance of multiple foes.

The problem for populism was that the forces it was battling against—those of economic change and mass migration—were problematically impersonal. Marxists, with their detailed worldview, might be satisfied with the ideas of historical process and class war, but less holistic ideologies required something more immediate, and therefore fluid. From the 1820s onward, there was a remarkable consistency in the language used to describe the threat to Americanism, but there was also a remarkable diversity of threats. These started with the Freemasons, against whose machinations the inventor of the telegraph, Samuel Morse, wrote an entire book in 1835. By the 1890s, the conspiracy was led by a group of bankers.

Financiers, who lent but never labored, and who foreclosed on farmers and small businesses, were the perfect target for populists. To them might be added the railroad owners, the mining companies, other big corporate battalions, and politicians, especially those from the east of the country. These relatively few powerful people were, it was argued, holding a whole nation to ransom, a view expressed thus by the late-nineteenth-century Minnesota populist Ignatius Donnelly:

> The newspapers are largely subsidized or muzzled; public opinion silenced; business prostrated, our homes covered with mortgages; labor impoverished and the land concentrating in the hands of the capitalists. . . . The fruits of the toil of millions are boldly stolen to build up colossal fortunes for the few, unprecedented in the history of mankind.[3]

Populism was particularly strong in the Midwest, where there were many small farmers and the frontier spirit was easier to invoke. Electoral revolts against the political Establishment were periodic, spiking at times of agricultural depression, when great stump orators roused the discontented to action—men like "Pitchfork Ben" Tillman, "Sockless Jerry" Simpson, "Alfalfa Bill" Murray, and William Jennings Bryan, who ran unsuccessfully for president on the Democratic ticket.

But progressive as it could be, American populism also lent itself to more reactionary impulses. Suspicious of big capital, it was equally hostile to the big state; and much as it claimed to champion the little man, it often took up cudgels against those seen as the conscript army of unwanted change—immigrants. Who these immigrants were depended on the most recent wave of arrivals. In the 1840s, it was the Irish and thus the Catholics; in the 1850s, the Germans; in the 1890s, the Italians—and therefore the Catholics again. It was also a fairly natural step from anti-big-business populism to protectionism, and almost as natural to progress from there to isolationism. The early-twentieth-century populists—unlike British jingoists—were largely unimpressed by anything smacking of imperialism or what Thomas Jefferson termed "entangling alliances." Big business might require empires and foreign policies, but prairie farmers certainly did not. It was this attitude that was to have a deep influence on those who opposed America's entry into the Second World War.

Flynn and the New Deal

Born in 1882 to a middle-class Irish Catholic family in New York, John T. Flynn started his career in the legal profession before deciding that he was more inclined to write. He got his first journalistic break in 1916, on the *New Haven Register* in Connecticut, and went on to become a regular, and increasingly celebrated, writer for the liberal *New Republic* magazine, with the column "Other People's Money." He also wrote a weekly syndicated newspaper column, "Plain Economics." But he differed from the other writers in this generally progressive stable in one important way: he was skeptical about big government, with its bureaucracies, subsidies, and inefficiencies. Though in November 1932 he had no difficulty supporting the presidential candidacy of the Democrat Franklin D. Roosevelt, who had promised prudent administration in the face of the Depression, he had considerable problems with the way Roosevelt subsequently chose to interpret this mandate.

The new president wasted no time in revealing his hand. Following the crash of 1929, U.S. unemployment had, by the time of Roosevelt's inauguration, soared from a low of just over 3 to a catastrophic 24 percent. All around the industrialized world, straight laissez-faire economics were increasingly falling out of favor, and the fashionable spectrum extended only from Keynesian interventionist economics at one end to corporatism or state socialism at the other, a spectrum that Roosevelt now began to explore. His inaugural address in March 1933 was uncompromising: he told the country just how far he was willing to go to pass the measures "that a stricken nation in the midst of a stricken world may require." His hope was that Congress would willingly agree to endorse the necessary programs, and then he continued:

> But in the event that the Congress shall fail to take one of these two courses, and in the event that the national emergency is still critical, I shall not evade the clear course of duty that will then confront me. I shall ask the Congress for the one remaining instrument to meet the crisis—broad Executive power to wage a war against the emergency, as great as the power that would be given to me if we were in fact invaded by a foreign foe.

The consequence of this determination was what the historian Hugh Brogan called an "orgy of lawmaking."[4] An armored column of acts and agencies poured out of Washington: the Agricultural Adjustment Act, the Federal Emergency Relief Act, the National Industrial Recovery Act, the Farm Credit Act, and many more. Even the FBI was hugely strengthened and given new powers. Where most on the center-left were glad to see such action, others like Flynn were dismayed. Their initial support became disillusionment, which hardened into an opposition that at times began to sound like fanaticism. Not only was the New Deal a mistake, Flynn came later to argue, it was very close to being evil:

> This is the complete negation of liberalism. It is, in fact, the essence of fascism . . . When you can put your finger on the men or the groups that urge for America the debt-supported state, the autarchial corporative state, the state bent on the socialization of investment and the bureaucratic government of industry and society, the establishment of the institution of militarism as the great glamorous public-works project of the nation and the institution of imperialism under which it proposes to regulate and rule the world and, along with this, proposes to alter the forms of our government to approach as closely as possible the unrestrained, absolute government—then you will know you have located the authentic fascist.[5]

How frustrating then that what was all too apparent to Flynn was so hidden from his colleagues and, more important, from the voters, who in 1936 compounded their forgivable error of 1932 by choosing to reelect Roosevelt by a landslide. Flynn—on the wrong side of the consensus—began a dogged and, in its own way, courageous campaign against Roosevelt's New Deal. It was his belief that it could not work unless the whole country—using Roosevelt's own metaphor—was mobilized as though for war. And what more effective way could that be managed than by having an actual war? It was therefore natural that the dominant politician of the day should use his powers to persuade the nation, should the occasion arise, to take part in armed conflict. Such a conflict, according to Flynn, could only lead to a horrific loss of American life for no real gain, the possibly permanent curtailment of freedoms at home, and economic disaster.

The War Conspiracy

This last sentiment, at least, was one that Flynn shared with most Americans. Wilsonian enthusiasm for engagement in the world, which had taken America into the First World War and then bestowed upon it the proselytizing role at the Versailles peace conference, had evaporated fairly quickly once normal business was resumed. The American elite had been disillusioned by the vengefulness and shortsightedness of the European victors, while ordinary Americans were more aware of the country's 263,000 dead, wounded, and missing in a war fought almost entirely a whole ocean away. And although the objective fact was that the United States emerged from the conflict richer and more powerful than when it went in, the perception was that these debatable fruits of victory had been unequally bestowed. In the 1920s, while heavy industry boomed and there were enormous increases in profitability, farm prices and wages fell. Then came the Depression.

So, although most populists had started out as supporters of the New Deal, they were absolutely united behind the idea that the Great War had been a disaster, and one that must not be repeated. By the mid-1930s, one of the most effective articulators of this view was the most decorated marine in U.S. military history, retired Major General Smedley Butler, twice winner of the Medal of Honor. As Hitler came to power, and the possibility of a new war in Europe became more tangible, Butler campaigned for neutrality. In 1935, he published a famous pamphlet—reprinted again and again in different versions up to 1941—*War Is a Racket*, in which he asserted that his own actions as a soldier had been, to his shame, dictated by the needs of war profiteers and big capital. In an earlier speech, Butler had confessed:

> I spent thirty-three years and four months in active military service as a member of this country's most agile military force, the Marine Corps. I served in all commissioned ranks from Second Lieutenant to Major General. And during that period, I spent most of my time being a high-class muscle-man for Big Business, for Wall Street and for the Bankers. In short, I was a racketeer, a gangster for capitalism.[6]

The First World War, said Butler, had indebted the nation but enriched companies such as DuPont, U.S. Steel, and, of course, the banks. He knew, too, why President Woodrow Wilson had changed his mind about entering the war. It was because he had been persuaded that an Allied defeat would be bad for the U.S. finance houses, to which Britain owed so much money. This, Butler argued, was the very essence of a racket. Or, indeed, a conspiracy. "A racket is best described, I believe, as something that is not what it seems to the majority of people. Only a small 'inside' group knows what it is about. It is conducted for the benefit of the very few at the expense of the very many. Out of the war a few people make huge fortunes."[7] He cited the "21,000 millionaires and billionaires" who "got that way" from the conflict.

There were plenty of politicians who saw things the same way that Butler did. One was the senator for the midwestern state of North Dakota, Gerald Prentice Nye. Ten years younger than John Flynn, Nye had enjoyed a similar career, working as a journalist in Wisconsin and

Iowa (and campaigning for Prohibition) before, in 1925, being selected by the Republicans to take a vacant seat in the Senate. In 1934, he was asked by Congress to head a committee to investigate whether the banks and munitions industry had profiteered from the Great War and whether the prospect of financial gain had indeed been a primary cause of U.S. involvement. Several of his fellow populist midwesterners joined him on the committee; Flynn was his chief researcher.

Starting on September 4, 1934, and over sixteen months and ninety-three hearings, the Munitions Investigating Committee questioned more than two hundred witnesses, and became an important reference point for those who wished to resist any future drift into foreign entanglements. The conclusion of its report, published in February 1936, was, however, too nebulous to be of any direct benefit to what would become known as the isolationist cause: "While the evidence before this committee does not show that wars have been started solely because of the activities of munitions makers and their agents," it stated, "it is also true that wars rarely have one single cause, and the committee finds it to be against the peace of the world for selfishly interested organizations to be left free to goad and frighten nations into military activity."[8] More helpfully, the committee noted that in the two years before entering the Great War, the United States had lent $27 million to Germany, compared with $2.5 billion to the Allies. The inference was obvious: 58,000 Americans had lost their lives for the cause of American banking. Nye himself said as much in a speech later that year, claiming that "the record of facts makes it altogether fair to say that these bankers were in the heart and center of a system that made our going to war inevitable."[9]

Neutrality and Isolationism

From quite early in his presidency, Roosevelt had become convinced that, in the event of a war between the European democracies and the European dictatorships, America could not permit a victory for the latter.

The problem was, as he knew well, that the American polity from voter to Congress was opposed to any repeat of 1917. Rhetorically, at any rate, Roosevelt was forced to portray himself as another isolationist. So, from 1934 onward, in a paradoxical reflection of what was happening in the rest of the world, the United States opted to stand apart. In that year, the passage of the Johnson Act prohibited American loans to countries that had not yet repaid their debts from the Great War. And in 1935, Congress began to pass a series of neutrality acts and other measures that required the administration to place an arms embargo on any nation at war, forbade the carrying on American ships of any weapons destined for countries at war, and authorized the president to prevent U.S. citizens from sailing on ships belonging to belligerent nations. Roosevelt did attempt to get Congress to make a distinction between aggressors and their victims, for the purposes of support and supply, but Congress—arguing that supplying one side was highly likely to provoke the other side into some kind of armed attack on U.S. interests—disagreed. Further acts in 1936 and 1937 effectively precluded aid to Abyssinia when it was invaded by Mussolini; to the Spanish Republic, whose rebels were being supplied by Nazi Germany and Fascist Italy; and to China when it was attacked by Japan. In each case, arguably, American neutrality served the interests of fascist aggression and acted against those of democracy and national integrity. Ironically, since it had never taken up membership in the very League of Nations that it had helped create, the United States found that it had effectively forsworn any way of intervening in the various crises that were beginning to engulf the world.

Unilateralists were happy, isolationists were content, the consciences of American pacifists were relatively clear. None of this, however, could obscure what Churchill was to call "the gathering storm." Roosevelt and his colleagues saw war coming and didn't think the United States would be able to keep out of it. While the neutrality acts were being discussed and enacted, the Rhineland was remilitarized, Austria forcibly integrated into the Reich, and Czechoslovakia occupied. On the other side of the world, an aggressive Japan was busy constructing the Asian empire it had begun with the annexation of Manchuria in 1931. The problem for the president was how to prepare his reluctant constituents for what might be asked of them.

America First

Roosevelt's task became even more urgent when Germany invaded Poland in September 1939 and the principal democracies—France and Britain—declared war. His first act was to affirm U.S. neutrality. His second, just weeks later, was to ask Congress to remove the arms embargo, his obvious intention being to regain the ability to supply Britain and France. Congress agreed. The game now was for Roosevelt to edge America further toward standing alongside the democracies while simultaneously presenting this as the best strategy for preventing direct U.S. involvement in a European war. By mid-1940, with the crushing German victories in Scandinavia and France, public sentiment—sympathetic to Britain but unwilling to fight—was supportive of this dubious compromise. Such feelings helped Roosevelt to win his third term in the presidential election that autumn. Soon after reelection, in one of his broadcast "fireside chats," while describing America's role as the arsenal of democracy, Roosevelt further elaborated his idea of the trade-off: "This is not a fireside chat on war. It is a talk on national security, because the nub of the whole purpose of your president is to keep you now, and your children later, and your grandchildren much later, out of a last-ditch war for the preservation of American independence and all of the things that American independence means to you and to me and to ours."[10]

Meanwhile, John T. Flynn was becoming one of the most strident advocates of American neutrality. His experience on the Munitions Investigating Committee with Nye had helped turn him from a financial journalist to an antiwar crusader. In 1938, he had participated in the formation of the Keep America Out of War Congress (KAOWC), alongside the socialist leader Norman Thomas, former editor of *The Nation* Oswald Garrison Villard, and a historian of rising reputation named Harry Elmer Barnes. Many well-known left-of-center intellectuals, social activists, and union leaders also signed up. Flynn warned his countrymen that fighting a war would wreck America. "Our economic system will be broken," he wrote, "our financial burdens will be insupportable. . . . The streets will be filled with idle men and women. The once independent farmer will become a government charge . . . and amidst these disorders we will have the perfect climate for some Hitler on the American model to rise to power."[11]

A year later he might have regretted the comparison, given the extreme bellicosity of the original Hitler. Even so, in the face of Germany's obvious and seemingly implacable expansionism, isolationists continued to warn their compatriots that any involvement at all could lead only to a hecatomb. "Did we have anything to do with the promises Britain and France made to Poland? No we didn't!" said Smedley Butler, before taking a fabulous swipe into empty air, and demanding, "Are *we* culpable in any way because Hitler started before the other side was ready?"[12] But the questionable relevance of this argument to the issue of whether America would be able to tolerate the total defeat of the democracies was balanced by Butler's much more effective appeal to the parents of the nation. "After you've heard one of those speeches and your blood is all hot and you want to go and hit someone like Hitler," he advised, "go upstairs to where your boy is asleep. Go into his bedroom. You'll find him lying there, pillows all messed up, covers all tangled, sleeping away so hard."[13]

Some of those boys themselves decided to move against their possible conscription into another conflagration. In early 1940, a petition was circulated in Yale University Law School, demanding that "Congress refrain from war, even if England [*sic*] is on the verge of defeat." The idea of the petition's sponsors was to set up a national organization of students to oppose involvement in the European conflict; instead they created something that became much bigger and endlessly controversial. By the end of July 1940, the movement had been backed by several Chicago businessmen, and was being presided over by the respected chairman of Sears Roebuck, General Robert E. Wood. In August the organization became the America First Committee (AFC).

It is interesting that these days membership in America First is consistently left out of obituaries, curricula vitae, and accounts of regional religious and peace organizations. In 1940, however, commitment must have been enormous, because the organization grew with tremendous rapidity. Its early supporters included novelists and poets like Sinclair Lewis, William Saroyan, John Dos Passos, Edmund Wilson, and e. e. cummings. There was the First World War air ace Eddie Rickenbacker, actress Lillian Gish, architect Frank Lloyd Wright, and American flying hero Charles Lindbergh, possibly the most celebrated American then alive. Among its student partisans were two future presidents, Gerald R. Ford and John F. Kennedy (who donated a hundred dollars to the cause), and future novelist Gore Vidal. In Congress it could number among its supporters a large number of midwestern and western progressives, men like senators Burton Wheeler of Montana, Robert La Follette of Wisconsin, Robert Taft of Ohio, William Borah of Idaho, and Gerald Nye. The New York branch, which at its zenith was to claim a membership of 135,000, was chaired by John T. Flynn.

The AFC's public position was that America should build up its defenses at home so that it would be impregnable, while desisting from offering any kind of aid to the belligerents—the implication being that the United States would then be able to contemplate in safety whatever kind of world emerged from the ashes of Europe. What was needed in the short term was that Americans "keep their heads amid the rising hysteria in times of crisis."[14]

Through the second half of 1940 and most of 1941, a public struggle of predictable bitterness ensued between isolationists and interventionists. Seen from London, the AFC and its supporters were in many ways as much of an existential threat as Hitler. Essentially a coalition that included friends of Germany as well as enemies of war, America First was open to accusations of appeasement and pro-Nazism. In retaliation, the rhetoric of AFC campaigners was just as impassioned in their claims that the administration and its financier friends were attempting to manipulate the American people into war.

Impassioned and increasingly desperate. Gradually, as the Battle of Britain was fought and won, and as Churchill came to personify defiance in the face of tyranny, Roosevelt was winning his political battle to supply America's democratic ally. Polls showed that a large majority of Americans wanted to see the defeat of Nazism, even if they didn't actually want to fight. Symbolizing this, the Lend-Lease Bill was passed in Congress in March 1941 by 60 to 31 in the Senate and 260 to 165 in the House. In September 1941, Charles Lindbergh, the effective leader of America First, fought back with a speech in Iowa. It expressed, in the most developed way, his sense of who exactly was behind the disastrous slide into armed confrontation:

> The three most important groups who have been pressing this country toward war are the British, the Jewish and the Roosevelt administration. Behind these groups, but of lesser importance, are a number of capitalists, Anglophiles and intellectuals who believe that their future, and the future of mankind, depends upon the domination of the British Empire... These war agitators comprise only a small minority of our people; but they control a tremendous influence... It is not difficult to understand why Jewish people desire the overthrow of Nazi Germany... But no person of honesty and vision can look on their pro-war policy here today without seeing the dangers involved in such a policy, both for us and for them. Instead of agitating for war, the Jewish groups in this country should be opposing it in every possible way, for they will be among the first to feel its consequences.[15]

The speech was a disaster. It included sentiments that might be commonly expressed in private but were too ugly for public consumption. Years afterward, the American writer, academic, and muscular liberal Arthur Schlesinger was asked whether in his opinion the Des Moines speech had destroyed America First. He replied that the movement had been shaken "very severely." He went on, "There are a lot of people in the America First Committee, like John T. Flynn for example, Norman Thomas, others who were really shocked by that speech and by its implications."

Shocked perhaps, but not necessarily by the sentiments. Lindbergh's own journals, published in 1970, suggest that his colleagues weren't as far away from sharing his opinions as Schlesinger suggests. Take this paragraph from the entry for Thursday, September 18, 1941:

> John Flynn came at 11:00, and we talked the situation over for an hour. Flynn says he does not question the truth of what I said at Des Moines, but feels it was inadvisable to mention the Jewish problem. It is difficult for me to understand Flynn's attitude. He feels as strongly as I do that the Jews are among the major influences pushing this country toward war. He has said so frequently, and he says so now. He is perfectly willing to talk about it among a small group of people in private. But apparently he would rather see us get into the war than mention in public what the Jews are doing, no matter how tolerantly and moderately it is done.[16]

Flynn's dissent from Lindbergh's demonology then was not about the facts but about the advisability of stating them publicly. In fact, Flynn, too, thought that there was a concerted and underhanded attempt at work to seduce the United States into armed struggle. In December 1940, he had told an AFC rally in Chicago, "The plain and terrifying fact is that this great and peaceful nation is in the grip of one of the most subtle and successful conspiracies . . . to embroil us in a foreign war."

And there was almost nothing, in the view of Lindbergh, Flynn, and others, that the infinitely unscrupulous Roosevelt was not prepared to do. Three weeks after Des Moines, Lindbergh confided to his journal that "regardless of the attitude of our people, it is a question as to whether the president will force us into war by actions and incidents which will make it unavoidable. He is in a position where he can force war on us whether we want it or not."[17] When, nine weeks later, on December 7, 1941, the

Japanese navy attacked the American naval base at Pearl Harbor, Lindbergh wrote in his journal, "Phoned Gen. [Robert] Wood in Boston. His first words were, 'Well, he [President Roosevelt] got us in through the back door.'"[18]

Roosevelt Knew

According to Flynn and many like him, Roosevelt had finally achieved the world war he had always wanted, the war he had been plotting for the last eight years. But the consequences of Pearl Harbor for America First were disastrous. It was now the AFC—the prophets, the enlightened peacemakers—not Roosevelt who were being reviled for their lack of patriotism. Pearl Harbor took some explaining, even to themselves. Furthermore, there could be no chance of rehabilitation, let alone eventual political victory, if the true nature of Roosevelt's duplicity were not exposed. There had been defeats for the movement along the way, of course, including the obstinate public sympathy in America for its anglophone relation across the Atlantic. But the one event that, by itself, had meant war had dropped on them all from out of the blue heavens of a mid-Pacific sky, and had blown America First apart as surely as it had destroyed the *Arizona*, the *Utah,* and the *Oklahoma*. It was with Pearl Harbor that the assault on the seemingly invincible Roosevelt would have to start.

Such an assault was never going to be easy. For the American people, Japanese perfidy was to blame for the disaster of what we might now call 12/7. Even so, war or no war, the Republicans had elections to fight in 1944, and Pearl Harbor had been, at the very least, a chapter of incompetencies. And while early inquiries had discovered the fault to be largely that of the local commanders, Admirals Kimmel and Short, the subsequent agitation by these men and their supporters against this conclusion suggested a possible line of attack. By the summer of 1944, a decision had been made by the Republicans to make Pearl Harbor an election issue. On September 11, 1944, a Republican congressman from Indiana even claimed that Washington had known from Australian sources that a Japanese carrier fleet had been heading for Hawaii but had neglected to inform the hapless admirals.

In October of the same year, shortly before the election, John T. Flynn published a thirty-two-page pamphlet, *The Truth About Pearl Harbor*, which he then expanded a year later, after the death of Roosevelt in April 1945. Flynn's thesis was important in that it added an extra dimension to the charge of presidential incapacity. It had, of course, been a blunder to "bottle" the fleet up in a vulnerable anchorage, a blunder to "strip" Pearl Harbor of its defenses, and a blunder not to warn Kimmel and Short that the serious deterioration in relations between Japan and America made some kind of attack quite likely. But Flynn added a new ingredient on top of incompetence, one that went beyond even deliberate carelessness. He charged Roosevelt with the specific intention of procuring just such a Japanese attack in order to bring America into the war. In other words, Roosevelt had conspired to provoke the exact action that he publicly so desired to avoid. Specifically, Flynn charged:

> By January 1, 1941, Roosevelt had decided to go to war with Japan. But he had solemnly pledged the people he would not take their sons to foreign wars unless attacked. Hence he dared not attack and so decided to pro-voke the Japanese to do so.
>
> He kept all this a secret from the Army and Navy. He felt the moment to provoke the attack had come by November. He ended negotiations abruptly November 26 by handing the Japanese an ultimatum which he knew they dared not comply with. Immediately he knew his ruse would succeed, that the Japanese looked upon relations as ended and were pre-paring for the assault. He knew this from the intercepted messages.[19]

In Flynn's mind, Roosevelt had miscalculated where the attack might fall. Flynn speculated—albeit in terms suggesting certainty—that Roos-evelt had anticipated a first Japanese assault against Singapore or just possi-bly the American bases in the Philippines or on Guam. "But if only British territory were attacked," Flynn asked, "could he [Roosevelt] safely start shooting? He decided he could, and committed himself to the British government." Not wanting to appear overprepared for war lest this spoil his case, Roosevelt decided to keep his military chiefs in the dark. But when Pearl Harbor and so many ships were lost, the president was "appalled and frightened." To save himself, Roosevelt "maneuvered to lay the blame upon Kimmel and Short," acting ruthlessly to destroy their reputations and to silence those who might exonerate them. "Now," concluded Flynn, "if there is a shred of decency left in the American people they will demand that Congress open the whole ugly business to the light of day."[20]

There were some obvious difficulties with Flynn's argument. First, it rested on the assumption that the Japanese needed to be provoked into making a surprise attack and a sudden declaration of war. Second, there was the absurd risk involved in provoking an attack: a risk that you might be taken utterly by surprise and defeated—not at all (even for the perfidious Roosevelt) the object of the enterprise. This Flynn dealt with by referring to the intelligence that the administration had with regard to Japanese intentions.

> A gift from the gods had been put into Roosevelt's hands. The British government had broken one Japanese code. It proceeded to hand over to the State Department the messages between Tokyo and various foreign representatives which it intercepted . . . Therefore on November 6, Roosevelt knew that the Japanese were playing their last card; that they would make no further concession and he knew also the very date they had set for action—November 25.[21]

On December 1, charged Flynn, a British intelligence report arrived in Washington telling of how Japanese aircraft carriers had left Japanese home waters.

> All this information was in the hands of Hull and Roosevelt. Nothing that could happen could surprise them—save undoubtedly the point of

the first assault . . . Roosevelt, the Commander-in-chief, who was now assured of the attack which would bring him safely into the war, went off to Warm Springs to enjoy the Thanksgiving holiday.[22]

For many years, these assertions formed the broad outline of the accusation against Roosevelt and the basis of the Pearl Harbor conspiracy theory. Believed by a number of Republicans and advocated by historians such as the America Firsters Harry Elmer Barnes and Charles A. Beard, the Flynn version of the story also attracted some military men, many of whom felt that Kimmel and Short had been badly treated.

For one celebrated American writer, this view of events was to persist for sixty years. Gore Vidal's novel *The Golden Age*, published in 2000, featured both Roosevelt's attempt to goad the Japanese into hostilities and the prewar "convergence on Washington of more than 3,000 British agents, propagandists, spies whose job it was to undermine the position of the anti-war movement." "Yes, I was there," Vidal wrote in defense of his thesis later that year. "At the heart of an isolationist family that 'entertained' as they used to say."[23] And, as we have seen, campaigned.

In May 2001, the *New York Review of Books* carried an exchange between Gore Vidal and Ian Buruma, a writer and specialist on Japan, concerning the prelude to war. Vidal was elegantly unpleasant about Buruma's acceptance of the notion of a warlike Japan. Citing the efforts of the peace faction in Tokyo, Vidal demanded, "Why is it, if we were not on the offensive, that so small and faraway an island as Japan attacked what was so clearly, already, a vast imperial continental power? You have now had over sixty years to come up with a plausible answer. Do tell."

Buruma's response was to cite the evidence, not least the series of Japanese imperialist and unilateral actions, each of which had demanded some kind of American response. As relations worsened in late 1941, a Japanese imperial conference was convened. One participant summed the conference up: "If we miss the present opportunity to go to war, we will have to submit to American dictation. Therefore, I recognize that it is inevitable that we must decide to start a war against the United States."

As to the "small and faraway island" (with its significant population and substantial armed forces), Buruma quoted a Colonel Tsuji Masanobu, who explained that "our candid ideas at the time were that the Americans, being merchants, would not continue for long with an unprofitable war." Ideology and hubris had combined to bring about a miscalculation on the part of the Japanese leadership. Whether Vidal thought the Japanese could win was beside the point; the fact seems to be that *they* thought they could.[24]

The Triple Conspiracy

One well-known historian was particularly persistent in his attacks on Roosevelt in the postwar period. Former America Firster Harry Elmer Barnes edited, in 1953, a seven-hundred-page collection of essays under the title *Perpetual War for Perpetual Peace* (the subtitle being *A Critical Examination of the Foreign Policy of Franklin Delano Roosevelt and Its Aftermath),* in which eight authors gave various and overlapping accounts of how Franklin D. Roosevelt had deceived America into abandoning neutrality, provoked the Japanese to attack Pearl Harbor, embarked upon an unnecessarily brutal war in which the Allies behaved as badly as, if not worse than, the Axis powers, and ended up selling out American interests to Stalinist communism at the conferences in Yalta and Potsdam. And all of this because of the false belief (signaled in the book's title) that only out of constant warfare could domestic peace be secured. Barnes also first developed the idea of the triple conspiracy. His belief was that, in addition to provoking the Japanese, Roosevelt had also been warned of almost the exact hour and place of the supposed surprise attack, and had decided not to pass the warning on lest defensive measures led to the attack being aborted and his plan foiled. Or as Barnes put it, "It appeared necessary [to Roosevelt] to prevent Hawaiian commanders from taking any offensive action which would deter the Japanese from attacking Pearl Harbor which, of necessity, had to be a surprise attack."[25]

Barnes thus took Roosevelt out of the category of scheming liar, into which he had been put by Flynn and others, and placed the still-revered late president firmly in a new grouping—mass murderer and infernal manipulator. The problem, however, for Barnes and others, was the overwhelming improbability of anyone taking such a risk as to invite enemy air attack on his undefended capital ships. Apart from a series of rumors and conjectures, the Harbor conspiracists just didn't have any substantial evidence. Where, for example, was the proof that U.S. intelligence had cracked Japanese naval (as opposed to diplomatic) codes? But in 1981, on the fortieth anniversary of the attack, the Pulitzer Prize–winning journalist John Toland published *Infamy: Pearl Harbor and Its Aftermath*, in which he claimed to have that important new evidence.

According to Toland, Dutch intelligence sources in the Far East had passed on information about the attack to Washington, and had received in return indications that the United States already knew an enemy fleet was en route for Hawaii. And an anonymous sailor—later revealed to be one Robert Ogg—who had worked in the intelligence office of the Twelfth Naval District headquarters in San Francisco told Toland that he had intercepted Japanese radio signals from which he had been able to plot the location of the carrier force as it headed toward Hawaii. Ogg said that he had passed this information on to his superiors and believed that they, in turn, had passed it to Washington. On this basis, Toland concluded that FDR was guilty, and then asked his readers to "imagine if there had been no war in the East. There would have been no Hiroshima and perhaps no threat of nuclear warfare. Nor would it have been necessary for America to have fought a gruelling and unpopular war in Korea and a far more tragic one in Vietnam which weakened [the] U.S. economy and brought bitter civil conflict."[26] I include this passage because, as partial hindsights go, this is hard to beat in its ambition and speculative range.

But even Toland's new evidence was more than problematic. Ogg's evidence is directly contradicted by Japanese sources, who claim that enormous efforts were made by the task force to maintain radio silence. (For obvious reasons. After all, even if there was a Rooseveltian plot, no one has yet claimed that the Japanese were in on it. They presumably were working on the assumption that, if discovered, they would be attacked.) To ensure against error or sabotage, the radios had been disabled, and the operators left in Japan. What was more, it was pointed out by the editors of *At Dawn We Slept*, Gordon W. Prange's magisterial history of the attack on Pearl Harbor, that in order to guarantee a successful Japanese surprise attack, the president would have needed to confide in the local U.S. commanders and persuade them to allow the enemy to proceed unhindered.[27]

The historian Stephen Ambrose took up this theme in a 1992 *New York Times* piece about conspiracy theories:

> About Pearl Harbor one must ask could Roosevelt, by himself, have kept information about an imminent attack from the commanders in Hawaii? Of course not. Teams of men were involved in breaking the Japanese diplomatic code in 1941; admirals and generals in Washington got the intelligence and took it to the President. They would have had to join him in a conspiracy. Can anyone believe the admirals would have allowed their men and battleships to go down without a protest? . . . MOST of all, the thesis that Roosevelt knew beforehand that there would be an attack on Pearl Harbor in December 1941 breaks down when Roosevelt's actual policy is understood. That policy, in December 1941, was to avoid war with Japan until Nazi Germany had been defeated. He did not take the back door to war; the Japanese attack at Pearl Harbor solved no problem for him, but rather made it worse. On Dec. 8, he asked Congress to recognize that a state of war existed with Japan—the war he did not want, at least not yet—but he did not ask Congress to declare the war he did want, against Germany. It was Hitler, not the Japanese, who solved Roosevelt's problem. On Dec. 11, in the craziest of all his loony decisions, Hitler declared war on the United States.[28]

But what if, despite all these objections and counter to all logic and experience, it were proved beyond most reasonable doubt that Washington really did know? In 1996, the National Security Agency transferred five thousand or so files from the records of the U.S. Signal Intelligence Service at Arlington Hall in Virginia to the U.S. National Archives. It was the first major release of documents relating to the time of Pearl Harbor. Four years later, in the spring of 2000, journalist and former sailor in the U.S. Navy, Robert Stinnett, published *Day of Deceit: The Truth About FDR and Pearl Harbor*. Stinnett's book, based on seventeen years of research and study of the newly released papers, was well received by reviewers in the quality press. Richard Bernstein wrote in the *New York Times Book Review* that it was "difficult, after reading this copiously documented book, not to wonder about previously unchallenged assumptions about Pearl Harbor" (though readers of this chapter may wonder what those "unchallenged assumptions" actually were); Rupert Cornwell of the *Independent* in London took the view that "the case put together by Stinnett is more than persuasive"; and Tom Roeser of the *Chicago Sun-Times* provided the publishers with their paperback cover blurb by announcing, "*Day of Deceit* is perhaps the most revelatory document of our time."

Stinnett's own feelings about his material were made clear in the preface. "As a veteran of the Pacific War, I felt a sense of outrage as I uncovered secrets that had been hidden from Americans for more than fifty years." What Stinnett claimed to have discovered was documentary proof that American intelligence had had access to Japanese naval codes at the time of Pearl Harbor and had therefore been in a position to anticipate and hence to prevent the attack. "Previous accounts," said Stinnett, "have claimed that the United States had not cracked Japanese military codes prior to the attack. We now know this is wrong. Previous accounts have insisted that the Japanese maintained strict radio silence. This too is wrong. The truth is clear: FDR knew."[29]

Day of Deceit

One problem with Stinnett's conclusions is that those officers involved in breaking the Japanese naval codes consistently and vehemently denied over the years that they had managed to achieve this before Pearl Harbor, only succeeding a year later. Could these men also be part of the plot? To accept Stinnett's conclusion you had to believe that, if anything, the conspiracy was even wider than alleged by Barnes and Toland. But there is a much greater objection to the accusations contained in *Day of Deceit*. Experts in cryptography, after studying his book, charged that Stinnett had either quite simply misunderstood the thousands of documents he had pored over or failed to read those that were most significant. In particular, he had failed to understand difficulties and time lags involved in breaking, reading, and decrypting a code.

The writer Stephen Budiansky has pointed out that the most authoritative account of the U.S. breaking of the code is contained in a document titled *History of GYP-1*, which was declassified and placed in the U.S. National Archives in 1998. This showed, according to Budiansky, that an initial, limited break *had* been achieved in September 1940, but that the Japanese had then changed their code and key books. Some of the decoded messages from that period, discovered by Stinnett in the archives, were perfectly explicable, but they had been decoded *after* the war. Altogether, concluded Budiansky, the documents "show unmistakably that not a single message sent throughout the year 1941 in the Operations Code was broken and read by the United States before December 7."[30] In fact, the earliest decoded message in the archives, according to Budiansky, has a decryption and translation date of January 8, 1942. Stinnett responded in part by accusing Budiansky—author of a history of Allied code-breaking—and other critics of having "close ties with the National Security Agency" and of launching "a two-year media campaign" to discredit his conclusions.

The Final Piece of the Jigsaw

It is hard to let the question of Pearl Harbor go without returning to Gore Vidal, probably the most internationally famous of those still alive who claim that Roosevelt had foreknowledge of the attack on Pearl Harbor and provoked it. In his collection of writings *The Last Empire: Essays 1992–2001*, Vidal included a letter sent to the *Times Literary Supplement* in response to one from the author Clive James. James had raised the tricky question of how risky and perverse it would have been for Roosevelt to assume that an attack by Japan would automatically lead to the war the president had really wanted all along—the one with Nazi Germany. Pouring scorn on James for his "received opinion," Vidal made the following argument: "On December 4th General Marshall had presented FDR, at his own request, with a war plan in which he proposed that, as Hitler was the principal enemy of the U.S. and the world, the United States should raise an expeditionary force of five million men and send it to invade Germany by July 1st 1943." The plan, Vidal reminded readers, was somehow leaked to the *Chicago Tribune*, where it was duly noted by Hitler. It thus provided a "rational, if odd reason," in Vidal's view, for declaring hostilities.[31]

In fact, Hitler gave many reasons for declaring war on the United States in his address to the Reichstag on December 11, 1941, as he always did when he decided to declare war on another country or to invade it. The speech suggests broader considerations than one leaked contingency plan:

> We know the power behind Roosevelt. It is the same eternal Jew that believes that his hour has come to impose the same fate on us that we have all seen and experienced with horror in Soviet Russia . . . We know that their entire effort is aimed at this goal: even if we were not allied with Japan, we would still realize that the Jews and their Franklin Roosevelt intend to destroy one country after another. The German Reich of today has nothing in common with the Germany of the past. For our part, we will now do what this provocateur has been trying to achieve for years. And not just because we are allied with Japan, but rather because Germany and Italy with their present leaderships have the insight and strength to realize that in this historic period the existence or non-existence of nations is being determined, perhaps for all time.[32]

A Brief History of Revisionism

What Vidal was demonstrating when he cited Marshall's leaked war plan, not least in his ascription to an adversary of the desire to cling to received opinion, was belief in a different history. He was suggesting that there is often, running parallel to the Establishment version of past events, another and truer version. A version uncontaminated by prejudice and what has come to be called spin. Such history is described as revisionist by its practitioners and supporters, and given a whole lot of other epithets by more established historians.

The study and writing of history have always been problematic. Primary sources disagree, and there are historiographical fashions. Some histories become almost canonical—unchallengeable retailers of the truth about the past. It is often said that history is written by the victors in any struggle, and that the identities of heroes and villains are therefore constructed so as to fit in with the requirements of the winner. Marxist historiography disputed the analytical usefulness of "bourgeois" history, and cast the passing worlds in terms of the struggle between social and economic classes. Social histories forswore the concentration on "great men," insisting that you only understand the past if you examine the lives of the masses. But revisionist history did something else. It was (and is) less an alternative way of studying than an adoption of deliberately alternative opinions about the past.

Probably the leading ideologue of American revisionism was Harry Elmer Barnes, the historian and America Firster who devoted so much time to proving that Pearl Harbor was a conspiracy. His definition of revisionism was that it constituted an "effort to revise the historical record in the light of a more complete collection of historical facts, a more calm political atmosphere, and a more objective attitude."[33] But the calmness is often hard to discern and the desire seems rather to destroy conventional wisdom than patiently to correct it. This destruction for many people became something of a pleasure. But it was also—in the case of the isolationists, who had comprehensively lost the fight against American intervention—a vindication of their beliefs.

A second direction for the revisionist impulse has been altogether less entertaining and more malign. Up to the end of the war, there was always a strong motive for isolationists to argue that the Nazi threat to the world was somehow less lethal than it had been painted. But after 1945, there was one overwhelming problem with any such position: to most people in America, almost any action taken against the regime that had authored the Holocaust could be seen as justifiable. Some revisionist historians therefore began to look around for other arguments. One such might be that the Allies, in the bombing of civilian areas and their use of the atomic weapon, had proved themselves to be bad guys too. But could it also be established that the Nazi horrors were actually less, well, horrific?

This was exactly the progression followed by Harry Elmer Barnes, who had always been disinclined to accept everything that was said about Hitler's aggressiveness. At some point in the early 1960s, his skepticism reached so far that he even began to question the claim that Hitler had ordered and presided over the near total destruction of Europe's Jewish population. Indeed, the very growth of knowledge and understanding about what had happened to the Jews was taken by Barnes as evidence of a lack of authenticity:

> These camps were first presented as those in Germany, such as Dachau, Belsen, Buchenwald, Sachsenhausen, and Dora, but it was demonstrated that there had been no systematic extermination in those camps. Attention was then moved on to Auschwitz, Treblinka, Belzec, Chelmno, Jonowska, Tarnow, Ravensbrück, Mauthausen, Brezeznia, and Birkenau, which does not exhaust the list that appears to have been extended as needed.[34]

That no systematic extermination was discovered in Dachau, etc., was hardly surprising, since the earliest camps to be liberated were work camps inside the Reich itself, and these had furnished a fair number of survivors. The second string of camps had wholly or in part been extermination camps, from which, by definition, almost nobody returned. But it is clear from Barnes's cynicism about how the list had been "extended as needed" that he regarded accounts of extermination as essentially manufactured. He continued: "The smother-out legend represents the German plan as the extermination of all Jews that the Germans could lay their hands on. No authentic documents have been produced that support any such contention." Barnes had clearly never heard of the Wannsee Conference.

The next step was to discover who was behind the attempt to smear the Nazis with the accusation of genocide. In 1964, the French writer Paul Rassinier, who had himself been incarcerated in one of the Reich's work camps, published a book titled *The Drama of the European Jews,* which questioned eyewitness and survivor accounts of the death camps, doubted the logistical feasibility of mass gassing, and concluded that there never had been a deliberate attempt by the German authorities to physically eliminate the Jews of Europe.

The elderly Barnes reviewed this work. Under the heading of "Zionist Fraud," Barnes agreed that the charges against Nazi Germany had been willfully exaggerated. Not that he denied altogether that atrocities had taken place, "committed by certain brutes in the concentration camps of the Third Reich, many of whom were Communists, who had infiltrated as guards." But Barnes agreed with Rassinier that the scale of the killings had been inflated from around a million to an absurd six million, a figure accepted by "shameless propagandists, doubtful witnesses, and others ill-informed." Rassinier showed, said Barnes, why this exaggeration had taken place:

> The courageous author lays the chief blame for misrepresentation on those whom we must call the swindlers of the crematoria, the Israeli politicians who derive billions of [German] marks from non-existent, mythical and imaginary cadavers, whose numbers have been reckoned in an unusually distorted and dishonest manner ... By presenting a reparations invoice based on the figure of six million Jews exterminated, each one representing an indemnity of 5,000 marks, the International

Zionist Movement has been concerned mainly with lightening the permanent deficit weighing on the bankers of the Diaspora; indeed, even to get rid of it and transform it into an appreciable profit.

This is very nearly the ultimate libel. The suggestion that the Holocaust had been invented largely to make surviving relatives a lot of money is uniquely offensive. Obliviously, Barnes plowed on: "It only weakens the case when, with the use of false documents, the weakest sort of testimony, and statistics outrageously inflated, the State of Israel claims indemnity for six million dead. This completely inaccurate figure only serves Communist and other political causes in Europe, and outright financial purposes in Tel Aviv."[35]

Barnes died in 1968, his name living on in a publication called the *Barnes Review*, ostensibly devoted to revisionism but, in fact, a repository of neo-Nazi, anti-Semitic, and Holocaust-denial writings. It is a sad memorial to an almost distinguished life.

Flynn and the Reds

But let us return to Mr. Flynn, whom we last saw declaiming about Roosevelt's duplicity in deliberately provoking a Japanese attack. The declaration of war and the dissolution of the America First Committee did nothing to daunt Flynn's ardor, and he continued to pursue his enemies throughout and after the war. Some of his targets were those he believed to have sabotaged the America First and antiwar movement. Even before Pearl Harbor, he'd had these people in his sights, laying before his friends and backers in the Senate his belief that Hollywood had been transformed into a mechanism for inculcating prowar sentiments. As a result, his old friend Gerald Nye of Montana had gone on the radio on August 1, 1941, to deliver an address that, according to Flynn's biographer John E. Moser, was largely written by the hard-talking journalist.[36]

Nye's argument was that the major motion picture studios were acting as "gigantic engines of propaganda" in an attempt to shift public opinion in favor of intervention. The reason, claimed Nye, was that the studios had financial interests in Britain, which gave them "a stake of millions of dollars annually in Britain winning this war." If Britain lost, "seven of the eight leading [motion picture] companies will be wiped out." Of course, the administration had been acting to ensure that movies reflected the government's line, an interference that had met with compliance from an industry that "swarms with refugees . . . from Russia, Hungary, Germany, and the Balkan countries" who were naturally "susceptible to . . . national and racial emotions."

At Nye's suggestion, the Senate agreed to hold an "investigation of war propaganda disseminated by the motion picture industry and of any monopoly in the production, distribution, or exhibition of motion pictures." The wording ensured that the inquiry would be conducted by the Senate Interstate Commerce Committee, chaired by fellow America Firster, Burton Wheeler of Montana.

The hearings began on September 9, 1941, just two days before Lindbergh's Des Moines speech. Flynn, who had quite possibly written the resolution calling for the investigation, now turned up as a witness before the committee. Nye also gave evidence. In the cinema, said Nye, "Mr. or Mrs. or Miss America sits, with guard completely down, mind open, ready and eager for entertainment," and instead received propaganda. His Senate cosponsor, Bennett Champ Clark, argued that "dozens of pictures are used to infect the minds of their audiences with hatred, to inflame them, to arouse their emotions, and make them clamor for war. And not one word . . . of the argument against war is heard." Clark's view was that the cinema was too great a force and "too dangerous a power for any democracy to permit, concentrated in the hands of a few men."

Three years on, in 1944, Flynn once again used his connection with Nye and Wheeler to attack the men behind some of the books and articles that he believed had smeared America First and the antiwar movement. The truth about them was, Flynn alleged in an article published in the *Washington Times Herald*, that they were either Communists or had Communist links. His claims led to a congressional investigation of the most offensive book, *Under Cover*. The investigation's conclusion was that there was a sinister Communist influence on American public life and that the party was deliberately making an "effort to create disunity among Americans," a charge which Flynn had previously dismissed in the 1930s as a scare story got up by America's wealthy elite.

From this point onward, communism and its apparent allies, rather than interventionism, were to become Flynn's principal targets. As the war in Europe ended, he penned an unpublished piece, "Why the Americans Did Not Take Berlin," charging Roosevelt with having allowed Stalin to occupy half of Germany and half of Europe in accordance with a secret promise made to the Soviet dictator at the Yalta conference in February 1945. Apparently, FDR, in addition to being a power-mad warmonger, was now soft on communism. No, worse: he was sympathetic to it. Quite how this accusation could be squared with Roosevelt's cozy relationship with big business and war profiteers was a problem for later.

As the United States emerged from the Second World War, it was obvious that none of the America Firsters' nightmares were coming true; their jeremiads were proved wrong in almost every conceivable way. Though thousands of Butler's tousle-headed boys had indeed died, the country was much wealthier and far more powerful than ever before. It was therefore fruitless, in political terms, to go back over the approach to war and try to argue that it should never have happened. Far more potent was the accusation that the benefits of America's hard-won triumph were being squandered. How had it come about, for instance, that the United States had gone to war against one totalitarian foe and made such sacrifices, only to find itself confronting another totalitarian power?

Un-American Activities

Long before the war, the American right had charged that the New Deal was communism in another guise, and that its leading proponents were sympathetic to Marxism. When, for example, the House Un-American Activities Committee (HUAC) was set up in May 1938, supposedly with the task of sniffing out pro-Nazi sedition, it soon became apparent that Communist subversion was the preferred target.

This prewar hunt for Red influence led to one of the most celebrated exchanges in modern American history. In December 1938, the head of the Federal Theater Project, Mrs. Hallie Flanagan, was called before the committee to answer the accusation that the project was full of Communists. Flanagan was questioned by Representative Joe Starnes from Alabama about an article on workers' theater that she'd written in an obscure periodical seven years earlier. Starnes read out a long passage that concluded with a reference to such theater having "a certain Marlowesque madness." Starnes then addressed Mrs. Flanagan directly.

MR. STARNES: You are quoting from this Marlowe. Is he a Communist?

MRS. FLANAGAN: I am very sorry. I was quoting from Christopher Marlowe.

MR. STARNES: Tell us who Marlowe is, so we can get the proper reference, because that is all that we want to do.

MRS. FLANAGAN: Put in the record that he was the greatest dramatist in the period immediately preceding Shakespeare.

MR. STARNES: Put that in the record because the charge has been made that this article of yours is entirely Communistic, and we want to help you.

MRS. FLANAGAN: Thank you. That statement will go in the record.

MR. STARNES: Of course, we had what some people call "Communists" back in the days of the Greek theater.

MRS. FLANAGAN: Quite true.

MR. STARNES: And I believe Mr. Euripides was guilty of teaching class consciousness also, wasn't he?

MRS. FLANAGAN: I believe that was alleged against all of the Greek dramatists.

MR. STARNES: So we cannot say when it began.[37]

With such heroic wielders of the broad brush as Starnes, a former school-teacher, it is hardly any wonder that, in short order, the HUAC had listed some 640 organizations, 438 newspapers, and 280 unions and labor groups as possible Communist fronts, including the American Civil Liberties Union and the Boy Scouts.[38] The anti-Communist impulse waned during the war as the United States allied itself with Soviet Russia, which it supplied with arms and which bore the brunt of the fighting and dying, but as the war ended, that alliance was fracturing. Even before V-E Day, it was clear from intelligence intercepts that the Russians were attempting to run a serious espionage network in the United States. Toward the end of 1945, the director of the FBI, J. Edgar Hoover, was once again describing Communists as "panderers of diabolic distrust." As the Iron Curtain, so famously named by Winston Churchill, descended, the balance of political argument tilted back from the liberals, the internationalists, and the pro–New Dealers, toward populism and the right. In 1946, the Republicans won substantial victories in Congress, with a disproportionate number of Democratic casualties occurring among the liberals in the north and west of the country. President Truman trimmed to the new wind by launching his own program to combat internal Communist subversion through administering loyalty tests to public servants.

The following year, 1947, saw the resuscitation of HUAC and the famous procession of movie directors, producers, and actors being questioned on whether they or their friends were or had ever been members of the Communist Party. The proposition was familiar to those who had watched the abortive hearings about alleged Hollywood propagandizing before the war: Communists or fellow travelers had consciously used their power over the industry to influence the (sometimes obscure) political messages contained in their movies. And indeed we now know, not least from the autobiography of screenwriter Walter Bernstein, that there was some limited truth in the notion that left-wing writers and directors would sometimes attempt to smuggle ideologically compatible material into their work. However, the institution of an effective blacklist in the entertainment industry was a reaction out of all proportion to the actual threat. And so, what Flynn had attempted unsuccessfully to do in 1941, was now accomplished with exemplary ruthlessness just six years later.

Though Truman narrowly won the presidential election of 1948, that was just about the only break that the center and center-left of American politics was going to get. In the summer of 1949, the Russians tested their own atomic bomb; in September, the nationalist Chinese government of Chiang Kai-shek was finally defeated by the Chinese Communists and fled to the island of Formosa; and in June 1950, the North Koreans moved south of their disputed border, and Americans found themselves once more involved in a foreign war. Who, the Republicans asked, was responsible for this series of disasters?

The notion that much of this was due to some kind of inside job stemmed, as we have seen, from the belief that the Roosevelt administration had contained many crypto-Bolsheviks, one of whose objectives had been to make the world safe for communism. The case that seemed to prove this imputation involved a man named Alger Hiss, who as a young lawyer had worked with John Flynn on the Nye Munitions Investigating Committee in the mid-1930s. From there Hiss had gone to the State Department, serving as special assistant to the director of the Office of Far Eastern Affairs, then as special assistant to the director of the Office of Special Political Affairs. At the end of the war, Hiss was intimately involved in the American effort to set up the United Nations. He was smooth, articulate, Ivy League, and an avid New Dealer, with powerful friends at the very top of the administration. He was everything, in short, that Flynn, American populists, Southern Democrats, and Republicans loathed. He had also, it turned out, been a Communist in the 1930s, and had handed American secrets over to the Russians via a clandestine agent named Whittaker Chambers.* Hiss's arraignment before the HUAC took place in a firestorm of publicity, but, as with Oscar Wilde, it was his

---

*For a balanced and almost painfully detailed account of Hiss's wrongly disputed guilt, see Allen Weinstein, *Perjury: The Hiss-Chambers Case* (New York: Alfred A. Knopf, 1978).

attempt to clear his name through a libel action that led to Hiss's eventual conviction and imprisonment for perjury.

Then, in the summer of 1950, Ethel and Julius Rosenberg, both American Communists, were arrested and charged with passing atomic secrets to the Russians. To many Americans, the wilder allegations of the anti-Communists now seemed to have substance. From California to the New York Island, the cry went up, *Nous sommes trahis!*

In this atmosphere, increasingly little distinction was made between espionage and subversion on the one hand, and legitimate political activity and agitation on the other. Historian of the McCarthy phenomenon David M. Oshinsky relates how "Indiana forced professional wrestlers to sign a loyalty oath. Ohio declared Communists ineligible for unemployment benefits. Pennsylvania barred them from all state programs with one exception: blind Communists would be cared for . . . Tennessee ordered the death penalty for those seeking to overthrow the State government." The government of the State of Tennessee, that is.[39] Another illustration of the folk appeal of this new Red Scare* was an incident in the small town of Mosinee, Wisconsin, where in 1950 veterans from the American Legion disguised as Russian soldiers took over the town, arrested the mayor, imprisoned the clergy, nationalized businesses, and allowed only potato soup to be served in the cafés, before allowing everyone to be liberated from communism at dusk.[40]

One of those elected in the 1946 midterm congressional elections was the young Californian Republican Richard Nixon. It was Nixon who, as a member of the HUAC, had first pursued the Chambers–Hiss case and Nixon for whom the outcome of the Hiss perjury trial was a personal triumph. The Soviets, argued Nixon, might be the ultimate enemy, but Soviet success was a homegrown disaster. It had happened "because President Truman treated Communist infiltration like any ordinary political

---

*The term has also been applied to the period of strong anticommunism in the United States between 1917 and 1920.

scandal. He is responsible for this failure to act against the Communist conspiracy, and has rendered the greatest possible disservice to the people of this nation."[41] The enemy without was not nearly as potent, he was implying, as the enemy within.

Enter McCarthy

In 1950, Senator Joe McCarthy of Wisconsin was no more or less anti-Communist than most of his fellow Republicans. He had a streak of that midwestern populism, but there was nothing to suggest that he was a monocausal crusader. A speech made by McCarthy in 1949 was, by the standard of the time, quotidian. "One of the major aims of the Communist Party," McCarthy told his audience, "is to locate members in important positions in newspapers—especially in college towns, so that young people will be getting daily doses of the Communist party-line propaganda under the mistaken impression that they are absorbing 'liberal' and 'progressive' ideas."[42] And, of course, subtracting the suggested underhandedness of this desire to spread the word, this was substantially true and mostly obvious. It's what all party activists do.

But in January 1950, McCarthy (according to most accounts) enjoyed a lunch with two friendly academics and a lawyer, and told them he was looking for an issue around which to base his campaign for reelection. One mentioned communism in government, to which McCarthy is said to have replied, "The government is full of Communists. The thing to do is to hammer them."[43] A few weeks later, McCarthy addressed a meeting of the Republican Women's Club at the McClure Hotel in Wheeling and was reported as telling his audience, "While I cannot take the time to name all the men in the State Department who have been named as members of a spy ring, I have here in my hand a list of 205 . . . that were known to the Secretary of State as being members of the Communist Party and who nevertheless are still working and shaping the policy of the State Department."[44]

This was a sensational charge, its impact due to its specificity and the fact that it was being leveled by a senator. The list itself was never published, but David Oshinsky has calculated that the figure was reached by taking the number of those employees whose loyalty screening back in 1946 had thrown up some damaging information, and then subtracting the number (seventy-nine) who had subsequently been discharged. McCarthy, comments Oshinsky, couldn't have known "whether those individuals were Communist, fascists, alcoholics, sex deviants or common liars. As a gambling man he was simply raising on a poor hand, searching for an ace or two before his bluff was called."[45]

On February 20, McCarthy took his charges to the floor of the Senate. In eight hours of innuendo, semi-connected suggestions, exaggerations, guilt by association, implied accusations, and invective, McCarthy elaborated on his essential charge that the American government and the administration of President Truman were riddled with Communists and Communist sympathizers conspiring against American interests. So wild were McCarthy's claims that the Democrats decided to undermine the man from Wisconsin by establishing an investigation to look at his accusations. Properly and publicly tested, they believed, these assertions would be revealed as false, thus casting doubt on other such allegations.

The Republicans agreed that such a body should be established, and McCarthy set up an investigation team with the objective of finding absolutely anything that would give substance to his contentions. Onside were a couple of ex-Communists, a handful of muckraking journalists such as Westbrook Pegler, and a number of right-wing ideologues. The HUAC helped out with access to their files, and the FBI may well also have given assistance. The posse was given the job of hunting down any signs that government employees had sympathies with the Reds, connections with the Reds, or relationships with anyone who did. It didn't matter how tenuous such links might be.

One of the earliest of McCarthy's targets was an academic and sinologist, Owen Lattimore, director of the School of International Relations at Johns Hopkins University. Lattimore had never actually been an employee of the government but had acted as an adviser, and in that capacity had long argued against U.S. support for the nationalist Chinese. During the war, he had insisted, correctly, that the Communists were more effective in the battle against the Japanese. But in the atmosphere of 1950 and the argument over who had "lost" China, Lattimore's past toleration of Mao looked like a fondness for communism. It didn't help that in 1938 Lattimore had been one of the credulous Westerners duped by the Moscow trials.

There were some problems for McCarthy, however. The most obvious was that Lattimore had himself been attacked in the Communist Party newspaper, the *Daily Worker*. Ah well, said McCarthy's team, wasn't it obvious that some party members and sympathizers would be protected from exposure by being criticized by party publications, or by being given special dispensation to deviate from the party line? "A new technique had been unveiled," comments David Oshinsky, "guilt by disassociation."* "Owen Lattimore had not been proved a Communist," *Time* commented on the case, "but he had not proved that he was not one." And how could he? Any more than he could prove that the *Daily Worker* wasn't criticizing him as part of a secret Communist strategy?

The comment illustrates how the ground had shifted. At the outset of the Red Scare, Communists might have been people with whom one absolutely disagreed but whose actions were broadly legal and acceptable. Then Communists per se came to be seen as disloyal and their activities semi-criminal. Then people who might have been Communists were added to that category, or people whose arguments were sometimes the same as the Communists. Assumption was piled on assumption, until you could have someone as nonrevolutionary as Lattimore, whose calvary could be justified because "he had not proved he was not" a Communist.

---

*The technique was not unsuccessful. Even those publications, like *Time* magazine, that were skeptical or hostile to McCarthy were unwilling to risk defending men like the reviled academic.

One feature of widely believed conspiracy theories may be that even those who do not accept them often cease to examine them properly; something that would otherwise be quickly seen as absurd is instead treated as if it were one genuine possibility among several.

John T. Flynn, now almost at the end of his ideological journey, was one of Joe McCarthy's most enthusiastic supporters. For him, the enemy was that group of fellow-traveling social democrats who had sold the New Deal, procured war, and were now revealed as having been in cahoots with the Reds. Owen Lattimore provided Flynn with a satisfying villain. In 1953, Flynn even wrote a book, *The Lattimore Story*, to expose "a conspiracy involving over four dozen writers, journalists, educators and high-ranking government officials—almost all Americans—to force the American State Department to betray China and Korea into the hands of the Communists." Lattimore himself was never successfully prosecuted, but departed America to teach at Leeds University in a United Kingdom that seemed unworried by Flynn's and McCarthy's accusations.

Before Lattimore left, McCarthy delivered an address to the Senate that stands as the perfect encapsulation of the Red Scare proposition and its psychology:

> How can we account for our present situation unless we believe that men
> high in this government are concerting to deliver us to disaster? This must
> be the product of a great conspiracy, a conspiracy on a scale so immense
> as to dwarf any previous such venture in the history of man. A conspiracy
> of infamy so black that, when it is finally exposed, its principals shall be
> forever deserving of the maledictions of all honest men.[46]

McCarthy's rhetorical question could have been answered by an analysis of twentieth-century history and any number of plausible hypotheses. But rather than attempt such a discussion, McCarthy begins his answer, "This must ..." The situation couldn't be the culmination of the effects of huge political, economic, and other forces, of mistakes and accidents; it "must be" the result of a deliberate and infernal calculation on the part of people whose avowed position—that they were trying to achieve the opposite result—was all a blindsiding lie.

The occasional Alger Hiss would not suffice. In his speech, McCarthy insinuated the involvement in the conspiracy of men like the secretary of defense, author of the Marshall Plan and wartime chief of staff General George C. Marshall, who had made a "baffling pattern of decisions" that always ended up serving the "world policy of the Kremlin." The aim of the conspirators, said the senator, was to make certain that America would "finally fall victim to Soviet intrigue from within and Russian military might from without."

This formulation recommended itself to Flynn, who was to endorse McCarthy's opposition "to admitting Americans who are enemies of our American system of government—Communists or Socialists—into the government of the United States." Unfortunately for Flynn, the Red Scare burned itself out over the next few years, with McCarthy himself being largely marginalized by the end of 1954. By then the Republicans were in the White House and less likely to give tacit support to McCarthy's rampage through American institutions. Flynn himself moved on to other targets. In a 1955 publication, Flynn took on the youthful United Nations, which in his view had nothing to do with preserving world peace. In a voice unmellowed by age, he thundered, "We must rid this nation of the United Nations, which provides the Communist conspiracy with a headquarters here on our own shores, and which actually makes it impossible for the United States to form its own decisions about its conduct and policies in Europe and Asia."[47] In his assault on the United Nations, Flynn anticipated the main thrust of American right-wing conspiracy thinking for the next forty years, certainly up to Oklahoma City and Timothy McVeigh. "They"—the forces of world domination and government—were seeking to hobble the independent United States and force it into submission, either to the advantage of communism or for the benefit of Zionism.

Why Flynnism?

The appeal of McCarthy, according to David Oshinsky, was that he provided "a simple explanation for America's 'decline' in the world. He spoke of a massive internal conspiracy directed by Communists and abetted by government officials who came to include the Republican President of the United States. He provided names, documents and statistics—in short the *appearance* of diligent research."[48] But there is a puzzle here, the existence of which is highlighted by Oshinsky's use of quotes around "decline." By any objective standard, America had risen, not declined. America was richer, victorious in war, and—in contrast to the pulverized continents of Europe and Asia—undamaged. The specter of communism might be repulsive, but it was a long way away and less obviously threatening than Nazi Germany and the Axis powers had been at their height. Yet for several years in postwar America, conspiracism was almost a majority pastime. And the targets of suspicion were far more exalted than the usual minorities or secret organizations of past demonologies. As the historian Richard Hofstadter put it:

> For the vaguely delineated villains of the anti-Masons, for the obscure and disguised Jesuit agents, the little-known papal delegates of the anti-Catholics, for the shadowy international bankers of the monetary conspiracies, we may now substitute eminent public figures like Presidents Roosevelt, Truman and Eisenhower, Secretaries of State like Marshall, Acheson and Dulles, justices of the Supreme Court like Frankfurter and Warren, and the whole battery of lesser but still famous and vivid conspirators headed by Alger Hiss.[49]

In one sense, however, those under suspicion conformed to the enemy of American populist folklore. They were East Coasters or Hollywooders; they were educated; they were city dwellers; they liked art and fancy music; they were separate from—and unsympathetic to—the daily travails of the American little man. And the American little man might be wealthier than before, but he was also facing greater change than ever before. One feature of Hollywood movies of the period is ambivalence about the transformation of small-town life. In Frank Capra's 1946 iconic *It's a Wonderful Life*, the hero battles against a monopolistic banker and his attempts to destroy small enterprise and thus the true values of the community. James Stewart is the champion of organic society, and as the sociologist Raymond Williams wrote, "the only sure fact about the organic society is that it has always gone."[50] To which the critic Lawrence Levine added another sure fact: "that almost invariably the organic society has barely just gone, leaving many nostalgic survivors in its wake."[51]

During the 1940s, small-town Americans had had direct experience of the strong state. They or their families had served in the armed forces, had been mobilized by the government and sent abroad. Young men, in particular, had met—often for the first time—other Americans from all the states of the Union. Mental and physical borders had been breached. Nothing would be the same. It is hardly too fanciful to suggest that the Communist menace was in some ways an externalization of internal fears about alterations to the passing world.

The originators and spreaders of the conspiracy theories of the 1950s were in the main the defeated of the 1930s and 1940s. Hofstadter's paranoid American of the postwar period was someone who "believes himself to be living in a world in which he is spied upon, plotted against, betrayed and very likely destined for total ruin. He feels that his liberties have been arbitrarily and outrageously invaded. He is opposed to almost everything that has happened in American politics in the past twenty years (1943–1963). He hates the very thought of Franklin D. Roosevelt."[52] The description perfectly fits men like John T. Flynn, who had battled against the "conspiracy" to take America into war, found themselves worsted by Roosevelt and history, and wondered how on earth it had happened. Their answer was to ascribe to Roosevelt the powers of a dark messiah. McCarthyism was in one sense a fightback by these politically defeated men, and their posthumous revenge on the dead president.

Passing the Baton: The Legacy of Harry Elmer Barnes

Within a decade of McCarthy's ascendancy, the strength of right-wing conspiracism had ebbed, partially because, with Eisenhower's victory in 1952, the more Establishment part of the insurgency had been co-opted (Richard M. Nixon, after all, was vice president) and partially because the Cold War had eased. Organizations such as the John Birch Society attempted to keep alive the flame of collective paranoia, but were limited to addressing a declining fringe of aging eccentrics. The new conspiracism was to be found elsewhere.

Toward the end of his life, Harry Elmer Barnes surveyed the terrain around him and understood that the right-wing isolationist impulse had faded. But he was not without optimism. In 1967, he wrote:

> About the only rays of light and hope on the horizon for the moment are by-products of the Vietnam War. For the first time in all American history, except for the Mexican War land-grab, the liberals are not the shock troops of the warmongers, and many are preponderantly "doves," notably the younger liberals or the "new left." This has encouraged many of them who, as a group, have been less subject to the World War II brainwashing, to look back over their shoulder at liberal bellicosity in the past and examine its validity more rationally.[53]

It was the young, liberal doves, wrote Barnes, who were now questioning the "impeccable soundness of interventionist propaganda and the historical blackout relative to the two world wars of this century." This skeptical and inquiring attitude, he thought, might grow. In fact, though he may not have realized it, the event that prompted a new liberal revisionism had already taken place. On November 22, 1963, a president had been shot.

4. DEAD DEITIES

I shouted out,
"Who killed the Kennedys?"
When after all,
It was you and me.

—ROLLING STONES, "SYMPATHY FOR THE DEVIL"

The entry in my late mother's diary for Saturday, November 23, 1963, begins: "Everyone abuzz with Kennedy assassination. Man called Lee Oswald arrested." Then she adds, "Wonder if it is a frame-up, he is billed as having comm[unist] associations." My mother, a member of the British Communist Party, was wary of any piece of reporting that sought to blame something as reprehensible as political murder on an unknown comrade. The next day she felt her suspicions had been justified: "Kennedy's alleged assassin now assassinated. More and more looks like a frame-up."

A few hours before Mrs. Aaronovitch took up her pen, the president of the United States of America, John F. Kennedy, traveling in a slow-moving motorcade through the city of Dallas in Texas, had been hit by two shots, and had died soon after. Although subsequent mythology attached a kind of contemporary sainthood to the dead leader, there had been much about Kennedy that, while he lived, had irritated many and enraged a few. He had presided over the resolution of the terrifying missile crisis of 1962, but he had also allowed support for an abortive invasion of Cuba—the Bay of Pigs fiasco—shortly after taking office, and superintended the escalation of American involvement in Vietnam. Domestically, his administration had become increasingly associated with civil rights for African-Americans in the Southern states and with the battle against organized crime. In short, not everyone loved him. Even so, the murder of this young and dynamic president was felt as a huge, almost personal shock by tens of millions of people around the world.

One conventional wisdom runs that it wasn't until September 1964, when the Warren Commission released its official report on the assassination in Dallas, that people began to question the official version of events that day. In this scenario, brave researchers then spent their nights sleeplessly sifting through the twenty-six volumes of proceedings and evidence, discovering, as they did so, how riddled with errors and evasions the commission's work had been. Only then, the wisdom continues, did faith in the idea that a lone gunman had carried out the assassination begin to crumble.

In fact, a substantial majority of Americans had hardly waited any longer than my mother before declaring for conspiracy. One week after Kennedy's murder, a major U.S. poll showed that less than a third (29 percent) of those asked believed that Oswald had acted alone.[1] And within four weeks such doubts were being theorized. The December 19 edition of the weekly *National Guardian* carried an article by a young lawyer, Mark Lane. In the tones of a Zola, Lane castigated the dash to blame one troubled young man—a young man himself conveniently eliminated before coming to trial—for the killing of the world's most powerful leader.

The magazine quickly sold out, and a complete extra press run also disappeared from the newsstands. As the pamphlet version of the article claimed, all too many heard the heavy echoes of past injustices: "The doubts and confusion in the aftermath of the assassination of President Kennedy have brought to mind the situation that was created by the Sacco–Vanzetti case and the case of Ethel and Julius Rosenberg." Within a month of his death, Lee Harvey Oswald was being listed in the honor scroll of left martyrology. (An irony here is that the anarchists Sacco and Vanzetti were very probably guilty of murder and the Rosenbergs certainly were guilty of treason.) Lane concluded:

> You are the jury. You are the only jury that Lee Harvey Oswald will ever have. A terrible crime has been committed. A young, vital and energetic leader of perhaps the world's most powerful nation has been killed by the cowardly act of a hidden assassin. The murderer or murderers were motivated by diseased minds or by such depths of malice as to approach that state. We will perhaps never know their motives. We must, however, know and approve of our own conduct and our own motives . . . We begin with a return to an old American tradition—the presumption of innocence. We begin with you.[2]

In the United States, Lane established the Citizens' Committee of Inquiry into the death of the president. Lane's call was also heard across the Atlantic by the great philosopher and peace campaigner Bertrand Russell. He believed the lawyer's evidence to be "so startling and so impressive" that another committee was needed, mirroring the American effort. The Who Killed Kennedy Committee (WKKC) soon comprised many of Britain's finest and most sensitive minds. The writers J. B. Priestley and Sir Compton Mackenzie, the Bishop of Southwark, Michael Foot MP (later leader of the Labour Party), the critic Kenneth Tynan, the publishers Victor Gollancz and John Calder, and the historian Professor Hugh Trevor-Roper all sat on it. Running the committee was a young American, Ralph Schoenman.

Russell and his committee were not to be mollified by the eventual publication of the Warren Commission Report. Even without reading it for himself, Russell knew (for Lane had told him so) that there had "never been a more subversive, conspiratorial, unpatriotic or endangering course for the security of the United States and the world than the attempt by the U.S. Government to hide the murderers of its recent President."[3]

The skepticism was catching. Throughout the mid-1960s, article followed article, theory was laid on top of theory, book followed book. By the 1970s, the conspiracy to kill Kennedy was an established "fact" of intellectual life in America and Europe, and the default view among the young and educated. Its purchase on popular culture is demonstrated by its incorporation into the routines of stand-up comedians. Woody Allen would tell audiences that he had just been working on a new movie script, which was "a nonfiction version of the Warren Report."

In the movie *Annie Hall* (1977), Allen even satirized his own preoccupation with the Kennedy conspiracy. A flashback bedroom scene involving the ineffectual Alvy (Allen) and his first wife has the hero breaking away from an embrace and pacing the room. She tries to talk him out of his obsession.

> ALLISON: Okay. All right, so whatta ya saying, now? That everybody on the Warren Commission is in on this conspiracy, right?
>
> ALVY: Well, why not?
>
> ALLISON: Yeah, Earl Warren?
>
> ALVY: Hey . . . honey, I don't know Earl Warren.
>
> ALLISON: Lyndon Johnson?
>
> ALVY: Lyndon Johnson is a politician. You know the ethics those guys have? It's like—a notch underneath child molester.
>
> ALLISON: Then everybody's in the conspiracy?
>
> ALVY: Tsch.
>
> ALLISON: The FBI, and the CIA, and J. Edgar Hoover and oil companies and the Pentagon and the men's-room attendant at the White House?
>
> ALVY: I would leave out the men's-room attendant.
>
> ALLISON: You're using this conspiracy theory as an excuse to avoid sex with me.[4]

Nearly two decades later, the comedian Bill Hicks was running a much angrier routine to another generation of young Americans.

I have this feeling that whoever's elected president, like Clinton was, no matter what promises you make on the campaign trail—blah, blah, blah—when you win, you go into this smoky room with the twelve industrialist, capitalist scumfucks that got you in there, and this little screen comes down . . . and it's a shot of the Kennedy assassination from an angle you've never seen before, which looks suspiciously off the grassy knoll . . . And then the screen comes up, the lights come on, and they say to the new president, "Any questions?"

"Just what my agenda is."[5]

Early on, as the desire to solve the Kennedy case burgeoned, housewives turned themselves into assiduous researchers, journalists turned geostrategists, and professors in humanities became experts in ballistics and forensic pathology. As Todd Gitlin, the writer and former political activist, put it, "Serious journals like the *New Republic*, the *New York Review of Books*, and *Ramparts* . . . regaled their readers with tale after tale about exit wounds, gunshots from the grassy knoll, missing frames of the Zapruder film, the accuracy of Mannlicher-Carcano rifles, exotic Cuban émigrés, mysteriously murdered witnesses, double agents, double Oswalds."[6] Among the most influential books on the subject were Lane's own *Rush to Judgment*, Harold Weisberg's *Whitewash*, Leo Sauvage's *The Oswald Affair*, and *The Second Oswald* by Richard H. Popkin.

Popkin was a professor at the University of California at La Jolla and previously best known for his *History of Skepticism from Erasmus to Descartes*, published in 1960. But in 1966, he glanced down from the study of Jewish and Christian millenarianism, put down *The Outlines of Pyrrhonism* by Sextus Empiricus, and considered instead the murder of the president. His ideas, which were given extensive play in that journal of liberal American intellectuals, the *New York Review of Books*, proved to be both similar to, and different from, the very many other books and articles being produced on an almost industrial basis elsewhere. The similarity lay in his objections to the conclusions of the Warren

Commission. The difference lay in his particular thesis about what had happened.

Descartes to Doppelgängers

If one reads the Warren Report, the circumstantial evidence that Oswald was the lone gunman seems overwhelming. He worked at the Texas School Book Depository, where, on the sixth floor, after the shooting, his rifle was discovered inside an improvised sniper's nest. People had seen a man at the sixth-floor window, had seen the rifle barrel, had heard the shots. Oswald was the only employee unaccounted for after the shooting, and he was picked up shortly afterward in a cinema, having just shot a policeman looking for someone of his description. The words "slam dunk" come to mind. One might wonder whether someone unknown had put the ex-marine and former defector to the Soviet Union up to the crime, but no one could seriously dispute that he had carried it out on his own.

But from the start, conspiracy theorists did exactly this: they challenged the notion that he acted alone. According to Popkin, the problem with the evidence was not that it "suggests that the 'official theory' is implausible, or improbable, or that it is not legally convincing, but that by reasonable standards accepted by thoughtful men, it is impossible."[7] The impossibility rested, in many people's minds, on the alleged physical unfeasibility of Oswald's achievement. As Popkin summarized it: "All of the Commission's obfuscation notwithstanding, Oswald was a poor shot and his rifle was inaccurate. Experts could not duplicate the alleged feat of two hits out of three shots in 5.6 seconds, even though they were given stationary targets and ample time to aim the first shot."[8] In addition, for the Warren findings to work, the first bullet to hit Kennedy must also have been the one that—having passed through the president—also transited Governor John Connally of Texas in the front seat and exited his wrist. Popkin, like many another unqualified American, looked at the ballistic evidence and the report on the autopsy, and made his decision.

The professor, however, recognized what many of his fellows didn't. Objections to the Warren version weren't enough. "All of this [criticism] usually builds up to a big 'So what?'" he wrote, "since the critics still have not been able to present a reasonably plausible counterexplanation of what could have happened. Why, for example, should Oswald have tried to implicate himself as the assassin?"[9] Popkin then went on to provide the answer. What followed was the theory that there were, in fact, two entirely separate Oswalds. One was the real, hapless Oswald, Oswald-Jekyll, if you like; and the other was the murderous Oswald (Oswald-Hyde), who might well have been an intelligence operative. "Second Oswald," theorized Popkin, "was an excellent shot, real Oswald was not. Real Oswald's role was to be the prime suspect chased by the police, while second Oswald, one of the assassins, could vanish . . . If the crime is reconstructed in this way, most of the puzzles and discrepancies can be more plausibly explained."[10]

Popkin agreed that his hypothesis was "tentative and conjectural," but that, even so, it was a more realistic explanation than that offered by Warren. He concluded his major piece in the *NYRB* with a call to action: "Many of us in this country are afraid to face reality, and part of our reality is living with our history. Can we continue to live a lie about what happened in Dallas on November 22, 1963, or has the time come to face what it means and what it involves for all of us? The public must cry out for a real examination and understanding of the events of that day."[11]

Whether the public cried out sufficiently to satisfy Professor Popkin or not, it is obvious that since 1966, examination at least has been plentiful. Understanding has been another matter. An industry of fluctuating intensity and volume of output has operated for four decades. Thousands of conspiracy enthusiasts continue to exchange theories, arcane pieces of information, and supposed expertise. The detail is overwhelming. Was Kennedy's brain stolen? Was his body swapped? Who were the tramps by the Dallas railway tracks? What was recorded on the walkie-talkie of a Texan patrolman? Was the smoke seen on the grassy knoll a sign of rifle fire or from a motorcycle's exhaust? Was Oswald's assassin, Jack Ruby, a Mafia hit man? Had someone tried to kill Kennedy earlier in Miami?

Was Oswald a CIA agent? A KGB agent? Authors and documentarists, mostly of the political left, insisted, variously, that their unique work and extensive research showed that the CIA, the FBI, right-wing freelancers, Vice President Lyndon Johnson, the Russians, the Cubans, the military-industrial complex, the military-industrial-intelligence complex, or the Jews were behind the assassination. As I began this chapter, a heavily marketed nine-hundred-page hardcover appeared in the bookstores, claiming that JFK was killed by the Mafia because of a failed plan to organize a coup in Cuba.

The Dead Left

It was I. F. Stone, one of the most prominent progressive U.S. journalists, who warned the left that they were falling prey to the same paranoias as the American right. Following Russell's denunciation of the U.S. government, Stone observed that, having lived through the McCarthy era, he had fought all his adult life "against conspiracy theories of history, character assassination, guilt by association and demonology," but now he saw the left "using these same tactics in the controversy over the Kennedy assassination and the Warren Commission Report." To Stone, it all seemed too improbable, and he voiced the instinctive objections of anti-conspiracists through the years. Were Lane and Russell and the others really arguing, he asked, that "the whole commission, from Chief Justice Warren down, and its whole staff, and the vast network of the police, the FBI, and CIA and the Secret Service all conspired to keep this secret? Not one man felt impelled by conscience to break out and tell the truth?" If so, then this was regrettable, because "people who believe such things belong in the booby-hatch."[12]

Unfortunately, there were many, besides Woody Allen's Alvy, ready for the booby-hatch. Take, for example, Sidney Blumenthal, White House spin doctor and confidant to President Bill Clinton, part of whose job in the 1990s was to trash the various conspiracy theories attaching themselves to the former governor of Arkansas. In 1976, as Sid Blumenthal the left-wing journalist, he had edited a book of essays titled *Government by Gunplay: Assassination Conspiracy Theories from Dallas to Today*, in which various skulduggeries were discussed, from the Kennedy assassination to the alleged murder of Martin Luther King, Jr., by the authorities. Hedging his bets slightly, Blumenthal exalted a new skepticism in the United States, and noted that "the idea that Lee Harvey Oswald was the lone assassin of President Kennedy runs against the grain of the new [suspicious, skeptical] American Character."

According to Blumenthal, the motor force behind such theorizing was a form of sublimated politics "based, in part, on the decline of the student radicalism of the sixties." On one level, conspiracy theory was, he suggested, "the doctrine of those still holding on to their faith; it is an attempt to defend the past."[13] Lest this leave the impression with the reader that Blumenthal himself might not quite buy the notion of the Mafia or the CIA organizing a gigantic cover-up, he went on to discuss the case of Sarah Jane Moore, the woman who tried to shoot President Gerald Ford in September 1975. Moore subsequently attempted to claim that she had been working for the government but had gone off the rails. She and Oswald were, wrote Blumenthal, malfunctioning operatives, "the epiphenomena of the politics of domestic destabilization."[14] Here, then, was yet another theory: conspiracy by accident.

Not all contributors to the book were so coy. Controversial chronicler of the CIA Philip Agee wrote an introduction in which he summed up the lesson to be learned from *Government by Gunplay*: "The ruling class conspiracy—whether acting through the CIA, government commissions, or a big business junta . . . can be stopped only by a countervailing grassroots movement of the American people." Some believed this ruling-class conspiracy had by 1976 taken the lives of the best and most popular leaders of the American left and center-left. And if you thought that JFK had been killed by "them," then why not his brother, gunned down in California in 1968? Or Martin Luther King, Jr., shot dead in Memphis in the same year? Or go back to 1965 and the New York slaying of black leader

Malcolm X? Or even, to assist Richard Nixon's reelection campaign in 1972, the shooting and wounding of the former segregationist governor of Alabama, George Wallace, whose candidacy threatened to split the right-wing vote? All supposedly the work of lone gunmen or radical factions, but all conveniently removed from the political stage.

To Carl Oglesby, a former president of the Students for Democratic Society, what was going on was essentially gang warfare, complete with hits, between the old East Coast establishment and new southwestern entrepreneurs:

> The facts surrounding the assassination conspiracies behind Dallas, Memphis, Los Angeles and Laurel, Maryland are like a storm of incomprehensible lightning. It changes everything, it changes colors, familiar components of the political landscape, it turns political parties that once we thought were strong and forceful into pawns and manipulated counters on a stage controlled by hidden forces. And the act of government is turned most fundamentally into an act of murder.[15]

Other, later writers discovered the true pattern of the murders. In *The Assassinations*, a comprehensive 2003 compilation of conspiracy theories, the authors claimed that "the cumulative effect of these assassinations is quite clear. They resulted in the death of the old Democratic Party and the birth of the new Jimmy Carter–Bill Clinton–Al Gore Democratic Party. And there is a huge difference between the two."[16] The authors then embarked upon a retrospective political wish list thwarted by old bullets. "If Robert Kennedy had lived he very likely would have won that nomination and defeated Richard Nixon. He would have gotten us out of Vietnam, and saved us from Watergate. This, of course, would have saved the rest of us from Carter, Strauss and Clinton."* Had Robert Kennedy and JFK and MLK and Malcolm X survived, they would have energized

---

*Leo Strauss is often thought to be the father of neoconservatism.

the Democratic base and re-created the New Deal coalition of FDR; the left would have been in and the right would have been out. As it was, the authors concluded, despondently, "what had once been a huge street movement now plays to small crowds with the likes of Noam Chomsky at small college auditoriums. What had been a large and growing majority is now a tiny minority."[17]

This book will have to park its sympathy for the undervalued Noam Chomsky alongside any attempt to detail each and every objection to the idea of a lone gunman. It is worth noting, however, that there are those who don't appear in the list of dead or wounded heroes. President Ronald Reagan was shot and injured in 1981, and Lincoln Rockwell was shot and killed by a sniper in 1967. But what theory of ruling-class malfeasance could possibly fit the attempt on Reagan? And Rockwell was, inconveniently, the führer of the American Nazi Party.

Lone Assassins

Reagan was shot by John Hinckley, the twenty-five-year-old son of an oil executive, who was trying to impress the actress Jodie Foster. Rockwell was killed by the editor of his Nazi newspaper, with whom he'd fallen out. Both events took place after the publication of the Warren Report, but the careers of the shooters wouldn't have surprised the report's authors. In 1881, they pointed out, President Garfield was assassinated by a man who wanted someone else to be president; in 1901, President McKinley was killed by an anarchist.

Both Roosevelts had been fired at: Teddy in 1912 by a deranged shop-keeper, and President-elect Franklin Delano in 1933 in Miami by another anarchist, Giuseppe Zangara. Zangara, who hit and fatally wounded the mayor of Chicago, Anton Cermak, was in Miami, according to reports, only "because it was warm and he was out of work, and he had lost $200 on the dog races." The FBI recorded that he had wanted to kill kings and presidents of wealthy governments since he was a teenager.

Two years later, the populist governor of Louisiana, Huey Long (known as the "Kingfish"), was shot and killed in the state capitol building in Baton Rouge by a Dr. Carl Weiss, whose father-in-law, a judge, had been gerrymandered out of office by the ruthless governor.

The assassinations of Robert Kennedy and Martin Luther King, Jr., were ascribed to an attention-seeking Palestinian Sirhan Sirhan and a white racist petty criminal James Earl Ray, respectively. Arthur Bremer, George Wallace's would-be assassin, was said by his defense to be schizophrenic, and in any case had left a journal, described by himself as a "diary of my personal plot to kill by pistol either Richard Nixon or George Wallace." (Some, including Gore Vidal, have described this diary as a forgery.) Plots seemed to be rare. Malcolm X was the victim of an organized hit by gunmen angry at his opposition to the Nation of Islam, and, in the autumn of 1950, two Puerto Rican nationalists, Oscar Collazo and Griselio Torresola, had attempted to murder President Harry Truman. So, in the run of presidents from Roosevelt to Kennedy, spanning 1933 to 1963, only Eisenhower was *not* the target of assassins.

It is fairly obvious from this list that lone gunmen were not a new phenomenon in American history when Kennedy's open limousine rounded the bend in the road below the Texas Schoolbook Depository. The question, of course, is whether Oswald was one of them. If there were a credible profile for a man who might want on his own account to kill a world statesman, would Oswald fit it?

The most startling, incontrovertible, and often overlooked fact about Lee Harvey Oswald is that seven months before the Kennedy assassination he had used the same rifle to try and assassinate another prominent American, Major General Edwin A. Walker.

Lee's Russian wife, Marina, maintained that on the evening of April 10, 1963, her husband had left home after dinner, and when he had failed to return by ten or ten-thirty, she had gone into his room and discovered a note addressed to her. The note, which survived, contained practical advice to Marina in the eventuality of Lee's not coming back, but also included, as point 2, "Send the information as to what has happened to

me to the Embassy and include newspaper clippings (should there be anything about me in the newspapers)," and as point 11, "If I am alive and
taken prisoner, the city jail is located at the end of the bridge through
which we always passed on going to the city (right in the beginning of the
city after crossing the bridge)."[18]

Marina testified under oath that when Oswald finally returned home
he was very pale. He told her that he had shot at General Walker, but
didn't know whether he had hit him. Next day, when newspaper and radio
reports revealed that an attempt had been made on Walker's life but that
the assassin had missed his target, Oswald told his wife that he "was very
sorry that he had not hit him." Later that week Oswald showed Marina a
notebook containing a map of the area where Walker lived and some photographs of the Walker residence. Though the notebook was subsequently
destroyed, three of the photographs were discovered after Oswald's arrest.
But what about the rifle used to shoot at Walker? Marina testified that
Oswald had told her that he had hidden it in some rough ground. Several days later, she said, he recovered it and brought it back home. A later
analysis of the bullet fired at Walker showed that it was "probably" from a
Mannlicher-Carcano, the same make as Oswald's gun.

Since no one has credibly suggested that Oswald was involved with
others to kill Walker, it's clear that he was already a would-be lone assassin long before anyone decided that Kennedy should visit Dallas or fixed
the route that he would travel. And Oswald's capacity for independent
mayhem is further proved by the again incontrovertible fact that, less
than an hour after the president was shot, he fired four bullets into Patrolman J. D. Tippit. He was seen shooting the officer, and his progress, followed by a number of eyewitnesses, culminated in his arrest in a Dallas
movie theater, while he was still holding the gun that had fired the bullets
that killed Tippit.

Even so, what was Oswald's motive? A clue lies in his own writings. A
troubled child and adolescent, Oswald defected to Russia in 1961, hoping
to discover a better form of society—and discovered instead the Soviet
Union. On his journey back to America in the summer of 1962, he jotted

down some of his thoughts about politics. He was disillusioned with what he understood of all political movements, writing, "I have offen wondered why it is that the Communist, capitalist and even the fasist and anarchist elements in America, allways profess patriotistism toward the land and the people, if not the government; although their movements must surly lead to the bitter destruction of all and everything [all *sic*]." The only solution, Oswald thought, was the destruction of all authority. "As history has shown time again the state remains and grows whereas true democracy can be practiced only at the local level, while the centralized state, administrative, political or supervisual remains their can be no real democracy a loose confederation of communitys at a national level with out any centralized state what so ever [all *sic*]."[19]

On November 22, 1963, chance routed the motorcade of the leader of the most powerful state in the world past Oswald's window.

It is suggestive that one of the eminent Americans who initially advocated the notion of a conspiracy changed his mind when he began to study Oswald the man. When *Oswald's Tale: An American Mystery* came out in 1995, the novelist Norman Mailer had, he said, moved away from his own "prejudice in favor of conspiracy theories" to the belief that Oswald was a "prime mover . . . a figure larger than others would credit him for being." If he blamed anybody, Mailer blamed the influence of Oswald's mother.

The "Magic Bullet"

Such a change of mind, apostasy almost, had to be accounted for in what is sometimes called the assassination community. One theory was that Mailer was somehow got at by his editor at Random House, Bob Loomis. It was pointed out that Loomis had also edited work by Gerald Posner, author of one of the best debunkings of Kennedy conspiracy theories, *Case Closed.*[20] The scale of Mailer's work and his own prickliness, however, would seem to make any such interference most unlikely.

Nevertheless, any discussion of Oswald's character would be academic if, as Professor Popkin claimed, Oswald could not plausibly have fired all the shots. In most conspiracy theories, there is a deal-breaker: the impossible fact that proves that the official version must be wrong and that some other, more ostensibly improbable or unspecified truth must be right. With Oswald, the impossible facts were the time taken to fire three shots and the course of the second shot, the so-called magic bullet. If Oswald could not have been the origin of all the shots, then someone else must have been firing on that day, and therefore there must have been a conspiracy. Furthermore, the conspiracy must have been covered up, not least through the assassination of the alleged assassin.

If, however, it was quite possible for Oswald to have fired all the shots in Dallas, and for the bullets he fired to cause the wounds that the president and Governor Connally suffered, the need for another theory more or less disappears. This is why the most arresting scene in *JFK*, Oliver Stone's celebrated movie of one man's investigation of the Kennedy conspiracy, is that in which the questing attorney Jim Garrison (played by Kevin Costner) runs through the sequence of shots and effects. The movie generates growing excitement as the full inconceivability of the Warren case is exposed.

But Oliver Stone was—as in just about every aspect of his film— wrong. For over a decade, using forensic techniques that were not available to Warren, we have known that Oswald's feat was by no means improbable.[21] In the first place, and contrary to Popkin's assertions, Oswald was a decent enough marksman in possession of a serviceable rifle with telescopic sights, firing at a target moving slowly along his line of vision, not across it. And the time that Oswald took between firing the first shot and the third was not the 5.6 seconds that Warren believed it to be (though this is quite doable, as Stone unwittingly demonstrated in *JFK*) but 7.1 seconds. Of these shots, the first missed, probably deflected by a twig or small branch on an intervening tree, the second was the magic bullet that hit Kennedy in the back and then wounded Governor Connally, and the third was the bullet that blew the president's brains out.

The literature on the magic bullet is voluminous, and over the years has dealt with trajectories, entrance and exit wounds, and the final condition of the bullet itself. But computer reconstructions based on the Zapruder film and other pictures, placing the victims in the same relative position that they occupied at the time, have allowed us to see that a bullet passing downward through the president's back and throat would indeed have struck the governor. Experiments carried out by Dr. John K. Lattimer in the early 1990s confirmed this, with his test bullet arriving in much the same condition as the one actually found on Connally's stretcher at the hospital in Dallas.[22]

The Disorder of the City

With this information, the last requirement for a conspiracy to be attached to Oswald's own obvious actions disappears. Yet most people who constitute part of that long-standing majority supporting a conspiratorial explanation have not read very much about the bullets or the timings. In other words, regardless of the facts, there has been a predisposition to believe that America's glamorous young president could not have been the victim of a lone gunman.

Some sociologists seem almost to believe that the underlying truth doesn't really matter. In his book *Conspiracy Culture*, Dr. Peter Knight of the University of Manchester argues, "The accusation levelled against conspiracy theories—that in trying to explain everything they explain nothing—could be turned back against lone gunman theories, which by contrast explain the assassination by declaring Oswald's motive inexplicable."[23] That is, one explanation is as good as another; what is important is what the belief tells us about the believer. Indeed Knight, while dismissing the Warren Commission's attempt to explain the "inexplicable" as "amateur psychobiography," feels confident enough in his grasp of history to speculate that "it is far from clear whether a lone gunman or a conspiracy theory is a priori the more politically naïve view."[24]

There is, of course, a confusion here. Oswald's motivations are not inexplicable at all, as we have seen, but they are unknowable. And if by "a priori" Knight means "before knowing any of the facts," then he would have a limited point if it weren't for all the other lone gunmen and deranged would-be assassins who crowd the historical stage. There is a good reason why the single shooter often succeeds where the corporate conspirator might fail, and that is because he is not only unafraid of being caught, he probably wants to be caught. Knight's analysis therefore fails to register just how far ordinary people are prepared to go in preferring to believe the improbable as opposed to the likely, and therefore risks underestimating the strength of the desire in society for the "higher" explanation.

Sections of the left, of course, looking back on how the promise of the Vietnam protests became first the Nixon years and then the Reagan era, had an interest in creating an account which somehow mitigated any sense of their own failure, or the failure of their ideas. But it should be remembered that for less partisan people, intellectual or otherwise, the Kennedy assassination was a genuinely appalling moment. The literary critic Irving Howe, writing a fortnight or so after Dallas, wailed his despair. It had been hard, he wrote, "these last two weeks, to feel much pride in being an American." Oswald was, according to Howe, "a man who embodies the disorder of the city, an utterly displaced creature, totally and (what is more important) proudly alienated, without roots in nation, region, class. *He cannot stand it*, but what it is he cannot stand he does not know."[25] Oswald was an unbearable manifestation of an unbearable society. The writer and critic Dwight MacDonald wrote that the sniper had created "a wound to our consciousness of ourselves as American . . . Now we see we are more in the class of Guatemala or the Congo."[26]

A lone shooter, far from suggesting an isolated act of homicidal madness, actually suggested a sick and chaotic society in which sudden and irrational violence could overtake anyone. That the target should have been young and one of the most famous men on the planet can only have made the feeling of dislocation and paranoia worse. Conspiracy theory, with its promise that the world was ruled by some kind of order, even if it was hidden, offered not the connection with reality that Popkin wanted but a flight from it.

Exit Marilyn

A rather more starry flight from reality surrounds the suicide of Hollywood icon Marilyn Monroe. The question is, whose flight was it? Hers, or those who believe she was murdered?

Marilyn died sometime during the night of August 4, 1962, fifteen months before the murder of President John Kennedy, her onetime lover. The Los Angeles coroner recorded a verdict of "probable suicide" by drug overdose, and the moviegoing world mourned the passing of the industry's most glamorous star.

That Monroe should die of barbiturate poisoning was not the greatest surprise for many who knew her. She was a chronic insomniac who needed pills to sleep and—eventually—to wake. In his famous essay on Monroe, "A Beautiful Child," Truman Capote paints a picture of Monroe in 1955, happily consuming pills, and she would sometimes have to be made up for performance while in a barbiturate-induced stupor. Monroe was famously afflicted by stage fright on set, maintained relationships with great difficulty, suffered from depression (in February 1961, she was briefly committed to a psychiatric hospital in New York), and at the time of her death was alone though contemplating her forthcoming remarriage to Joe DiMaggio. Some biographers also see significance in the fact that her psychoanalyst, Dr. Ralph Greenson, was away at the time of her death. Greenson himself had confided in Anna Freud (Sigmund Freud's psychoanalyst daughter, who practiced in London) that he was concerned that Monroe might kill herself.

The early debates, then, were not about whether Marilyn died by her own hand but whether her death was intentional and who should bear the greatest measure of blame. Had Hollywood killed her? Or her shrinks? Or her men? Or all of us?

It took nearly two years for a revisionist version of Monroe's death to appear. *The Strange Death of Marilyn Monroe*, self-published in 1964 by Frank Capell, was more of a pamphlet than a book. Capell's orientation may be illustrated by the fact that his previous work was titled *The Threat from Within: The Truth About the Conspiracy to Destroy America*, to be followed a few years later by *Henry Kissinger: Soviet Agent*. Capell, in conformity with his general worldview, was of the opinion that Monroe had been murdered by Communist agents possibly in the pay of Robert F. Kennedy.

The "impossible fact" in Marilyn's death is supposed to be the body's incapacity to ingest as much barbiturate as was found in Monroe's bloodstream. Over the years this has given rise to two main thoughts: either that she was forcibly injected or—given the complete absence of any marks of injection—that she was treated to a barbiturate enema. Donald Spoto (*Marilyn Monroe: The Biography*, 1993) abjured vulgar murder theories and hypothesized that it was all a terrible mistake. He has Dr. Greenson instructing Monroe's housekeeper, Eunice Murray, to give her employer an enema of chloral hydrate, not realizing that it would react with the Nembutal that he had also prescribed. In this account, Greenson emerges as a kind of negligent Svengali, hugely influential over his patient and almost entirely stupid. Spoto, by positing an enema by consent, at least avoided the image created by Chuck and Sam Giancana, respectively brother and godson of the Mafia boss of the same name, in their 1993 book *Double Cross*. This had Mafia hit men, who had been spying on the star, going to Monroe's bedroom, where she was lying on the bed face-down, and forcibly administering a Nembutal enema.

In Joyce Carol Oates's best-selling fact-novel *Blonde* (2000), someone known only as the "Sharpshooter"—sent by an agency that wants Marilyn dead because her views are a bit progressive—gives her a lethal injection. Donald Wolfe's *The Assassination of Marilyn Monroe* (1998) has several men—including RFK, Rat-Packster Peter Lawford, and Greenson—visit Monroe on the night of August 4 in what one critic called "the conspiracy sub-genre's reductio ad absurdum: Bobby Kennedy and Sam Giancana and

Marilyn's psychotherapist tripping over each other in an effort to commit the great pointless homicide."[27]

Though Marilyn theories have taken longer to emerge and have less purchase on the popular consciousness than their JFK counterparts, they have become every bit as diverse in their demonology. The mob did it to implicate the Kennedys; the mob did it at the behest of the Kennedys; Jimmy Hoffa did it; the Russians did it; the FBI or the CIA did it. Somehow the film star's death succeeded in linking together those four great arenas for popular culture—politics, crime, sex, and show business—and, once the parade started, the floats kept on coming.

Secret Marriages, Hidden Tapes, Duped Reporters

Marilyn-themed conspiracy theories were always going to be lucrative. The seven hundred or so biographies of Monroe bear witness not just to authors' fascination with the subject but also to the calculation on the part of publishers that such books will sell. But each book, each documentary, each major magazine article required something new—a twist, a revelation, a unique selling point. In such circumstances, the incentive to produce novel information and evidence is obvious. And so, too, is the desire to use it.

In 1974, a certain Robert Slatzer published *The Life and Curious Death of Marilyn Monroe*, in which he claimed to have been secretly married to the star—albeit briefly—in 1952 and to have been her lifelong confidant. In this capacity, he discovered her "affair" with Robert Kennedy and saw her little red diary, in which she mentioned "Murder Incorporated." This, she explained to Slatzer, was in the context of Bobby telling her "that he was powerful enough to have people taken care of if they got in his way." At least one other biographer has proved that on the day Slatzer was supposed to be marrying Marilyn in Mexico the star was actually shopping in Hollywood, yet Slatzer's version of Monroe's demise has been used as the basis for many more biographies and articles since.

Slatzer's were not the only revelations of forgotten diaries or hidden recordings. Indeed, all the various agencies already mentioned, plus— according to some more way-out theorists—a paranoid Marilyn herself and Twentieth Century–Fox, were supposed to have bugged the Monroe house. Yet not one of the dozens of tapes that must have been made has ever surfaced for examination. There have been only "transcripts" or "eyewitness accounts" of the hard evidence, which has always conveniently disappeared from history.

One prime example of this kind of Monroevian evolution is afforded by the work of Matthew Smith, a Sheffield-based writer who has presumably made a good living out of Kennedyana in recent years, publishing *JFK: The Second Plot* in 1992 (Patrolman J. D. Tippit was in on it, apparently), *Vendetta: The Kennedys* (1993), *Say Goodbye to America: The Sensational and Untold Story Behind the Assassination of John F. Kennedy* (2002), and *The Kennedys: The Conspiracy to Destroy a Dynasty* (2006). In this last book, Smith constructs an overarching theory that connects the deaths of Marilyn, JFK, RFK, and Mary Jo Kopechne, the girl who died in Edward Kennedy's car at Chappaquiddick in 1969. It was all—all of it—the work of elements within the CIA. They saw JFK as being too left-wing and bumped Marilyn off to discredit the Kennedys, both of whom were having affairs with the star at her bugged bungalow in Los Angeles. Unfortunately, that didn't work, so they killed JFK the next year, and then, for some reason, waited another five years before getting rid of Bobby. The next year they arranged for Ted to drive his car, complete with a young woman, off a bridge, thus destroying his chances of the presidency.

Two difficulties with Smith's thesis are that there is no evidence of Monroe having entertained JFK at the Los Angeles bungalow—their one attested liaison having taken place in 1960—and no real evidence that she ever had an affair at all with Robert. Until, that is, previously unknown recordings surfaced, to form the basis of Smith's 2003 book *Victim: The Secret Tapes of Marilyn Monroe*.

In the preface to this work, Smith explained what had happened. A man named John Miner, who had been the head of the Los Angeles DA office's medical legal section, had approached him with transcripts of two tapes made by Monroe herself shortly before she died. These tapes had been recorded for Ralph Greenson as part of a free-association exercise in which Monroe unburdened herself of various thoughts and memories, and were played by Greenson for Miner in the days after Monroe's death on condition of the strictest confidentiality. Greenson's aim, according to Smith, was to give Miner some idea of the star's state of mind in the last days of her life. Despite the agreement with Greenson, Miner subsequently made "nearly verbatim" notes from memory, only breaking his silence when the by-now-deceased psychoanalyst was himself named as a possible Marilynicide.

As partially reproduced by Smith, the transcripts (not "tapes," as he describes them) are both commercially comprehensive and properly incriminating. Marilyn begins by telling Greenson that this recording business is "really easy. I'm lying on the bed wearing only a brassiere. If I want to go to the refrig or the bathroom, I can push the stop button and begin again when I want to."[28] And she reminds Greenson (and thus Miner and thus Smith and thus the readers) that "you are the only person who will ever know the most private, the most secret thoughts of Marilyn Monroe." And there it all is: her orgasms, her lesbian fling with Joan Crawford, the glitz, the sex, the high politics, and, of course, the Kennedys. And she finishes, "But Bobby, Doctor, what should I do about Bobby? As you see there's no room in my life for him . . . I want someone else to tell him it's over. I tried to get the president to do it, but I couldn't reach him." She was going to give Bobby the kiss-off, and then she was dead. It was, as Sarah Churchwell puts it in her serious biography of Marilyn, *The Many Lives of Marilyn Monroe*, "thoughtful of Marilyn to dispose of so many of our questions about her life just before she died and to offer summary versions of all her most famous relationships to the psychiatrist she'd been seeing daily for two years."[29]

So where were the original tapes? Greenson's wife had never heard of them. No suggestion of them ever turned up in the Anna Freud archives. The first time they were ever mentioned was by Miner himself in a review of the Monroe case in 1982, and even then, despite Greenson's death in 1979, Miner made no mention of any transcripts. In fact, there was only Miner's word that the tapes had ever existed at all. Smith has told the *Los Angeles Times* that he believes Miner to be "a man of integrity." He also said, "I've looked at the contents of the tapes, of course, and, frankly, I would think it entirely impossible for John Miner to have invented what he put forward—absolutely impossible."[30]

Even a fairly casual look at what has been published reveals the absurdity of this claim. It would have been entirely possible for someone who had followed the theories about, and biographies of, Marilyn over the years to concoct such a story. Indeed, as Churchwell suggests, the transcripts seem credible only as a fabrication. Wearing only her brassiere, indeed!

And the motive for any such hoax is obvious too: Smith, of course, paid Miner an undisclosed fee for the use of the transcript. As rival Marilyn biographer and conspiracy theorist Anthony Summers revealed in 2005, Miner had been hawking his supposed transcript around the theorizing community for the best part of a decade. "What happened in 1995," Summers told a television interviewer, "was that Miner got in touch to say he was going to let go what he claimed to have heard Monroe say on the purported tapes. He said he had seventy to eighty handwritten pages of what he called manuscript-type notes of what he supposedly heard back in 1962. He obviously wanted money . . . and he spoke of having been offered six-figure sums for his story."[31] Skeptical about how anyone could reconstruct from memory eighty pages' worth of Monroe speaking, Summers had asked to see the original shorthand notes. After a few months, all that Miner produced was a thirty-five-page condensation written on a yellow legal pad only a few weeks previously. "I said thanks, but no thanks," said Summers, adding, "I don't understand why any reputable paper like the *New York Times*, like the *LA Times* would decide to run the material."[32]

More Forgeries

If Smith was taken in, he wasn't the only one. One of the legendary investigative reporters of the last fifty years is Seymour Hersh, who currently writes for *The New Yorker*. In his book debunking the golden myth of the Kennedys, *The Dark Side of Camelot*, Hersh states as fact what can only be supposition, that Miner "was given confidential access to a stream-of-consciousness tape-recording Monroe made at the recommendation of her psychoanalyst . . . Miner put together what he considered to be a near-verbatim transcript of the tapes." These tapes, said Hersh, helped to prove that "Monroe's instability posed a constant threat to [John F.] Kennedy."[33]

In Hersh's book, the reference to Miner nearly had to play second fiddle to spectacular new evidence linking Kennedy to Monroe. For Hersh had come across a separate cache of astonishing documents and agreements—this time proving, among other dark things, that JFK had agreed to pay the film star $1 million in hush money to keep her quiet both about their affair and also about JFK's supposed relationship with Mafia boss Sam Giancana. The source of these hundreds of new documents was Lex Cusack, whose father had worked as a lawyer for Marilyn Monroe's mother before her death. Cusack found them, he claimed, when his father died in 1991, and over the next few years he would go on to earn up to $7 million through sales of the documents to dealers and middlemen. It was one of these, John Reznikoff, president of the University Archives at Stamford, who introduced the documents to Seymour Hersh, then in the process of researching his Kennedy book. Hersh was excited, clearly believing them to be genuine: one journalist wrote of him brandishing the documents in a restaurant and shouting, "The Kennedys were . . . the worst people!"[34]

Whatever Hersh agreed to pay Cusack or anyone else for the documents, they certainly seemed worth it, since NBC television agreed to pay $1 million for the rights to a documentary based on the forthcoming book. However, as was later revealed by the *New York Times*, NBC started to express doubts to Hersh about the authenticity of the documents and then pulled out of the project.[35] ABC took up where NBC left off, and it was ABC's investigation, involving forensic testing, that demonstrated that the Cusack documents were fakes. Hersh removed all reference to them from his book, and in 1999, Lex Cusack was sentenced to ten years in prison and ordered to pay restitution of $7 million to his victims.

Hersh had had a narrow escape. Of course, there are those who question why he did not himself have the documents forensically analyzed, given the obvious questions about their provenance and the amount of money riding on their authenticity. One possibility is that they suited him so well he couldn't bear them to be fakes—so they weren't.

Belief is all-important. In the foreword to Smith's book of dubious tapes, Monroe's fellow actor Donald O'Connor writes, "I knew her well enough to believe she could not have killed herself; it was not in her nature. She was murdered, but by whom?"[36] It is impossible to ask the late Mr. O'Connor just what kind of "nature" he thought a suicidal person may have. Perhaps it was simply that he didn't *want* to believe that she could have killed herself. Certainly, for many of her fans and contemporaries the thought of the self-slaughter of someone so wealthy, popular, talented, and, of course, beautiful was almost too much to bear. And if she was killed, the thought didn't have to be borne. It was far easier to see her as a pawn of powerful political forces.

"The conspiracies surrounding Monroe's death are *always* about the intersection of her story with politics," wrote Sarah Churchwell. "There are not similarly powerful theories surrounding the untimely death of any other celebrity except Diana Princess of Wales."[37]

And Exit the Princess of Hearts

Bernie Taupin wrote "Candle in the Wind," the famous song about Marilyn Monroe, for Elton John. Almost a quarter of a century later, Taupin updated it for the dead Diana, Princess of Wales.

The week of August 31 to September 6, 1997, which ended with Elton John's singing "Goodbye England's Rose" in Westminster Abbey, was one of the strangest that I can remember. The news of the death of Diana in a Paris car smash was followed by a public grieving completely unexpected in a nation that had previously understood itself to be phlegmatic in a crisis; the Spirit of the Blitz was somehow replaced by Men Can Cry Too. TV presenters wept on air; men and women spoke of how Diana's death had acted as a point of contact between the public world and their own private agonies and disasters; commentators told us all about the new feminization of society and how this moment marked a break with the past. Outside Buckingham Palace and in Kensington Gardens, hundreds of thousands of still-wrapped bouquets created plateaus of cellophane. Every day brought some surprise. One of these wonders was the hostility shown by the public, and articulated by a guilty media, toward the surviving royal family. "They" had driven her to her death with their repressed emotions, their coldness, their affairs, their lack of empathy. At best, it had been a case of neglect: Diana was a fabulous plant needing warmth and water, and had received instead a windy place on a north-facing step. At worst, "they" wanted to be rid of her.

Twenty-one months earlier, in November 1995, Diana had given an extraordinary interview to Martin Bashir of the BBC's *Panorama*, an interview whose planning was kept secret by top executives from the corporation's royalist chairman, Marmaduke Hussey. Among many other revelations, the encounter emphasized Diana's own belief that she was now victim of a paranoia gripping her husband's family and their entourage. In a question almost certainly agreed upon with Diana beforehand, Bashir asked the princess whether she would ever be queen:

> DIANA: I'd like to be a queen of people's hearts, in people's hearts, but I don't see myself being queen of this country. I don't think many people will want me to be queen. Actually, when I say many people I mean the Establishment that I married into, because they have

decided that I'm a non-starter . . . I just don't think I have as many
supporters in that environment as I did.

BASHIR: You mean within the royal household?

DIANA: Uh-huh. They see me as a threat of some kind, and I'm here to
do good. I'm not a destructive person.

BASHIR: Why do they see you as a threat?

DIANA: I think every strong woman in history has had to walk down a
similar path, and I think it's the strength that causes the confusion
and the fear. Why is she strong? Where does she get it from? Where
is she taking it? Where is she going to use it? Why do the public still
support her?

When Diana died, one obvious and common question was "What
exactly happened?" The answer to this question seemed apparent enough.
But if one were to ask "Who stood to gain?" then the answer might lead
the questioner in a very different direction. Every week thousands of
people are killed in car crashes: a truck drives into the back of a stationary car, a bus goes through a median, a hatchback full of teenagers fails to
negotiate a sudden bend. It is rare for the immediate reaction to be "Who
gets the insurance money?" This is just as well, because it is always a short
step from a suggested motive to a suggested crime.

Princesses are not immune to the malign coincidences of poor high-
speed driving, impulsive decision-making, and bad luck. In an abrupt
change to an earlier plan, Diana, leaving the Paris Ritz, was put in the back
of a Mercedes and driven recklessly fast by a man who had been drinking
into a tunnel with a disguised ramp. Since nobody, it seemed, could have
had advance notice of the journey or its timing, the idea that an elaborate and well-planned conspiracy ended the princess's life seemed, almost
intuitively, more than usually difficult to support.

Even so, in the decade following the accident, a steady fifth to just
under a third of British people, and a similar proportion of Americans,
continued to believe that Diana was murdered. Even higher numbers

could be found supporting the notion that aspects of Diana's death had been covered up.* Less reliably, self-selecting phone polls conducted by pro-conspiracy newspapers invariably tripled or quadrupled the numbers of those backing the conspiracy theory. In the meantime, more than $13.4 million and countless hours of police and juridical time were spent investigating whether or not the princess was the victim of an implausible murder plot. It was a lengthy process, but finally, on April 7, 2008, ten years, seven months, and eight days after the Paris crash, a jury gave the verdict that Diana, Princess of Wales, died by accident: the fatal Paris car crash had been caused not by malicious conspirators but by the gross negligence of the dead driver, Henri Paul, and the actions of the infamous paparazzi.

How had this absurdly elongated investigation come about?

Executive Intelligence

The persistence of Diana conspiracy stories after August 31, 1997, owed much to the work of two men: the first, Harrods owner and father of Dodi, Mohamed Al Fayed; the second, the lesser-known Lyndon LaRouche. A former Trotskyist and prison inmate (he was sentenced for mail fraud and tax evasion), LaRouche has been a presidential candidate in most U.S. elections for the last thirty years, and his adherents continually attempt—with little success—to infiltrate the Democratic Party. According to LaRouche, the world is dominated by a financial oligarchy centered on the City of London and partly directed by the British Establishment, headed, naturally, by the British royal family. The queen, among her other duties, is behind the world trade in narcotics, and not only did her retainers

---

*For example, in a poll carried out for the *Daily Express* in August 2003, 49 percent of respondents said they believed there had been a "cover-up" of the circumstances of her death, while 34 percent disagreed.

murder the People's Princess, but they have also planned to assassinate Lyndon LaRouche. This would be bad for the world because LaRouche is, according to his own publications, "the world's foremost economic fore-caster, who has inspired a worldwide political movement to reverse the depression collapse and bring about a new classical renaissance."[38]

Of course, such an ideology makes great demands on those encounter-ing it for the first time. Too great, in fact. But most people coming across a LaRouche-initiated campaign will not be inducted into the full pro-gram. Instead they may see a TV documentary or visit a website featuring Jeffrey Steinberg, the "counterintelligence" editor of the *Executive Intel-ligence Review*, where it is revealed that his research indicates this or that hypothesis or suggests this or that conclusion. It was in *Executive Intelli-gence Review* that LaRouche's Diana conspiracy theories were given their most substantial airing. Brushed with a patina of scholarship, as a forger of old manuscripts applies egg white to give the effect of age, the LaRou-chian view of the Paris accident was sold to a largely unsuspecting world as "disturbing questions" or "troubling anomalies" in the official version.

From the beginning, Jeffrey Steinberg acknowledged that without Mohamed Al Fayed, the Diana conspiracy theories would probably never have taken off. It was, he told readers, Al Fayed who "brought the whole tempo of developments around the case to a kind of a fevered pitch when he . . . said he's 99.9 percent certain it was murder.

"And, I frankly happen to agree with him, and I'm privy to less evi-dence than he has." In the reflexive world of conspiracy, such evidence can be circular. On Al Fayed's own, rather impressive website, the Har-rods millionaire revealed, "One of the world's leading magazines, *Execu-tive Intelligence Review,* is supporting my campaign to shed light on the truth surrounding the crash."

In the years after the crash, Al Fayed's website would display a pleth-ora of newspaper articles and speculation about who was responsible for Diana's death. Set against such memorabilia as portraits of Dodi and Di framed by interlinked D's, adorned with Mediterranean foliage and supported by a bronze fountain, "which plays into reflecting pools of water—the symbol of eternal life," the message was clear: it was the secret services or the royal family rather than a series of unfortunate decisions leading to the princess being chauffeured by an inebriated and incompetent Al Fayed employee that were responsible for the deaths. Al Fayed related, for example, how Annie Machon, a former employee of MI5 and the partner of another former MI5 officer, David Shayler, had written a book, *Spies, Lies and Whistleblowers*, in which she speculated that the accident was planned by British intelligence but not supposed to be fatal. Al Fayed quoted Machon as saying, "The vast majority of the British people, of course, now believe that the crash was no accident. Although the British media continues to call the matter a 'conspiracy theory,' we feel there is compelling information to indicate that events were anything but accidental."

Al Fayed's tone has always been impressively committed: agreement represents confirmation of his views concerning a plot, but so does disagreement. When one journalist questioned his assertion that Princess Diana had been pregnant with Dodi's child, he wrote that the reporter and his cronies were "the very worst kind of establishment and Royal family arse-lickers," claiming that the article could "only have been prompted by the Security Services who are clearly very nervous about the positive findings the investigation is uncovering." And, for years, many of the stories suggesting that Diana's death was not accidental had their origin in activities carried out by employees or agents of Mr. Al Fayed. One interesting example of this process came in a story in the *Sunday Express* from June 23, 2002. Billed as an "exclusive" with the byline Gordon Thomas, the piece began: "Explosive tapes on the secret life of Princess Diana will prove that she was pregnant and intended to marry Dodi Al Fayed, it was claimed last night," and continued:

> American secret agents regularly monitored Diana's conversations and collated 1,000 secret documents using its [*sic*] "spy in the sky," the National Security Agency. They were obtained by its Echelon satellite surveillance system and contain highly sensitive material including her

marriage plans, her views on Prince Philip, who was known to be highly critical of her, and new details of her love affair with James Hewitt. Now, lawyers acting for Mohamed Al Fayed are trying to obtain the tapes through America's Freedom of Information Act.[39]

The source of the claims, in other words, was Al Fayed. The suggestion that these tapes monitoring Diana existed at all also came from Al Fayed. But Thomas is himself a major player in the conspiracy business. He is the author of several dozen books ranging from *The Jesus Conspiracy* to *The Assassination of Robert Maxwell* and, important for the particular conspiracy theory under discussion here, an account of the history of Mossad, *Gideon's Spies*—which, worryingly, is often quoted by mainstream journalists as a respectable and reliable source of information about Israel's intelligence agency.

The 2000 edition of *Gideon's Spies* begins with these words: "When the red light blinked on the bedside telephone, a sophisticated recording device was automatically activated in the Paris apartment near the Pompidou Center in the lively Fourth Arrondisement."[40] This supposedly happened on the night Diana died, and was connected to the fact that Henri Paul, variously asserted by other theorists to be an employee of French and British intelligence, was, actually, according to Thomas, a Mossad asset. Mossad it was, said Thomas, who also helped bring down Jonathan Aitken, the pro-Saudi British Cabinet minister, following his famous and ultimately disastrous stay at the Ritz.

Thomas got both stories from one of his most fertile sources, Ari Ben Menashe, who, he claimed, had been a major figure in Mossad for many years. Menashe had also advised Thomas on how Mossad had done away with its own agent, the tycoon Robert Maxwell, making his fall from his yacht look like an accident. Thomas, by his own account, put Menashe in direct contact with Al Fayed, and the Israeli told the Egyptian that, yes, there was a chance of Mossad involvement and that he, Menashe, would hunt it down in return for a retainer of $750,000 a year.[41] The impatient Al Fayed, however, wanted some material up front and Menashe refused—being, in Thomas's words, "more used to dealing with governments than 'a man with the manner of a souk trader.'" Interestingly, the government for which Menashe worked as a consultant was the Zimbabwean regime of Robert Mugabe—until, that is, Menashe was involved in trying to trap the leader of the Zimbabwean opposition into a taped act of treason against Mugabe. Unfortunately, the Zimbabwean court preferred to believe Morgan Tsvangirai rather than Menashe, and threw the case out.[42] But despite Menashe's failure to strike a deal with the Harrods owner, the Al Fayed–Thomas combination was still able to create a newspaper headline in the middle of 2002. Al Fayed got his coverage; what Thomas got by way of payment we don't know.

The death of Diana, though nothing like as lucrative as the life of Diana, has always been seen as financially exploitable. There have been books on Diana's loves, Diana's dresses, Diana's boys, Diana's mother; there have been memoirs of her butler Paul Burrell, of her housekeeper, of her bodyguards, of her "spiritual adviser," and of her "dream analyst." And there have been the conspiracy theories.

Landmines

Almost all conspiracy theories about Diana start with the same basic "doubts" about the accident: the mysterious white Fiat Uno that was struck by Henri Paul's Mercedes and then disappeared, the disputed blood tests on the dead driver, the mysterious money that Henri Paul may have earned . . . They then add speculative motives, possible additional facts, and purported culprits.

Some of the conjecture has been easily dealt with. For example, according to both Diana's closest friend and to those who examined her body, she was not pregnant, which removes the satisfyingly straightforward theory that action was taken to prevent the birth of a Muslim who would be a half brother or sister of the heir to the throne. But the loss of one piece of supposed evidence or motivation for murder did not seem to diminish the life force of the conspiracy creature itself. For example, nine years after her death, a former *Mirror* journalist, Nicholas Davies, in his book *Diana: Secrets and Lies*, speculated that Diana was killed because of her plans to highlight the plight of the Palestinians. Early theorists may have missed this possibility because back in 1997, with the peace process in the Middle East still in play, a possible link between Diana and the plight of the Palestinians might have seemed somehow less topical. By 2006, when Davies was publishing, the subject was far more fashionable.

Where there is money there is often considerable ingenuity. A stereotypical Diana conspiracy book, selected almost at random, is David Cohen's *Death of a Goddess*. Most of Cohen's previous works had been about popular psychology, including works on Piaget and behaviorism. But in the winter of 1994, he somehow became involved in making a documentary for Channel 4, about a cult called the Order of the Solar Temple, fifty-three of whose members had burned themselves to death that December.

Not long after this documentary was aired, Cohen was approached by a Frenchman designated only "Guy," who claimed to have been the "driver, personal assistant, and enforcer" for a senior member of the order. What Guy told Cohen formed the basis for another Channel 4 film—one of those revisionist documentaries that were so popular on Britain's television channels in the mid-1990s—this one about the film star and Monegasque princess, Grace Kelly. Kelly, said Guy, had been a member of the order, had been inducted in a weird sexualized ritual, had paid $8 million to the cult, and had finally been murdered by them, her death disguised as an automobile accident on the winding roads of the Riviera.

Despite having just made this questionable film, Cohen claims that "as a trained psychologist" he was "skeptical about conspiracy theories"[43] and that initially his only contact with the Diana story was to be called into the TV studios after her death (as many of us were) and pumped for his limited expertise. But then, nineteen days after the Paris accident, Guy made contact again. This time, Guy's story was that two months earlier he had been asked to launder $500,000. "His client," said Cohen, "was a man

I will call Roland, who had been in the East German secret services and had gone to live in Cuba after the fall of the Berlin Wall. Roland had done some freelance jobs for Jo di Mambro, the leader of the Solar Temple, which was why he had turned to Guy for help."[44]

According to Guy, Roland had been paid the money—probably by British intelligence—to organize the assassination of the princess. This he accomplished by playing on Henri Paul's secret homosexuality, setting him up with a lovely young transvestite "who called herself Belinda." The treacherous Belinda at some point on the fatal evening planted a "tiny pin-like device" on Paul's clothing. An instrument of death, this gadget was designed, on signal, to emit the nerve agent VX, which acts as a "synaptic disruptor." Sure enough, when Paul's vehicle was in the Alma Tunnel, the device sprayed him with the deadly chemicals, his synapses were disrupted, and bang![45] This was also apparently the way Roland, a serial assassin of European princesses, had accounted for Grace Kelly in September 1982.

Cohen never met Roland himself—though he did speak to a man with a deep voice on the telephone—and therefore could only conclude of Roland's story, "I cannot prove it is true. I remain unsure." But Cohen was struck when he found out that the dry cleaner in a village frequented by Solar Order members had once cleaned Prince Charles's dressing gown. As Cohen pointed out, "This would place the Prince and Di Mambro in a tiny village at the same time."[46] And if this evidence seems a little thin, then there are always the collateral arguments. Doesn't Charles, asks Cohen, share a lot of interests—stuff like spirituality—with the Solar Temple? Haven't British intelligence plotted to assassinate people before? Such as the plan to kill Nasser in 1956, the preemptive murder of the IRA members on Gibraltar in 1988, and "possibly, Hilda Murrell, a peace activist in the 1980s."[47] It seems almost redundant to point out that, according to one source at least, Guy, a former customs officer, is a fairly well-known con man and hoaxer on the Continent.[48]

Cohen's credentials, sources, and analytical method are representative. I could as easily have chosen *Princess Diana: The Hidden Evidence* by Jon King and Jon Beveridge. These two are billed by their publishers as "investigative journalists," whose claim to that title comes from their both having worked for one magazine, apparently called *Reality,* and who now work for another, called *Odyssey.* In fact, *Reality* magazine was actually titled *UFO Reality,* and Jon King, far from being an investigative journalist, is a UFOlogist who has written several other books, including *Cosmic Top Secret* and *The Ascension Conspiracy. Princess Diana: The Hidden Evidence* was supposedly based on information received "from a veteran CIA contract agent one week prior to the crash in Paris" and "other highly placed sources." It shows how the princess was done away with by MI6 *and* the CIA because she "threatened to expose the Crown's vested interests in Angola by pursuing her 'landmines campaign.'" There is a foreword by "Prince Michael of Albany" (a Belgian, Michel Lafosse), who claims to be the lost Stuart heir to the throne of Scotland, and the book has been hailed as "the most historically and politically important book of its time"—by Stephen Reid, who is (or was) the book review editor of *Odyssey* magazine.

Studying the competing claims of various secret sources, one can see that to believe one is to disbelieve the others. Whether the authors who used these sources were complicit in what must, at the very least, have been a series of hoaxes, is impossible to say. But if one were to ask the old conspiracist question *Cui bono?* (Who benefits?), the answer seems obvious. I say "seems" because in this world, every debunkable theory could actually be disinformation put out by the Establishment/security services to throw investigators and the public off the scent. Such a hypothesis was put forward by the former MI5 officer Annie Machon on Channel 4's *Richard and Judy* in 2005. It was the very stupidity of some of the theories surrounding Diana's death, she told her interviewers, that first convinced her that the accident was, in fact, murder. She had been alerted to the conspiracy by the classic MI6 disinformation technique of suggesting conspiracies.[49] Or, as Umberto Eco put it, "The Rosicrucians were everywhere, aided by the fact that they didn't exist."[50]

Filing Down the Pins

This seems an appropriate point to celebrate another feature of conspiracy theories: the way in which they can mutate to accommodate inconvenient truths. There are a lot of inconvenient truths in the Diana story. For example, it stretches credulity to argue that the Diana conspirators would have been able to know what car she and Dodi would be traveling in on the fatal night, who would be driving it, where they would be going, and by what route. Indeed, it wasn't at all impossible that the couple would just stay in the Ritz that evening. To overcome these objections, one has to imagine that Henri Paul was part of the conspiracy, either as a well-paid suicide or as a dupe, and that the route was prearranged. After that, we have to accept that one or more security agencies, the Parisian hospital service, and the French police were all in on the plot. But even this elaborate construction is destroyed by the simple observation that, had the princess been wearing a seat belt, then—like her bodyguard Trevor Rees-Jones—she probably would have survived. What kind of conspiracy founders on the ability of the principal victim to save herself by taking the most elementary safety precautions?

This was the problem dealt with by Nicholas Davies, ex–*Daily Mirror* journalist and, according to Gordon Thomas, Mossad asset (but then who, according to Gordon Thomas, is not a Mossad asset?). In his 2006 book *Diana: The Killing of a Princess*, Davies (whose "contacts within the intelligence services" had told him as early as 2001 that Diana had been murdered by MI5 together with French intelligence, because of—you will recall—her pro-Palestinian proclivities) confronted the seat-belt problem in the following way. The security services ensured that the couple would use the Mercedes, having first installed listening devices and having tampered with the rear seat belts. Technicians had filed down the pins, so that with minimum pressure the belts would spring open, though for some reason they left the front passenger's seat belt intact. Di and Dodi thought they had buckled up, but in reality they were totally vulnerable.

Davies's explanation necessarily added one extra layer of complexity to an already absurdly complicated intrigue. The powers that be had not only to suborn the driver, know the route, arrange for and drive a white Fiat, have it sideswiped, create a flash, delay the ambulance, switch the blood samples, turn off the CCTV, and corrupt the investigators; they now had to identify, tamper with, and deliver the death-trap vehicle too. There must surely be simpler methods of killing someone. And even all this doesn't square every circle. For example, a crash investigator, Dr. Vic Calland, told a 2006 Sky TV investigation that the crash was very nearly nonfatal. "It was a matter of inches as to whether the car would actually glance off [the pillar] or be spun," said Dr. Calland. "If it had not actually hit the pillar at the angle that it did, it would probably have carried on down the tunnel having a chance to come to a halt and there probably wouldn't have been a fatal accident at all."[51]

Short of there being some infernal mechanism that can make a crashing car describe a precise and predictable path, it looks unlikely that any theory will be able to deal with this objection.*

Papers, Mags, and TV Programs: The Transmission of Credulity

If one reason for the large number of Diana conspiracy theories was that they earned money for their discoverers or originators, another is media proliferation. Simply, there are ever more news and light current affairs outlets competing with fewer resources for a market whose size does not increase and which is under pressure from new media. The British *Express*

---

*Praise is due here to the journalist Martyn Gregory, the Gerald Posner of Diana conspiracism, whose research into the Paris crash and the various murder theories has sometimes been all that has stood between the mundane but important truth about that night and the Al Fayed–fed nonsense machine.

newspaper titles have made Diana stories their main marketing ploy for several years, using and reusing the princess's name and picture to try to maintain a circulation that has been declining badly over three decades. For years, practically any story or quote from Mohamed Al Fayed was guaranteed a place in the *Daily* or *Sunday Express*.

In January 2004, Lord Stevens, former commissioner of the Metropolitan Police—Britain's top police post—at the behest of the queen's coroner, started work on Operation Paget, a criminal investigation into the deaths of Diana and Dodi Fayed. The report of the inquiry took nearly three years to produce, appearing in December 2006, and covered almost every widely touted theory about how the couple had met their deaths. As the inquiry progressed, Lord Stevens, who had been conducting a simultaneous and similarly high-profile inquiry into corruption in British soccer, issued a number of gnomic comments. He suggested the existence of "new forensic evidence" from the crash meant Mohamed Al Fayed was right to raise some—unspecified—questions about the deaths, and commented that the case was "far more complex than any of us thought." These remarks gave rise to a large number of stories. However, it is probable that Stevens made them to suggest his impartiality while conducting the investigation.

As any spin doctor or publicist can tell you, the modern media beast requires feeding. The publisher's publicity for King and Beveridge's *Princess Diana: The Hidden Evidence* boasted that Jon King "has appeared on numerous TV shows—including the UK's number one morning show, *GMTV*; as well as Channel 4's *The Diana Conspiracy* and many other TV and radio shows." And this is almost certainly true, though it should be noted that *The Diana Conspiracy* was a debunking of conspiracy theories, presented by Martyn Gregory. Even what theorists like to call "the mainstream media" can sometimes be very undiscriminating about who finds his way into a studio as an interviewee.

Modern TV schedules in Britain, America, and elsewhere teem with daytime and evening talk shows, and the last two decades have seen the proliferation of twenty-four-hour news channels. This quantity of programming generates an enormous demand for items and guests, who have to be contacted and vetted by a relatively small number of hard-pressed and usually very young assistant producers and researchers. These trawl the PR handouts and publishers' lists for stories that will divert viewers and are easy to grasp. The consequence is that conspiracy theorists, like royal biographers, security experts, or crime experts, manage to find their way onto factual TV programs, where their claims are treated with undiscriminating credulity.

With television documentaries, the process is slightly different. Here commissioners are looking for factual ideas that combine novelty with shock value. The "hidden truth" behind a life or an event can often provide just such value—always supposing that there isn't a serious risk of legal proceedings for libel or slander. For example, a 2002 BBC program looking at the 1967 Israeli attack on an American warship, the USS *Liberty*, was made entirely from the conspiracist point of view, which stated that the attack, far from being accidental, as the Israelis claimed, was deliberate, and that this was subsequently covered up. One may imagine the bored response from the producers had Judge Jay Cristol, the author of the most painstaking of the studies of the event, approached the BBC with a proposal to make a documentary saying that the attack had indeed been accidental.*

There is a gulf, however, between the almost cavalier way in which some documentaries are produced and marketed by TV companies, and the way they are perceived by the public. In 1998, ITV aired a prime-time documentary fronted by a senior newsman that gave almost complete credence to all of Al Fayed's claims about Diana: the pregnancy, the engagement, the happy couple going apartment-hunting, the notion of secret-service involvement. The next morning, the *Daily Mirror* reported that over 90 percent of those phoning a special polling line now believed that Diana had been murdered. Whether the executives who had commissioned the documentary were similarly convinced is anyone's guess, but it feels too cynical to believe that journalists and writers are incapable

---

*See chapter 8.

of extraordinary credulity. An illustration of unexpected naivety is provided by Diana's prophetic letter, disclosed in the autumn of 2003 by Paul
Burrell, her former butler.

The letter, apparently written ten months before the Paris smash,
claimed that X (the name was blanked out but was later revealed as that
of Prince Charles) would somehow manufacture a car accident involving
"brake failure and serious head injury" and leading to her death, allowing him to remarry. The *Daily Mirror* described this as Diana "predicting
exactly how she would die," though brake failure has never been credibly
suggested as a possible cause of the accident. The paper accompanied this
observation with a series of "unanswered questions" such as "Was she
pregnant?" and "Had she taken drugs?"—most of which self-evidently
could have had nothing to do with the Mercedes's crashing into the wall
of an underpass at high speed. But most surprisingly, in the upmarket
and venerable weekly magazine the *Spectator*, the writer, former newspaper editor, and media commentator Stephen Glover told the readers that
he had once scoffed at Diana conspiracists, but "now I am not so sure."
He continued, echoing the *Mirror*, "Isn't it extraordinary that she foresaw
almost exactly how she died?" adding that the letter was evidence that
would "make anyone save the boneheaded and smug wonder a little."[52]

But had he stopped and turned it over in his mind, as perhaps the boneheaded and smug did, Glover would have realized that the letter constituted supporting evidence for her murder only if you believed one of three
very unlikely things. The first possibility was that Diana was genuinely
psychic and could forecast the future. The second possible causal explanation was that the future assassins, having got hold of the letter, looked
at it and agreed with her that this would indeed be a good way of arranging her permanent exit. Or third, that Diana was warned by someone else
that a car accident was the preferred method of her execution, but that
for some reason she neglected to include this information in her letter.
None of these seems ordinarily plausible, and we are therefore left with
Glover's simple desire to believe. As the journalist and Paris correspondent
for the *Daily Telegraph* Colin Randall noted in his online diary, "I long ago

accepted that in any gathering of five otherwise sensible people, there will probably be at least two who sincerely believe Diana was murdered."[53]

It was not wholly unexpected that the conclusions of the Stevens Report failed to satisfy Mr. Al Fayed, though its 832 pages, written in agonizing forensic detail, answered and countered almost every aspect of the main conspiracy claims from motive to aftermath, its failure to get around to the Order of the Solar Temple notwithstanding. Nevertheless, it might have been anticipated that Stevens had shown to any reasonable and intelligent observer that there was no evidence of a conspiracy. Sadly, this was not so. The day after publication of the report, the *Independent* newspaper, founded in 1986 to be an impartial journal of record, declared itself unhappy with Stevens's conclusions. "No one," its editorial began, "likes to be labeled a conspiracy theorist" and therefore to be associated with the kind of people "who believe the world is run by aliens disguised as humans," but the newspaper was concerned that too officious a desire to avoid such a label might impair its capacity to ask questions. "Skepticism," it pointed out, "can be a healthy instinct."

This proposition is, in abstract terms at least, undeniable. But where would such skepticism lead one in the case of the Stevens Report? There were, concluded the *Independent*, a number of awkward questions that had not been resolved. For example, there was the issue of the white Fiat Uno belonging to a conveniently dead French paparazzo, which might just have been the one clipped by the princess's Merc in the Paris underpass. There was also the problem of "all of the closed circuit television cameras monitoring the underpass [which] inexplicably failed to record the incident." In addition, said the newspaper, "the question of whether anyone had the motive to murder the couple remains unresolved. The report says there is no reason to believe Diana and Mr. Fayed were preparing to marry. Mr. Fayed's father maintains that there was."[54]

These observations came close to being perverse. In fact, Stevens, in exhaustive detail, showed both that the Fiat Uno in question could not conceivably have been the one in the Paris tunnel, and revealed, camera by camera, that almost all the CCTV installations en route were trained on the entrances of the buildings to which they belonged. Furthermore, Stevens established that everybody in whom Diana had regularly confided did not believe that she was planning marriage, and some said that she had explicitly ruled it out. In fact, only Mohamed Al Fayed, owner of the Mercedes that crashed and employer of the man who was driving the car at the time, testified to having been told that there was to be a wedding.

It wasn't clear whether the writer of the *Independent* editorial had plowed his or her way through the Stevens Report or not, but in any case, the newspaper allowed itself two tangential arguments that by now may be familiar to the readers of this book. The first was that the absence of complete certainty ("We should beware the assumption that all the circumstances of this case have now been fully explained and all the loose ends neatly tied up") somehow permitted an almost impossible explanation to be regarded as being as true, if not truer than a likely one. The second was that the prevalence of an opinion somehow conferred a degree of truth upon it. "According to a recent poll," said the *Independent*, "a third of the British public believe what happened to Diana was not an accident. This cannot be written off as a fringe belief."

Conspiracy on Trial

But there are other ways of determining whether a belief is justified. It seldom happens that conspiracy theories are held to the same evidential standards as official versions; the 1934 trial of the Swiss publishers of *The Protocols of the Elders of Zion* was a rare example of the propagators of a theory being forced to substantiate it in court. However, this is more or less what occurred between October 2007 and April 2008 in London's Royal Courts of Justice. In the beechwood environs of Court 73—many of the press and public accommodated in a large overspill room, watching on TV monitors—coroner Lord Justice Scott Baker presided over what became, in effect, a trial of the assertions that Diana was murdered. Despite Lord Scott Baker's early suggestion that the process was not an adversarial one, the jury of five men and six women saw highly paid counsel for the various protagonists cross-examine witnesses with antagonistic vigor.

Al Fayed's team was led by one of the most celebrated and radical Queen's Counsel in England, Michael Mansfield—as one *Guardian* journalist put it, "the light shining off the silver highlights in his well-coiffed hair, his brilliantly colored silk ties illuminating an otherwise drab courtroom."[55] A TV technician covering the event described Mansfield to me as "chasing every hare he could; trying to force open every little chink. But they were all dead ends."

One dead end was the possible role of the queen's husband, the Duke of Edinburgh, for a decade the target of accusations by Mohamed Al Fayed. Al Fayed's team simply could not provide any evidence that would make the octogenarian consort a material witness at the inquest. But major figures within the Establishment certainly did testify, including Lord Stevens, Sir Richard Dearlove (former head of MI6), and Lord Fellowes, the queen's private secretary and also brother-in-law to Princess Diana.

The most theatrical performance belonged to Al Fayed himself, who, during his day in court, named as conspirators the duke; former Prime Minister Tony Blair; two former commissioners of the Metropolitan Police, including Stevens; Lord Fellowes; Diana's older sister; the former ambassador to Paris; and the Prince of Wales. His own former bodyguard, Trevor Rees-Jones, the only survivor of the crash, was a "crook" and also in on the plot, according to Al Fayed. Others were castigated. Dodi's former girlfriend Kelly Fisher was "just a hooker" and Diana's former boyfriend, the heart surgeon Hasnat Khan, was dismissed as a man who "lived in a council flat and has no money." However, none of this talk, so colorful on the page, seemed convincing in court, especially as the props of conspiracy collapsed one by one, to be replaced by evidence of the incompetence of Al Fayed's own security operation, an incompetence originating with the Al Fayeds themselves.

Diana could not have been pregnant, as Al Fayed had insisted she had told him she was. Postmortem examination established this fact, and it was corroborated by Dodi's former masseuse, as well as the yacht *Jonikal's* former stewardess, giving evidence on a videolink from New Zealand, who had seen contraceptive pills in the princess's bedroom. The accident itself could easily have not been fatal, a collision investigator told the court. The Mercedes hit the corner of a column in the tunnel, creating a much greater impact than had it struck the column's face or the opposite wall. Furthermore, some key conspiracy witnesses, who had testified to such phenomena as the "blinding light" in the tunnel, turned out under questioning to be fantasists. "A number of people," said Lord Justice Scott Baker in his summation, "seem to have had a compelling desire to pretend they were there when, in truth, they were not there at all." Worst of all, former MI6 employee Richard Tomlinson, who had originated the strobe-gun theory based on plans he recalled from his secret-service days, now admitted that he might have got the whole thing wrong, and that there was no blinding-light plan after all. As a BBC reporter put it at the time, Tomlinson's credibility had been damaged "because he doesn't have really the evidence to back up what he told Mohammed Al Fayed nine years ago."[56]

What was established as fact, however, was that Henri Paul, the driver called in by Dodi Fayed to drive the couple that night, had been drinking and was well over the alcohol limit. "Henri Paul was not fit to drive when he got into that Mercedes," concluded a leading toxicologist. Worse, Al Fayed employees had then lied to the press about how much Paul had drunk. What also emerged in court was the culpability of Dodi and Mohamed Al Fayed for what had happened. Mansfield suggested that the Al Fayed bodyguards should have resisted the plan to have Henri Paul do the driving. Michael Mansfield interrogated bodyguard Kes Wingfield on this point.

MANSFIELD: You see, at the very least—at the very least—although you weren't in the car, there was a responsibility by your colleague to ensure that Princess Diana did have her safety belt on before they moved off. Do you agree?

WINGFIELD: Without a shadow of a doubt, Trevor will have mentioned that, but he can't physically grab the Princess of Wales and put a seat belt on her.

And later:

> MANSFIELD: You didn't get authority or clearance . . . for this plan, did you?
>
> WINGFIELD: When we spoke to Dodi, he told us the plan had been okayed by Mr. Fayed.
>
> MANSFIELD: I am so sorry, just answer the question and we will be much quicker.
>
> CORONER [JUDGE]: I think the witness is answering the question.
>
> MANSFIELD: You didn't telephone through?
>
> WINGFIELD: I personally never telephoned, no.
>
> CORONER: Would there have been any point if it had been authorized by the boss?
>
> WINGFIELD: No, sir, because Mr. Fayed is so hands-on with every aspect of his organization . . . Once Dodi had said to me, "It's been okayed by my father," that really closed the door on any further discussion.
>
> MANSFIELD: I am going to suggest to you that whatever you are being told . . . it's part of the instructions that you are given when you do this job to make sure that his name is not taken in vain, particularly by those offspring who have bodyguards. That was well known to you, wasn't it?
>
> WINGFIELD: I wouldn't call him "offspring."
>
> CORONER: What age was Dodi?
>
> WINGFIELD: He was forty-two, sir.[57]

In the end, Al Fayed's counsel was forced to admit that he hadn't sufficient evidence—in fact, hadn't any evidence at all—even to support the accusations of a conspiracy. Mansfield accepted that there was no evidence incriminating the Duke of Edinburgh, MI5, MI6, the police, the unknown driver of the white Fiat Uno; no medical evidence of a Diana pregnancy, nor a plot to cover up such a pregnancy; no evidence that the French medical services were involved in a deliberate delaying of necessary treatment.

At one point, toward the end of the inquest, the following, rather pathetic exchange took place between Mansfield and the coroner. It concerned the allegations made by Al Fayed against Trevor Rees-Jones, and is worth quoting in full:

> CORONER: Are these allegations being maintained by Mr. Al Fayed? Because, if so, Mr. Rees[-Jones] is entitled to be told of any evidence in support of them and to give us his explanation.
>
> MANSFIELD: Sir, I have been very careful in the examination. I have not maintained those and I am not in a position to produce any material to support them.
>
> CORONER: Why haven't they been withdrawn by Mr. Al Fayed since February 9, 2006? They are very grave allegations, and one would have thought that a man with any decency who was not going to pursue them would withdraw them.
>
> MANSFIELD: May I say this with regard to that? I appreciate the nature and gravity of the allegations and I hope that in the longer term his position will be appreciated, and that is this: that he has been very concerned from the beginning to discover the circumstances of the crash and obviously what lay behind it. There have been many beliefs that he has held, and in my submission he was quite entitled to hold certain beliefs and obviously to see whether, in the longer term, when those beliefs were, as it were, exposed to this inquest, whether there was material which supports them . . . It's very difficult for those people in those circumstances to relinquish a belief that has been firmly held, even though, as it may turn out, there is very little material to support the belief that they have, for example that it's not suicide or it is suicide, whatever it is, and therefore I hope that it will be understood that obviously it's for the person individually to obviously make that clear.[58]

Even that humiliating climbdown wasn't quite the end. An actor friend of Al Fayed's, Keith Allen, revealed that he had been making an undercover documentary, filmed partly in the press overspill room at the inquest. "It's not about a conspiracy before the crash," said Allen, "but there definitely was a conspiracy after it." And it was announced that filmmakers were seeking backers for a movie titled *Underpass*. Based on Gordon Thomas's *Gideon's Spies*, it would tell the tale of "the infiltration by Mossad into the Ritz."[59]

Such projects, though, appeared to be doomed. For the first time since her death, a feeling of satiety concerning the princess seemed to be creeping in. Not perhaps among the most obdurate of theorists, but on the part of the general public, whose reading and buying habits, and whose answers to pollsters, had helped to maintain the conspiracy theories for so long.

The Untidiness of Reality

Toward the end of his great work of journalism *In Cold Blood*, Truman Capote noted how the people of the town of Holcomb, Kansas, near where the murder of four members of the Clutter family had taken place, were not entirely satisfied when they discovered the true identity of the killers. "The majority of Holcomb's population," wrote Capote, "appeared to feel disappointed at being told the murderer was not someone from among themselves," but that the killings had been carried out instead by two sociopathic drifters. Capote quoted the formidable sub-postmistress, Myrtle Clare: "Maybe they did it, those two fellows. But there's more to it than that. Wait. Some day they'll get to the bottom, and when they do they'll find the one behind it. The one wanted Clutter out the way. The *brains*."[60]

Myrtle Clare's impulse—the belief that the explanation being offered for an event is in some way deficient—runs through much theorizing. The Clutter murders were the greatest event in that part of Kansas for many years, but the solution to the murders led nowhere. There was no proper motive, and once the killers were caught, all that was left to do was hang them. The lack of an overarching reason for the murders must also have been worrying: apparently, anyone in small-town America was as much a potential target as Herb Clutter and family. To return to Sarah Church-well's discussion of Marilyn's death, "it is only narrative that promises a reason for early death; reality offers no such assurance."[61]

Even so, it takes a great deal more than the untidiness of reality to launch an entire generation of conspiracy theories. What makes the deaths of JFK, Marilyn Monroe, and Princess Diana so fascinating is the victims' iconic status and their youth. All were considered beautiful, all were world figures whose images existed inside the homes of billions. Kennedy was forty-six when he died; Monroe had just turned thirty-six, almost exactly the same age as Princess Diana. They were, all of them, whatever their internal demons, exceptionally successful, wealthy, and attractive. Consequently, they drew both admiration and envy, and much of the latter was (and is) unconscious.

Consider for a moment the repressed sadism that seems to lurk behind a lot of assassination conspiracism: the descriptions of the death, the reports from the autopsy, the photographs of the body. The British con-spiracy theorist Robin Ramsay, in his small book on assassination litera-ture, writes almost pornographically of "parts of JFK's skull bounc[ing] onto the boot of the presidential limousine." Marilyn is injected or has medicines inserted into her anus. Whatever we might have envied in these people, we sure don't envy them now.

And if we do have such feelings, one way in which we might want to exorcise them is through constructing or accepting a version of history in which they were extinguished by something clearly "other" than our-selves. It was not our thirst for gossip about celebrities that killed Norma Jean or England's Rose, but the CIA. It wasn't an ordinary Joe with a rifle who murdered the young president, but the Mafia or the FBI. "What is assassination, after all," wrote Todd Gitlin, "if not the ultimate reminder of the citizen's helplessness—or even repressed murderousness?"[62] Con-spiracy theory may be one way of reclaiming power and disclaiming responsibility.

5. A VERY BRITISH PLOT

It was a time of ruthlessness in government and of the crushing of enemies.

And everywhere, there was the shadow of the secret state, arrogant and apparently omnipotent.

— NICK DAVIES, ON THE TENTH ANNIVERSARY
OF THE MURDER OF HILDA MURRELL[1]

Death of a Rose Grower, Part One

It was as though, instead of investigating murders, Agatha Christie's Miss Marple had been murdered herself. Friends and admirers of the dead woman told of a redoubtable elderly English country spinster whose acute sense of right and wrong, inquiring mind, and independence of spirit had perhaps led her down dangerous paths. And enlightened minds believed the murderer to be, far from an everyday criminal or pervert, the shadowy forces of the secret state itself.

The woman's name was Hilda Murrell, at the time of her death seventy-eight and retired. The younger Hilda Murrell, an expert on roses and the manager of an old-fashioned rose-growing business, had assisted the writer Vita Sackville-West in creating the White Garden at Sissinghust Castle in Kent, and had supplied roses to the royal family and the Churchills. Three weeks before her death, in the early spring of 1984, she had agreed to have a rose named after her. A medium-to-large fragrant plant with pink blooms, you can still find it in catalogs.

By then, Hilda Murrell was living alone in the suburbs of the Shropshire town of Shrewsbury in a large brick house called Ravenscroft, and taking part in as many activities devoted to conserving the countryside and its habitat as someone of her age and suffering from rheumatism reasonably could. Some of these were not obviously political—the Soil Association and the Council for the Protection of Rural England were both beneficiaries of her activism—but others were more controversial. Hilda was a supporter of the European Nuclear Disarmament group; was involved with the Shropshire Anti-Nuclear Alliance, and, in 1983, had traveled to London for a Campaign for Nuclear Disarmament (CND) demonstration that was, by the standards of the time, enormous. And Hilda's aversion to nuclear fission went beyond the manufacturing of bombs: increasingly, it encompassed its use as a source of power. By 1982, she had decided to become a formal objector at the forthcoming public inquiry into whether a new nuclear power station should be built at Sizewell on the coast of East Anglia. For the next year and more, she worked on a paper concerning that abiding problem of the nuclear industry, the management and disposal of radioactive waste. Then she was killed.

On the morning of Wednesday, March 21, 1984, a bright day in early spring, Hilda Murrell drove her white Renault 5 hatchback into central Shrewsbury, shopped at the Safeway store, and drove back. She parked in her gravel driveway and went straight to a neighbor's to pay sixteen pence owing on a raffle ticket, before returning home. That was the last time she was seen alive. She was due for lunch at her friends' in the nearby village of Kinnerley but didn't turn up; later, nearly seventy witnesses were to relate how they saw her small white hatchback being driven fast and badly northeast out of Shrewsbury. One woman was forced to swerve to avoid a collision. She saw the passenger, an elderly woman, "fall across" the driver, who appeared to push her back. A second woman driver, also alarmed about a possible collision, described how the man driving the car was "staring as if he'd lost control." At just after a quarter past one, a local farmer came across a white car that appeared to have been dumped in Hunkington Lane, a minor road that runs between the village of Withington and the ruins of Haughmond Abbey. Some miles to the west, Miss Murrell's failure to turn up for lunch had led her friends telephoning her at Ravenscroft, but there was no answer.

The next day, Thursday, was notable only for what didn't happen. The owner of a small wood off Hunkington Lane, known as the Moat, visited it in order to count the trees. He saw nothing, telling the police later that he had "examined the place so thoroughly I would have seen if there'd been a dead rabbit there, let alone a person."[2] On Friday, there was more activity. The farmer who had found the car in Hunkington Lane discovered that it was still there, and once again reported it to the police. By the evening, the police had traced the vehicle to Hilda Murrell. Also on the Friday, and significant only in retrospect, a local sex counselor was visited by Shrewsbury police, who asked him if he could "think of anybody who might have a sexual hang-up about elderly ladies." He subsequently told campaigners inquiring into the Murrell case that he realized only "when I read the first reports in the paper the next evening of the finding of Hilda Murrell's body that it seemed that the police had been describing the murder." Also that evening, there were, according to later claims by a person living close to the Moat, "lights and movement" visible among the trees.[3]

The body was found on Saturday the twenty-fourth, although not by the first policeman to visit Ravenscroft that day. At eight-thirty a.m., Hilda Murrell's gardener, Brian George, found an officer about to leave the house. The policeman apparently told him that he had found nothing untoward, although the house was a bit untidy. He hadn't gone into Hilda's bedroom, not wanting to disturb her. Once the officer had left, George and two other people decided to look around Ravenscroft themselves. They discovered laundry on the floor, handbags on the scullery table, three days' worth of newspapers and mail beside the front door, and the telephone—when they tried to use it to call the police—not working. A superintendent arrived sometime before ten-thirty a.m.

Meanwhile, a PC Robert Eades had been investigating the abandoned

Renault. Along with a local farmer and her Labrador dogs, Eades went to the Moat copse, the nearest bit of cover, and at ten-thirty a.m. found a body lying in a shallow depression. It was that of Hilda Murrell. She was lying on her front, was naked from the waist down, and her skirt lay nearby. Her knees were abraded and bloody; there was bruising to her hip and shoulder, a cut under her right eye, another to her hand; her collarbone was fractured; and there were nonfatal stab wounds to her arm and abdomen, one of which had slightly penetrated the liver. The police pathologist who examined her later decided that none of these injuries was responsible for her death, which had probably occurred between five and ten hours after her injuries as the result of hypothermia. The corpse had not, he thought, been moved after death; Hilda Murrell had died at the Moat. In a nearby hedge were found the old lady's hat, spectacles, and a weapon—an eight-inch cook's knife later identified as having come from Ravenscroft. Her car keys were in the pocket of her coat. A closer inspection of the house itself now revealed signs of a struggle in a back bedroom, clothes scattered over the floor and a stair banister knocked out. The telephone had been disconnected. Subsequent forensic tests established that tissues found in the bedroom carried traces of semen, as did Miss Murrell's clothing.

The crime appeared, as the police admitted, rather bizarre. If it was, as seemed most likely at first sight, a burglary gone wrong, it involved an atypical criminal. Burglars tend to be opportunists who try to escape at the first sign of interruption, but this one had stayed in the house after Miss Murrell had parked her car in the drive and ignored the opportunity to escape provided by her short visit to her neighbor. After she had come back home and, presumably, found him, the burglar had assaulted her, physically and sexually, then taken her outside in broad daylight, placed her in her own car, and driven her through Shrewsbury. Crashing into a ditch in Hunkington Lane, he had abandoned the car and lifted or dragged Miss Murrell a hundred yards or so into an obscure copse, where he had left her to her fate. The criminal, if working alone, had then been forced to leave the site, again in daylight, on foot.

And, embarrassingly, this strange and surely incompetent burglar was nowhere to be found. Neighbors said that they had noticed a "young man in jeans and a pipe [*sic*]" loitering in the area some days before the break-in, one suggesting that this man "had a military look about him."[4] On the morning of the murder, someone else had seen a man jump over a low wall and walk toward Ravenscroft. This man wasn't traced. A "jogging man" aged between twenty-five and forty was recalled by several witnesses running alongside the road in the area of Hunkington Lane and into Shrewsbury. And a red Escort car was reported to have been seen in several locations: in Sutton Lane, passing Ravenscroft on the morning of Hilda Murrell's death, and also near Haughmond, where her Renault was found.

Then, one week after the murder and with no one either arrested or charged, the local newspaper, the *Shropshire Star*, ran a story on the Murrell case with the intriguing headline "Murder Victim Left an Unfinished Report." Miss Murrell, the *Star* revealed, had been writing a paper on the dangers of nuclear waste, which had been close to completion at the time she was killed. With this news, a gentle exhalation was heard in many parts of liberal Britain. In Eliza Doolittle's words, the suspicion now was that "they done the old woman in." It was, after all, 1984.

THE ENEMY WITHIN

If ever a death had a context, Hilda Murrell's did. Though 1984 might not have dawned on the total dystopia of Orwell's fantasy, it was nevertheless a tense and unpleasant year, especially for those of a progressive or nervous cast of mind. In the weeks before the murder, news watchers had heard or read about a formal Russian protest concerning alleged American arms-control violations and a subsequent Soviet nuclear test in eastern Kazakhstan, events that were mere wraparounds for the news that on February 9, the general secretary of the Soviet Communist Party, Yuri Andropov, had died after only fifteen months on the job and been replaced by another Politburo geriatric, Konstantin Chernenko. On the day of the murder itself, March 21, a Soviet submarine crashed into an American warship off the coast of Japan.

In the months following Hilda's death, a woman police officer was shot dead outside the Libyan embassy in London, killed by shots fired from inside; the IRA nearly succeeded in assassinating the British prime minister in a bomb explosion at her hotel in Brighton during the Conservative Party conference; a Polish dissident priest, Father Jerzy Popieluszko, was abducted and murdered and his death later attributed to four state security officers; Indian Prime Minister Indira Gandhi was killed by her Sikh bodyguards; the Los Angeles Olympics were boycotted by the Soviet Bloc countries; there was a catastrophic explosion at the Union Carbide chemical factory in Bhopal, India, resulting in thousands of deaths; and the Cold Warrior Ronald Reagan won reelection to the presidency of the United States in a landslide, defeating Democrat candidate Walter Mondale. This was despite his famous, inadvertently on-mike joke, "My fellow Americans, I've signed legislation that will outlaw Russia forever. We begin bombing in five minutes." One American cartoonist had depicted a grim-looking Konstantin Chernenko responding, "We begin bombing in ten minutes. Is no joke."

But more important in setting the immediate psychological context for how the murder of Miss Murrell came to be seen by a section of the British population was a speech made by Margaret Thatcher to a gathering of Conservative backbench MPs in July 1984. At this private meeting, she drew a parallel between the battle for the Falkland Islands, won in 1982, and the struggle against trade union militancy in Britain. "In the Falklands," she reportedly told her audience, "we had to fight the enemy without. Here is the enemy within."[5]

The particular enemy referred to by Mrs. Thatcher was the leadership of the National Union of Mineworkers (NUM) and its supporters. On March 5, 1984, two weeks before Hilda Murrell's death, miners at Cortonwood colliery in Yorkshire—threatened with closure by the National Coal Board—walked out on strike. The next day flying pickets from the Yorkshire coalfield appeared, uninvited, at pitheads in Nottinghamshire, traditionally a more moderate area. There was well-publicized violence as striking miners attempted first to persuade and then prevent their colleagues from working. On March 12, Arthur Scargill, the noisily militant president of the NUM, declared that despite the absence of a national ballot, the strikes in the various coalfields now constituted a national stoppage that all members were expected to observe.

From the beginning, the strategic objective of the NUM was to achieve a full strike in all areas, using pickets to enforce it; the objective of the authorities was to prevent such picketing and gradually to wear the strikers down. Coordinated police action, sometimes based on inside intelligence, anticipated the movement of pickets, and intercepted them, often miles from the collieries they were about to visit. The strike, which lasted nearly a year, saw more than 11,000 arrests, unprecedented police mobilization, and scenes of industrial violence and strikers' hardship not witnessed in Britain since the 1920s.

There was significant sympathy for the miners, even among those who disapproved of their tactics. The job itself was associated with a certain labor nobility—tough men from tough communities doing tough things— that was now passing into history. There was the contrast between the strident certainty of Mrs. Thatcher and her (inevitably wealthy) supporters in the press, and the circumstances of striking miners' families, deprived of money and forced to fall back on what was offered by churches and volunteers. Despite being depicted by some parts of the press as adjuncts to the KGB's efforts to subvert British democracy, the truth was that in some ways the miners better represented a comfortable idealization of the country's past than did the economics of the new right. Moreover, those non-miners who had such feelings easily persuaded themselves that they, too, were now regarded as being, in the state's eyes, part of the enemy within. It may not have been an altogether unexciting feeling. Nor was it altogether untrue.

THE TIME IS OUT OF JOINT

In May 1979, Margaret Thatcher's Conservative Party had secured a majority in the British general election—to the surprise of some commentators, who had expected her avuncular Labour opponent, Jim

Callaghan, to overcome the problems of his incumbent Labour administration and defeat the somewhat shrill and "extreme" Tory leader. This
domestic shock to Britain's political system was soon to be matched by
greater shocks to the process of détente—mutual tolerance—which
had been going on between the Soviet Bloc and the West since the early
1970s. When, in December 1979, Soviet troops entered Afghanistan in an
attempt to prevent the bloody disintegration of the pro-Soviet government in Kabul, the entire edifice of East-West cooperation appeared to
collapse.

It was a particularly bad time for all this to happen. The recent deployment in Eastern Europe and the western Soviet Union of intermediate-
range nuclear weapons—the SS-20s—was about to be matched by the
controversial stationing of U.S. intermediate-range nuclear weapons on
European soil. Cruise and Pershing missiles were to be located at sites in
Great Britain and West Germany, a decision which, in conditions of dete-
riorating relations between the superpowers, seemed to many Britons and
Germans almost outrageously provocative. In the view of some, the threat
of nuclear war, having lessened throughout the 1970s, was now growing
once more. The election in November 1980 of derided right-wing former
actor Ronald Reagan to the leadership of the free world revived images of
Slim Pickens in the movie *Dr. Strangelove* sitting astride a Russia-bound
bomb like a cowboy at a rodeo.

Britain saw a sudden expansion in the membership of CND, an organization that had been in decline since the mid-1960s. In September 1981,
a march, attended mostly by women, terminated at the U.S. Air Force
base at Greenham Common in Berkshire, one of the sites chosen for the
stationing of cruise missiles. There, some of the women set up what was
later called the Greenham Peace Camp, a permanent site that became a
cultural fixture. From across Britain, activist women of all ages (though
mostly of middle-class backgrounds) came to Greenham to pin woolly
favors to the fence, write poems, sing songs about the earth, and, occasionally, try to enter the base. The Greenham woman became a kind of prototypical citizen activist, the Women's Institute plus politics. My mother,

last heard of in this book in November 1963, was one of those who visited Greenham.

By 1983, tension was rising. Mrs. Thatcher, partly as a consequence of her victory over Argentina in the matter of the Falkland Islands, had been reelected by a landslide in the general election, this despite a full recession and unprecedented levels of unemployment. Ronald Reagan, in a speech to an evangelical group in Orlando, Florida, described the Soviet Union as the "focus of evil in the modern world," and a human chain of fifty thousand or so CND protesters linked the Greenham base with an arms factory fourteen miles away.

The British government was far from relaxed about the resurgence of the CND, as it was far from relaxed about almost any enemy. Thatcher's supporters often gave the impression that opposition to the government and sedition were much the same thing. So the government took pains to counter CND's arguments overtly and, as Britons discovered, state security also made efforts to monitor CND covertly. One year after Hilda's murder, in March 1985, a departing MI5 officer, Cathy Massiter, went on television to reveal how the telephones of CND members had been bugged and an agent infiltrated into the London office of the organization. The same tactics, she told viewers, had been used against the National Council for Civil Liberties (now known as Liberty), because both bodies had been officially classified as "subversive." Massiter had blown the whistle because she believed that the surveillance operation had been "getting out of control."[*6] This wasn't all. The case of a woman named Madeleine Haigh, who wrote a pro-CND letter to a local newspaper in 1981, only to find Special Branch on her doorstep, seemed to justify any paranoia on behalf of simple sympathizers with dissident causes. Nearly two decades later, the rationale for such intrusions was supplied by Sir Philip Knight, chief constable of West Midlands Police from 1975 to 1985.

---

[*]It is an interesting comment on these operations that four of the activists on whom files were maintained later became ministers in the government of Tony Blair.

KNIGHT: It was perceived that CND had links to the Communist Party, and it was automatically, I think, assumed, that there would be people in there who had subversion as their main aim, and we wanted to try and find out who they were.

QUESTIONER: So if I had gone on a CND demonstration in the early eighties I was therefore a legitimate person for investigation?

KNIGHT: Unfortunately yes, you probably could have been, yes.

QUESTIONER: And a knock on the door.

KNIGHT: Possibly, yes, possibly.

QUESTIONER: By Special Branch officers.

KNIGHT: Possibly. Yes. Unless you inquire, you don't find out. You can't just pick it out of thin air whether somebody is a subversive or not. You have to inquire.[7]

The same series revealed that at around the same time Special Branch had had a mole inside the National Union of Miners.[8]

Thatcher's enemies extended from the peripheral (New Age travelers in convoys of old buses who insisted on setting up camp on other people's land) through the irksome ("loony-left" local councils trying to operate little oases of socialism in what they saw as the wasteland of Thatcherism) to the, in the case of the Provisional IRA, genuinely threatening and murderous. In 1984, as we have seen, the IRA came close to murdering the prime minister herself, and in that year killed fifty-one people in Northern Ireland, most of them civilians.[9] The intelligence operation against the IRA was characterized by the employment of informers and agents, whose cover sometimes necessarily involved them in the commission of crimes.

Death of a Rose Grower, Part Two

The summer of 1984 saw the police make no progress on catching the murderer of Miss Murrell, and soon some of those scrutinizing their efforts began to focus on supposed inconsistencies in official accounts of the crime. For example, the police had described Ravenscroft as having been "ransacked" as though by a burglar searching for anything of value, and the telephone wires as having been pulled out of the socket. But to a number of observers, the scene-of-crime video seemed rather to suggest that the "intruder or intruders had systematically gone through everything, including Hilda's papers and books, which had then been replaced in their original positions."[10] Brian George, her gardener, also said that the telephone wires seemed to him to have been expertly disconnected rather than simply yanked out. And then there was the sexual aspect of the attack. At various times, the police were supposed either to have suggested that the traces of semen were too slight to be able to obtain a blood-group match, and at others that the sperm count was low enough to indicate that the attacker had had a vasectomy.

Such relatively minor discrepancies were first pulled together and described in print in the magazine the *New Statesman* in the autumn of 1984. A freelance writer and member of CND, Judith Cook, published an article speculating on whether, far from being a botched burglary, the Murrell murder might, in fact, have been the consequence of a political decision. Cook had discovered, she wrote later, that "there were those in Shrewsbury who had been convinced, almost from the outset, that the answer did not lie close to home but a good deal further away; that Hilda, either by accident or design, had been the victim of something a good deal more sinister than a simple burglary followed by assault."[11]

In part, this suspicion was based on Hilda Murrell's own fears, now given posthumous voice. According to acquaintances to whom Cook had spoken, before her death Hilda had been "frightened and very secretive." On February 25, she had called her friend and antinuclear campaigner Gerard Morgan-Grenville, and in the course of the conversation had said to him something like, "If they don't get me first, I want the world to know that one old woman has seen through their lies." Morgan-Grenville's account of this phone call comprised the first interview in a program in the prestigious *World in Action* current affairs series transmitted a year after the murder. Hilda had also spoken of the existence of a "nuclear brøderbund," some sort of shadowy organization.[12]

Cook pointed out that Hilda had, a few days earlier, finished her paper for the Sizewell B inquiry, and noted that another comrade from the Shropshire Peace Alliance later claimed that Hilda had called him between eleven and eleven-thirty a.m. on the day of her abduction to ask him to come over and look after some papers of hers because "she was under some kind of surveillance and she was expecting a visit from Inspector Davies or Davy."[13] The inference was clear: Hilda had felt herself to be under scrutiny from the authorities because of her antinuclear activism. They, not burglars, had been the stuff of her nightmares.

And then, argued Cook, there was the diligence, or lack of it, being displayed by the police investigators. In the summer of 1984, she wrote, "three senior officers involved in the murder hunt were discovered to have been playing golf when they should have been out pursuing their enquiries." This mattered because "the suggestion was made that possibly the police had their own reasons for not wanting to pursue the killer with too much enthusiasm."[14] But what might those reasons—aside from the desire to play golf or a degree of fatalism because the case was now going cold—actually be? Logic suggested one possible alternative: the police knew or suspected who had done the old lady in but didn't want to catch them. And if that was the case, then the question was, why?

At the time of Hilda's death, her closest living relative seems to have been her nephew Rob Green, who at that time was living in Dorset and training to be a thatcher. Green soon tended to the view that his aunt's death was somehow connected to her involvement in protests against nuclear power. Others, however, became convinced that it was Hilda's connection to Rob Green that had provided the motive for her murder, for Green was bound up with that great cause célèbre of the first Thatcher term, the sinking in 1982 of the Argentinian battle cruiser *General Belgrano.*

The *Belgrano* affair had entered British folklore partly because it seemed to provide the one chink in Mrs. Thatcher's adamantine exoskeleton. As the British task force had steamed toward the occupied Falkland Islands, and before full battle was joined, various diplomatic initiatives were under way in attempts to avert conflict. These were unpromising, given the mutually exclusive positions of the two sides. At the same time, Britain declared an area around the Falklands a "total exclusion zone," within which hostile ships should expect to be attacked. The *Belgrano* was close to but not inside this zone when the submarine HMS *Conqueror* fired three torpedoes, which sank the ship, killing 323 of her crew.

A year later, in the course of her general election campaign, the one moment of awkwardness for the Iron Lady came when she was questioned on a live TV show by a middle-aged woman named Diana Gould. Combative but polite, Gould forced Thatcher to admit that the *Belgrano* had been heading away from the Falklands and suggested that the attack might have been part of a deliberate attempt by the government to forestall peace negotiations and ensure the issue would be decided by force of arms. It was widely, almost plaintively, believed on the center and left in Britain that had the Falklands not been invaded and an atmosphere of jingoism thus created, then the Tories would have lost the 1983 election. That being so, it was natural to invert this proposition and to suggest that, guessing this in advance, Thatcher had opted for war to improve her election prospects. If so, this was a major scandal and might even lead to Thatcher's downfall.

And who were best placed to expose any such scandal but those who had been part of the *Belgrano* operation? The men on the *Conqueror* perhaps, or those in Thatcher's war cabinet, or the men and women of naval intelligence, who saw all the signals sent on that day? As it happened, one of those men was Commander Robert Green of the Royal Navy, nephew of Hilda Murrell—a fact that immediately captured the attention of that British parliamentary phenomenon, Old Etonian Labour MP Tam Dalyell.

Dalyell, once described as "more a campaigning journalist than an MP,"[15] had made the fate of the *Belgrano* his life's obsession since the sinking. Indomitable and unembarrassable, the MP for Linlithgow in

Scotland was regarded by many as a somewhat absurd figure. But as the journalist Andrew Brown was to comment later, Dalyell, "by dint of an almost ludicrous persistence, which involved getting himself thrown out of the chamber five times, managed to implant in the national consciousness the idea that there had been something markedly less than heroic about the action which, more than any other, secured the safety of the task force that recaptured the Falklands."[16]

On December 20, 1984, as the police investigation into the Murrell murder entered its ninth fruitless month, Dalyell rose in the House of Commons to tell the world that he had effectively solved the crime. The police version, he argued, had always been improbable because it "did not tally with what was obviously a sophisticated break-in, in which the telephone had been cut, leaving it so callers could ring in but not out." Such circumstances "pointed away from a random murder." No, it was more likely that the intruders were looking for something—that this was an intelligence operation that had gone "disastrously wrong." Dalyell was unconvinced by the Shrewsbury view that the botched search concerned nuclear documents, not least because he knew people high up in the nuclear industry and couldn't believe that they "would dream of authorizing minions to search the house of a seventy-eight-year-old rose grower who had elegantly expressed, but quite unoriginal, views on reactor choice and nuclear waste disposal." No, the issue was, of course, the *Belgrano,* and he had received tips from two "reliable sources" about exactly what had happened:

> I am informed that the intruders were not after money, not after nuclear information, but were checking to see if there were any *Belgrano*-related documents of Commander Green in the home of his aunt . . . They had no intention of injuring, let alone killing, a seventy-eight-year-old rose grower. Yet being the lady she was, and in her home, Hilda Murrell fought and was severely injured. She was then killed or left to die from hypothermia—and the cover-up had to begin because the searchers were members of British intelligence, I am informed.[17]

While the notion of members of the British security services going around bumping off little old ladies in English market towns (more or less the exact opposite of their official role) may have amazed most MPs, it simply angered Mr. Dalyell. "On whose ministerial authority, if any," he demanded to know, "did the search of Miss Murrell's home take place? Was there clearance, or was this the intelligence services doing their own thing?" And he concluded: "Of one thing I am certain—that there are persons in Westminster and Whitehall who know a great deal more about the violent death of Miss Hilda Murrell than they have so far been prepared to divulge."

Commander Green's own MP, the Liberal member for Yeovil, Paddy (later Lord) Ashdown, requested that, in light of Dalyell's revelations, there should now be a formal inquiry into the murder. The next day, there was substantial press coverage. The *Guardian* reported that the Home Office was investigating Dalyell's claims and added (somewhat randomly, given that Dalyell had firmly dismissed the nuclear connection): "At the time of her death Miss Murrell, who was an active anti–nuclear power campaigner, was working on a document to be presented to the Sizewell B inquiry . . . It was this activity which fuelled earlier speculation about the reasons for the break-in at her home."[18] The London *Evening Standard* carried the headline "MP's Amazing Murder Story," and there was a speculative piece in the *Sunday Times* in which a senior officer was quoted as saying that the Murrell murder "doesn't follow the accepted pattern of burglaries, not in my experience as a policeman."[19]

Dalyell subsequently elaborated on his information and his theory. Two days before the March abduction, Dalyell had asked Defense Secretary Michael Heseltine some very pointed questions in the House concerning the *Belgrano*. The substance of his questions concerned material leaked to him (it later transpired) by a Ministry of Defense civil servant, Clive Ponting. But the questions had caused "a flap in Downing Street" and a demand that the source of the leaks be found at all costs. According to Judith Cook, with whom Dalyell was in contact, his sources had told him, "there had indeed been a semiofficial break-in at the home of Hilda

Murrell . . . What Tam was told was that the operation had not been organized at a very high level. There had been no intention of harming Hilda, but it had been decided to search her house to see if she had any copies of documents or raw signals." There had been two intruders in Ravenscroft when Hilda had come home unexpectedly and disturbed them. There was a struggle, she was hurt, and taken away, and left to die.[20]

There were many problems with the Dalyell story, however impeccable his anonymous sources. For example, why was Hilda's return so unexpected given she had only gone shopping in Shrewsbury? But perhaps the biggest difficulty was the picture it painted of the security services: functionally incompetent in matters of basic tradecraft and, given the forensic evidence, sexually perverse. How could such a force deal with the threat from the IRA or Middle Eastern terrorism when it couldn't even conduct a search of an old lady's detached house without having to murder her? It simply wasn't credible.

Unless. In the spring of 1985, the *Sunday Telegraph* carried a story about a private detective who had allegedly told Special Branch officers that the Murrell murder was a surveillance operation in which "something went badly wrong and it involved officialdom." The next day the *Guardian*'s security specialist Richard Norton-Taylor reported that West Mercia Police were "believed to be considering the possibility" that the murder had been carried out by "a private detective acting for MI5 or another security service." Norton-Taylor then lobbed in this bombshell: "It is known that private investigators . . . work from time to time for the security service. It is also known that private detectives were investigating objectors to plans to build a pressurized water nuclear reactor (PWR)—in which a number of companies, British and American, have a stake—at Sizewell, Suffolk, at the time Miss Murrell died in March 1984."[21] Here was a way to square the obvious circle: the crime had been carried out not by professional spooks but semi-amateurs, the dross of the policing and security world.

One such private operator was a Mr. Peter Hamilton, formerly an officer in military intelligence, who ran a company called Zeus Security

Consultants and admitted that he had been asked by a "private client" to conduct clandestine investigations into the activities of Sizewell objectors. Judith Cook claimed that she had been given information that Zeus had then subcontracted some of this work out to even smaller outfits, such as Sapphire Investigation Bureau, based in the village of Acle near Norwich, and Contingency Services of Colchester.[22] Contingency Services was run by Victor Norris, who, in addition to being a convicted pedophile, also operated a company selling Nazi memorabilia. The sexual connection was not perfect, since attraction to old ladies would appear to be a philia at the opposite end of the scale to that suffered—or enjoyed—by Norris. But it was highly suggestive, thought Cook, that just three weeks after the Murrell murder, the boss of Sapphire, one Barry Peachman, got into his car with a shotgun, placed it in his mouth, and shot half his head away. True, conceded Cook, Peachman had been having an affair, and this had led some to speculate that his suicide was caused by domestic difficulties, "but as we know, it was not quite like that."[23]

Cook, Dalyell, and the Shrewsbury peace set were far from alone in their suspicions. Granada's prime-time *World in Action* program of March 1985 had begun by suggesting that the police "know that there's evidence that points toward two quite different and disturbing explanations for Hilda Murrell's death" and concluded, twenty-six suggestive minutes later, by talking about the "possibility that some kind of conspiracy had occurred."[24]

Then, in the early 1990s, a writer, Gary Murray, claimed that the truth behind the whole story had been vouchsafed to him by a prison inmate. The tale he heard (and believed) was that anxiety in Number 10 about *Belgrano* leaks had led an unidentified security agency to employ a northern firm, Ceres, to search Hilda's house. On the fateful day, a Ceres team consisting of a leader code-named Demeter (a moonlighting garage owner), a woman named Helga, and a right-winger who used the nom de guerre Spengler turned up at Ravenscroft, looking for papers. When Hilda interrupted them, she was restrained and Spengler (who else?) set about torturing her to reveal the location of the documents. Unfortunately, the sadistic Spengler became aroused and felt compelled to leave his DNA over various items. Judith Cook was clearly of two minds about Murray's analysis but asked, in a question worthy of an Umberto Eco novel, "If Zeus exists, then why not Ceres?"[25] The whole thing was like some surreal updating of the Ealing comedy *The Ladykillers*.

Over time, there were plenty of theories and even confessions. The magazine *Private Eye* ran with the notion, probably originating with Rob Green, that Hilda's body had been dumped in a roadside ditch on the night of the twenty-first, and only afterward was it placed in the Moat wood. Green still believes, as he recently told one interviewer, that his aunt's death was "a result of a state-sponsored abduction, with her car used as a decoy." His sense that the authorities were involved had been heightened, he said, by a series of odd occurrences. Hilda's Welsh cottage had been set on fire; his tires had been slashed; his telephone and post "were often interfered with"; and he believed that on several occasions he had been followed when driving in Shropshire. As late as 1994, his father's house—where he was living at the time—was broken into, but nothing was stolen. Meanwhile, Judith Cook reported getting intimidating phone calls suggesting that she leave the Murrell case alone.[26] And in 2002 a Scottish journalist claimed that a member of a Nazi organization, the National Socialist Movement, was "suspected of the murder of elderly CND activist Hilda Murrell." It isn't clear whether or not this was the demonic Spengler.[27]

The comments made by police pathologist Dr. Peter Acland in January 1985—as the conspiracy theories were beginning to cohere—caused less of a furor. "I don't know who killed Miss Murrell," he wrote, "but I have a strong suspicion that some two-penny-halfpenny thief is gloating over a pint of beer in a pub not many miles from Shrewsbury about all this media interest." We'll see later in this chapter whether or not he was right. By the time he said it, however, Hilda was ceasing to be an ordinary elderly lady and was metamorphosing via "gutful, courageous, seventy-eight-year-old Edwardian woman" (Tam Dalyell) into a kind of secular martyr of the antinuclear and peace movements. She was a woman who had suffered and died for her beliefs. She was a victim of the notion of the enemy within.

Her posthumous celebrity came quickly. The year 1985 saw two books published about her murder as well as numerous articles and features. The writer Maggie Gee based a novel on her death. Three years later, an English band, Attacco Decente, recorded a song about the murder, titled "The Rose Grower." And three separate dramas were fashioned out of the story. In the summer of 1986, you could have gone to see *Who Killed Hilda Murrell? An Investigation* at the well-regarded Tricycle Theater in Kilburn in north London, taken a brief holiday, and returned for a performance of *Celestial Blue: The Life and Death of Hilda Murrell* by an entirely different author at the equally acclaimed Gate Theater in Notting Hill in West London. *Unlawful Killing*, Judith Cook's own play, was put on at the Theater Royal Stratford East in the spring of 1991. After that, interest in the Murrell case waned, though even now (late 2008) you can visit the Hilda Murrell website maintained by her nephew Rob Green.[28]

CONSPIRACY—COMING TO A SCREEN NEAR YOU

A striking phrase recurred in the descriptions of the case by many of those who thought that Hilda Murrell might have been killed by the secret state. She was, or might have been, they suggested, the "British Karen Silkwood." In their minds was the famous case of an employee at a plutonium fuel plant in the United States, who had died in a mysterious car accident on an Oklahoma highway ten years before. Or, at least, the *movie* of the famous case, since Silkwood's death made very little impression on the British public until it was turned into a film starring the most celebrated Hollywood actress of that moment, Meryl Streep—a film that had been playing in cinemas all over Britain only months before Hilda's death. In real life, Karen Silkwood was a union activist who had criticized the safety of the plutonium fuel plant where she worked and was killed in a road accident that involved no other vehicle. Her death was soon regarded as a setup by some of her fellow activists, who suspected her employers, Kerr-McGee, of having somehow arranged for this irritant to be removed. The plant itself closed down the following year.

In the film, Silkwood is depicted as an ordinary woman with problems in her marriage, struggling to keep everything together but possessed of an extraordinary amount of courage and integrity. On becoming ill, she begins to realize that the safety practices at the plant are endangering the workforce, and develops an obsession (to the predictable detriment of her love life) with discovering evidence to prove neglect. Having collected this evidence into a dossier, she is en route to meet a reporter from *The New York Times* when her "accident" takes place. The authorities blame it on a combination of alcohol and tranquilizers; the movie draws no definite conclusion but leaves the filmgoer with the strong impression that Silkwood was somehow assassinated.

That Karen Silkwood earned movie eponymity owed something to fashion. Five years after her death came one of those coincidences of fact and fiction that filmmakers must have interesting dreams about. On March 28, 1979, there was a partial core meltdown at the Three Mile Island nuclear generating station near Harrisburg in Pennsylvania, with observers following in real time the debate about whether or not to evacuate the local population. Although no such decision was taken, no one was killed,* and the reactor was brought under control, the impact on public consciousness was profound.

The coinciding fictional event had occurred less than a fortnight earlier, when the movie *The China Syndrome*, about a possible accident at a nuclear plant in California, had opened in the United States. Carrying the ominous tagline "Today only a handful of people know what it means . . . Soon you will know," *The China Syndrome* took its name from the proposition that a nuclear core meltdown might be so powerful that nothing could prevent it from burning its way right through the earth until it came out on the other side—in China. In the movie, Jane Fonda plays a Califor-

---

*Although critics of the nuclear industry believe that a substantial release of radiation from Three Mile Island may have led to an increased incidence of cancer among local people.

nia TV news anchor, Kimberly Wells, who just happens to be filming at a nuclear power plant with her cameraman (Michael Douglas) when there is a minor earth tremor and panic breaks out in the control room. Even if her TV bosses are unimpressed, the incident interests Wells. She soon comes into contact with head technician Jack Godell (Jack Lemmon), who, on investigating what happened during the earthquake, discovers that short-cuts were taken by the contractors when they built the plant. Godell tries to warn his bosses, but, parsimoniously, they refuse to shut operations down while he sorts things out. In an obvious echo of the Silkwood case, Godell is attacked while he is driving to give evidence at a public hearing, but he survives. Desperate that there might be a catastrophic accident, Godell commandeers the plant control room at gunpoint, and is broadcasting via Wells to the public when the transmission is cut off and a police team break into the room and shoot him dead.

The themes that run through the Godell, Silkwood, and Murrell cases—fictional or historical—are similar. On the one side, there is the dissident who gradually becomes aware of the dangers of nuclear power and decides to speak out to prevent disaster. On the other, there is the secret state and its commercial partners whose objective is to prevent dissent from interfering with their concept of national security or, more venally, the profits that may accrue from the harnessing of perilous technologies. And somewhere in the middle is the media.

The dissident—though emotionally damaged or eccentric—is good; the state—though powerful and seemingly benign—is bad. But the media has the capacity to be either. It may try to cover up or ignore the truth, but in the hands of courageous or farsighted journalists it can become a tool for the exposure of wrongdoing. Don't, however, hold your breath.

A VERY BRITISH EDGE OF THE REALM

After *Silkwood*, as we've seen, came Hilda Murrell, and after Hilda Murrell came a remarkable series of conspiracy-theory dramas produced for British television and cinema. For four years, these films and programs captured middlebrow imaginations in Britain and then—just as suddenly as they had arrived—they disappeared.

British television drama in the early 1980s had been dominated by two hugely expensive serialized epics: Evelyn Waugh's *Brideshead Revisited*, which turned the lugubrious Jeremy Irons into a star, and Paul Scott's *Raj Quartet*, broadcast as *The Jewel in the Crown* in 1984. Superficially, both series could be seen as nostalgic, being set in an England and an empire still within living memory but now gone. But both series also portrayed the worm in the bud, the internal corruption of lost, aristocratic England and of British India. When, however, the director of *The Jewel in the Crown*, Christopher Morahan, unveiled his next project, it was set very much in the present—or, rather, in a very dark version of the present.

In the Secret State, shown on the BBC on March 10, 1985, was an adaptation of a book by Robert McCrum. In a very minor version of the Three Mile Island coincidence, the drama was shown just two days after Cathy Massiter's revelations about MI5 surveillance of CND members and others, and in the same week as the *World in Action* program about Hilda Murrell. This time, the whistle-blowing hero is a civil servant who discovers that his department's new computer is being used both to create false files on political opponents of the government, such as an awkwardly crusading radical MP, and also to perpetrate a gigantic and lucrative tax fraud on behalf of certain crooked businessmen. The civil servant is just about to solve the whole puzzle when he is blown up by a bomb placed in his car. The opening sequence was memorable for its shot of a large rat suddenly emerging from a garbage bag, an image that dovetailed with the obviously significant words of one of the main characters: "Suspicion. It's a virus. We are the carriers. We're like rats scuttling through medieval sewers."

Coincidentally, *In the Secret State* was in production at the same time as another British feature film about whistle-blowers and bombs, released in November 1985. In *Defense of the Realm*, Gabriel Byrne played Nick Mullen, an amoral young reporter on an amoral British tabloid newspaper. Mullen is following a story of a scandal that, on the face of it, discredits a crusading opposition MP. But with the help of an older and more principled colleague, he investigates further and finds out that the original scandal has been manufactured to prevent the MP from raising in the House of Commons an embarrassing question about a missing boy. The principled old journalist is killed (quite possibly by Special Branch) in a way that makes it look as if he died from natural causes. Nevertheless, Mullen discovers that the boy was killed in a runway accident on an American nuclear base in England—an accident that very nearly led to a nuclear explosion. Mullen has his scoop, but the newspaper's knighted owner, who has interests in the armaments business, orders the story to be spiked. A frustrated Mullen then makes sure that the foreign press gets the information and provokes a major scandal, but this is the audience's only consolation, as Mullen is then killed when a bomb blows up his flat.

If British audiences hadn't yet got the point about the secret state, its allies, and its enemies, there was a TV series to come in the winter of 1985. *Edge of Darkness* was first shown in six episodes on BBC2 in November and December, and then, following critical praise and high audience figures, was immediately repeated in three jumbo episodes on consecutive evenings on BBC1. The series later won four BAFTA awards and, according to the British Film Institute, also achieved "cult status." In *Edge of Darkness*, one of the most popular actors then working on the British stage, the tall, serious Bob Peck, plays Craven, a senior policeman whose student daughter Emma is shot dead on the steps of the family home in what appears to be a botched attempt by criminals to kill her father. Determined to discover the truth about Emma's death, Craven follows a convoluted trail that leads to a cover-up of the illegal production of weapons-grade plutonium at a British nuclear reprocessing plant. This, in turn, links to an American plan to militarize space. In the course of his investigations, Craven is contaminated by plutonium, but together with a rogue CIA agent manages to tell the world about the conspiracy before, presumably, expiring from the effects of radiation.

The narrative similarities between these dramas are extraordinary. The questing hero starts out as an apolitical or even Establishment figure who almost unwillingly uncovers secrets that invariably involve nuclear power or nuclear weapons. There is always dark cooperation between corporate and state forces—which usually combine to murder the protagonist, but only after he/she has made the vital disclosure, thus creating a martyr. It is left unclear whether the impact of the hero's sacrifice is lasting or momentary. In its own way, the genre displays all the uniformity of the 1950s Western.

In 1988 came the culminating expression of this fashion. *A Very British Coup*, shown in three parts on Channel 4 and based on a novel by left-wing journalist Chris Mullin, posed the question of what this same nexus of spooks, Americans, and tycoons—the military-industrial-newspaper-intelligence complex—would do if the British people were impertinent enough to elect a socialist Labour government. The answer was that the new administration would be subjected to financial pressure by the Americans, spied upon by the security services, and undermined by a press seeking scandal.

But by now the conspiracist moment was over. The circumstances that had created the specific paranoia of the early 1980s had changed. The accession to the Soviet leadership of Mikhail Gorbachev, and the astonishing speed with which his reform and openness programs (named *perestroika* and *glasnost*, respectively) dissipated fears of nuclear confrontation, began with the Reykjavik summit in 1986, and progressed through an arms control treaty signed in Washington at the end of 1987. Ronald Reagan departed the presidency at the beginning of 1989; barely eleven months later, the Berlin Wall had fallen, and a year later Mrs. Thatcher, too, had gone, to be replaced by an altogether more emollient kind of Conservative—the sort of man who didn't look as though he would authorize the assassination of journalists in their own flats.

Death of a Rose Grower, Part Three

But what of Hilda? Her case was forgotten by all but her closest friends, and remained unsolved throughout the 1990s, as the Soviet Union fell and Bill Clinton followed Bush and Bush followed Clinton. Technology, however, marched on, and in the spring of 2002, West Mercia detectives announced they were conducting a cold-case review of the Murrell murder, reexamining all the testimony and, most critically, the physical evidence.

Just over a year later, police knocked on the door of a flat in Meadow Farm Drive, Harlescott, in northeast Shrewsbury, no more than three miles from where Hilda's body was found. The man they arrested was a thirty-five-year-old laborer with a long criminal record. Andrew George had been sixteen and resident in a local children's home at the time of the murder, and it was his DNA that the police cold-case team had found on the semen-stained tissue and on Hilda's clothes. When the case came to trial at Stafford Crown Court, the jury heard that George had been burgling the house—he had noticed that the door was sometimes left open—when Hilda had come home and found him. She had then been bound to the banisters with an ironing-board cover, sexually assaulted, stabbed three times, bundled into her own car, and driven for six miles. After crashing the car, George had stabbed Hilda again and then dumped her close to a tree. Although he refused to answer any police questions about the murder, George did tell his girlfriend during a prison visit that he was not guilty, blaming his brother Steven. They had been looking for money. On Friday May 6, 2005, over twenty-one years after Hilda Murrell's murder, Andrew George was found guilty and sentenced to a minimum of fifteen years in prison. The judge told George that the sentence reflected his age at the time of the offense and added, "If you had committed that crime recently as an adult, I would have considered a whole-life order—no release ever."

It was just as the police had said all along. Looking back at the police reaction to the various conspiracy theories suggested by the questioners on the 1985 *World in Action* program, one can see clearly that what was made to seem like confusion on the part of the police was, in fact, incomprehension. For years, they were told by Tam Dalyell, Rob Green, various journalists, and TV producers that their theories of a walk-in burglar were just not credible, yet they were right.

At the time of writing, neither Dalyell nor Green has admitted his error. Dalyell, now retired from politics, has stuck to the objection that Hilda's body could not have lain undiscovered from the Wednesday to the Saturday. On June 1, 2006, the *Shrewsbury Chronicle* reported that Rob Green, now living in New Zealand, was "heading to Britain armed with information he claims will shed new light on her case." Green had appeared on New Zealand television stating that he had new evidence that he would present at Andrew George's appeal. "His announcement," said the *Chronicle*, "is set to revive conspiracy theories that the secret service was involved in the murder." Green himself told an interviewer that he had "reason to believe" that the conviction was "an outrageous miscarriage of justice." Quite how a twenty-one-year-old DNA sample could have been faked, and by whom, is not clear. It would have required, at the very least, a renewed twenty-first-century conspiracy, featuring an entirely new cast of conspirators. Certainly this notion seems not to have recommended itself to the three Appeal Court judges who, on Friday June 9, 2006, finally rejected Andrew George's appeal against his conviction for the murder of the Shropshire rose grower.

The conspiracy theories, in this instance, seem to have faded away, for the obvious reason, one suspects, that their moment has passed. The particular set of demons that haunted the mid-1980s—the nuclear state with its thuggish minions—has vanished, to be replaced by others. But at the time, Hilda Murrell had been a powerful symbol. She had represented an ideal that the embattled campaigners of the period had of themselves. Politically defeated, marginalized even, they had an existence in their own minds that was simultaneously heroic and doomed. If they were unsuccessful, it wasn't due to any deficiency in their cause or their actions, nor was it down to the fact that the majority of British (or American) people simply disagreed with them. It was explained, instead, by the strength and ruthlessness of the forces they were up against.

6. HOLY BLOOD, HOLY GRAIL, HOLY SHIT

"What if, instead, you fed the computer a few dozen notions taken from the works of the Diabolicals—for example, the Templars fled to Scotland, or the Corpus Hermeticum arrived in Florence in 1460 and threw in a few connective phrases like, 'It's obvious that' and 'This proves that'? We might end up with something revelatory. Then we fill in the gaps, call the repetitions prophecies and—voilà—a hitherto unpublished chapter of the history of magic at the very least!"

"An idea of genius," Belbo said. "Let's start straight away."

—UMBERTO ECO, *FOUCAULT'S PENDULUM*

Different aspects of life seem to run on different timelines. Does punk really belong to the era of Jimmy Carter, or did *Baywatch* really begin in the same year as the French sank the *Rainbow Warrior*? The cultural and political worlds often seem autonomous. So, as Margaret Thatcher and Ronald Reagan were being elected, as the Greenham women began their vigil, as Leonid Brezhnev, for sixteen years the top man in the USSR, lay dying, unconscious preparations were being made for the sensational trial involving thriller writer Dan Brown, which took place in London's Royal Courts of Justice in the Strand in March 2006.

These proceedings involved three antagonists—two plaintiffs and a defendant—all of whom (remarkably, some may think) hailed from former English colonies beginning with the word "New." Was it just coincidence that, in Court 61, Dan Brown of New Hampshire was defending himself against the charge of plagiarism, accused by Richard Leigh of New Jersey and Michael Baigent of New Zealand? Some conspiracists might have thought not, since theirs is a world that thrives on rebuffing coincidence. And thrives financially, too: as we'll see, large amounts of money can be made by people able to spin far-fetched but portentous-sounding yarns about coincidences. But that same money can also be lost in the pursuit of absurd cases of law, as Messrs. Baigent and Leigh were about to find out.

Their claim was infringement of copyright: specifically, that Brown's thriller *The Da Vinci Code*, a book that had by this point earned its author over $45 million, replacing *Harry Potter* as the most ubiquitous item on train, plane, and beach, used a plot that had been directly plagiarized from their own work of "history," *The Holy Blood and the Holy Grail*. This book, published in 1982, had also made its authors (Baigent, Leigh, and a third man, Henry Lincoln) a considerable fortune, as had its sequels. But for Baigent and Leigh, it seemed, the money wasn't the issue: they had more high-minded reasons for objecting to the Dan Brown phenomenon. "We are being lumped in with Dan Brown's work of fiction and that degrades the historical implication of our material. It makes our work far easier to dismiss as a farrago of nonsense," Michael Baigent was quoted as saying. And then he addressed a slightly different question. "Whether our hypothesis is right or wrong is irrelevant. The fact is that this is work that we put together and spent years and years building up. Issuing the writ is not something we have done lightly, but we feel that we have no choice."[1]

Baigent's claim that *The Da Vinci Code* undermined the authority of *The Holy Blood*'s "historical implication" sat uneasily with the idea of plagiarism. If Baigent and Leigh's book was essentially history, then surely anyone writing what was clearly a novel would be entitled to use it, provided they didn't quote great chunks of it without attribution or permission. So it wasn't surprising that after three weeks, the judge, Peter Smith—described by journalists in the court as "portly and ruby-faced," and clearly enjoying every moment of the proceedings—ruled in favor of Dan Brown, holding that Baigent and Leigh's argument was "vague and

shifted course during the trial and was always based on a weak foundation." Baigent and Leigh's costs were estimated at over a million dollars,
and they were also told to pay 85 percent of Brown's more than $2 million
legal bill. A year later, an appeal by Baigent and Leigh was dismissed, by
which time their costs had risen to $5 million.

In the course of the trial, Judge Smith's textual analysis of the two
works allowed a glimpse into the private process of authorship. It had been
Brown's wife, Blythe, an art expert, who had read *The Holy Blood and the
Holy Grail* and who had offered her husband some kind of synopsis of its
contents. Though Brown's debt to the book is acknowledged in the character of Leigh Teabing, whose improbable name is an amalgam and an
anagram of the surnames of the two authors, the judge concluded, "In
reality, Mr. Brown knew very little about how the historical background
was researched. He, in my view, simply accepted Blythe Brown's research
material when incorporating it into the writing of part two of *DVC*."[2]

This insight into the questionable thoroughness of Dan Brown's research
techniques seemed slightly at odds with Brown's own reaction to the trial's
conclusion. Judge Smith's findings were, he suggested, a great victory for
artistic expression, because "a novelist must be free to draw appropriately
from historical works without fear that he'll be sued." The author's formulation accidentally echoed one of the great ironic newspaper headlines of
our generation: "Da Vinci Case Pits History Against Art."[3] Though, as the
judge suggested, 40 million book buyers can never be wrong in the eyes of
publishers, *The Da Vinci Code* is probably not great art. And in what sense
can *The Holy Blood and the Holy Grail* be described as history?

Henry Lincoln and the TV Quest for the Holy Grail

At around the same time as the trial in London was closing, the movie
of *The Da Vinci Code* was opening in cinemas across the world. Its

thunderous trailer, shown a million times already, claimed that the film would tell the story of "the greatest cover-up in human history," which readers of the book knew to be that supposedly perpetrated by the Catholic Church, which for two millennia had deceived its adherents into believing that Jesus was a bachelor and Mary Magdalene a whore. So intense had the controversy over Dan Brown's theology become that bishops denounced the film, and the very day I tried to see it in the Indian city of Hyderabad, it was banned by the state government of Andhra Pradesh because it might lead to demonstrations and civil disorder. "The minority organizations," said a state spokesman, "have pointed out that the film's storyline attacks the very heart of the Holy Gospel, destroying the divinity of Jesus Christ."

This may have been India, which is very careful about its minorities for good historical reasons, but even so, it seemed surprising that such an extreme stance should have been taken. Surely everybody knew how to distinguish a farrago of exciting nonsense involving psychotic albino monks and centuries-old secret societies from a genuine claim about historical truth? But perhaps the Andhra Pradeshis were right, after all, because, as we've seen, at least two groups central to the creation of *The Da Vinci Code* weren't making the crucial fact-fiction distinction. Indeed, Dan Brown included this categorial foreword at the beginning of all editions of *The Da Vinci Code*: "FACT: The Priory of Sion—a European secret society founded in 1099—is a real organization. In 1975, Paris's Bibliothèque Nationale discovered its parchments known as the Dossiers Secrets, identifying numerous members of the Priory of Sion, including Sir Isaac Newton, Sandro Botticelli, Victor Hugo, and Leonardo da Vinci." Brown elaborated later in a television interview that while the murderous albino and the angry French police officer named Fache might have been made up, "all of the art, architecture, secret rituals, secret societies, all of that is historical fact."

Meanwhile, Baigent and Leigh were adamant that there was also a historical basis to their work: in the publicity for their 1986 follow-up, *The Messianic Legacy*, they argued that "*The Holy Blood and the Holy Grail—* the book in which the Priory of Sion was unveiled—rocked the very foundations of Christianity." With pilgrimages being organized to the historical sites where this alternative history had supposedly been played out, and with Church employees being harassed by eager neo-heretics, it was perhaps little wonder that the popular triumph of *The Da Vinci Code* so irked the Catholic Church. But where had it all started?

Strangely, given the prominence in the court action of Baigent and Leigh, the story of *The Holy Blood and the Holy Grail* didn't begin with them at all, but rather with their absent coauthor, Henry Lincoln. In his incarnation as popular historian, television presenter, and writer of serious books, Lincoln was the personification of a new breed of scholar unhampered by prejudices of the past. His goatee beard, longish hair, turtleneck sweaters, and mellifluous voice lent a plausible dignity to his inquiries and discoveries. When, as a teenager, I first saw him on the BBC *Chronicle* program in the early 1970s, I was both convinced and captivated by him. Here was the kind of hippie pedagogue I wanted to be taught by.

There were things, however, I didn't know about him, though they weren't hidden. His real name is Henry Soskin, and Soskin/Lincoln was not, in fact, in any proper sense, a historian, but an occasional actor and a successful scriptwriter for TV shows and science fiction programs such as the children's series *Doctor Who* and the early medical soap opera *Emergency Ward 10*. In 1968, he appeared on the credits of the Boris Karloff movie *The Curse of the Crimson Altar* as cowriter. So Lincoln was, in his working life, a moderately successful storyteller.

And his greatest story began with words nearly as good as "Once upon a time . . .": "In 1969, en route for a summer holiday in the Cévennes," he writes in the preface to *The Holy Blood and the Holy Grail*, "I made the casual purchase of a paperback."[4] This providential holiday reading, *The Accursed Treasure*, written in French by Gérard de Sède, was, according to Lincoln, a "lightweight, entertaining blend of historical fact, genuine mystery, and conjecture," and told a tale of an obscure nineteenth-century country priest in the small Languedoc village of Rennes-le-Château who had found something extraordinary in his church, and who used his knowledge to amass vast wealth.

Most readers of *The Accursed Treasure*, English or French, would have enjoyed the story, lent the book to someone else, and then forgotten about it, but Lincoln was cut from a different cloth. The book contained, he noticed, a "curious and glaring omission": although it depicted "cryptic documents" supposedly uncovered by the fortunate *curé*, it never actually bothered to decipher them. Yet, from the reproductions of two of these documents contained in the book, Lincoln himself was able to make a decryption. If he could manage that with a fairly cursory inspection, why hadn't the author done the same? This incongruity nagged at Lincoln and from time to time motivated him to return to the documents. When he did so, they rendered up to him "tantalizing new glimpses of layers of meaning buried within the text."

These "glimpses" were enough to earn Lincoln a remarkable commission to research an item for the BBC's main historical and archaeological series, *Chronicle*. Remarkable because Lincoln, as we have seen, was neither a historian nor an archaeologist, nor was his tale based on anything more than photographed documents in an obscure "lightweight" work of French popular history. Nevertheless, the BBC paid for him to travel to France to meet the author of *The Accursed Treasure*, Gérard de Sède, in Paris in the winter of 1970. There, Lincoln asked de Sède repeatedly why he hadn't published the decryption of the documents. "This time de Sède's answer was calculated: 'Because we thought it might interest someone like you to find it for yourself.'"

Lincoln was indeed interested, and de Sède began to feed him further fragments of information, including an encoded message that mentioned the painter Poussin. De Sède told Lincoln that a tomb resembling the one depicted in the painter's famous *Shepherds of Arcadia* had been found at Pontils close to Rennes-le-Château. When Lincoln saw photographs of the discovered tomb, he realized he was on to something big. "It was clear that our short film on a small local mystery had begun to assume unexpected dimensions."

There were eventually to be three *Chronicle* films on the stories of Rennes-le-Château. The first, in 1972, was *The Lost Treasure of Jerusalem?*;

the second, *The Priest, the Painter and the Devil*, appeared two years later. With their emphasis on medieval mysteries and codes hidden within famous paintings, both were popular with British viewers, and little or no criticism of their tenuous historicity surfaced—perhaps the historians were busy on the nights of transmission, and this was before videotape or DVDs. After the second film, Lincoln found himself some important collaborators. At a summer writing course in 1975, he spent some leisure time discussing the Knights Templar with one of his fellow lecturers, the novelist Richard Leigh. Leigh offered to help with the part of Lincoln's project that involved the knights, and also introduced him to Michael Baigent, in Lincoln's words, "a psychology graduate who had recently abandoned a successful career in photojournalism to devote his time to researching the Templars." Together, the trio made for *Chronicle* the documentary *The Shadow of the Templars* (1979), thus completing the trilogy of films that, according to Richard Leigh, were "regarded by the BBC as the most successful documentaries they had ever done."[5] "The work we did on [*The Shadow of the Templars*]," said Lincoln with characteristic suggestiveness, "at last brought us face to face with the underlying foundations upon which the entire mystery of Rennes-le-Château had been built." It was a mystery that he, Baigent, and Leigh finally revealed in their 1982 book, *The Holy Blood and the Holy Grail*. As Lincoln writes, "In 1972 I closed my first film with the words, 'Something extraordinary is waiting to be found . . . and in the not too distant future, it will be.' This book explains what that 'something' is—and how extraordinary the discovering has been."[6] People obviously wanted to know. The popularity of the films passed to the book. On the first day of publication in Britain, 43,000 hardcover copies of *The Holy Blood* were sold. I waited for the paperback.

The Second-Greatest Story Ever Told

The 1996 edition of *The Holy Blood and the Holy Grail* comprises 495 pages of dense text plus thirty-six pages of footnotes, a thirteen-page bibliography detailing works in English, French, and German, and twenty-four pages of photographs. It has the cover of a thriller and the interior of a work of popular scholarship, and the story it tells, in essence, is this.

Jesus and Mary Magdalene are lovers, as suggested in the so-called Gnostic Gospels found in "scrolls" (actually, they were in book form) at Nag Hammadi in Egypt in 1945. The Gnostic Gospels also hint that Peter, the first pope, was jealous of the couple's intimacy. The pair have a child or children, and after the crucifixion Mary takes him/her/them and flees across the Mediterranean to southern Gaul, where she goes into hiding within the local Jewish community.

Four hundred years or so later, in the early Dark Ages, one of the descendants of Jesus and Mary marries into the aristocratic family then beginning to unite what will become France. This family, known as the Merovingians, therefore becomes both a royal dynasty and the bearer of the authentic bloodline of the Messiah. Appropriately, the Merovingians establish Christianity in France but, alas, King Dagobert II is the last of his line to rule. In the seventh century A.D., France is taken over by the Carolingians, whose most famous member is Charlemagne.

Ousted, the bearers of the holy genes go underground and metamorphose into the aristocratic House of Lorraine. They only become royal again when the head of the family, Godfrey de Bouillon, joins the First Crusade and somehow manages to get himself crowned first king of Jerusalem. Helping him achieve this satisfying fulfillment of prophecy has been a secret group who now found a priory on Mount Zion and name themselves the Priory of Sion. This group is also behind the establishment of the Knights Templar, and it is through them that the buried Jewish Temple of Solomon is excavated, revealing something that might have been documents, the remains of Jesus, or the Ark of the Covenant.

The Priory remains secret, but the Templars are highly visible until, in 1307, at the command of the king of France, the order is suppressed, supposedly for heresy, and many of its members tortured and killed. So now the Priory of Sion is left to bear the great truth, and maintain the bloodline, in secret, which it does, though not without yielding to the temptation to scatter clues about its existence and mission around medieval and Renaissance Europe. One such is the story of the Grail, usually rendered as the San Graal (the cup of tradition) but really signifying the Sang Real—the Royal Blood.

Over the next 650 years of clandestine existence, the Priory passes the secret on from generation to generation and from grand master to grand master. Some of these are from the sacred House of Lorraine itself; some are men who dabble in alchemy; some are great scientists; some are great artists. Holders of the office, according to a list later helpfully deposited in the Bibliothèque Nationale in Paris, include Robert Fludd, Robert Boyle, Sir Isaac Newton, Victor Hugo, Claude Debussy, Jean Cocteau, and of course, Leonardo da Vinci.

Obscure hints of what is going on are left in such works of art as the French painter Nicolas Poussin's *The Shepherds of Arcadia*, in which some rustics are seen by a tomb on which the words *Et in Arcadia Ego* are inscribed. However, this habit of scattering clues catches up with the Priory when, in 1885, the priest of Rennes-le-Château, Bérenger Saunière, discovers some parchments inside a hollow Visigothic pillar. Saunière, with the help of a local bishop, cracks one of the codes hidden therein and discovers that it reads: "To Dagobert II king and to Sion belongs this treasure and he is there dead." Somehow Saunière works out that this refers to the bloodline of Jesus and blackmails the Church authorities (who presumably realize too, otherwise they wouldn't have minded), thus accounting for his sudden *richesse*.

And there this ancient mystery would have rested, had not Gérard de Sède published his book, had not Henry Lincoln read it and wondered at it, had not the BBC commissioned no less than three historical documentaries from him, had not someone deposited a lot of documents in the Bibliothèque Nationale, had not the Priory of Sion been publicly registered by its own most recent grand master in 1956, and had not Michael Baigent, with his strong opinions on the bloodline of Christ, been brought aboard to write *The Holy Blood and the Holy Grail*.

So it was that Lincoln and company eventually met Pierre Plantard de St. Clair, then extant grand master of the Priory of Sion, by direct descent Merovingian claimant to the throne, and therefore—disconcertingly, given his resemblance to the incompetent Irish builder in *Fawlty Towers*—the descendant of Jesus. Plantard, they concluded, was now breaking cover because he was intending to launch a political movement of extraordinary importance, though they didn't know what it was.

The Greatest Royalties Ever Earned

Surprisingly, the book was not immediately dismissed. While the Anglican Bishop of Birmingham, Hugh Montefiore, was unimpressed and told the authors so in the course of a TV discussion on the day before the book's official publication, and although the *Times Literary Supplement* thought the book "worthless" and "rather silly," other reviewers were quite friendly. The *Times Educational Supplement* allowed that it was "compulsive reading"; the *Oxford Times*, read by many a don, attested to its "well-documented and often sinister facts." The reviewer in the conservative *Sunday Telegraph* speculated, "no doubt this one will infuriate many ecclesiastical authorities," then continued sunnily, "but the authors may still be proved right." On the other side of the world, the *Los Angeles Times* agreed there was enough "to seriously challenge many traditional Christian beliefs, if not alter them." In a large number of bookshops, *The Holy Blood* was elevated from the unrespectable realms of "New Age" or "Spiritual" (i.e., analytically worthless) books, and placed in either "History" or "Archaeology." It leapfrogged over the alien abductions, the anal probes, and Atlantis exotica, to land in the world of scholarship. Where it sold in the hundreds of thousands.

As ever, like seagulls behind a trawler, in its wake flew an army of sequels. The authors themselves released *The Messianic Legacy* (or *HBHG 2*) within three years. Baigent and Leigh, alone or together, produced *The*

THE DEARBORN INDEPENDENT

One Dollar   Dearborn, Michigan, May 22, 1920   Five Cents

The International Jew: The World's Problem

The Jewish conspiracy in America: Henry Ford's *Dearborn Independent*.

Piotr Ivanovich Rachkovsky, tsarist agent and father of *The Protocols of the Elders of Zion*.

Die Protokolle der **Weisen von Zion** und die jüdische **Weltpolitik** von **Alfred Rosenberg**

Hitler associate Alfred Rosenberg's own edition of the *Protocols*.

The young Georgy Pyatakov
during the heroic era.

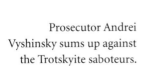

Convinced by Stalin: the novelist
Lion Feuchtwanger.

Prosecutor Andrei
Vyshinsky sums up against
the Trotskyite saboteurs.

John T. Flynn—from left-winger to McCarthyite.

Senator Joe McCarthy, discerner of the immense Communist conspiracy.

America First rally, Chicago, 1941.

A still from the Zapruder film: The magic bullet has just hit JFK.

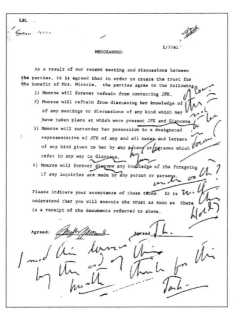

Marilyn, JFK, and the Mob: a page from the Cusack forgery.

Mohamed Al Fayed waves the damning Diana letter.

ABOVE: Victim of a
security blunder?
Hilda Murrell.

RIGHT: Tam Dalyell, MP,
whose obsession was
the *Belgrano*.

Antinuclear demonstration at Greenham Common, England, 1980s.

Holy costs: Richard Leigh and Michael Baigent at the High Court, London.

Pierre Plantard: hoaxster or
direct descendant of Christ?

David Ray Griffin,
the Dean of 9/11 Truth Studies.

RIGHT: Stylish poster for a
screening of *Loose Change*.

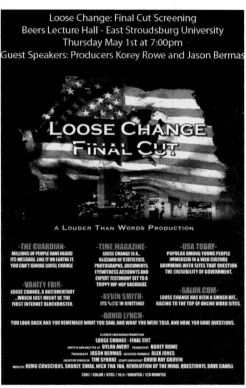

The home page of the Scholars
for 9/11 Truth website.

David Kelly testifies, two days before his death, July 2003.

Pooter of the Yard: Norman Baker, MP, at Harrowdown Hill, where David Kelly's body was found.

Temple and the Lodge, The Dead Sea Scrolls Deception, The Elixir and the Stone, and *The Jesus Papers.* Henry Lincoln has specialized for over twenty years in Rennes-le-Château penumbra: guides, videos, DVDs, lectures, maps, and so on. And there have been many other cashers-in. The last twenty years have seen the publication of dozens of Rennes-le-Château books, Mary Magdalene books, Templar books, Grail books, Poussin books, Leonardo books, sacred geometry books, decoded painting books, and Jesus bloodline books. Like those far-left groups whose names offer reluctant proletarians every permutation of the words "worker," "social-ist," "revolutionary," "party," and "group," post-Templar titles seem almost invariably to include one or more of the following key terms: hid-den, secret, mystery, treasure, revelation, discovery, conspiracy, scroll, lost, Jesus, goddess, knights, quest, Messiah, unlocking, and legacy. You can make up your own. Several writers in the genre have managed to achieve publishing success that very few novelists and almost no histo-rian has enjoyed. They have sold books in the tens of thousands, have marketed follow-up audiotapes, videos, CD-ROMs, and DVDs. They have joined the lecture circuit, have appeared as apparent authorities on doz-ens of radio and TV shows, and have even been rewarded with the ulti-mate industry salute of having their original books republished in special deluxe or updated anniversary editions.

The accolade of most ubiquitous writer across conspiracy genres has been earned by an American, the "award-winning journalist and *New York Times* best-selling author" Jim Marrs, whose 2001 contribution to Templariana was titled *Rule by Secrecy: The Hidden History That Connects the Trilateral Commission, the Freemasons, and the Great Pyramids.* Marrs is also the author of *Crossfire: The Plot That Killed Kennedy,* a number of books on UFOs, and more recently, *The Terror Conspiracy,* about how the attacks of September 11, 2001, were probably an inside job, and *The Rise of the Fourth Reich: The Secret Societies That Threaten to Take Over America.* Here is a man who must think very deeply before taking a decision about whether to cross the road.

The New Scholarship of Lincoln, Baigent, and Leigh

Viewers of Henry Lincoln's three *Chronicle* programs and those who bought *The Holy Blood* largely because of what they'd seen on the television will have assumed, probably without thinking about it, that these were products of something like the usual scholarly process, just particularly exciting ones. They would not have doubted that the authors had used standard techniques of inquiry and research to establish the known facts, had weighed probabilities, had created hypotheses, and, as far as possible, tested these hypotheses. If Lincoln, Baigent, and Leigh had turned up such wonderful discoveries, it was due to luck or the particular quality of their explorations.

Of course, it was noticeable that the areas the trio delved into seemed more diverse than in more orthodox chronological or thematic histories. They were looking at aspects of the Bible, the early Church, Christian heresies, Freemasonry, anthropology, alchemy, Renaissance art, Middle Ages politics, and myths and legends. But as long as the authors held to the same general standards as other historians, this capacity to think widely was admirable.

The trouble is that the trio weren't holding themselves to those standards, or anything like them. Not only did Lincoln, Baigent, and Leigh claim to have discovered the Grail, they also claimed to have discovered a new form of historiography. Note a paragraph that appears early in the first chapter:

> It was necessary for us to synthesize in a coherent pattern data extending from the . . . Gospels and Grail romances to accounts of current affairs in modern newspapers . . . For such an undertaking the techniques of academic scholarship were sorely inadequate. To make the requisite connections between radically diverse bodies of subject matter we were

obliged to adopt a more comprehensive approach, based on synthesis rather than conventional analysis.[7]

It is easy to miss the significance of these lines on a first reading. You skim the passage perhaps, marking only key words (academic, techniques, analysis, scholarship) and pass on happily to treasure and Merovingians. Look at it again, however, with the attention Henry Lincoln gave to decoding de Sède's parchments. What do these sentences actually mean? Why exactly would the techniques of scholarship be inadequate? If the evidence was present to be able to make a decent hypothesis, then where was the problem?

The interesting word here, the one that stands out like Dagobert in a Sion document, is "requisite." Presumably, what made any particular connection "between radically diverse" subjects "requisite" can only have been the needs of the hypothesis; it was the authors' theories that required links to be made that normal standards of analysis weren't going to permit. So to provide these hookups, the authors abandoned scholarly methods of analysis, describing—with considerable chutzpah—their alternative method as "a more comprehensive approach."

This rationalization of an act of anti-scholarship was to be partly justified by the subject matter itself, since "much of what we were exploring lay in spheres deemed academically suspect." This is a tricksy psychological inversion of meaning, since the authors are really wanting to convey that potential critics are (in their word) "conventional." The implied image is of one type of narrow learning, belonging to fusty old academics or college pedants, versus another, far more exhilarating form of erudition. In this battle, Lincoln, Baigent, and Leigh are the new boys, the rebels. Like buccaneers they range wide, sailing free on the limitless seas of the past, unconstrained by the crabbed island existences of other scholars. They are cool, boasting, as they do, the historian's inquiring mind but, more important, the novelist's imaginative capacities. The novelist, they explain, is superior to the historian even when trespassing on the latter's field, because "he recognizes that history is not confined to the recorded facts, but often lies in more intangible domains . . . in the psychic lives of both individuals and entire peoples."[8]

Novelists have another obvious advantage over historians: facts don't really matter that much. They are imaginatively free. So *The Holy Blood* authors liberate themselves, where it is "requisite," from fact, but without ever quite admitting it. And their connecting technique is evident throughout every one of their books. Take this passage chosen, in a way that should surely please them, entirely at random—my copy of the book fell open at this page because it was next to the photos. We are near the beginning of chapter 13, "The Secret the Church Forbade." Speculation about Jesus, the authors are claiming, is necessary because there is a vacuum of real information. They continue:

> If Jesus was a legitimate claimant to the throne, it is probable that he was supported, at least initially, by a relatively small percentage of the population—his immediate family from Galilee, certain other members of his own aristocratic social class, and a few strategically placed representatives in Judea and the capital city, Jerusalem. Such a following, albeit distinguished, would hardly have been sufficient to ensure the realization of his objectives—the success of his bid for the throne. In consequence he would have been obliged to recruit a more substantial following from other classes—in the same way that Bonnie Prince Charlie, to pursue a previous analogy, did in 1745.[9]

One must admire that first "If," which is the keystone holding up what follows. Then we have "it is probable." Why is it "probable"? Why is he of the "aristocratic" class? Why a few "strategically placed" representatives? Why not many? Why not none? If it was many, then why not enough to realize his objectives? If. Probable. Would. Would. Each possibility is banked, turning into a probability upon which the next mini-hypothesis rests. The whole thing is like this, built brick by unreliable brick.

Such a technique, allied to (as Lincoln, Baigent, and Leigh would have it) the synthesizing of radically diverse subject matter into the requisite coherent pattern, creates a scholarship where absolutely anything is possible, granted first the authors' desire for it to be possible. Consider the section of *The Messianic Legacy* where they attempt to get a second wind out of the miasmic Priory of Sion. This body, they claim, has in modern times been operating in a murky sphere "where Christian Democratic parties of Europe, various movements dedicated to European unity, royalist cliques, neo-chivalric orders, freemasonic sects, the CIA, the Knights of Malta and the Vatican swirled together, pooled themselves temporarily for one or another specific purpose, then disengaged again."[10] One would like to have been present at a swirling involving, say, the CIA and the Knights of Malta on one side, and the Freemasons and the Vatican on the other.

The playful Henry Lincoln has also been fond of using the partiality and contradictory nature of New Testament interpretations to sanction his own liberties. Is it more likely, he asks, that a man should have been born of a virgin, been able to walk on water, and rise from the dead than that he should have been born as other men are born, married, and raised a family? It's a good line, but the trouble is that while the Gospels do create some evidence for a man called Jesus who led a religious movement in the early years of the Roman Empire, there is no evidence whatsoever from any source at all that that man might have been married or had children. None. And it's hard not to be amazed by Lincoln's own recollection, some years after *The Holy Blood*, of how the sacred Merovingian bloodline occurred to him and his colleagues. During a discussion, one of them remarked that there was something "fishy" about the Merovingians. And then, said Lincoln, "the penny dropped with an almighty clang!"[11] Merovingians, fishy. Fish, early Christian symbol. Early Christian symbol, Jesus. Jesus, Jesus's kids. Therefore, Merovingians, Jesus's kids. And this was "a book that cannot easily be dismissed" according to the Reverend Neville Cryer, then general director of the British and Foreign Bible Society.

The Grail Upturned,
the Blood Congealing

Even before discovering the real story of how *The Holy Blood and the Holy Grail*—and hence Dan Brown's fact box—came about, nitpickers and academic pedants were noticing some of the inconvenient improbabilities of the core story. Let's begin with the key proposition, that the bloodline of Jesus was safeguarded in the persons of the Merovingian kings and their descendants. A moment's pause should make us realize what an exhausting proposition this is. By the time the Jesus descendant married into the Merovingian house (four centuries and twelve generations after the supposed progeny of the Messiah first disembarked on the Riviera), there must have been thousands upon thousands of other Jesus descendants, or else we'd be talking about inbreeding that would make Pitcairn Island look like Piccadilly Circus. By now there would be millions of Jesus folk walking the earth, and yet, perversely, only one of them would be guarded by the Priory of Sion.

You can illustrate this point with reference to Elizabeth Windsor, who may trace her ancestry back to Edward the Confessor, but in the company of hundreds of thousands of others. At various times, the British monarchies have been fairly arbitrarily decided—by invasions, civil wars, coups, and revolutions—giving Scots, English, and Welsh the Normans, the Plantagenets, the Bruces, the Yorkists, the Tudors, the Stuarts, the House of Orange, the Hanoverians, and so on. Any branch of any of the alternatives would have thrown up, over time, a complete city's worth of claimants to the thrones. Whom would a Confessor-bloodline support group have chosen from among the stadia full of possibilities?

The next problem is that Pierre Plantard, the supposed descendant of Jesus at the time that Lincoln et al reached their sensational conclusion, while certainly claiming to be the heir to Dagobert II (and who wasn't?), never claimed to be a long-distance offspring of the Lamb of God. In fact, in 1983 he went to some lengths to disavow the claim made on his behalf by the questing Holy Blooders.

Third, the entire story of the Grail itself—cup, blood, and everything else—seems not to have existed before being invented in the late twelfth century by the poet Chrétien de Troyes. De Troyes, whose patron was Count Philip of Flanders, wrote *The Story of the Grail* as one of several knightly romances, and the popularity of the poem led to it being copied, altered, reedited, and retold over succeeding years. But, as the historian Richard Barber wrote, "In 1180, as far as we can tell, no one would have known anything of the 'holy thing' called the Grail."[12] The claim about the Sang Real, adds Barber, is based on a fifteenth-century English author's mistranslation from the original French.

Fourth, there was no secret about where Bérenger Saunière, the priest of Rennes-le-Château got his wealth from: for just under a decade, between 1896 and 1905, Saunière supplemented his Church stipend by selling masses, actively advertising his Mass-saying services in newspapers and taking payment in the form of postal orders. At one point, Saunière was receiving as many as 150 postal orders a day, often from religious communities and frequently from outside France. Despite this, he wasn't actually that rich: when he applied for a loan in 1913, he was assessed by a bank as being worth only 13,000 francs.

Fifth, the hollow Visigothic pillar in Saunière's church wherein lay the cryptic parchments is actually solid and unable to contain anything. Sixth, the tomb near Rennes supposedly depicted by Poussin was built in 1903 to mark the burial of the local landowner's wife and grandmother; the painting *The Shepherds of Arcadia* was completed 250 years earlier, somewhere between 1637 and 1639. There are many other objections, but six is enough.

You Knew It All Along

Things truly began to unravel, however, when people started to look into the life story of Jesus-descendant Pierre Plantard. In late 1940, when most of France was under occupation, a man signing himself Varran de Varestra wrote a letter from Paris to Marshal Pétain, the venerable head of state of the rump government of France in Vichy. The letter requested that Pétain do everything in his power to prevent the country being involved in further conflict. "You must," begged Varestra, "put an immediate stop to this terrible 'Masonic and Jewish' conspiracy in order to save both France and the world as a whole from terrible carnage," and added, "At present I have about a hundred reliable men under me who are devoted to our cause. They are ready to fight to the bitter end in response to your orders."[13]

Seven weeks later, a report for the French secretary of state for the interior stated that Varestra was "none other than PLANTARD, Pierre Athanase Marie, born in Paris on 18 March 1920 (7th), the son of Pierre and RAULO, Amélie Marie, of French nationality, a bachelor." Plantard senior, said the ministry report, had been a butler who had died after an accident at work, and Plantard junior now lived in a two-room apartment with his mother, whose small pension kept them both. It then detailed Plantard's youthful activities in setting up or running various groups, some of them avowedly anti-Semitic and anti-Masonic. His current organization, La Renovation Nationale Française, the official detailed laconically, "seems to be a 'phantom' group whose existence is purely a figment of the imagination of M. Plantard. Plantard claims 3,245 members, whereas this organization currently only has four members (the executive committee). It is worth noting that one member of this committee, Mme. Grubius, is the daughter of the concierge at 22 Place Malesherbes."[14] Then, "Plantard . . . seems to be one of those dotty, pretentious young men who run more or less fictitious groups in an effort to look important."[15]

The dotty Plantard turns up again in police records in 1954, which reveal that he was held by the Germans, who did not approve of secret societies, for four months in Fresnes prison toward the end of the war. In June 1956, the mayor of Annemasse in Haute-Savoie, where Plantard was now living, wrote a letter to a sub-prefect, referring to Plantard's imprisonment at the end of 1953 after being found guilty of offenses against property. Also in the summer of 1956, and also in Annemasse, the registration took place of a new organization—the Priory of Sion. Pierre

Plantard was one of the four founding signatories to the statutes of an organization pledged to "the defense of the rights and the freedom of low-cost housing." Thereafter the Priory fades even from recent history.

In January 1956, there was a series of stories in the French press, stories that originated with Noel Corbu, a restaurant proprietor in Rennes-le-Château who now owned the Saunière estate. Corbu may have been trying to get publicity for his rather isolated Hôtel de la Tour, which had opened the previous Easter, and his chosen method was to tell a wonderful tale of treasure and hollow columns. One headline to an interview in a local newspaper with Corbu read, "The Billionaire Priest of Rennes-le-Château's Fabulous Discovery."[16]

At some point in the next five or so years, Pierre Plantard went to Rennes and met Corbu. The Saunière fable captivated him; perhaps he also understood its value both financially and in creating a basis for his longtime fantasy of establishing his own importance. Whatever his motives, he set to work on writing a book about the treasure, incorporating new details such as the parchments supposedly found inside the Visigothic pillar, with their link to Dagobert II and the lost Merovingian line. His friend Philippe de Cherisey, a boozy but bright aristocrat, forged the parchments on Plantard's behalf, and these, along with a number of other manufactured documents, were placed by the pair in the Bibliothèque Nationale, where they might be discovered to give corroboration to Plantard's story.

Unfortunately, no publisher could be found who wanted to buy Plantard's book; perhaps it was too badly written. But Plantard did have one acquaintance, Gérard de Sède, who could turn a word. In 1967, de Sède's *L'Or de Rennes* appeared in print. The contract for the book included Philippe de Cherisey, entitling him to a share of what the book might earn. Extant from this period, there are dozens of letters exchanged between Plantard, de Cherisey, and de Sède detailing the progress of the hoax and discussing strategies for how to deal with the inevitable refutations of their stories.[17] One of the elaborations was to construct a history and a role for Plantard's fictitious Priory, and deposit that, too, in the

Bibliothèque Nationale. There it lay, awaiting discovery by Henry Lincoln, intrigued by the de Sède book, indulged by the BBC, and conned by the French hoaxers.

All this was revealed in 1983—so, not long after the publication of *The Holy Blood and the Holy Grail*—by Jean-Luc Chaumeil, a journalist on the fringe of the Priory hoaxers who still has the letters and a forty-four-page confession to forgery given to him by Philippe de Cherisey. Chaumeil's accusations were borne out in this country by researchers such as Paul Smith, Robert Richardson, and the BBC producer Henry Cran, who all did what the original *Chronicle* team so signally failed to do, and checked the Priory story out. Cran, in the BBC's 1996 *Timewatch* program "The History of a Mystery," even managed to trace the Plantard line back to the sixteenth century, where they found a peasant who grew walnuts.

It was all a hoax, every bit of it. It began with a story, which then developed into a massive fantasy, support for which was manufactured by forging documents. Many of these were lists of names copied from other genealogies and registers, and then tinkered with; others were invented travelogues. The motives of the participants varied. De Cherisey was interested in surrealism and in the 1960s was involved in an organization called the Workshop for Potential Literature (Oulipo), in which the members played around with puzzles, ciphers, and codes. Plantard, as we have seen, had been trying most of his life to give himself some significance through shadowy or secret organizations, joining the many people through the centuries who have been attracted to the idea of membership in a clandestine society with elite, and sometimes occult, powers to organize the world. Finally, there were those motivated simply by money.

And one can only imagine their enjoyment at playing Lincoln along, constructing a clue here, suggesting an answer there, and perhaps wondering how on earth their deception managed to keep the BBC man and his associates in programming for the best part of a decade. Eventually, however, even Plantard exhausted his capacity for invention, admitting under oath in the mid-1990s that the entire business had been a fraud.

When Plantard died in 2000, almost everyone who had followed the story knew that the world had just lost one of its more harmless and entertaining con artists. Everyone, that is, except Michael Baigent, Richard Leigh, and Dan Brown.

Plantard's Willing Victims

As for Henry Lincoln, in 2004 he told an interviewer that the late Pierre Plantard was so inscrutable and unreadable that he would have made a wonderful poker player. "In fact," he went on, almost vehemently, "we don't know anything about Bérenger Saunière the priest, we don't know anything about Pierre Plantard, we don't know anything about the Priory of Sion. We *know* almost nothing. That's the word. The demonstrable facts are very few. All the rest is hearsay evidence, guesswork, and interpretation. None of the books written, including my own, have any validity whatsoever."[18] Though his words are revealing, Lincoln was quite wrong. By the time he gave this interview, we knew a great deal. In fact, we knew categorically that the Priory didn't exist and that the documents were a con. But what we now want to know—for the purposes of this book—is whether the *Holy Blood* team were themselves the innocent (if materially enriched) victims of a hoax, or whether they effectively agreed to be deceived, or whether they were in some way complicit in the deception.

Chaumeil's own book exposing the Priory scam went to press after the last of the *Chronicle* programs in 1979 but before *The Holy Blood and the Holy Grail* appeared in 1982. Chaumeil told Channel 4 television that he had alerted the *Holy Blood* trinity to the fact of the scam up to a year before they completed their book. This allegation was subsequently put to Michael Baigent by the actor and TV historian Tony Robinson. Was it true? "I don't recall that," replied Baigent, adding, almost surreally, "but then Chaumeil was never necessarily very close to the inner groups of the Priory." Robinson persisted. How did Baigent respond to Chaumeil's revelation that the Priory was a surrealist fantasy?

> BAIGENT: He's wrong.
> ROBINSON: Why are you so sure that he's wrong?
> BAIGENT: Because I've seen the documents, I've researched them, I spent six years looking at the Priory and I'm satisfied that the Priory existed.[19]

Baigent's claim is, and always has been, that his team checked all the information it was given, and that, "in the end everything we could check proved accurate." This checking must, at the very least, have been carried out in the most forgiving way, since by 1993 everyone involved at the French end of the Priory had admitted that it and its documents were fraudulent. In the afterword to the 1996 edition of *The Holy Blood,* its authors argued that they "granted a novelist might fabricate a comparable precision. But M. Plantard had no aesthetic justification for doing so. Neither did he stand to gain financially or in any other way. In the absence of any plausible reason for fabrication, we had no reason to doubt his word."[20] In their inverted world, Leonardo and Jean Cocteau could easily be guarding the Merovingian bloodline, but Pierre Plantard really couldn't be an impostor.

They had an almost heroic way of fending off evidence of the Priory's real origins. This is how they put it in *The Messianic Legacy* published in 1987. One wonders if their counsel had read this passage before the Dan Brown trial.

> Nothing appeared straightforward; nothing could be taken at face value; everything had an alternative explanation. The Prieure de Sion had begun to seem to us like a holographic image, shifting prismatically according to the light and the angle from which it was viewed. From one perspective it appeared an influential, powerful and wealthy international secret society, whose members included eminent figures in the arts, in politics, in high

finance. From another perspective it seemed a dazzlingly ingenious hoax devised by a small group of individuals for obscure purposes of their own. Perhaps, in some fashion, it was both.[21]

And perhaps Lincoln, Baigent, and Leigh are, in some fashion, a group of Zulu women from the high veld. My instinct is that Baigent's background heavily influenced his thinking. His personal history suggests someone rejecting the Establishment of his childhood, looking for other spiritual keys to unlock the world and thinking, for a time at least, that he has discovered them. He was brought up in an intensely Catholic family in New Zealand, attending church three times a week and given private tuition in Catholic theology from the age of five. In partial rebellion, the young Baigent looked for his own answers, attending, in turn, "every Christian church in our town, including Methodist, Anglican, Presbyterian, and Mormon churches." At university, he changed from a science degree to comparative religion. He then joined a Christian Kabbalah group called the Builders of Adytum. By 1976, he was in London, sharing a flat in north London with Richard Leigh, through whom, as we've discovered, he was drawn into the Henry Lincoln *Chronicle* series. By then working as a photographer, Baigent sold his cameras and worked night shifts at a soft-drinks factory so that he could afford to be involved in the Priory research. "With hindsight," he said in his court deposition, "I became obsessed with it."[22]

Obsession occurs again in relation to Baigent. The skeptic Paul Smith visited him in Winchester in early 1993. "I found him very hospitable," wrote Smith, "courteous to talk with, but still believing in the Priory of Sion, in Merovingian Bloodlines existing to the present day, and his Line of David obsession was evident." Smith discovered that among Baigent's papers were several effectively proving the Saunière story was a myth. The problem was that this evidence, Smith thought, lay "in the possession of somebody who did not know how to use it properly because they preferred to pursue non sequiturs relating to pseudo-history."[23]

In short, arguably Baigent had looked the other way because he had found what he always wanted to find. He interpreted every bit of evidence in favor of his heart's desire and discounted every objection. In the mid-1990s, recalled Matthew d'Ancona, later editor of the *Spectator*, a lunch took place at L'Amico, a restaurant in central London. On one side was "a motley right-of-center bunch" all of whom were unhappy with Britain's being part of the European Union, and on the other a couple of "men who don't get out very much"—Baigent and Leigh. "What they wanted to know," said d'Ancona, "was this: had we Euroskeptics ever come across anything, well, peculiar? Did we ever get the strangest, tingly feeling that Europe's covert intention was not so much to . . . establish a federal superstate, but—for instance—to restore the bloodline of Jesus?" They were genuinely searching, he thought, for the Holy Blood and the Holy Directive.[24]

The overwhelming desire to believe is one explanation. But Henry Lincoln, one suspects, has probably known for many years that the Priory story is nonsense. Like *Doctor Who* or the *Curse of the Crimson Altar*, perhaps it was fun, and the money turned out to be even better. Or was it that, as a faux archaeologist, Lincoln achieved fame and popularity that even writing *Emergency Ward 10* had not provided? Or maybe he was simply entranced by a great story, and the historical truth of the matter was never as important to him? In one of his myriad post–*Da Vinci Code* appearances, Lincoln agreed that the Priory documents "are proof of absolutely nothing, beyond the fact that they have been written." In fact, all documents of all kinds, he says, are like this.[25] Nothing is better than anything else, and in history, as in novels, nothing is real, so there's nothing to get hung up about. Or is there?

The Hidden-Hand Redux

One of the great early figures of conspiracism was a nineteenth-century French priest, the Abbé Barruel. Appalled by the French Revolution, Barruel decided that Jacobinism, and indeed most of the ills of the world, were the product of a great, historic plot. For Barruel, as Norman Cohn put it, "A revolutionary conspiracy has existed down the ages, from Mani to the medieval Templars and thence to the Freemasons. As for the Jews, he believed them to have made common cause with the Templars."[26]

Readers of *The Holy Blood* have, in a reduced fashion, bought into Barruel's view of history. True, there is no blaming of the Jews in the work of Lincoln, Baigent, and Leigh; what there is instead is an adaptation, for their own purposes, of the *Protocols of the Elders of Zion*. The *Holy Blood* authors agree that the *Protocols*, "at least in their present form," are a forgery, and that their object was to incriminate the Jews, but—and it's obvious a "but" is coming—"The 1884 copy of the Protocols," the authors state, "surfaced in the hands of a member of the Masonic lodge." (This was, as we have seen, an allegation first made by "Gottfried zur Beek," in reality Captain Ludwig Müller von Hausen, in 1919, but for which there was no evidence whatsoever.)

Furthermore, according to Lincoln, Baigent, and Leigh, Maurice Joly, the originator of the dialogues on which the *Protocols* were partly based, "is said to have been a member of a Rose-Croix order."[27] Said by whom?

Then comes the point at which the authors have been driving. "Modern scholars have dismissed them as a total forgery . . . and yet the *Protocols* themselves argue strongly against such a conclusion." This is because there was an original text on which the *Protocols* were based, which was, they argue, authentic and issued from the Masons. This "may well have included a program for gaining power, for infiltrating Freemasonry."[28] As we've seen, Joly's original text was a satire on Napoleon III, and was crudely altered by Rachkovsky and his acolytes to fit the Jews instead. The idea that such an absurd plan for world domination actually existed, but for another group altogether, is really only slightly better than the original libel.

But the desire to "reclaim" the *Protocols* does reveal something about the eternal appeal of the hidden-hand theory—the idea that history is guided by secret organizations, whether for woe or weal. Like a joke or gossip, once you know what the secret is, not only do you hold the key to understanding but you can also pass the information on yourself, becoming the storyteller, the wise one.

A Brief History of Pseudo-Scholars

The first grand wizard of the Universal Order of Mass Pseudo-Scholarship may have been the psychiatrist Immanuel Velikovsky, whose "study" of the mythologies of China, India, Mesopotamia, and ancient Greece, as well as the Bible, led him to argue that the planet Venus had originated only 3,500 years ago. In the form of a huge comet, it had come close to earth, setting off a series of events that were recorded as catastrophes by the then inhabitants of the planet, including the Hebrews in Egypt, who experienced them as the various Mosaic plagues in the Book of Exodus. In 1950, Velikovsky had his theory ("about which I no longer have any doubt") published by Macmillan under the title of *Worlds in Collision*.

Velikovsky's technique was similar to that of the *Holy Blood* authors. He deployed evidence that favored his hypothesis, ignored anything that didn't, and accounted for the lack of specific records of the Venus comet by arguing that mankind had suffered from some kind of planetary repressed-memory syndrome. So, in a tone now familiar, he set down the nature of his task, which was "not unlike that faced by a psychoanalyst who, out of disassociated memories and dreams, reconstructs a forgotten traumatic experience in the early life of an individual."[29] By correctly reading the unconscious clues, he alone had found the truth.

Scientists hated *Worlds in Collision*, loathing its reduction of the achievements of astronomy to the half-baked interpreted neuroses of ancient Assyrians. What made things worse was that Velikovsky was lionized by the scientifically illiterate literary elite, who, according to the popular scientist Carl Sagan, placed the questing shrink on the same level as Einstein, Newton, Darwin, and Freud. Apparently, some scientists who published their works with Macmillan's textbook division threatened to take their books elsewhere, not wanting to be associated with Velikovsky's theories. As a result, Macmillan dropped the book and it was taken up by Doubleday, where it continued to sell remarkably well.

Velikovsky's successor—who was fifteen at the time of the publication of *Worlds in Collision*—was the Swiss hotelier and convicted fraudster Erich von Däniken. Living on money in most cases honestly earned by working in hotels and bars across Switzerland, the young von Däniken financed an interest in archaeology and visits to ancient sites. At Palenque, a site in the Chiapas province of Mexico inhabited by the Mayans between the fifth and ninth centuries A.D., von Däniken came across the tomb of King Pacal, inside the Temple of Inscriptions. First discovered in 1952, the tomb displays an unusual carving on the five-ton stone coffin lid. In the middle of it, wrote von Däniken,

> a being is sitting and leaning forward (like an astronaut in his command module). This strange being wears a helmet from which twin tubes run backward. In front of his nose is an oxygen apparatus. The figure is manipulating some kind of controls with both hands. The fingers of the upper hand are arranged as if the being was making a delicate adjustment to a knob in front of him. We can see four fingers of the lower hand which has its back to us. The little finger is crooked. Doesn't it look as if the being was working a control such as the hand-throttle of a motorbike? The heel of the left foot rests on a pedal with several steps.[30]

And if that's what it looked like, reasoned von Däniken, then that's what it was. This then was evidence for what he called "paleo-contact": aliens had landed on Earth thousands of years ago, amazed men with their extraordinary technology, and simultaneously given rise to the great civilizations of the world. Other traces of the extraterrestrials were to be discerned at Stonehenge, on Easter Island, and in a ship-borne navigation aid found off the coast of Greece.

Von Däniken's odd manuscript did not attract publishers, and he received twenty-two rejections, with one describing his work as "emotional ramblings." Only when the book was rewritten with the (very terrestrial) help of a sci-fi author and promoted as archaeology did *Chariots of the Gods? Unsolved Mysteries of the Past* find a publisher. And a lucky publisher at that. Brought out in 1967, it was a phenomenal success. Even an awkward interruption of three years in prison for tax fraud and embezzlement did the author's sales no harm. In his Landsberg, von Däniken completed a second book, *Return of the Gods*, and by the time he emerged from jail in 1971 (his conviction was subsequently overturned), he had sold 2.5 million copies of both books in at least twenty languages. Today, enjoying the sobriquet "the most successful nonfiction writer in history," von Däniken has published a Trollopian twenty-six books on paleo-contact, been translated into thirty-two languages, and sold sixty-three million copies.

Inevitably, his theory was disputed from the first day of its appearance. Von Däniken reacted to criticism in the usual way: the Establishment was out to get him, but he wouldn't be got. "Even if a reactionary army tries to dam up this new intellectual flood," he told readers, "a new world must be conquered in the teeth of all the unteachable in the name of truth and reality." And then he commended both himself and his fans: "It took courage to write this book," he said, "and it will take courage to read it."[31] It isn't clear whether more or less bravery was required to watch von Däniken's theories on television—as tens of millions have, especially in America and in Germany. As recently as 1996, the network RTL showed a film made by ABC in America, which was seen by nearly eight million viewers.

But extraterrestrialism was yesterday's thrill by the mid-1980s. The moon landings were becoming a memory, space was no longer quite so glamorous, a decade of UFOlogy had led to the Roswell autopsy hoax, and Steven Spielberg had moved on to other things. Even with von Däniken still alive, his seal and sepulcher passed into the hands of British writer Graham Hancock.

Hancock, who became the archetypal practitioner of the book-TV-book-DVD cycle, is a sociologist by training. He worked as a journalist on several mainstream British newspapers and was something of a specialist on Africa and poverty, writing several books on international aid from rich countries to poor. And then in 1987, according to him, he had a revelation in Chartres Cathedral, which eventually led him to write his own *Holy Blood*–style work of pseudo-history. "Following obscure clues found within ancient stories and biblical tales," explains his publisher, "through the occult knowledge gleaned from the coded Grail epic of Wolfram von Eschenbach, and the obscure and secretive workings of the enigmatic Knights Templar, [he] traces the Ark from its source in ancient Egypt, to Jerusalem, and from there to its final resting place in Africa."[32] Two uses of "obscure" in one sentence should be a bad sign, but when *The Sign and the Seal* appeared in 1992, unlike his earlier works on Africa, it was a bestseller.

Hancock's big triumph was yet to come. By 1995, he had evolved a theory that was rather larger than anything about Templars, however enigmatic. He had decided that his observations of ancient cultures pointed in one direction: 10,500 years ago there was a supercivilization of superterrestrials who built the Sphinx and passed on their knowledge to the Egyptians, who came along some 6,000 years later. "If I'm right," said Hancock, "and our whole conception of prehistory is wrong, then the foundations upon which we have built our idea of what our society is are crumbling."[33] Three million copies of the resulting book, *Fingerprints of the Gods*, have been bought worldwide.

Hancock has variously theorized that Atlantis was actually Antarctica, inhabited before the ice covered it, and that there are formations on Mars that also suggest the activities of ancient civilizations. In a more recent book, *Supernatural*, he promises to answer such questions as "Why did Nobel Prize–winner Francis Crick keep concealed until his death the astonishing circumstances under which he first 'saw' the double-helix structure of DNA? And why did he become convinced that the DNA molecule did not evolve naturally upon this planet but was sent here in bacteria by an alien civilization?"[34]

I don't know. Drugs, perhaps? But skepticism has not been universal. Hancock's books have been described as "persuasive and scholarly" by the *Observer*, as containing "an elegant theory that reads like a detective story" by the *Daily Mail*, and as representing "a discovery about the pyramids that could change our whole view of human history" by the London *Evening Standard*. Hancock's work has been expensively filmed and given prime-time airing on the BBC and Channel 4 in Britain, and his lecture tours of America have been hugely successful. Millions have watched, millions have read, millions have bought.

A quick look through Hancock's Amazon reviews shows how few purchasers seem inclined to doubt Hancock's "research," but those few who do track down his claims discover basic errors in archaeology and astronomy. One American, writing about attending a Hancock illustrated lecture in the mid-1990s, comments on the author's claim that the Gateway of the Sun at Tiahuanaco in Bolivia contains a carving of an elephant. Hancock's point was that the gateway dated from around the sixth century A.D., while elephants had been extinct in Bolivia since the eleventh century B.C. The American gentleman points out, perhaps with British humor, "This is a carving of a parrot . . . Of course, someone could respond: 'Well, you think it looks like a parrot because that's what you want to see.' Fair enough. But what's more likely, that it's an incongruous, extinct elephant carving from 10,000 years ago or a more recent carving of an existing, common indigenous species?"[35]

At the end of 1999, two BBC *Horizon* programs demolished Hancock comprehensively. They showed that the best archaeological evidence was that civilizations had developed incrementally and individually and did not derive from a common source. They also showed that Hancock's claims about the astronomical positioning of the Pyramids to reflect the night sky in 10,500 B.C. could also be applied to twentieth-century Manhattan, so was he saying that the super-ancients were somehow influencing the architects and planners of the modern era?

The BBC giveth ground to the pseudo-historians, and sometime later taketh it away.

And a Byway: Schonfield and the Bible

When it comes to Bible studies, an area where facts are even harder to ascertain, the door is wide open for far-out theories. One strand was begun in 1965 by Dr. Hugh J. Schonfield, a British academic and Bible scholar. *The Passover Plot* consists of the extended hypothesis that Jesus engineered his own arrest and crucifixion in order to fulfill the Jewish prophecy about the Messiah, but that he had an elaborate plan for survival, which would be sold as a resurrection. "These things had to come about," wrote Schonfield, "in the manner predicted by the Scriptures and after preliminaries entailing the most careful scheming and plotting to produce them . . . A conspiracy had to be organized of which the victim was himself the deliberate secret instigator. It was . . . the outcome of the frightening logic of a sick mind, or of a genius."[36]

Almost all went to plan: Jesus set Judas up to betray him, and events took their intended course. Jesus knew that crucifixion was a slow death and swallowed a special potion to make it look as though he had expired more quickly than usual, so that he would be cut down still alive. He and others had arranged a tomb "conveniently placed" on Joseph of Arimathea's land, to which he would be taken off and revived, making it clear to all that he was indeed the Chosen One. Unfortunately, a Roman soldier, in an uncharacteristic and unlucky moment of compassion, decided to speed Jesus' end by thrusting a spear in the suffering man's side. After that the disciples spirited the body away and made the rest up as though nothing had gone wrong. Ironically, Christianity survived; Christ didn't. Schonfield's book (a bestseller, need I say) reminded people how disputed much of New Testament history really was. A whole variety of speculations and theories on the story of Jesus followed. Was he black? Was he gay? Was he a she? Did he really die? And so on.

With sections of the established Church still professing to believe in saints, miracles, and manifestations, in the liquefying of sacred blood and the transubstantiation of comestible items, such theories seemed no more far-fetched. But while Schonfield genuinely was a scholar, some of those who came later have made their lesser learning go much further. Particularly threatening was the promise, made as this chapter was being researched, that the British duo of Lynn Picknett and Clive Prince were finishing a book called *The Masks of Christ*, for which the advance publicity read, "As the phenomenal sales of *The Da Vinci Code* continue to fuel a growing global appetite for questioning the old certainties and assumptions about Christianity and what it says about its founder, never has there been a more perfect time to launch *The Masks of Christ.*"

Lynn Picknett and Clive Prince have enjoyed several perfect times. Their slightly disturbing hair has graced just about every documentary made on the subjects of the secret Leonardo, the mysterious Templars, and the hidden wife of Christ in the last decade, and they have an impressive publishing record. Between them, they have managed *The Templar Revelation, The Sion Revelation, The Stargate Conspiracy, Mary Magdalene: Christianity's Hidden Goddess,* and *Turin Shroud: How Leonardo da Vinci Fooled History.* Published in 2006, *The Sion Revelation* is a particularly adept bit of sophistry, succeeding as it does in turning the proof of Plantard's hoax on its head. True, say P & P, the Sion skeptics "do undoubtedly have the weight of evidence on their side," but it isn't as simple as that, because the hoax was "as intricate a hoax as any in history" and therefore presumably beyond the resources of a group of French con men. So we should be careful before we decide to consign the story to the big Book of Swindles, and wary lest "the evidence that the Priory has lied, ever, on any subject—automatically means that it can be dismissed out of hand."[37]

In fact, the evidence is that those who invented the Priory lied all the time and on every subject. You can see, however, where this is going. The Priory was a front for other shadowy forces—Freemasons, French nationalists, Francoists—and Prince and Picknett have discovered the real conspiracy behind the false conspiracy, so that just when you thought it was safe to go back into the bookshops, they manage to cobble together another possible bestseller out of the discarded carcasses of the old ones. And here I cannot forgo the pleasure of pointing out the error that appears on the cover of their book. Under "Praise for Picknett and Prince," you may read: "'Astonishing, gruesome, shocking and sensational'—*Washington Post*." On their website, however, we discover—among comments about their book suggesting that Leonardo painted the Turin Shroud—the full quote, except it's from the *Washington Times*: "This is a book to which all the tabloid adjectives truly apply. It really is astonishing, gruesome, shocking and sensational. It even appears to be true." The *Washington Post* is, of course, a very different publication, an altogether more serious animal than the *Washington Times*. It is, one feels, a mistake that was unlikely to have been made the other way around.

The Anti-Stratfordians

Some of the theories discussed in this book have had disastrous consequences. You can't say that about Templariana. No one has been killed seeking the Priory of Sion, though one may live in hope. There is a certain soft violence inflicted upon the idea of scholarship, but the only real damage done is that people might have been reading better books or, more questionably, watching better television.

There is, however, a psychological or anthropological question to be answered about our consumption of pseudo-history and pseudoscience. I have now plowed through enough of these books to be able to state that, as a genre, they are badly written and, in their anxiety to establish their dubious neo-scholarly credentials, incredibly tedious. So, if we're not reading them for the prose, why are we? Why do we read bad history books that have the added lack of distinction of not being in any way true or useful, and not buy in anything like the same numbers history books that are often far better written and much more likely to give us an understanding of who we are and where we came from?

In one of the best of the several dozen books seeking to explain the success of *The Da Vinci Code*, Dan Burnstein speculates that the Dan Brown phenomenon owes a great deal to the author's erudition and his cerebral ambition. "Our culture," wrote Mr. Burnstein, meaning, I think, the United States, "is hungry for the opportunity to feed the collective mind with something other than intellectual junk food . . . All too few are writing novels that deal with big philosophical, cosmological or historical concepts."[38] In fact, there are plenty of novels being written which are stuffed to the bindings with those three -icals and more. But however hungry the culture might be for them, the paradox is that no one much wants to buy these books. The appeal surely lies elsewhere, and Mr. Burnstein has a second stab at locating it. Elevating *The Da Vinci Code* high above its station as a mere thriller full of characters with unconvincing, daft names, Burnstein connects it with the jittery zeitgeist. The book resonates with readers because, in a way, it's true:

> The modern American church concealed heinous cases of sexual abuse for years; the president of the United States may have launched an invasion of a foreign country based on concocted evidence of weapons of mass destruction; executives of companies like Enron and WorldCom deceived shareholders and regulators about billions and billions of nonexistent value. One can't read *The Da Vinci Code* without hearing the echoes of these contemporary incidents of lying and cover-up—and the truth coming out in the end.[39]

The albino monks and Priory grand masters may be far-fetched, but the idea that the authorities are hiding the truth from us, manipulating us to believe that fact is fiction and are, in reality, doing what Sir Leigh Teabing is doing fictionally, is apparently all too believable.

Perhaps. There is also the element of fashion and genuine interest. Eco's 1982 medieval thriller *The Name of the Rose* was set in the world of heresy and early science of the Middle Ages. At the same time, the Cathars were becoming a popular subject for historical research. Books appeared about the Templars, the Bogomils, with Gnosticism and Manichaeanism. In 1957, Norman Cohn's *The Pursuit of the Millennium* examined medieval mystical sects, and in 1971, Keith Thomas published *Religion and the Decline of*

Magic, on the transition in Europe from magical and folkloric practices to formal religion and science. There was a weird world out there, which had run in parallel to what was depicted in the usual histories, in the same way as there was more to be said about women in history or the precolonial histories of America, Africa, and Asia. Novelistic treatments of subjects like these can create a painless entry point into more complex study.

There is also the playfulness associated with breaking codes and solving puzzles, from the silent clues supposedly offered by architecture and paintings to the Enigma code and Sudoku. Finally, there is the seductiveness and the romance of believing in the possibility of hidden treasure, of "wonderful things" to be seen through a sudden hole in the rock face, of the Lost World and Shangri-La.

In Umberto Eco's spoof novel of the faux-archaeological genre, *Foucault's Pendulum*, the worldly publisher Signor Garamond says to his employees, "It's a gold mine, alright. I realized that these people will gobble up anything that's hermetic, as you put it, anything that says the opposite of what they read in their books in school. I see this as a cultural duty: I'm no philanthropist, but in these dark times to offer someone a faith, a glimpse into the beyond."[40] Signor Garamond knows he has to give his buyers "anything that says the opposite of what they read in their books in school." That way, when they have read his magical nonsense, they will think they know more than those who instructed them.

It's a theme taken up by the American playwright and screenwriter/director David Mamet. In his short book *Three Uses of the Knife: On the Nature and Purpose of Drama*, Mamet throws a dart at those writers who over the years have decided to argue that the hidden truth is that Shakespeare didn't write Shakespeare's plays. This denial Mamet calls anti-Stratfordianism. The purpose of the writers, and by extension the purpose of their readers, is somehow to make themselves greater than even the greatest poet, partly, of course, by making him lesser. In this, says Mamet,

> they invert the megalomaniacal equation and make themselves not the
> elect, but the superior of the elect . . . They . . . consign the (falsely named)

creator to oblivion and turn to the adulation of the crowd for their deed of discovery and insight . . . They appoint themselves as "eternity"—the force that shall pass on all things . . . The anti-Stratfordian, like the flat-earther and the creationist, elects himself God—possessed of the power to supervene in the natural order—and the most deeply hidden but pervasive fantasy of the above is the ultimate delusion of godhead: *I* made the world.[41]

They also understand what everybody else doesn't, what everybody else would most like to deny. They are the lonely custodians of the truth, and they got there through the quality of their minds—and by being brave enough to read a book.

7. A FEW CLICKS OF A MOUSE

We have become entranced by demonic power, so focused on lust for wealth and control that almost anything becomes possible.

—DAVID RAY GRIFFIN, AMERICAN THEOLOGIAN[1]

Friends House is a square building in the neoclassical style, built in 1927, whose stone has become so engrimed by the passage of traffic down the busy Euston Road that you can no longer tell what color it once was. For decades, its large hall, let out by the Quakers for next to no charge, has provided the venue for lost or unfashionable causes. The room is paneled, with tiered seating and a high stage at the end, upon which—on a mild day in early summer 2005—there is a high screen showing tropical fish swimming in a large tank, edited to a relaxation-therapy soundtrack. For a moment, I think I have come to the wrong fringe meeting, a discussion of homeopathy and ley lines perhaps, instead of the gathering billed to rail against the cover-up of the capitalized Truth of what happened in New York on September 11, 2001.

When the fish swim off, the music dies and the lights go down, the hippie feel is heightened by the fact that our host is the actress Susannah York, most famous as an open-faced flower-power girl movie star in the late sixties and early seventies. Now short-haired, York is still beautiful, but her manner, far from thespian, is hesitant and vague. "What is the truth about 9/11?" she asks us, though most of the audience seem to have a good idea. Apparently, whatever this truth is, it is being hidden from us, because, according to York, it is "increasingly the norm to prevent the people from knowing what's going on." She then goes on to suggest that cover-ups have been consistently deployed over time, listing a series of historical events that might have been taken from the *Ladybird Book of Conspiracies* under "Plots to Get Us into War." Her timeline starts in 1898, with the sinking in Havana harbor of the USS *Maine*. Then she cites 1941 and Pearl Harbor, a "subtly engineered ploy by Roosevelt," followed by the 1964 Gulf of Tonkin incident, in which President Lyndon Johnson used an alleged attack on a U.S. destroyer as a pretext to begin the bombing of North Vietnam, thus providing much fodder for conspiracy theorists. All of this culminates in 9/11, when the Pentagon "wanted a new evil empire to justify their expansionist policies."

York's job is to introduce the other speakers, who include veteran conspiracy theorist Lisa Pease, described as a "lifelong information activist"; Canadian Barrie Zwicker, "author and media critic"; and Webster G. Tarpley, writer of a book on "the role of Prescott Bush in the rise of Hitler." There is also in the audience a special guest star, David Shayler, "former counterterrorist staffer with MI5." It is a prototypical panel for a 9/11 Truth event, missing only an academic, though Zwicker has been a visiting professor in his time. The speakers seem to suit the audience of four hundred mostly white, middle-class Britons, dressed in their most casual clothes, some sporting The Who and eco T-shirts.

First up is Lisa Pease. An American in middle-middle age, Pease puts 9/11 into an almost personal historical context: "The government has been trying to sell us a pack of lies," she insists, "since I was born." She is followed by fellow American Tarpley, a wide, shiny sixty-year-old, bald and slick, who possesses the menacing amiability of a big-tent evangelist smilingly consigning sinners to eternal torment. "My new book," he tells us, reveals how 9/11 was "an own goal by a faction within the intelligence community . . . A faction that has been around for a hundred years. The Secret Team. The Invisible Connection. The Parallel Network."

What is arresting about Tarpley is his absolute contempt for the very idea that Islamist fanatics could have been in any way responsible for the attacks on the Twin Towers and the Pentagon. This version is, he emphasizes, "One of the most absurd stories of all time . . . an insult to your intelligence!" He doesn't so much argue with the notion as seek to annihilate it. The Arab hijackers were "patsies, dupes, useful idiots, fanatics, police agents, Oswalds." And just as Oswald "did not have the physical ability to shoot the shots," so the nineteen Arabs "did not have the ability to do what they were accused of." Mohamed Atta, the Egyptian generally thought to be the hijackers' leader, was clearly a "double agent." What kind of life, after all, demands Tarpley, was that for a good Muslim boy? "Cocaine, prostitutes, the Beastie Boys." (At this, the girl in front of me laughs at the wonderful absurdity of anyone thinking that Atta was a genuine jihadi.) No, in Tarpley's view, 9/11 was "state-sponsored false-flag terrorism," which is the true threat to democracy and liberty, whereas the Islamist threat is the purest of confections. "Terrorism," declares Tarpley, "is the myth of the twenty-first century." And as for the Twin Towers, "The 9/11 myth is the way George Bush controls America."

This assertion receives some support from the last panel speaker, David Shayler. Shayler's time with MI5 lends him an authenticity denied to Tarpley, and allows him to use phrases such as "I stand here as a personal witness" and sound credible, even though, rather than the field agent that some of those present may imagine him to have been, Shayler was actually a desk operative. His view is that 9/11 was the "first attempt at a new Pearl Harbor." Then Shayler makes one of the distinctions that are increasingly important in the growing 9/11 Truth movement. "I used to think they let it happen," he says, and pauses. "I have come to believe, with my counterterrorist hat on, that they made it happen." This conversion earns Shayler applause, because it marks his transition from the less full-on let-it-happen-on-purpose (LIHOP) position to the more full-hearted made-it-happen-on-purpose (MIHOP). The acclamation dies down, and then is renewed when Shayler tells us, "We are, in fact, looking at a coup d'état."

The Power of Conspiracy

The Internet has created shadow armies whose size and power are unknowable. Cyberspace communities of semi-anonymous and occasionally self-invented individuals have grown up, some of them permitting contact between people who in previous times might have thought each other's interests impossibly exotic or even mad. At the same time, the democratic quality of the Net has permitted the release of a mass of undifferentiated information, some of it authoritative, some speculative, some absurd. But increasingly, material originating on the Net has turned up in popular culture—a millennial version of the word-of-mouth route to popularity. The online encyclopedia Wikipedia has, at the time of writing, become a first resource for many students, despite the amusing randomness of its reliability.

Around the time of the Friends House meeting, dozens, perhaps hundreds, of English-language websites were springing up specifically devoted to proselytizing for the 9/11 Truth movement. In addition, many "independent" or "alternative" media sites routinely replicated 9/11 conspiracy material uncritically, and many of these sites linked to or cited each other. And then there were the thousands of bloggers who had 9/11 conspiracy constructions as part of their individual cyber-*Weltanschauungen*. How many individuals were represented by these sites, contributed to them, or, indeed, read them was conjectural in the absence of any substantial study. What was obvious, however, was that sites endorsing 9/11 conspiracy theories, and those subscribing to them in passing, far outnumbered sites devoted to debunking or refuting such theories.

The Internet has also allowed the construction and circulation of audio and visual material devoted to 9/11 revisionism. Cheap movies, often made using material not cleared for copyright, made and narrated by nonprofessional filmmakers, have been posted on Google video, YouTube, and other sites specializing in moving pictures. Invariably, such items make the same claims to accuracy and balance as do mainstream

TV programs, but have been concocted with the smallest fraction of research and resource, though no little ingenuity.

The collision of new media with the 9/11 movement created new, young celebrities. In 2005, a video coproduced by three friends in upstate New York became one of the most popular items on the Web. Dylan Avery had begun "researching" 9/11 at the age of eighteen. "I found an article [on the Internet] on the World Trade Center," he told *Vanity Fair* magazine. "Someone had posted a picture of a controlled demolition and then a picture of the World Trade Center collapsing. And I was like, wow, OK. And then you find one article and that article links to ten others, and before you know it you're up until six in the morning. It's crazy, the information takes over."[2]

Avery's Net-inspired film ran eighty minutes, was made in contemporary pop-video style with quick edits and short interviews, and was boosted by a lively soundtrack contributed by his friends. *Loose Change* claimed to be an examination of the WTC and Pentagon attacks in the light of the official investigation by the 9/11 Commission, and over the course of a year competed with some of the Web's most celebrated videos—the comedian who was rude to the president, the chubby teenager singing along to a Romanian pop tune. By May of 2006, *Loose Change* had, in part or in its entirety, been viewed some ten million times. "We beat the woman getting punched in the face," Avery told *Vanity Fair*. "We beat the guy who beats his computer with his keyboard," added his coproducer. "The viral videos," said his researcher, "we dominate them."[3]

Radio coverage of their film soon meant Avery and team being invited to address college meetings all over America. Their objective in spreading the 9/11 word, they claimed, was just to get the truth out there, and certainly they seemed to have no discernible political ideology aside from a pleasure in making waves. Avery gleefully predicted a second American Revolution when people fully understood it was the U.S. government itself that had brought down the Twin Towers. "The shit is gonna hit the fan. People are going to be upset. You can't stop it. People say, Aw, we need a peaceful revolution. We need to peacefully change things. Trust me, that's a great idea—I'm all for it. But Americans are violent, especially when they've been lied to, especially over something like this . . . So many people have just got—fucked. It's the only way to put it."[4]

And a lot of people were indeed getting upset, or at least preparing to be upset. In 2003, a third of young Germans, for instance, were of the view that the attack was an inside job. In August 2004, a poll conducted by the Zogby opinion research company found nearly two-thirds of New Yorkers under thirty agreeing with the proposition that the administration "knew in advance that attacks were planned on or around September 11, 2001, and that they consciously failed to act." Two years later, another Zogby poll found 42 percent of all Americans believing that there had been some kind of cover-up and that the authorities, both the government and the 9/11 Commission, had "concealed or refused to investigate critical evidence that contradicts their official explanation of the September 11th attacks." A Scripps Howard poll of July 2006 (which measured belief in a Kennedy conspiracy at 40 percent) had 36 percent of respondents suspecting government participation of some kind in the attacks, with just over one in six believing that explosives had been used to bring down the Twin Towers. These beliefs were particularly prevalent among younger respondents, Democrat voters, the less educated, and racial and ethnic minorities.[5]

Little by little, the idea of a 9/11 conspiracy leached into the mainstream. In March 2006, Charlie Sheen became the first Hollywood star to declare himself a supporter of the Truth movement. His doubts, he told a radio host, had begun on the day of the attacks, watching coverage of the planes flying into the World Trade Center. "It just didn't look like any commercial jetliner I've flown on any time in my life and then when the buildings came down later on that day I said to my brother, 'Call me insane, but did it sorta look like those buildings came down in a controlled demolition?' "[6] In September 2006, on the fifth anniversary of the 9/11 attacks, the cult film director David Lynch, when asked about *Loose Change* in an interview on Dutch television, said that it wasn't necessary to believe everything in Avery's documentary to still have significant doubts about the generally accepted (or official) version of events.

"You look back," said Lynch, "and you remember what you saw, and what you were told, and now, you have questions."[7] That same week, James Brolin, the actor husband of Hollywood and music legend Barbra Streisand, interviewed on the ABC show *The View*, had urged the program's audience to look at a 9/11 Truth website.

"Mobile Phones Don't Work from Altitude, Simple as That"

It was early 2006, and I was writing a piece in Florida, and I found myself, along with others, having a salad lunch with Bob, a very young-looking sixty-year-old who had made his money in property and retired early. When the subject of 9/11 came up, Bob was all over it like a lurching puppy. He was certain that 9/11 was a conspiracy by the government, and what made him certain, the magic bullet, were the mobile phone calls from the flights. It was scientifically impossible, said Bob, for a mobile phone call to be made from an airplane once it was in the sky. There had been studies; there was a report by a leading professor; there had been attempts to replicate the circumstances of mobile calls; and all had concluded that it couldn't be done.

The 9/11 Commission report (the official "official" version) contained details of a number of calls made between passengers and crew on the hijacked planes and people on the ground. The accounts given in these calls were critical in determining the means by which the hijackers had taken over the planes and in suggesting what weapons they had used or had access to. They included a call made by Peter Burton Hanson to his father, Lee, in Connecticut from United Flight 175 from Boston to Los Angeles at 8:52 a.m. Hanson told his father that hijackers might have taken over the cockpit, adding, "An attendant has been stabbed, and someone else up front may have been killed." Seven minutes later, on the same flight, a male attendant spoke to the United Airlines office in San

Francisco and said that the plane had been hijacked, another attendant had been stabbed and both pilots killed, and that he thought the hijackers were flying the plane. At 8:59 a.m., Brian Sweeney called his mother, Louise Sweeney, and said that the passengers were thinking of storming the cockpit. A minute later, Lee Hanson got another call from his son: "It's getting bad, Dad. A stewardess was stabbed. They seem to have knives and Mace. They said they have a bomb. The plane is making jerky movements. I don't think the pilot is flying the plane. I think we are going down. Don't worry, Dad, if it happens, it'll be very fast. My God, my God." At 9:03 a.m., the Commission reported, both Lee Hanson and Louise Sweeney saw on their TVs an aircraft slam into the South Tower of the World Trade Center. It was carrying their children.

Or so the world believed—as it believed that Betty Ong, flight attendant on AA11, the plane that hit the North Tower, called American Airlines and was speaking to a supervisor in Reservations, Lydia Gonzalez, as the aircraft headed across the water toward lower Manhattan. On the same flight was attendant Madeline Sweeney, whose last words to colleagues on the ground were: "I see the water. I see the building. I see buildings . . . Oh my God!" Most famous were the calls made by the dozen passengers and crew from Flight 93, who spoke to relatives, colleagues, and emergency services. From these conversations, it was concluded that they had rushed the cockpit.

Naturally, when Bob told us around that Miami table that all these calls were impossible, we were in no position to contradict him. I had certainly never tried to make a call on my mobile from altitude, nor had the other three at lunch that day. It's probable that Bob's information originated in a "study" carried out by Professor A. K. Dewdney of the University of Western Ontario in Canada, a longtime contributor to *Scientific American* magazine. This exercise consisted of him boarding planes and making a large number of calls at various altitudes, from which he concluded that mobile phones were altogether useless at altitudes above eight thousand feet and pretty much useless below that level.

If this were true, then how might one account for the parents who say they spoke to their children, the ground staff who were audio witnesses

to their colleagues' last moments, or the widely available recording of
Betty Ong's dialogue with Lydia Gonzalez? They would have to have
been manufactured, as charged by Dylan Avery in *Loose Change*. "For
starters," he argued, "the calls themselves are extremely peculiar. Most
of them are only a couple of sentences long, before the callers end the
conversation, only to call back later." Betty Ong did not sound to him
like a woman on a hijacked plane who had just witnessed several murders should sound. "Why is nobody in the background screaming?"
he demanded. As to Madeline Sweeney's call, Avery was contemptuous.
"'I see buildings. Water. Oh my God!' Madeline was a flight attendant out
of Boston for twelve years. I think she would have recognized Manhattan.
The cell phone calls were fake. No question about it."[8]

One fairly obvious problem with judging the provenance of the calls is
that many of them seem to have been made through the Airfone service
but were reported, usually in the early days after 9/11, as having been cell
phone calls. Reporters may not have been aware of the difference, and
those receiving the calls were hardly likely to have made the distinction.
Even so, mobile use at altitude is, in fact, possible. According to Marco
Thompson, president of the San Diego Telecom Council, if a plane is slow
and flying over a city, mobiles in it will work to an altitude of around
ten thousand feet. Even at thirty thousand feet, a cell phone "may work
momentarily while near a cell site, but it's chancy and the connection
won't last."[9] Other mobile service providers concur with Thompson.

Anecdotally, there are plenty of examples of people who have successfully used their mobiles on planes, or who have witnessed other people
doing so. But at least as relevant is a piece of research carried out in 2004,
into the possible dangers of the use of mobiles and other emitting elec-
tronic devices on aircraft. On the incidence of use, the authors revealed,
"Our research shows clearly that, in violation of FCC and FAA rules, calls
are regularly made from commercial aircraft. Results from our analysis
imply that calls from on board scheduled commercial aircraft in the eastern United States occur at a rate of one to four per flight." The research,
using specialized equipment, was carried out by Bill Strauss, an expert

in aircraft electromagnetic compatibility; M. Granger Morgan, head of Carnegie Mellon's department of engineering and public policy and a professor in the department of electrical and computer engineering; Jay Apt, professor in the department of engineering and public policy; and Daniel D. Stancil, professor in Carnegie Mellon's department of electrical and computer engineering.[10] Bob's likely source, Alexander Keewatin Dewdney, is, by contrast, not an engineer or an expert in electronics; he describes himself as "a mathematician, environmental scientist, and author of books on diverse subjects," though he was the coordinator of a group calling itself the Scientific Panel Investigating Nine-Eleven.

A convert to Islam in the mid-1970s, Dewdney has written extensively on the near impossibility of Muslims' being involved in suicide bombings, and to support this view evolved a detailed hypothesis—which he named Operation Pearl—as to what had really happened on September 11, 2001. For people who found the long version of this scenario "too convoluted to understand" or had "a slight comprehension problem," Dewdney devised this synopsis:

> Four commercial passenger jets (American Airlines Flights 11 and 77 and United Airlines Flights 93 and 175) take off and shortly after the pilots are ordered to land at a designated airport with a military presence. Two previously prepared planes (one a Boeing 767, painted up to look like a United Airlines jet and loaded with extra jet fuel) take off and are flown by remote control to intercept the flight paths of AA 11 and UA 175 so as to deceive the air traffic controllers. These (substituted) jets then fly toward Manhattan; the first crashes into the North Tower and (eighteen minutes later) the second crashes into the South Tower. A fighter jet (under remote control), or a cruise missile, crashes into the Pentagon. Back at the airport the (innocent) passengers from three of the Boeings are transferred to the fourth (UA 93). This plane takes off, flies toward Washington, and is shot down by a U.S. Air Force jet over Pennsylvania, eliminating the innocent witnesses to the diversion of the passenger planes. Under cover of darkness later that evening the other three Boeings are flown by remote control out over the Atlantic, are scuttled and end up in pieces at the bottom of the ocean.[11]

Enter the Dean

In 2004, two major changes happened in the life of American academic David Ray Griffin, longtime resident of Claremont, a prosperous medium-size college town hugging the mountains thirty miles east of Los Angeles. The first was that he retired after teaching for thirty-one years at the Claremont School of Theology and became professor emeritus of philosophy of religion and theology. The second was that he wrote a book effectively accusing the American government of murdering nearly three thousand of its own citizens so as to take over parts of the world, before pinning the blame on innocent Muslims.

As millennial theologians went, Griffin was a celebrated one. When a *Handbook of Christian Theologians* was compiled in the mid-1990s, Griffin was one of the sixty selected for inclusion. At the Claremont School of Theology, Griffin had been an advocate of process theology, a religious metaphysics based on the teachings of the late-Victorian English-born philosopher Alfred North Whitehead. The essential idea of process theology seems to be to pull together and integrate the various different aspects of human existence—religion, science, art—into a single coherent explanation. It is, in a sense, suspicious of "facts," seeking instead to capture the experience of change, which makes one wonder whether a Henry Lincoln or a Michael Baigent might not have been very much at home in Griffin's Center for Process Studies in Claremont, where the professor remained codirector even after retirement, pleasantly running down his years in a town (annual average temperature 63 degrees Fahrenheit) nicknamed the "City of Trees and Ph.D.'s."

Then along came 9/11, or, rather, along came 9/11 conspiracy theories on the Internet. As Griffin told it to the *San Francisco Chronicle*, he was at first skeptical. "I can remember my exact words . . . I said, 'I don't think that even the Bush administration could perpetrate such a thing.'" The spark that helped him change his mind was provided by a "fellow professor" who sent Griffin an e-mail with links to 9/11 conspiracy websites.

"Knowing her to be a sensible person," Griffin later wrote, "I looked up some of the material on the Internet." What he found was a timeline from an "independent researcher," Paul Thompson, which highlighted the failure of the U.S. military to scramble planes to intercept the hijacked aircraft. After that, wrote Griffin, "I happened to read" Gore Vidal's book *Dreaming War*, "which pointed me" to *The War on Freedom* by Nafeez Ahmed, "an independent researcher in England." Griffin also discovered the writings of "French researcher" Thierry Meyssan, which argued that no plane had ever hit the Pentagon.[12]

In other words, Griffin, the dispassionate scholar, didn't go out looking for conspiracies; they came looking for him. OK, he was inclined to be very critical of the administration, but he was skeptical nonetheless about the idea of an inside job. But then things happened or pointed him in certain directions. Of course, another kind of skeptic might observe that there were certain other directions, such as those in which researchers debunked conspiracy theories, that Griffin was obviously not pointed in. In any case, the professor's retirement was over before it had begun.

The first fruit of Griffin's studies was his book *The New Pearl Harbor: Disturbing Questions About the Bush Administration and 9/11* (2004). This turned out to be one of those rare works where the reality of the book exceeds the purported ambition. Griffin stated that he sought merely to raise "disturbing questions" about the accepted version of the events of 9/11, with the aim of persuading Americans that a full inquiry would be justified. He was not himself arguing that there had been a conspiracy, but that the problems raised by certain researchers and critics needed an answer. "I have not independently verified the accuracy of this evidence," he admitted, "I claim only that these revisionists have presented a strong prima facie case for official complicity ... If a significant portion of the evidence summarized here holds up, the conclusion that the attacks of 9/11 succeeded because of official complicity would become virtually inescapable."[13]

The New Pearl Harbor was greeted in certain circles with something approaching rapture. "A courageously impeccable work ... Griffin painstakingly marshals the evidence pro and con, and follows where it leads," wrote a professor of philosophy and fellow of the Royal Society of Canada. Where it led, according to the Carpenter Professor of Feminist Theology at Berkeley, was to "demonstrate a high level of probability that the Bush administration was complicit in allowing 9/11 to happen in order to further war plans that had already been made." The professor of religion and political science at Bucknell University in Pennsylvania felt that Griffin had created "a list of unresolved puzzles strongly suggestive of some sort of culpable complicity by U.S. officials in the event."

This last comment gave the game away. A list of unresolved puzzles isn't really suggestive of anything other than a lack of resolution, unless you think you know the answers. Griffin's book, far from being a dispassionate look at the conflicting evidence, was in fact a lengthy argument in favor of a conspiracy theory implicating the U.S. government in the murder of its own citizens. Griffin simply hadn't decided which conspiracy theory he favored. The comment in the paperback edition of *The New Pearl Harbor* by British former government minister Michael Meacher, that Griffin's technique was "to raise questions fearlessly and then test possible answers rigorously against all the available evidence," was misplaced. In fact, although Griffin's work did include some critical analyses of the official version, at no point did he subject the claims of the revisionists to the same scrutiny, or indeed any real scrutiny at all. He bought the whole shop.

Almost immediately, *The New Pearl Harbor* filled a large gap in 9/11 conspiracism. Its author, with his conventional clothes, soft and rather boring voice, and low-key didacticism, was the antithesis of a swivel-eyed Idaho conspiracy nut. Possessing the easy authority of the teacher who has been lecturing to the slightly inferior for several decades, he appealed to the middle-aged professionals—the doctors, teachers, social workers, lawyers, and academics (often retired)—who felt sidelined by Republican administrations. At meetings from Santa Rosa, California, to West Hartford, Connecticut, Griffin received standing ovations from some of America's best-educated people, after he had finished his speech with a peroration like this: "It is already possible to know beyond a reasonable doubt one very important thing: the destruction of the World Trade Center was an inside job, orchestrated by domestic terrorists. The welfare of our republic and perhaps even the survival of our civilization depend on getting the truth about 9/11 exposed."[14]

This was conspiracism for the most delicate of constitutions, and Griffin was generous. After *The New Pearl Harbor* came *The 9/11 Commission Report: Omissions and Distortions* (2005), *Christian Faith and the Truth Behind 9/11: A Call to Reflection and Action* (2006), *Debunking 9/11 Debunking: An Answer to "Popular Mechanics" and Other Defenders of the Official Conspiracy Theory* (2007), *9/11 Contradictions: An Open Letter to Congress and the Press* (2008), and *The New Pearl Harbor Revisited: 9/11, the Cover-up and the Exposé* (2008).

Fairly soon, David Ray Griffin had been nicknamed the "dean" of the 9/11 Truth movement, the man who seemed to give to the assortment of geeks, teenagers, far leftists, far rightists, strange millionaires, and perpetual dissidents composing the coalition that characteristic they lacked above all—gravitas. Yet Griffin's books all exhibit the same general and fatal tendency: lofty incredulity about the official accounts of September 11 and tolerant credulity toward the arguments of anyone challenging them. In itemizing the critiques of the accepted account and in seeming to endorse them, Griffin generally ignored the problem that most, if not all, of these arguments had been rebutted, and usually by people with far better qualifications or expertise than those who promoted them. The magazine *Popular Mechanics*, for example, created a team of nine researchers, who consulted more than seventy experts and professionals in the fields of engineering and aviation with the goal of examining the sixteen most common claims about 9/11 made by conspiracists. The result, said the editors, was that the magazine was able to debunk every single one by dint of "hard evidence and a healthy dose of common sense."[15] One example should suffice to demonstrate the ease with which Griffin's contentions can be demolished: the question of what exactly hit the Pentagon.

The Hole That Was Too Small

"[Thierry] Meyssan's arguments," wrote Griffin in that first 2004 work, "combined with those of other critics, do provide many reasons for concluding that it was not Flight 77 that hit the Pentagon."[16] There were, Griffin argued, "insuperable difficulties" for the contention that the plane had crashed into the headquarters of the United States Department of Defense because "whatever did hit the Pentagon simply did not cause nearly enough destruction for the official story to be true."[17] This was evident largely because "the orifice created by the impact . . . was at most 18 feet in diameter. Is it not absurd to suggest that a Boeing 757 created and then disappeared into such a small hole? . . . Can anyone seriously believe that a 125-foot-wide airplane created and then went inside a hole less than 20 feet wide? . . . It was actually technically difficult to do as little damage to the Pentagon as was done." Whatever else the evidence suggested, it "proves that it was not a Boeing 757 that went inside the Pentagon's west wing."[18]

There were not many precedents in 2004 for a large commercial airliner being flown deliberately and at speed into the side of a substantial building. So, throughout Griffin's discussion of the crash of Flight 77, there was a notion, only partly expressed, of what he thought ought to have happened when plane and structure came together so cataclysmically. This idea seems to have been informed to an extent by *Tom and Jerry* cartoons in which the cat, Tom, when propelled through a wall, leaves his entire profile, whiskers and all, outlined in the brick. So, argued Griffin, if you had a plane, consisting of fuselage and wings, you broadly ought to see a hole equal to or larger than the shape of a fuselage with wings. Since that wasn't what you saw, it couldn't have been a plane, no matter what other evidence there was for it being just that.

In fact, Griffin's measurements were wrong. The 2003 report into the Pentagon crash compiled by the American Society of Civil Engineers and the Structural Engineering Institute gave a width of ninety feet to the hole but explained that the wings had been destroyed by the reinforced columns of the Pentagon as the plane entered the building and disinte-grated. Mete Sozen, professor of structural engineering at Purdue University, Indiana, designed several simulations of the disaster, and their results were all consistent with Flight 77 striking the Pentagon.

Professor Sozen would have had difficulty otherwise, because the physical evidence for the official version, far from being absent was overwhelming. Fully 184 of the 189 people known to have been aboard Flight 77 or killed in the Pentagon, were identified (mostly through DNA testing) from remains found at the site. Wreckage from a large plane was also found, as one might expect, though few of the pieces were very big. There are photographs of parts of the plane on the lawn in front of the building, and pictures of engine and other parts inside. Aviation engineers from the website Aerospaceweb.org examined photographs of two pieces of wreckage from the Pentagon "and found them to be entirely consistent with the Rolls-Royce RB211-535 turbofan engine found on a Boeing 757 operated by American Airlines. The circular engine disk debris is just the right size and shape to match the compressor stages of the RB211, and it also shows evidence of being attached to a triple-shaft turbofan like the RB211."[19]

But there is always the possibility, however extraordinarily remote, that DNA might have been planted to the exact specifications of the missing passengers, crew, and employees, that wreckage might somehow have been placed at the scene within minutes of the crash, and that the real occupants of the missing Flight 77 might have been spirited away to some unknown place, there to be butchered or to live in the world's weirdest witness protection program. Those possibilities must be facts if, as David Griffin also averred, the attack on the Pentagon was "so difficult and so perfectly executed . . . no pilot with the minimal training the hijackers evidently had could have executed this maneuver."[20]

Aerospaceweb takes issue with this idea. "It is unclear what has prompted this belief," it comments, detailing the evidence from those eyewitnesses to the crash who had remarked on the way in which Flight 77 was flown. Sitting in traffic near the Pentagon, Afework Hagos noticed the plane "see-sawing back and forth" as the pilot struggled for control. The aircraft was "tilting its wings up and down like it was trying to balance." Penny Elgas observed the same thing, as did Ann Owens, James Ryan, Albert Hemphill, and David Marra. The site also reported the comments of a pilot, who remarked that "crashing a plane into a building as massive as the Pentagon is remarkably easy and takes no skill at all. Landing one on a runway safely even under the best conditions? Now *that's* the hard part!"[21]

The number of people who claimed to have seen not just an aircraft, but one with an American Airlines logo on it, might be regarded as an insuperable problem for Griffin's critique of the official version. James Ryan said that he had identified the AA on the tail: "The plane was low enough that I could see the windows of the plane. I could see every detail of the plane. In my head I have ingrained forever this image of every detail of that plane. It was a silver plane, American Airlines plane." "I was close enough (about a hundred feet or so) that I could see the American Airlines logo on the tail as it headed toward the building . . . I clearly saw the AA logo with the eagle in the middle," recalled Steve Riskus. A pilot, Donald "Tim" Timmerman, who lived in an apartment on the sixteenth floor of a building overlooking the Pentagon, had "quite a panorama . . . It was a Boeing 757, American Airlines, no question."[22]

None of this counted for Griffin, since, in a conflict between physical evidence (the size of the hole) and eyewitness recollection, a court of law would favor the former "because the human testimony might be wrong for all sorts of reasons, such as misperception, faulty memory, or outright lying (perhaps because of bribery or intimidation)." Nor was he prepared to credit the claim made by the solicitor general of the United States, Ted Olson, that his wife, Barbara, a passenger on Flight 77, had made a phone call from the plane. There were "at least four reasons to doubt Ted Olson's testimony," the first that he was "very close to the Bush administration" and the fourth that "Ted Olson is the only person who reported receiving a call from Flight 77."[23] In fact, another passenger, Renee May, had called her mother, Nancy, at 9:12 a.m. to tell her that the aircraft had been hijacked. Nancy May was not, as far as anyone has established, an intimate of anyone in government.

Even so, despite the debris, the DNA, the eyewitnesses, the fact that Flight 77 indubitably went missing and none of its passengers has ever turned up alive, Griffin persisted in claiming throughout his books that it was far more probable that something else had happened to the Pentagon than that Flight 77, piloted by a hijacker, had flown into it. Against all the freely available evidence, Griffin, a Christian theologian, portrayed a bereaved man as a conspiring monster, implicated hundreds in the worst act of treachery in recent history, and was punished by having his books sell in their thousands and retired professionals from one coast to the other applaud his accusations.

Murderous Holograms and Other Fancies

A summary of what a made-it-happen-on-purpose 9/11 Truth activist—taking his or her cue from David Ray Griffin—was likely to believe as of January 2007 goes something like this. Certain forces in the Bush administration wanted a pretext to use overwhelming military force in the Caspian area and the Middle East, either to procure oil supplies, or to weaken opposition to Israel, or both. Accordingly, they or their agents organized a false-flag operation, which would accomplish what Pearl Harbor was supposed to have accomplished for the Rooseveltian war party in 1941, causing a large number of Americans to die on the territory of the United States itself, with the blame wrongly being put on Islamist extremists. The plot they devised involved three airliners being flown into the World Trade Center main towers and, possibly, a Washington target. There were either no hijackers or the ones on board were patsies, and two of the planes were guided remotely into the World Trade Center. What brought the towers down, however, was a "controlled demolition" using explosives planted there at some earlier time. The same devices also toppled the structure now known as World Trade Center 7, though no plane flew into that building. The Pentagon was not hit by an airliner but by a guided missile. The fourth airliner, United 93, possibly heading for the capital, was either shot down because the passengers threatened to land it successfully, thus exposing the plot, or else it was never found. Various ruses, including faked mobile phone calls and fraudulent claims of such calls (for example, by Ted Olson), were used to disguise the true nature of the crime.

That was the basic theory, although different people in the Truth movement might agree or disagree with various parts of it. To accept it, you have to believe that elements of the American government engaged in a conspiracy of exceptional complexity and enormous risk of failure. This group of conspirators would have had to suborn, dupe, or train nineteen hijackers, create elaborate background stories for them, send them to flying schools to be seen around Florida and other parts of the United States, before disposing of them either in the crashes or, in the case of Flight 77, in a manner unknown.

The conspirators would have had to have sent experts in to rig the two main towers and WTC 7 with sufficient explosives to be sure of bringing the first two buildings down sometime after the planes had hit them, and WTC 7 whenever it was felt expedient to do so. But the explosives had to be sufficiently inert not to be triggered either by the impacts of the planes or by the thousands of gallons of burning aviation fuel, an especially tricky proposition since no precedent existed for the crashing of a large civil airliner into a thousand-foot skyscraper. The planes also had to be guided into the exact locations of the explosives. The towers had to come down because the destruction by terrorists of planes full of passengers and the unknowable number of casualties in the areas of the towers hit by the aircraft might not, in themselves, have been sufficiently provoking to cause the reaction needed by the plotters. On the other hand, it was apparently thought excessive to rig the towers in such a way as to have them topple over and possibly destroy half of lower Manhattan. A balance had to be struck.

For reasons unknown (a liking for variety, perhaps) the plotters decided not to repeat the trick in Washington. Believing that an attack that could kill up to 30,000 people in New York might not provide an adequate *casus belli*, the plotters trained a missile or an explosives-laden small military plane on the Pentagon, trusting that onlookers would accept that it must have been an airliner, either for the positive reason that Washingtonians are more suggestible than New Yorkers or the negative one that it was too tall an order to get a big plane to strike the Pentagon in the right way. There was, however, quite possibly a plane targeted on another Washington building (perhaps you don't want too much variety), Flight 93. This was the one that supposedly crashed into a Pennsylvania field. Not so. It had to be shot down by the government when the passengers unfortunately got wind of what was planned and stormed the cockpit—to find the autopilot, or the patsies, or whatever they found. Although another theory, favored by the makers of *Loose Change*, is that Flight 93 didn't crash and wasn't shot down, but, like Flight 77, was made to disappear.

Of course, it was essential that no air defenses were deployed properly against the two or three planes containing "hijackers," because the premature destruction of these aircraft would have meant the towers would have to be blown with no obvious culprit. So it was necessary to effectively stand down those defenses, by scrambling fighters deliberately late and issuing them with intentionally vague orders.

Then there was postproduction. One aspect of this was simple: the faking of videos of Osama bin Laden and others claiming responsibility for the attacks. Another was more complex: the passengers of Flight 77 and possibly Flight 93 were either murdered in a secret location and their bodies disposed of beyond any chance of discovery, or else they were relocated, lost forever to their families and friends, somewhere they could never be found. This would have been slightly easier if, as the millionaire 9/11 Truth activist Jimmy Walters has claimed, they were "all working for the government." Finally, investigators belonging to the disaster agency FEMA, to the National Institute of Standards and Technology, to the fire, police, and other emergency services, were paid off or intimidated to produce reports favorable to the official version.

Although the ingenious A. K. Dewdney has calculated that this whole plot would only require forty-four agents, it seems obvious that the intimidation alone would need as many if not more operatives than that. Hundreds, if not thousands, would have to have been directly involved in different aspects of the conspiracy. And all of them would have to have been either fanatically committed to the project or else almost unimaginably immoral. Think for a moment about the men who rigged the Twin Towers with explosives.

As if this plot weren't sufficiently challenging, there were Truth activists who became persuaded of even more technologically complex possibilities. On the fifth anniversary of the attacks, the *New Statesman* carried an interview with David Shayler and his partner Annie Machon, also a former employee of MI5.* The interviewer describes Machon as looking uncomfortable when Shayler decides to reveal his true opinion.

> "Oh, fuck it, I'm just going to say this," [Shayler] tells her. "Yes, I believe no planes were involved in 9/11." But we all saw with our own eyes the two planes crash into the WTC. "The only explanation is that they were missiles surrounded by holograms made to look like planes," he says. "Watch the footage frame by frame and you will see a cigar-shaped missile hitting the World Trade Center." He must notice that my jaw has dropped. "I know it sounds weird, but this is what I believe."[24]

It seems likely that Shayler hadn't seen the pictures of wreckage from Flight 175 on top of WTC 5. Even so, this "intelligence expert" believed that a cabal that couldn't plant weapons of mass destruction in the vastnesses of the Iraqi desert could fly hologram-shrouded missiles in plain daylight into one of the most public places in the world. But Shayler's selective credulity was only very slightly different in scale to that of David Ray Griffin and, presuming that they had thought through the implications of the conspiracy charge, those of Griffin's applauding audiences. It is surely remarkable that anyone should believe a story like the one

---

*See chapter 4.

effectively invented by the 9/11 Truth movement, let alone senior academics in American universities charged with instructing the young.

The Structural Engineers with a Special Place in Hell

Yet believe it they did. Griffin's success in drawing into the 9/11 Truth movement a number of people who defied the stereotypical image of the deluded paranoid was both striking and unexpected. But Griffin was just one man. It took other adherents to his formula to disseminate the word on an almost institutional level. In December 2005, Professor James Fetzer, a philosopher from the University of Minnesota in Duluth, and Steven Jones, a professor of physics at Brigham Young University, Utah, formed Scholars for 9/11 Truth (or, as they liked to call it, S9/11T). Fetzer at least was a veteran conspiracist, having previously argued, among other things, that President Kennedy's brain had been swapped with someone else's for the benefit of the autopsy X-rays, and that the Zapruder film had somehow been faked.

Unsurprisingly, from the start, S9/11T seemed to be making two contradictory pitches. According to its founding statement, the organization was both "devoted to applying the principles of scientific reasoning to the available evidence, 'letting the chips fall where they may,'" but also to contending that it was already established that "the World Trade Center was almost certainly brought down by controlled demolitions and that the available relevant evidence casts grave doubt on the government's official story about the attack on the Pentagon." Far, therefore, from being allowed to fall unhindered, the chips had been nudged firmly, if not remotely controlled, into their final position. Indeed, leading members of Scholars for 9/11 Truth, despite their commitment to an open-eyed search for veracity, turned out to have a rough way of dealing with rebuttals from other, invariably more qualified scholars who disagreed with the "science" underlying most 9/11 conspiracy theories. To Professor

Fetzer, this opposition came down to moral deficiency. "These people lack integrity, or they are corrupt," he told a radio audience in the summer of 2006. "I am disgusted, disgusted with the structural engineers who know the truth and have kept their mouths shut. There's a special place in hell reserved for them."[25]

Despite this ambivalence, the website for the Scholars gave evidence of something approaching hyperactivity, as its leading members addressed meetings, wrote articles, did interviews, attended symposia, and organized conferences. But who, exactly, were they? What were they scholars of? A researcher following up on the names discovered that, as of late 2006, out of seventy-six named Scholars for Truth there were no Middle Eastern experts and only two engineers, one of whom thought the United States was plotting to bomb the planet Jupiter with antimatter weapons while the other devoted himself to studying the mechanics of dentistry. Nine (the largest number) were philosophers, five were English experts, five were psychologists, five were physicists, and four were theologians. One, Webster G. Tarpley, was the president of the "Washington Grove Institute," an institution traceable only via a PO Box on Tarpley's website.

A Long, Digressive Note on Webster G. Tarpley

The story of 9/11 conspiracy theory is, as much as anything else, a story of the way in which the Internet has brought unlikely people together across geographic and political distances. Who, for example, is Webster G. Tarpley? It was a question I asked myself when I attended the 9/11 Truth meeting at Friends House in 2005. I didn't know the name. Nor, I suspected, did the majority of the audience, and yet they were lapping up what he was telling them. Almost as though I were uncovering a conspiracy myself, I began to research the backgrounds of the key members of the 9/11 Truth movement. Who were they all, and what did they, in sociological or historical terms, represent?

Twenty years ago, such an exercise would have been easy, and the grouping of people around any particular cause might have been described by its political or class affiliations. A campaign might be left-based, involving trade unions, socialists, and left-liberals, or it might be center-right and include business representatives and conservatives. One could, by dint of reading a select few far-left journals, develop the ability to distinguish between the various revolutionary parties, who in any case were always anxious to publicize themselves.

The 9/11 movement, as it calls itself, obeys none of these rules. It is composed of people whose other interests are so diverse, from Buddhism to nativism, as to defy any categorization. Even so, this movement has developed an ideology that it, itself, barely recognizes. When I delved into the background of Princeton-educated Tarpley, for example, I discovered that he was, in fact, a longtime associate of Lyndon LaRouche, the wealthy cultist who, you may recall from chapter 4, believes that the British royal family conspires with finance capital to run the world. Should you browse the back catalog of the *LaRouche Connection** videotapes, you can find Tarpley variously hosting "A Conversation with Helga Zepp-LaRouche" (Lyndon's German wife), interviewing Lyndon himself on the topic of "Food and Metals Hoarding," taking part in a press conference to demand an end to "The British Whitewater Assault on the [Clinton] Presidency," and, on a similar theme, warning against "The British Oligarchy: America's Mortal Enemy."

Although he is supposed to have left the LaRouche movement in the mid-1990s, the same strain of historical eccentricity runs through all Tarpley's work. In his book *Against Oligarchy*, Tarpley charges, "the events leading to the Great Depression are all related to British economic warfare against the rest of the world"; in *Surviving the Cataclysm*, one of his targets is Karl Marx, who is described, possibly for the first time, as an "Anglo-Venetian ideologue." *Surviving the Cataclysm* argues that to beat

---

*An American cable television program.

the coming crash (there is invariably a coming crash—and occasionally they even come) the United States must colonize space. Tarpley's 1991 work *George Bush: The Unauthorized Biography* claimed that the father of George W. Bush, then president, was a psychotic whose mental health would be the main election issue in 1992.

Something significant about the diversity of 9/11ers is exemplified by the active participants in another event involving Webster G. Tarpley, which I came across only because I was looking for video evidence of his various speeches. The First Axis for Peace Conference took place in Brussels on November 17–18, 2005. According to its organizers, it gathered together 150 leaders from thirty-seven countries, including "intellectuals, politicians, diplomats, and military officers," with the twin aims of promoting world harmony and criticizing the hegemonic and imperialist plans of the United States of America, with the latter being rather more prominent than the former.

A few years earlier, such a prospectus would have placed the conference firmly on the left of the political spectrum, and during the Cold War might even have suggested the possibility of sponsorship by a Soviet-funded body such as the World Peace Council or the International Union of Students. But the Axis for Peace event, as much a product of globalization in its own way as many of the phenomena that it deplored, could certainly not be said to be mainly a gathering of progressives. It was organized by Réseau (Network) Voltaire, a French private think tank named after the great figure of the Enlightenment. Originally set up to combat racism and to resist legislation seen as repressing free speech, the Network's organizing genius and president was a former student of theology, Thierry Meyssan, who had been active in the small French center-left Parti Radical de Gauche, and had subsequently become both a campaigner against far-right organizations and a proselytizer for the decriminalization of hard drugs. One aspect of the Network's operation was to supply with information a series of independent media outlets, particularly in Latin America.

But in February 2002, Meyssan, who must have worked extraordinarily quickly, published one of the very first books to argue that 9/11 was an inside job carried out by the Bush administration. *L'Effroyable Imposture* (published in the United States and Britain as *9/11: The Big Lie*) became a bestseller in France following an appearance by Meyssan on a popular current affairs show on France 2, one of the main television channels, in which he was able to outline his thesis apparently without being challenged. According to the *New York Times*, 100,000 copies of *L'Effroyable Imposture* were sold in the fortnight following the broadcast.[26] "Copies have been flying off shelves," a bookstore clerk told the BBC. The book topped Amazon France's best-seller list.[27]

Where there is Tarpley there is also Lyndon LaRouche, so it was no surprise to find among those addressing the Brussels conference LaRouche's wife and head of the LaRouchian Schiller Institute, the rhythmically named Helga Zepp-LaRouche, along with the editor of the French LaRouchian newspaper and the head of the French LaRouchian political party. Also present was a pair of colorful British mavericks, at that moment with no careers or clear means of support: Craig Murray, the former British ambassador to Uzbekistan, who had left his job, some said pushed for political reasons and others because of his exciting private life, and the ubiquitous former MI5 man David Shayler.

Then there were two European politicians who had been elected representatives in their home countries. The first, Andreas von Bülow, had been a minister in the SPD government of Helmut Schmidt, serving as state secretary in the West German Ministry of Defense and the Ministry for Technology. Out of politics since 1994, von Bülow, like Meyssan, had written a book accusing the Bush administration of having carried out the 9/11 attacks. The second, Giulietto Chiesa, a member of the European Parliament, had been a correspondent in Moscow for the Communist newspaper *L'Unità*. Latterly, in several books, Chiesa had been advancing the view that a new-world super-elite, the "super clan," acting without check in the United States, was destroying liberal democracy and trying to bring about "a world much worse than the Orwellian." Only Europe, argued Chiesa, could resist the super clan.

Charles Saint-Prot, former chairman of the French Peace Committee for the Middle East, was described by the event organizers as an "Iraq specialist." He had also, I discovered, interviewed Saddam Hussein in 1982–1983. The interview was published as a booklet by the Al-Huria Printing House of Baghdad, and a copy was discovered in one of Saddam's palaces in 2003. In this interview, Charles Saint-Prot asks various obsequious questions, such as, "Concerning Franco-Iraqi relations, I believe Your Excellency has talked about them favorably. Is Your Excellency pleased with the results of the talks recently held in Paris by [Iraqi minister] Tariq Aziz?"

For Lebanon, there was pro-Syrian former Prime Minister Selim Ahmed al-Hoss; for Belgium, Michel Collon of the Workers Party (PTB), member of the International Committee to Defend Slobodan Milosevic. From Russia had come the former chief of staff of the Russian defense forces and current vice president of the Academy of Geopolitical Studies, Colonel General Leonid Ivashov. Ivashov had already expressed the view that only a government agency could have organized an attack on the scale of 9/11, concluding, "Osama bin Laden and Al Qaeda cannot be the organizers or the performers of the September 11 attacks. They do not have the necessary organization, resources, or leaders. Thus, a team of professionals had to be created and the Arab kamikazes are just extras to mask the operation."[28]

Ivashov's primary concern, however, was that modern Russians were failing to discern that the main enemy of their nation was not Chechen rebels but the West. "Young people are confused," Ivashov had written, "they are disoriented and cannot see the long-term threat. Yes, NATO troops do not shoot and bomb Russia today, and this creates the impression that the threat is not real . . . In addition, Western values are being planted in Russia, while its own historical and cultural roots are coming into oblivion."[29]

From America came two representatives, who were on the face of it from different sides of the political divide. One was an academic and self-professed socialist revolutionary with a dispiriting line in dense polemic, James Petras. Petras's view of 9/11 had, between the event itself and the

Brussels conference, undergone an interesting metamorphosis. Initially sharing the belief that the attackers were terrorists of Middle Eastern origin, Petras was eager to explain their motives. "This was not an indiscriminate attack against 'America,'" he claimed, "but a political attack against a major military-financial target which is central to U.S. global empire." The Pentagon was vital to U.S. imperialist military designs on the world, and the World Trade Center the obvious symbol of its economic imperialism. So "September 11 was a complex act in which human tragedy and strategic political issues were intertwined . . . The terrorists acted with rational forethought: if the intention was to challenge the empire, they chose a significant target, although the 'collateral damage' to civilians is excruciating." Even so, he re-assured readers, "Some of the victims in the WTC are known swindlers."[30]

Within a few months, however, Petras wasn't so sure that the power behind the attacks was quite so benignly anti-imperial and the atrocities quite so understandable. "The lack of any public statement concerning Israel's possible knowledge of 9/11," he argued, "is indicative of the vast, ubiquitous, and aggressive nature of its powerful diaspora supporters." In 2006, he would go on to widen the scope of his assault on the "Zioncons" (neoconservative Zionists) by claiming that Mossad was behind several cartoons depicting the Prophet Muhammad, the publishing of which in the Danish newspaper *Jyllands-Posten* led to riots, the burning of Scandinavian consulates, and the murder of a Catholic priest in Turkey. Petras's causal chain was as follows:

> Given Mossad's long-standing penetration of the Danish intelligence agencies, and their close working relations with the Right-wing media, it is not surprising that a Ukranian [*sic*] Jew, operating under the name of "Flemming Rose" [the editor of *Jyllands-Posten*] with close working relations with the Israeli state (and in particular the far-Right Likud regime) should be the center of the controversy over the cartoons . . . Prior to being placed as a cultural editor of a leading Right-wing Danish daily, from 1990 to 1995 "Rose" was a Moscow-based reporter who translated

into Danish a self-serving autobiography by Boris Yeltsin, godchild of the pro-Israeli, post-Communist Russian oligarchs, most of whom held dual citizenship and collaborated with the Mossad in laundering illicit billions.[31]

Interestingly, Flemming Rose had a similar accusation made against him by the other American speaker at the Axis for Peace conference, Christopher Bollyn, then a journalist for the ultra-right-wing *American Free Press*. In early 2006, Bollyn was to demand, "Are we likely to see cartoons in *Jyllands-Posten* calling into question the force-fed Zionist myth of the Holocaust, which has become the new 'Holy Cause' of Europe? . . . Take a good look at the non-Danish 'cultural' czar of *Jyllands-Posten* and ask yourself." The accompanying photograph shows a man, presumably Rose, who has a moderately prominent nose.[32] Bollyn seemed to be suggesting that the nose was indicative of its owner's Jewishness.

The Voltaire Network described Bollyn as an "investigative journalist," but this professional label rather understated his political associations. The *American Free Press* was originally founded by Willis Carto, a disciple of the historical revisionism of Harry Elmer Barnes[*] and also a white supremacist and possibly America's leading anti-Semite. Carto's other legacy to American politics, the *Barnes Review*, named for his hero, is available for purchase on the Internet. Leading *Review* articles have included items such as "Of Teutonic Blood: German and German-American Contributions to Civilization as We Know It Have Been Massive," and the intriguing-sounding "Adolf Hitler: An Overlooked Candidate for the Nobel Prize." Carto's erstwhile publishing company, Noontide Press, was responsible for publishing, among other books, *The Myth of the Six Million*, by a David Hoggan, which, as the title suggests, was a rejection of the historical truth of the Holocaust. Though the *American Free Press* tended to be somewhat circumspect about its attitude toward Jews, its concentration on stories involving Israeli perfidy, Israeli spies, Israeli brutality, and "Zionist" financial and political

---

[*]See chapter 3.

influence suggests that this may have been more a matter of marketing than political difference. Bollyn's specialism at the magazine became articles on 9/11 conspiracy theories, although these, as we shall see, were not lacking in allusions to Israeli perfidy.

As if to personify the ideological melange occurring at the conference, one of the two Polish representatives was another MP, Mateusz Piskorski, elected for Stettin in the 2005 parliamentary elections on the ticket of the Self-Defense (Samoobrona) Party. Samoobrona is an unusual amalgam of populist left-wing economics and xenophobia, but Piskorski, still in his twenties, had, as revealed in the mainstream Polish newspaper *Gazeta Wyborcza*, a previous history of far-right activism, including the translation and publishing of neo-Nazi material, including "skinzines" for the movement's more physically militant elements. Now, Piskorski, sitting on the platform next to the onetime antifascist Meyssan, was applauded for expressing his shame that Poland had committed troops to the occupation of Iraq.

The exemplar of the politics of the event may have been the French comedian Dieudonné Mbala Mbala, who contributed to one of the panel sessions of the Axis for Peace, arguing for the need for new political movements to replace those that had, he claimed, "given in to the Zionist lobby." A formidable stand-up comedian, the half-Cameroonian Dieudonné had received a UN special award for antiracism in 2000. By 2004, however, his main targets appeared to be not the racist right in France but Israel, Zionism, and Jews. Interviewed in *Le Journal du Dimanche* that February, he accused all Jews of being "slave-traders who have turned to banking or show business and, today, to terrorist action to show their support for Ariel Sharon's policies."[33] When challenged about this assertion in a subsequent interview for the *Ha'aretz* newspaper of Israel, Dieudonné elaborated: in the fifteenth century, much wealth was earned from trading in slaves, and every person who became wealthy exploited slavery in some way or another. "History tells us that many Jews earned their fortune during that period," said Dieudonné. "Do you think it's logical that businessmen throughout the world got rich out of this and Jews had nothing to do with this?"[34] The comedian was careful to differentiate between being an anti-Zionist, which he admitted to, and being anti-Semitic, which he denied. His interviewer, Raney Cohen, had found it hard to appreciate the distinction when attending a Dieudonné show in 2004:

> Dieudonné said—with a serious expression on his face—that he had decided to apologize to "the Chosen People." When he finished his request for forgiveness, he was quiet for a moment, then glanced all around suspiciously and explained in a whisper that "When the cowardly Zionists attack someone, it's always from behind." Then he smiled mischievously to the audience and concluded with a crude gesture and shouts, "You can shove my apology up your ass, Chosen People!" as the crowd went wild.[35]

A British journalist, John Lichfield, witnessed a similar Dieudonné skit.

> He is greeted with roars and whoops by a packed, multiracial audience, which is young, trendy, intellectual, and Left-wing. Many of them have come straight from the latest demo against the government's new jobs law for the young . . . However, something else intrudes, something darker and more sinister. Dieudonné is obsessed with Jews. All races, including his own mixed black and white origins, get a gentle mickey-taking in his show. When Jews are mentioned—and they are mentioned often—the tone becomes more aggressive, even violent. In one skit, Bernard-Henri Lévy, the Jewish-French philosopher, haggles with a street potato seller. Dieudonné/Lévy says: "How can you ask me to pay so much when six million of us died in the Holocaust?" Roars of delight from the audience.[36]

Dieudonné's trajectory and his embracing of diverse themes previously thought to be contradictory is emblematic of the Axis for Peace and of a certain kind of radical politics that forms the ideological spine of the 9/11 Truth movement. This politics is a loose coalescence of impulses: antiglobalization, broadly antimodernist and anti-imperialist—with imperialism being inevitably and solely associated with American power.

These impulses are easily felt both by the far left and the far right, and the consequence has been an unofficial and almost, but not quite, unconscious alliance. What binds this alliance even tighter is its anti-Israeli bent. In February 2005, three members of the administration council of the Voltaire Network resigned precisely because of what they called the organization's "redbrown" (far-left/far-right) orientation. "The pretext of resisting American Imperialism, [plus] lenience toward Chinese and Russian imperialisms and closeness with Islamists," they protested, "is symptomatic of a latent anti-Semitic drift among the leadership."[37]

The Missing Four Thousand

In David Ray Griffin's *The New Pearl Harbor*, the work of "independent researcher" Eric Hufschmid is frequently cited: his book *Painful Questions* is described as "most valuable," and his notion of the Twin Towers collapsing at "free fall" speed is accepted uncritically. But Hufschmid believes, "Most wars and terrorist attacks of the past century were instigated by Zionists. They pretend to be Americans, Communists, Russians, Liberals, Republicans, Greens, Christians, Muslims, and 9/11 researchers. They infiltrate, bribe, and blackmail our governments, militaries, news agencies, and police."[38]

As the 9/11 Truth movement gathered momentum, Hufschmid began to worry that the Zionists were somehow arranging for the truth about their involvement in the attacks to be obscured by other theories, which concentrated on the culpability of the Bush administration. One example, according to Hufschmid, might be the inexplicable popularity of Avery's *Loose Change* video over his own effort, *Painful Deceptions*. As a consequence of this belief, Hufschmid recorded an hour-long telephone conversation in April 2006 between himself and Dylan Avery, who was accompanied by his sidekicks Korey Rowe and Jason Bermas.

As Hufschmid pressed his notion of crypto-Jewish conspiracies at work in the anti-conspiracy movement, the response from the *Loose*

Change men became ever more agonized, like children whose favorite uncle has begun to behave strangely. They were, said Avery, "well aware of the Illuminati, we're aware of the New World Order, and we're well aware that there are people who want an all-Jewish state, but that's not what we're about . . . If you're going to say crypto-Jew, you have to have something to back it up. Until you get a Kabbalah or a Torah or a yarmulkah, how can you say that?" Bermas conceded that maybe Mossad was behind the bringing down of the Twin Towers. "It's not that [the theory is] not legitimate, I just haven't seen enough information to say that this Zionist cabal that everybody's talking about is responsible."[39]

Since September 12, 2001, there have been theories linking Israelis/ Jews/Zionists (the names always indicating the same people) to the worst terrorist incident in history. Christopher Bollyn, last seen in this chapter joining Thierry Meyssan at his anti-imperialist colloquium in Brussels, was one of the leading American protagonists of this strand, along with his *American Free Press* colleague Michael Collins-Piper. To Bollyn, there was "a preponderance of evidence pointing to Israel's intelligence agency, the Mossad, being involved in the terror attacks."[40] Some of this evidence was circumstantial but, to a certain cast of mind, suggestive, such as the case of the five young Israelis picked up by the FBI after they were seen watching the attack on the Twin Towers from the George Washington Bridge and supposedly "speaking in a foreign language and hugging each other."

But the story that provided the initial impetus for the claims of a Zionist plot was the urban myth, repeated by Bollyn, that four thousand Jews or Israelis (the description varies) mysteriously stayed at home on the day of the attacks, clearly forewarned about what was to happen. On September 15, the Syrian newspaper *Al-Thawra* stated that "four thousand Jews were absent from their work on the day of the explosions." Al-Manar television in Lebanon, linked to the militant Hezbollah organization, also referred to Israelis who "remarkably did not show up in their jobs the day the incident took place." If these were the first instances of the charges, they certainly weren't the last: in January 2007, an Internet search on Google turned up over 33,000 references to "4,000 Jews" and the WTC attacks.

The origin of the figure is probably the September 12 Internet edition of the *Jerusalem Post*, which stated, "the Foreign Ministry in Jerusalem has so far received the names of 4,000 Israelis believed to have been in the areas of the World Trade Center and the Pentagon at the time of the attacks." This story, almost certainly based on panicky inquiries about relatives visiting or living in the Washington and New York areas, was given the utterly misleading headline "Hundreds of Israelis Missing in WTC Attack." Later, when four thousand Israelis did not turn up dead in the WTC, this permitted those who wanted to, such as Bollyn, to note a nonexistent discrepancy.

In fact, 2,071 workers in and visitors to the World Trade Center were killed on 9/11, and as far as can be ascertained, between 10 and 14 percent were Jewish, roughly correlating to the percentage of Jews in the population of the New York area. This should have surprised nobody except perhaps an anti-Semite or a Syrian newspaper. From Bollyn, who belongs to the section of the openly racist far right that also believes the Holocaust to be a hoax or an exaggeration, such an argument might be considered run-of-the-mill. Far more extraordinary was that he kept company with, among others, a German Social Democrat and a black American Marxist poet.

Andreas von Bülow, the German former government minister who had also attended the Brussels conference, was asked about the Israeli connection by a journalist from *Der Spiegel*. There were, said von Bülow, "a number of indications . . . point[ing] to some connection between the Mossad and the act and perpetrators of 9/11," including the fact that there was "only one Israeli victim on 9/11." There then followed this slightly surreal exchange:

> VON BÜLOW: They [the Israelis] didn't know about it, [but] they had an idea.
> Q: And why isn't any of them talking today?
> VON BÜLOW: That has happened. They say a little Pakistani boy said, "The towers will no longer be standing tomorrow."[41]

At the time of 9/11, the official poet laureate of New Jersey was the sixty-six-year-old black left-wing writer Amiri Baraka (born Everett LeRoi Jones). In 2002 he published a poem titled "Somebody Blew Up America," the essence of which was to contrast the demonization of militant Islam with the lack of attention paid to other, worse criminals, such as those who became rich from slavery. The technique Baraka used was to ask who was responsible for each of the other historical offenses against humanity. So the poem included, according to one supporter of Baraka's, a "provocatively poetic inquiry about who knew beforehand" about the WTC attacks:

> *Who knew the World Trade Center was gonna get*
> *bombed?*
> *Who told 4,000 Israeli workers at the Twin Towers*
> *To stay home that day?*
> *Why did Sharon stay away?*

It seemed 9/11 had drawn together a lifelong foe of racism and a foot soldier in the ranks of the modern neo-fascists. They could agree (or provocatively inquire, poetically) that the Jews were somehow to blame. Or if not the Jews, as such, the evil manipulators of the Jews, the Zionists, themselves an almost invincible form of super-Jew.

Mind the Gap

The growth in belief in conspiracies about 9/11 owed as much to what occurred after the attack as to what happened before it. In October 2001 coalition forces went into Afghanistan, removed the Islamist Taliban government, and chased Osama bin Laden out of his bases. Then in March 2003, American and British forces invaded Iraq in what was to prove the most controversial and divisive foreign-policy decision for both countries of the post–Cold War era. There were huge protests, followed by a widespread belief that somehow the American and British people had been lied to. Many books have covered and will cover that territory, but one consequence was a flood of conspiracy theories discussing almost every aspect of Western (here defined as American, British, Israeli, and, if you have less parochial tastes, Australian) foreign and counterterrorist policy.

Within a day of the Madrid train bombings in March 2004, it was being suggested that the United States might have planted the devices to "consolidate broader social support for coming imperial wars, restrictions of civil liberties, and general social paranoia, phenomena from which Spain had been relatively exempt until today."[42] The following month, the capture and filmed beheading in Iraq of an American contractor, Nicholas Berg, led to widespread speculation that the event had been staged to make the Iraqi insurgency look bad. His captors didn't wear their headgear the way real Arabs would; a doctor said there wasn't enough blood, and so on. In the same week that Berg was kidnapped, the doyenne of the antiglobalization movement, Naomi Klein, wrote from Baghdad that the burgeoning civil war might be being deliberately fomented by the American administration, "creating the chaos it needs" to avoid having to hand over power to the Iraqis.[43]

Inevitably, the London bombs that killed fifty-six people on July 7, 2005, gave rise to a whole raft of speculation about government involvement, and in 2006, two British versions of *Loose Change* appeared on the Net. One was called *Ludicrous Diversion,* and the other (after a public service announcement made at certain London Underground stations) *Mind the Gap.* David Shayler was the author of the second, arguing in it that the 7/7 bombings were probably a false-flag operation designed to instill a false fear of terrorism into the British people and permit the government to do whatever nefarious thing it had on its collective mind at the time. *Mind the Gap* came complete with supposed warnings to Israelis, disturbing questions about evidence and photographs, and CCTV shots allegedly so badly forged that they were evidence of elements in the new world order wanting to reveal themselves, saying, "Look, we're sick of lying. We've had enough."[44] The aftermath of the bomb blasts didn't look like the product of peroxide bombs to Shayler, who as a deskbound operative for MI5 would, one must imagine, have seen very few peroxide bombs exploding. What was more, the so-called bombers were nice boys who liked cricket, and the train timetables for the jihadists to arrive in London were all wrong.

One piece of evidence, a potential magic bullet, was accepted by all the 7/7 conspiracists, and this was the impossible locations of the blasts. The official version was that the lethal explosives had been carried in backpacks by the bombers, who set them off on three trains and a bus, killing themselves and the people around them. But if the bombs could be shown to have detonated somewhere else—underneath the trains, for example—then they couldn't have been associated with the so-called terrorists. This, stated the theorists, was exactly what eyewitnesses had claimed to see happen when the bombs exploded. Ultimately, all such reports could be traced to one source—*Guardian* journalist Mark Honigsbaum. In June 2006, Honigsbaum gave an account of how the idea of the blast from below had come into existence. On July 7, he had been sent by his news desk to Edgware Road, the site of one of the explosions, where among scenes of complete confusion he had managed to grab quick interviews with some of the survivors as they left a makeshift triage center in a local store.

Two of them told Honigsbaum that when the bomb exploded, the covering on the floor of the carriage had "raised up." With no time to check what the passengers had said, Honigsbaum phoned in an audio report to the *Guardian*, which was used on its website. It was Honigsbaum who added the elaboration that it "was believed" that the explosion had happened underneath the train, and "some passengers described how the tiles, the covers on the floors of the train, flew up, raised up." After filing, Honigsbaum spoke at greater length to more survivors who had been much closer to the blast, and they told him that the explosion had happened inside the carriage. His earlier report, admitted Honigsbaum, had been "flawed," but unfortunately "my comments, disseminated over the Internet where they could be replayed ad nauseam, were already taking on a life of their own." Ruefully, the reporter concluded that in the old days of telephones and books it would have taken some time for Rumor to paint itself full of tongues, but today "such networks can be created instantaneously with a few clicks of a mouse."[45]

In Defense of Extreme Improbability

It is a contention of this book that conspiracy theorists fail to apply the principle of Occam's razor to their arguments. Nowhere is this better exemplified than in the attempts by Dr. David Ray Griffin to justify the wild improbability of the alternatives to the generally accepted story of 9/11. He constructed three lines of defense. The first was that the conspiracy theories, no matter how far-fetched, might be found to be quite believable, if properly tested. "The questions they [conspiracy theorists] have raised about the official account," he wrote, "are based on conflicts between this account and known facts, whereas the questions just now raised about complicity theory [the theory that the government was complicit] are rhetorical questions, implying that no answers could be given to any of them. But perhaps answers CAN be given at least to some of them." For example, hazarded Griffin, on the problem of why none of the thousands of conspirators had spoken out, "the revisionists could reply, people raising this question have probably never experienced the kind of intimidation that can be brought to bear on individuals by threats of prosecution, or worse."[46] Here, of course, he was entering that inevitable circular plea of conspiracism, that the objections to the theory tended, if anything, to prove the theory right. The very fact that no one had talked could almost be seen as evidence of the sheer ruthlessness of the plotters.

Griffin's second defense—linked to the first—was that the arguments of 9/11 Truth activists somehow belonged in a different ontological category from those of their critics. Challenged on radio by a left-wing American conspiracy skeptic, Griffin reasoned, "What I have presented is a cumulative argument which relies on a massive amount of evidence that I do take to be prima facie reliable . . . If you're presenting a deductive argument, that's when we say that no chain is stronger than its weakest link, then it is important to point out if there are a couple premises of the argument that are at fault, then the whole thing falls. But with the cumulative argument that isn't the case."[47] As we've seen, Griffin's evidence was far from reliable to say the least, but even so, for his argument to fail one would have to refute specifically almost every single element of it. This supposed separation between deductive and cumulative arguments is reminiscent of the *Holy Blood* authors' scholarship of synthesis, which explicitly didn't require the old, more academic way of looking at evidence but a new willingness to make impossible connections between disparate phenomena. Both have the same quality—the need for a leap of faith.

Griffin's third defense was, in essence, if you think my theory is silly then take a look at your own. If there was a choice between the received conspiracy theory (Osama did it) or the revisionist conspiracy theory (Bush did it), was the latter really more unbelievable than the former? Was it not deeply unlikely that a man in a cave together with a few mad Arabs could pull off something so truly devastating? This unlikelihood, suggested Griffin, dwarfed all the other unlikelihoods.

It is certainly true that the 9/11 plotters, if we believe them to have been al-Qaeda members, carried out an audacious and imaginative plot, in the execution of which they enjoyed very little bad luck, and before which they went about their business relatively free of harassment by the authorities. It was, if you accept the evidence, something of a judo throw in which the opponent's very weight was used against him.

There was, however, one other obvious factor that Griffin might have considered when seeking to compare unlikelihoods. Most people, even ones we think of as bad, do what they think and profess to be good, or else invent excuses as to why they can't. Osama bin Laden and his deputy Ayman al-Zawahiri said several times that their organization was behind 9/11. Their particular ideology justified such attacks, and saw them as both laudable and central to Islamist strategy. What's more, jihadis operating as part of bin Laden's group had already exploded huge bombs at the U.S. embassies in Nairobi and Dar es Salaam, attacked a U.S. destroyer in Yemen and Israeli holidaymakers in Mombasa, and tried to shoot down an Israeli airliner. In 1993, Islamists later associated with bin Laden had also exploded a huge bomb under the World Trade Center itself, with the objective of destroying the buildings. So bin Laden's responsibility for 9/11, if proved, would make him exactly what he wanted to be, a hero of the Islamic resistance to American/Zionist/Crusader imperialism, and every jihadi would have understood that. By contrast, if it were to have been established that President Bush had been in some way involved, then he would become the greatest traitor and liar in American history, a kind of super Benedict Arnold. We may guess that every Bush-ite collaborator would have known this too.

Cui bono?

This kind of tangle occurs through the conspiracy theorist's use of the *cui bono?* (who benefits?) question to establish motive. If you can make a case that X, in some way and at some time, derived some benefit out of an event, no matter how much X may have declared their opposition to it, then you are justified in asking whether X might not have been in some way involved. That's the way the planets move, the way the world is. David Ray Griffin provides a classic example of *Cui bono?* when he quotes in his book someone named Patrick Martin. "The principal beneficiaries of the destruction of the World Trade Center," Martin argues, "are in the United States: the Bush administration, the Pentagon, the CIA, the FBI, the weapons industry, the oil industry. It is reasonable to ask whether those who have profited to such an extent from this tragedy contributed to bring it about."[48]

Readers will note the yoking of a highly questionable assertion made as obvious fact to the professed mildness of the conclusion. It is not at all clear, for example, that the CIA and the FBI, charged above all with protecting the United States, would have expected to benefit from allowing the worst terrorist attack in world history to take place on U.S. soil. Describing them as among the "principal beneficiaries" of such an atrocity must therefore be regarded as eccentric, and to use the idea of benefit to ask the question whether they "contributed to bring it about" seems not to be the act of any reasonable seeker after truth, but rather of someone who has already decided where the truth lies.

An agreeably simple and often quoted *cui bono?* sentiment was formulated by the late George Seldes, an American muckraking journalist. "If you look for the social-economic motive," Seldes wrote, "you will not have to wait for history to tell you what was propaganda and what was truth." The problem with this seductive proposition is that it is hopelessly reductionist, completely failing to appreciate that people act from many other motives. It rejects the accidental, the complex, the unforeseen or the ideological, substituting an unpredictable economic outcome as the test of a subjective intention.

So, who plotted the First World War? Not those people who danced in the streets in Vienna, London, Berlin, and Paris in August 1914; they couldn't benefit because they weren't rich and were too likely to suffer in one way or another. Not the German kaiser, the Russian tsar, or the Austro-Hungarian emperor, because they all lost their thrones in the end. Not the American administration, because it obviously entered the war too late and too reluctantly to be considered a prime mover. But who emerged, secretly smiling, from the hecatomb? The armaments manufacturers, the war profiteers, and, behind them, the bankers. And, for those inclined to ask the extra question, what religion did many of the bankers profess?

That is where over-schematizing gets you. A further problem with the *cui bono?* line is that it assumes the supposed protagonist knows at the outset what is going to happen. In other words, it falls prey to the historian's fallacy.

The Historian's Fallacy

The term "historian's fallacy" was coined in 1970 by the scholar David Hackett Fischer to describe the "ludicrous" but common error in the assumption "that a man who has a given historical experience knows it, when he has it, to be all that a historian would know it to be, with the advantage of historical perspective." Fischer is not talking about what we call the benefit of hindsight, but about the tendency to forget that the actors in a historical drama simply did not know, at the time, what was coming next. Subsequent to an event, we may recall the clues and warnings that it was about to happen, but, warns Fischer, "our memory does not extend with equal clarity to many other signs and signals which pointed unequivocally in the other direction."[49]

You can apply Fischer's insight both to specific charges and to the bigger picture of the 9/11 attacks. In one very clear example, David Ray Griffin took the North American Aerospace Defense Command to task for its suspicious tardiness. He demanded to know "why, if NORAD had been told at 9:24 [a.m.] that Flight 77 appeared to be headed back toward Washington, the Pentagon was not evacuated. In 13 minutes, it seems, virtually everyone could have gotten out. The strike would not have caused the death of 125 people working in the Pentagon."[50] Griffin knew, as did we all, that Flight 77 was supposed to have struck the Pentagon. That's because we saw the damage to the Pentagon and were told a plane had flown into it. But thirteen minutes earlier, the Pentagon was not the only target that Flight 77 could have been heading for. It could just as easily have been bound for the Capitol or the White House or the CIA headquarters at Langley, or have been a hijacking aimed at securing the release of prisoners. Griffin never suggests that all of these other places should also have been evacuated or other possibilities entertained, because he assumes a prior knowledge of the target.

On a more general level, the picture painted by the commission of inquiry into 9/11 was one of an Establishment taken utterly by surprise by the events of September 11—events that, from the time Flight 11 was seen to crash into the WTC to the confirmation by Pennsylvania police of the destruction of Flight 93, lasted only 123 minutes. In the form it took, the attack was neither expected nor predicted; once it was under way, it took some time to realize what was going on, and no one knew what might happen next. For example, at 1:44 p.m. on 9/11 the Pentagon announced that a task force of two aircraft carriers and five other warships would sail from the U.S. naval station in Norfolk, Virginia, both to protect the East Coast from further danger and to reduce the number of ships sitting in port and therefore vulnerable to attack. It was quite possible to imagine then that the WTC and Pentagon attacks might be supplemented by hijacked transatlantic flights only now arriving at the coast. In the skies over the eastern United States, with the planes' transponders turned off by the hijackers, the signals from the individual hijacked flights had melted into the usual swarm of radar spots. We might also mention the understandable unwillingness of the authorities to send fighters into the sky with instructions to shoot down any passenger airliner that seemed to fit an offending profile.

One radical academic wary of falling into Griffin's error was the great linguist and veteran campaigner Noam Chomsky. In constant e-mail contact with his public, Chomsky found himself under some pressure to join the Truth movement. In 2002, taxed with some of Gore Vidal's "disturbing questions" and asked whether they didn't add up to a government plot, Chomsky replied, "The world is full of unexplained data. Intelligence agencies and military forces are deluged with low-quality information which may, in retrospect, seem significant, but cannot seriously be evaluated . . . It would also be quite mad, in my opinion, for any government to try something like what [Vidal] suggested."[51]

8. MR. POOTER FORMS A THEORY

A man of middle age and middle height with a receded chin and receding hairline, Liberal Democrat MP Norman Baker is not a terribly arresting figure. He is distinguished neither in oratory nor dress sense, and his career before Parliament was almost exceptionally ordinary: he was a regional executive for a retail record chain, ran a wine shop, taught English as a second language, and was a local councilor in Sussex. It was the electoral train wreck involving the Conservative Party, rather than any obvious leadership qualities, that in 1997 allowed Mr. Baker to become the MP for Lewes, Sussex.

Having entered Parliament, however, Baker underwent an interesting transformation: he began to make himself un-ordinary. He did this by becoming one of the most prolific questioners in British parliamentary history. After three months in the job, Baker had asked more parliamentary written questions of ministers than his Conservative predecessor had in twenty-three years. By the end of ten years, it was estimated that he had asked eight thousand such questions, an average of more than two per day, including every weekend, holiday, and bank holiday. Now, answering a written question requires some minimal amount of civil-service time, and a cautious estimate puts the cost of each query in the region of £150. It is therefore reasonable to cost Mr. Baker's super-interrogatory decade at a minimum of £1.2 million. Though it is bad manners in a democracy to dwell on the price of information, and offensive to speculate on its cost-effectiveness, it is perhaps reasonable to comment that had every non-governmental member chosen to behave in the same way as Mr. Baker, then the bill would have been over half a billion pounds.

Nevertheless, Baker's questioning won him accolades. No matter that he was dull. "You sit up in the middle of what he is talking about," said one parliamentary sketch writer, "stunned and amazed that anybody could be so boring." But, he then added, "You underestimate him at your peril . . . He has a habit of being right. He sticks to his guns and I think his constituents are very lucky to have him."[1] In 2001, the *Spectator* magazine named him Inquisitor of the Year, and in 2002, Channel 4 News awarded him the title Opposition MP of the Year. His support for complete disclosure of MP's allowances and expenditures won him fierce praise from those journalists who tend to see politics as something of a racket. "Is Norman Baker the greatest man in politics?" asked one, replying, "He is a deeply honest man of utter integrity who is determined that British voters should know the truth about how we are governed. Baker is neither flashy, smooth nor glamorous. He does not sit on the Front Benches.* But he is, in his own way, the most admirable and heroic MP at Westminster."[2]

A less idealistic observer of the Baker technique might note a some-what scatter-gun approach to the business of accountability. For example, in 2008 he asked how many people had been killed in a small earthquake on the Tibetan border, how much bottled water was consumed in Parliament, and what progress was being made in reducing aircraft noise pollution in the national parks. The previous year he was eager for Prime

---

*Correct at the time, but Mr. Baker has held a number of front-bench positions since.

Minister Tony Blair (something of an obsession with Mr. Baker) to tell Parliament about his attendance at the Bilderberg conferences to discuss global economics and politics. Bilderberg, essentially an informal transatlantic elite networking group, is a favorite subject among those who believe that there is a global organization that attempts to run the affairs of the planet. Mr. Blair replied that he had not attended such a conference. In January 2007, Mr. Baker was asking the same question of the Chancellor of the Exchequer, Mr. Gordon Brown.[3]

Mr. Baker's main preoccupation in the years 2006 and 2007 was elsewhere. Between March 2006 and June 2007, fifty-four of Mr. Baker's parliamentary written questions were on the subject of a man whose death in July 2003 had created a scandal that had threatened to bring down the prime minister: government scientist Dr. David Kelly. For that period, Mr. Baker stood down from his responsibilities with the Liberal Democrat front bench in order to complete a book, *The Strange Death of David Kelly*, in which he claimed that Dr. Kelly's death—presumed to have been suicide—was in fact murder.

The Death of a Government Inspector

In the summer of 2003, the British press was dominated by the media firestorm that was the "Kelly Affair." It began with a series of reports on BBC Radio 4's combative and important *Today* program. Following the invasion of Iraq, it was becoming clear that stockpiles of supposedly extant Iraqi weapons of mass destruction were unlikely to be found. BBC correspondent Andrew Gilligan suggested on *Today* that a dossier released by the government the previous September, which claimed that there was strong evidence of WMD in Iraq, had in part been published against the wishes of the intelligence community, and in the knowledge that sections of it were untrue or exaggerated.

The implication of Gilligan's revelations—amplified by him in a newspaper the following weekend—was that the British government, far from having been mistaken about Iraqi weapons, had connived at the creation of false evidence for them. In this context, Gilligan's assertion that his information came from a senior intelligence source—whose identity, naturally, he could not be expected to reveal—seemed disastrous for the prime minister and even more so for his controversial press secretary, Alastair Campbell, who had had some responsibility for the production of the dossier. Very publicly and very angrily, Campbell demanded that the BBC issue an apology and a retraction of its allegations, saying that the source, if it existed, could not be a senior intelligence officer, and that this fact, if revealed, would show Gilligan to be, at best, wrong.

But there were far more than just three players in this tragedy. Other journalists had been digging in the same field, and at least two parliamentary committees—jealous of their rights and prerogatives—were looking into the question of the dossiers. There was widespread, almost feverish, speculation about who Gilligan's source might be. Then Dr. David Kelly, an employee of the Ministry of Defense but not an intelligence official, informed his superiors that he had spoken to Andrew Gilligan, but added that he had not said the things attributed by Gilligan to his source. It was probably inevitable that this would become public, and the government took no very stringent steps to ensure that it didn't. The result was that a besieged Kelly, transformed overnight from private to public figure, found himself giving televised evidence to the parliamentary committees, and it was at one of these—on July 15—that some of his denials that he was Gilligan's source for certain quotes were shown, though not immediately, to be misleading.

Two days later, in the mid-afternoon of July 17, Dr. Kelly told his wife at their home in a small Oxfordshire village that he was going out for a walk. Just before midnight, one of his adult daughters called the police to say her father was missing. His body was discovered at 9:20 the following morning in a small wood not far from his home. Pathologists attributed his death to the combination of three factors: the severing of his left ulnar artery, the ingestion of a large number of co-proxamol painkiller tablets, and an existing atherosclerosis—deterioration of the arteries. Tony Blair, informed of the news while in midair between Washington and Tokyo, announced the setting-up of an independent inquiry to look into the circumstances of Dr. Kelly's death.

This inquiry, chaired by Lord Hutton, concluded in January 2004 that Dr. Kelly had committed suicide, and disappointed many in Britain by attributing most of the blame for the events leading up to his death to the BBC and not to the government. Subsequent controversy centered on this perceived injustice, rather than on the suicide verdict itself. Doubts about the latter were left to a small number of doctors in a letter-writing campaign coordinated by a British woman, Rowena Thursby. "During 2004," she subsequently wrote, "I made contact with a Dr. C. Stephen Frost who had written a list of thirty-five questions about Dr. Kelly's death on the *Independent* Internet forum. Working together, and liaising with the rest of the medicolegal team, we managed to get five letters published in the *Guardian*."[4]

The group, a collection of surgeons and specialists that included a retired orthopedic surgeon, a radiologist, a specialist in anesthesiology, a public health consultant, a vascular specialist, and a retired pathologist (none of whom had personally examined Dr. Kelly), cast doubt on the likelihood of Kelly having died as described by the original pathologists. Their intervention caused, according to Thursby, a "media storm." "We were inundated with requests for radio and TV appearances . . . The *Evening Standard* ran a headline on the evening prior to the publication of the Hutton Report: 'Was Kelly Murdered?'" Thursby herself did not sign the letters. This may have been wise, since she had an Internet pedigree of conspiracist thinking that suggested a general disposition toward a belief in plots rather than simple skepticism occasioned by specific doubts. "Beyond Belief" she had titled one abortive attempt at a blog, which she subtitled "Freedom from the Known." It continued:

I base my search on a suspicion—from books and information available on the Net—that the truth about political events is a world apart from what we are led to believe. For example: Were both world wars engineered? What about other wars—were they deliberately "arranged" for a purpose? Is there a plan for world government? If so, who is behind it? Was 9/11 the prime catalyst? This site hopes to peel back the veneer, and address the big questions:

Who is really behind the the [*sic*] terrorist atrocities? Where lies the true source of political power? What part do secret societies play in the politics today?[5]

That, however, is where the blog ends.

The Suicidal Type and Other Norms

In his book advancing the thesis that David Kelly was murdered, Norman Baker acknowledges the pioneering work of Ms. Thursby ("a remarkable woman") and of the small group of doctors. Though he doesn't say so, it seems likely that it was the *Guardian* letters that began Baker's interest in the theory that Kelly might not have committed suicide. In origin, then, the involvement of the politician in the construction of a conspiracy theory concerning the death of a prototypical English citizen seems similar to that of Tam Dalyell MP in the Hilda Murrell case nearly a quarter of a century earlier.

There are other similarities, too, although Dalyell didn't go as far as to expound his ideas at length in a book. It is Baker's lengthy and, in its way, courageous, exposition that is so fascinating and revealing, because it demonstrates the techniques Baker used, not least on himself, to try and persuade skeptics that David Kelly had been the victim of a complex conspiracy. Above all, it becomes possible to track the method by which Baker makes the likely—that Kelly did indeed commit suicide—seem very unlikely, and the unlikely—that he was murdered with the connivance of the British government—seem not just likely but inevitable. Given the ratio of suicides (there were 4,300 suicides or undetermined deaths in England in 2003) to murders of Britons in Britain by external forces, this is no small achievement.

Baker's starting credo is the following: "I am personally convinced beyond reasonable doubt, to apply that test," he writes, "that it is nigh-on clinically impossible for Dr. Kelly to have died at his own hand in the manner described, and further that both his personality and other circumstantial evidence strongly militates against suicide."[6]According to Baker, Kelly was psychologically not the type of man to commit suicide—his inhibitions against self-slaughter were too great—and his behavior just before his disappearance gave little support to the idea that he might have been contemplating his own death.

The notion that Kelly was not the type does not result from any scrutiny, as far as the book goes, of suicide statistics, of major studies into the causes of suicide, or of the work of psychiatric or health professionals. It comes from the opinions of a small number of occasional colleagues and friends, including two cribbage players from the local pub, who expressed surprise at Kelly's death, and from Baker's own belief that there is a suicidal type. He does not enumerate the characteristics of this type; he merely asserts that Kelly didn't fit it. In fact, as we will see, David Kelly had at least one characteristic that, in statistical terms, probably made him an enhanced suicide risk.

But what about the supposed inhibitions? One was that "Dr. Kelly was an adherent and relatively recent convert to the Bahai faith, which strongly outlaws suicide."[7] As an argument, this is irrelevant, and as a fact, it is—in relative terms—wrong. Irrelevant because there are, of course, adulterous Jews, thieving Catholics, and highly uncharitable Muslims. And suicide is often associated with deep depression, in which such external restrictions may well seem to belong to a different world. Wrong, because the Bahai strictures on suicide are, if anything, much less stern than those of other faiths. Jews, Muslims, and Catholics regard suicide as murder, and several religions famously deny the consolation of burial in the faith to those who kill themselves. The Bahai do, as Baker writes, "forbid" suicide, but also, as he neglects to mention, they say that a suicide "will be immersed in the ocean of pardon and forgiveness and will become the recipient of bounty and favor."[8]

A second Baker objection to the suicide verdict is that Dr. Kelly had long been concerned for his wife, Janice, who suffered poor health and required to be looked after. "It is hardly likely, then, given that approach, that he would want to exacerbate matters in the worst possible way for his wife by committing suicide that day."[9] That "hardly likely" is a blind guess on the basis of no evidence. Almost all acts of suicide can be expected to have an impact on family or friends. Sometimes the suicide seems to be persuaded that his or her death will come as relief, or remove some obstacle, or avert some greater disaster. Since we know very little about the intimate relationship between Dr. and Mrs. Kelly, we have no way of knowing—let alone judging the likelihood of—how Kelly may have imagined the consequences of his own death.

The third objection is based on a particular reading of Dr. Kelly's state of mind on his last morning. "Indeed the evidence from Dr. Kelly's e-mails written that morning suggests his mood was, if anything, upbeat." Dr. Kelly had, Baker points out, booked aircraft flights. "It must be said that none of this fits with the profile of a man about to commit suicide. People about to kill themselves do not generally first book an airline ticket for a flight they have no intention of taking."[10] As we will see, both Mrs. Kelly and a professor of psychiatry felt—one from direct and the other from clinical experience—that Dr. Kelly's state of mind was anything other than "upbeat." Again, Baker's assumptions are of the man-in-the-pub kind. He has absolutely no evidence that those who may soon attempt suicide very rarely or never do anything which might suggest a future.

He applies the same kind of reasoning to his fourth objection: that there was no suicide note. Baker claims, "While suicide notes are not an invariable feature, they are very common and one might have been expected in this case."[11] "Very common but not invariable" is one way of saying that the majority of those who commit suicide leave no note at all, perhaps up to two-thirds. Why then, in Norman Baker's opinion, might a note not be anticipated in the bulk of cases of suicide but be "expected" in the case of Dr. Kelly? Mr. Baker simply doesn't say.

So what, in a case of suicide, might reasonably be expected? As Baker concedes, David Kelly's own mother committed suicide. The day before his twentieth birthday, she died from an overdose of sleeping pills. Though there is a great deal of debate, opinion among health professionals tends to favor the notion that the suicide of a close family member or friend helps create an enhanced risk of suicide in the bereft. A 2002 American study proposed that children of parents who had attempted suicide were up to six times more likely to attempt suicide themselves. Some psychiatrists see this as due to a heritability of depression, others argue that such a death is deeply suggestive, or induces "pathologic bereavement."[12]

Baker does not acknowledge such evidence, but instead deals with the problem in this way. "The question inevitably arises whether this tragic incident was on Dr. Kelly's mind on 17 July 2003."[13] A more interesting question would surely be whether his mother's suicide was *in*, rather than on, Dr. Kelly's mind—in other words, whether he carried it with him at all times. Mr. Baker feels that, in any case, Dr. Kelly had got over it, because in discussions with others concerning the death of his mother, "his tone, by all accounts, was slightly dispassionate and quite balanced."[14] You don't have to be a mental health professional to find such a mechanical interpretation rather ludicrous. Dr. Kelly did not weep, sob, or wail when speaking of his mother's suicide, therefore we may believe he was relatively unaffected by it.

A second, fairly common indicator of possible suicidal intent is a mental dress rehearsal. After the Kelly death, an acquaintance, David Broucher, came forward with an account of a conversation he had had with him some time earlier. As Baker reports it, Broucher "asked what would happen if Iraq were invaded. Dr. Kelly replied that he 'would probably be found dead in the woods'—as indeed he was." Baker goes on to make the following deduction: "At the inquiry, this was construed as meaning that he already had suicidal thoughts. That, of course, is patently absurd . . . Nobody can seriously suggest that Dr. Kelly was suicidal at the time the meeting took place."[15] In fact, no one can know what Kelly's state of mind was at the time of that conversation, including Norman Baker. But one detail stands out and is incontrovertible, if we trust Mr. Broucher:

it was David Kelly and no one else, as far as we know, who associated his being found dead with "the woods." This makes Baker's next observation grimly and unintentionally comic, as well as a model of inversion. "It is uncanny that he [Kelly] should have alighted on that very phrase."[16] But if Kelly committed suicide, then it isn't uncanny at all.

Baker's book shows him to be ignorant of, and uninterested in, suicide as a phenomenon. When writing about it, he operates at the level of vulgar prejudice masquerading as common sense. But even here he has a problem, since Mrs. Kelly herself gave evidence to the Hutton Inquiry suggesting that her husband was in a severely depressed state in the period before his disappearance. "I just thought he had a broken heart," she said. "He had shrunk into himself." If you accept this, then it becomes easy to believe that a man in such a state might kill himself.

Baker is ruthless in his dismissal of Mrs. Kelly's testimony. "In terms of evidence," he writes, "this is clearly reinterpreting what was to pass with the benefit of subsequent knowledge of the official explanation of her husband's death."[17] A truly remarkable sentence, this, suggesting that Mrs. Kelly alone among all the acquaintances, cribbage players, and others cited by Baker was incapable of distinguishing her impressions before the death from her views following the verdict of suicide. Their generalizations were more to be trusted than her close-up observations. Baker continues to drive the knife in. "It is perhaps surprising," he writes, "given how 'shrunk into himself' her husband had seemed to her at lunchtime, that she did not worry earlier. That again suggests that any thoughts that he might harm himself were far from her mind. It is also odd that she appears not to have tried to contact him on his mobile phone . . . Surely that is the first thing a concerned spouse would do in such circumstances."[18]

Nor is the rest of the family let off. "It is still somewhat surprising that the police were not called until twenty to midnight. The family must have had no serious concerns for his health to leave it that late."[19] Once again Baker displays unearned omniscience. Is it not possible to imagine that Mrs. Kelly, herself an invalid, and her family might have worried about her husband's absence from, say, six in the evening, but that they were debating as to whether or not to call the police? Was there perhaps some reluctance to bring in the authorities, and certainly cause massive public interest at a time when Dr. Kelly was desperately trying to avoid further exposure?

Janice Kelly's inconvenience to the Baker theory leads the MP to add this strange codicil: "With a huge headache, being physically sick and [sic] painful arthritis, it seems to be Janice Kelly, rather than her husband, who was well below par."[20] The inference seems to be that Mrs. Kelly was simply too sick and self-preoccupied to notice properly what kind of state her husband was in. No second-party evidence is cited to back up this suggestion. What is more, Baker ignores second-party evidence that supports Mrs. Kelly's claim that her husband "had a broken heart." A friend of Dr. Kelly's, Professor Alastair Hay, was widely quoted in July 2003, recalling the fears that he had felt on seeing Kelly give evidence to the Foreign Affairs Committee: "I was so worried after I saw extracts of his evidence to the committee," said Hay. "He just looked so beaten by the process."[21]

Suicide: The Baker Method

Such views wouldn't matter much, however, if it could be established that it was "well-nigh impossible" for Dr. Kelly to have killed himself in the manner described at the Hutton Inquiry. And this is exactly what Baker attempts to do. The doctors' letters had concentrated on two aspects of the pathologist's findings. These were the implausibility of death from severing the ulnar artery, and the low level of co-proxamol in Dr. Kelly's body. Baker puts it thus: "It is extremely difficult to kill yourself by cutting your wrists. Of course, people can die from wrist or arm cutting, but it requires some basic medical knowledge to be successful."[22] Furthermore, he says, it is "generally accepted that concentrations of drug in the blood can increase by as much as tenfold after death, leaving open the possibility that Dr. Kelly consumed only a thirtieth of the dose of co-proxamol necessary to kill him."[23]

But the forensic pathologists who had actually examined the body thought that it was entirely possible for Dr. Kelly to have died from the severed artery, the co-proxamol, and his existing arterial problems. Other than suggesting that these experts were somehow in on the plot, how might one reasonably explain the difference between their verdict and those of the *Guardian* doctors? Baker achieves this in the first instance by quoting one of the letter writers, retired trauma surgeon David Halpin, who says to Baker, "surgeons know rather more about arteries than pathologists do."[24] However, on a BBC program screened some nine months before Baker's book was published, Home Office forensic pathologist and president of the British Association in Forensic Medicine, Dr. Allen Anscombe, anticipated this line of argument. Clinicians concentrated on patients surviving, he told the BBC, while "forensic pathologists are biased in terms of seeing what people actually die from." He was "quite happy" to accept that often severing a small artery might not be fatal, but knew from his experience that occasionally it certainly would be.[25]

According to national statistics, two deaths occurred as the result of a severed ulnar artery in 2000, one in 2001, and one in 2004. So Baker's "well-nigh impossible" is statistically quite possible even if rare. But of course, the original pathologists had also attributed Kelly's death to two other causes: existing atherosclerosis, only diagnosed postmortem, and the ingestion of co-proxamol tablets.

A combination of paracetamol and an opioid, dextropropoxyphene, co-proxamol—usually used to alleviate back or arthritic pain—began to be withdrawn from use in the United Kingdom just two years after Kelly's death, because the drug, as even Baker's book admits (though in a footnote),[26] was by 2003 responsible for up to four hundred fatal overdoses every year, many unintentional. The Medicines and Healthcare products Regulatory Agency (MHRA) subsequently claimed that taking as few as ten tablets in a twenty-four-hour period could slow the respiratory system, cause abnormal heart rhythms, and lead to possible cardiac arrest.[27] Among forensic toxicologists, there wasn't much doubt that the number of tablets apparently consumed by Dr. Kelly could, by themselves or in combination, lead to death. The president of the Forensic Science Society, Professor Robert Forrest, told a British news station in March 2004, "Twenty-nine tablets of co-proxamol would kill most people."[28] There is no mention of Forrest or his opinion in Norman Baker's book, despite the fact that it was entirely researched and written after this interview. Forrest went on to tell the BBC in early 2007:

> We normally see higher concentrations than that in a person who has died of an overdose of co-proxamol. But if you've got heart disease, and if there is something else going on like blood loss, then all three of those are going to act together . . . I've got no doubt that the cause of Dr. Kelly's death was a combination of blood loss, heart disease, and overdose of co-proxamol. Not necessarily in that order. If I was going to put it in order I'd put the overdose of co-proxamol first. But it's important that all of them had interacted to lead to the death.[29]

Had Baker shared the views of Britain's leading forensic toxicologists with his readers, the impression he was attempting to create would, to say the least, have been dissipated. But he was prepared to throw everything, including the kitchen sink, into trying to inject a spurious oddness into the verdict of suicide. "A further objection," he writes, "is that Dr. Kelly undoubtedly knew more about the human anatomy than most people, and the idea that he would have chosen such an uncertain and painful method to commit suicide is not easy to sustain."[30] He pursues this argument: "At the very least, Dr. Kelly would have known that to overdose on co-proxamol could have left him alive but medically damaged . . . Similarly, he would have known that to cut the ulnar artery could well have left him alive, suffering in extreme pain, and with a hole in his wrist."[31] And it comes again, ratcheting up the incredulity: "Are we really expected to believe that someone of the knowledge and maturity of David Kelly would have decided upon such an inept, uncertain, and painful way to kill himself?"[32]

Any failed bid can leave the attempted suicide badly wounded: one thinks of people who have managed to shoot their jaws off or put holes in their chests. The point is that they believe they are going to die. Actually, as we have seen, co-proxamol was a good method, and if Kelly took the tablets first, the artery severing might have been an attempt to hurry things along. But one wonders what certain and painless methods Baker thought Kelly should have chosen. One of the most common forms of suicide, hanging, is believed to be one of the most agonizing. Perhaps hemlock was unavailable.

Baker's demolition of Dr. Kelly's suicide method is lengthy and detailed, employing cumbersome sarcasm in order to suggest strained credulity. "We are told," he writes, "that the police found twenty-nine of the tablets had been removed from their trays—doubtless the one that David Kelly thoughtfully left helped the police with their inquiries. Dr. Kelly had apparently also very considerately replaced the empty blister packs inside the pocket of his waxed jacket, found at the scene."[33] As opposed, one imagines, to committing one final caprice and carefully digging a hole and putting the tray in it so as to bamboozle any investigators. Much is made out of an aversion that Dr. Kelly was supposed to have had, according to one source, to swallowing tablets. "If this is right, we are then being asked to believe that Dr. Kelly indulged in a further masochistic act in the attempt to take his life."[34] One hardly needs to point out that suicide is an act of self-destruction. Is it really hard to believe that someone intent on killing themselves and with the means on hand would do so?

Previously, Baker points out, Dr. Kelly's wife had offered a friend, Mai Pederson, some of her tablets for a headache. "Ms. Pederson accepted, but Dr. Kelly criticized his wife for offering tablets prescribed for her alone. If true, this can only reinforce the doubts that exist that Dr. Kelly would actually have chosen to ingest twenty-nine of these tablets."[35] Actually, of course, it does no such thing. If anything, it reminds us that Kelly knew how dangerous these drugs could be. So did Baker really think that Dr. Kelly—intent on suicide—wouldn't have taken an overdose of tablets unless they'd been prescribed to him personally?

Almost any argument would do. "Common sense tells us that quite a lot of water would be required to swallow twenty-nine tablets, particularly ones such as these, oval with a long axis of about half an inch. It is frankly unlikely, with only a small water bottle to hand, that any water would have been left undrunk."[36] There seems to be no evidential basis whatsoever, and no authority, for Baker's claim of what was and wasn't "frankly unlikely." However, a reader might like to see if they can wash down twenty-nine jelly beans with rather less than half a liter of water. It's pretty easy.

"Yet what person, intent on cutting their wrists, or indeed swallowing large numbers of tablets, would do so on their back? The natural position, if such a term can be used, is surely sitting, which in a wood does suggest against a tree."[37] Once again, there is no support for the claim about the "natural position" for a wrist-cutting or tablet-swallowing suicide to adopt. But anyway, there had been no suggestion from the pathologists or the police that Kelly had been lying "on his back" at the point when he took the tablets and cut his wrist. He was found with his head slightly propped up at the base of a tree.

Dark Hints

We have already seen, in the case of Janice Kelly, how Baker's tactic when dealing with inconvenient evidence is to "vanish" the troublemaker. Like a rather desperate defense counsel whose client has been found standing with a bloodied knife above the body of his victim, a fresh £100,000 life insurance policy in his pocket, Baker sets about the naysayers with impressive vim. First up is Dr. Nicholas Hunt, the pathologist chosen by the Oxfordshire coroner (judge), Nicholas Gardiner, to take on the case. Dr. Hunt was, according to Baker, underqualified. "It is curious therefore that the Oxfordshire coroner should have made this choice," he writes. "Under the circumstances Mr. Gardiner could have been forgiven for employing the most experienced pathologist he could find from the register, or even employing two such people."[38] There is an insinuation here, but we don't know of what.

Anyone in the way of Baker's theory gets this dark-hint treatment. Tom Mangold, one of the most experienced investigative reporters in British journalism, knew and liked Dr. Kelly, who had helped him in the past. Mangold is an abrasive and outspoken man with no time for conspiracy theories about Kelly's death, and therefore became a prime Baker target. "Tom Mangold's role overall is a singular one," he writes. "Even before Dr. Kelly's body was officially found on the Friday morning, he was on the phone to Mrs. Kelly." There isn't anything "singular" about this at all, since the fact of Kelly's disappearance was known hours before his body was found. But Baker continues: "Indeed, Mr. Mangold seemed strangely keen to declare the death a suicide and to discredit any suggestion to the contrary."[39] "Strangely" is surely used to convey the impression that Mangold was complicit in a cover-up, or else means nothing at all.

Baker then sets about abnormalizing the police operation, beginning with the search. "It is difficult to understand the purpose of sending a dog through the house," he writes.[40] Is it? In fact, it is surprisingly common for initial searches to miss bodies that are actually concealed in that most expected of places, the home. To give a recent famous example, in the 2006 case of Neil Entwistle, the Englishman who murdered his wife and child in Boston, two searches of the family home failed to discover the shot bodies under a duvet on one of the beds. Why then should it be so unexpected for the police to double-check the Kelly home using dogs? "It is surprising, given that the helicopter was equipped with heat-seeking equipment . . . that Dr. Kelly's body could not be found."[41] Try entering "heat-seeking equipment" and "failed to find" in a search engine and you'll find out just how surprising this is. Because something is better doesn't mean it is infallible. "Could army personnel not have been used on this search?"[42] In other words, was there something untoward about the usual procedure not being ditched, and the army (which bit?) not being called out at midnight on a police search?

It goes on and on. A sniffer dog did not behave as Norman Baker feels it should have done. "Oddly, although the dog was trained to take his handler toward what he has found, on this occasion he did not do so."[43]

Is this odd? Or does it happen quite frequently? And what does it matter? Baker is also unhappy with the policeman who, once the body was found, was left to guard the scene of the crime, and who testified that he applied standard procedure and went no closer than seven or eight feet. "It is difficult to accept that he went no nearer than this. Surely the natural human reaction would have been to approach the body, without touching it, to observe the situation more closely."[44] Once again, Baker is master of the human condition, able to assert that a constable would be far more likely to break procedure than not.

With the scientist missing, a police communications mast was placed in the garden of the Kelly house. An anonymous chief constable subsequently told Baker that such a mast would usually only be fifteen feet tall, but this one was considerably higher. Aha! Clear evidence of a plot here. And yet the Oxfordshire police explained to Baker that the mast needed to be tall because the garden was in a "communications blackspot." Baker didn't accept this explanation. "What was the purpose of this very high mast? It seems clear that normal police communications would not require such a structure." Then he adds this suggestion: "It might, however, have been required if it were thought necessary to contact an aircraft in the sky a very long way away, such as the one at the time carrying the Prime Minister to Washington."[45] There is much to admire in this argument. Having dismissed a perfectly testable explanation for no given reason, Baker reaches instead for a rationalization based on no evidence whatsoever.

Finally, we come to former Prime Minister Tony Blair. Inevitably, Blair gets the insinuation treatment in spades, with Baker pointing out how convenient politically it was for the PM "that Dr. Kelly's body should have been found less than a day after Parliament broke up for its long summer holiday and a time when Blair himself was out of the country far away."[46] A reader might imagine that a parliamentarian like Baker would be in a good position to judge exactly how convenient it was for the prime minister. In fact, Baker's assertion was inane. Blair was informed of Kelly's death on a plane over the Pacific full of lobby journalists all looking for a story. There was nowhere to hide, no question of not immediately facing the press. Reports unanimously agree that Blair looked shaken and pale. On landing in Tokyo, Blair was famously asked on camera, "Have you got blood on your hands, Prime Minister? Are you going to resign over this?" The timing was about as inconvenient politically as it could possibly have been.

Liberty and Truth

We shall see in a moment who exactly Norman Baker thinks murdered Dr. Kelly, but before we do, let's look at how he justifies his belief in such a plot. In case one should dismiss his hypothesis as a mere conspiracy theory, Baker devotes considerable time in his preface to previous examples of government deceit. "Does such a concept deserve to be dismissed out of hand?" he asks. "History teaches us otherwise." And he points to events through history that corroborate his view. One is the setting on fire of the Reichstag in Berlin at the end of January 1933, after which several Communists were put on trial for arson. "In fact the Nazis themselves were responsible for the fire," writes Baker, "precisely in order to achieve the double objectives of discrediting the Communists and benefiting themselves."[47]

There is no footnote to provide support for Baker's confident assertion. It is certainly true that such a version of events is widely believed, and has been for seventy years. The problem is that there isn't much evidence to support it. As books like the anti-Nazi Fritz Tobias's *Der Reichstagbrand*[*] show, the firm belief of the Berlin detectives who were the first investigators of the fire was that the man they caught red-handed, Dutch revolutionary Marinus van der Lubbe, was solely responsible for the crime. The Nazis, of course, were determined to prove that the fire had been a Communist

---

*Published in Britain and the USA as *The Reichstag Fire: Legend and Truth*.

conspiracy, and the Communists were equally intent on proving that it was a Nazi plot. The former were now in power in Germany and commanded a powerful propaganda machine. The Communists, under the direction of their brilliant clandestine publicist Willi Münzenberg, for their part issued the famous Brown Books, in which the argument against the Nazis was put forward. However, throughout the pretrial, the trial itself, and right up to his execution, one man insisted that Marinus van der Lubbe had committed the deed unaided. That man was Marinus van der Lubbe.

Another of Baker's examples is asserted at slightly greater length, although, once again, it is unsourced. "In 1967," he writes, "during the Six Day War, the CIA intelligence ship, *Liberty*, was bombed by unmarked Israeli planes in an apparent case of mistaken identity. It is now widely accepted that the attack was ordered by President Lyndon Johnson himself. Other U.S. ships in the area were prevented from assisting the *Liberty*. The bombing of the *Liberty*, with the loss of 34 crew members and the wounding of 171 others, was designed to look like an Egyptian attack, thus giving the U.S. a pretext to enter the war. This was only averted and the episode ended when a Soviet spy ship appeared on the scene."[48]

No one, apart from Mr. Baker, as far I am aware, has claimed that the *Liberty* was a CIA ship. It wasn't; it was a U.S. Navy ship. But once again, though a series of official investigations in both the United States and Israel found that the attack was essentially a friendly-fire incident, there are many people who, from a mixture of motives, argue that it was no mistake. Foremost among these are a group of survivors of the incident, whose insistence that the Israelis knew that they were firing on a U.S. ship has acted as the springboard for many books and TV documentaries.

Quite apart from some of the factual objections to the no-mistake theory (and there are many),[49] the obvious problem has always been one of motive. Why would the embattled Israelis choose to try to sink a ship belonging to the friendlier of the two superpowers? It doesn't make much sense. So the theories of the no-mistakers have taken on a complex, almost baroque quality. Some have argued, for example, that the Israelis wanted it to be believed that the attack was undertaken by Egyptian planes, and thus bring America into the war more directly. Possibly the most far-fetched of the theories, however, is that expounded by the journalist Peter Hounam in his 2003 book *Operation Cyanide: Why the Bombing of the USS Liberty Nearly Caused World War III*. As a *Sunday Times* writer, Hounam played a major part in revealing Israel's nuclear weapons program in the 1980s, a substantial journalistic achievement, but by the early 2000s he was to be discovered writing books suggesting that Princess Diana might have been the victim of a conspiracy.[50]

Unusually, given the BBC's attention to being seen as impartial, *Operation Cyanide* was given a preface by John Simpson, the corporation's rather grandly titled world affairs editor. A flavor of the body of the book can be gained from his endorsement. "Suppose," wrote Simpson, "in an attempt to shore up his critically damaged presidency, Lyndon Johnson deliberately engineered an event in which American lives were sacrificed and the United States was brought disturbingly close to an all-out nuclear war with Russia?" He added, "It sounds, I know, like one of those depressing conspiracy theories which cluster round every big controversial event, from the death of Princess Diana to the attack on the World Trade Center . . . yet this book is based on careful, rigorous investigation by a well-known and respected journalist . . . As with the assassination of President John F. Kennedy four years earlier, the official version is even more unlikely than some of the conspiracy theories."[51]

At the most basic level of believability—given the history of friendly-fire and mistaken-identity incidents (including, for example, the attack twenty-six years earlier by British torpedo bombers on the cruiser HMS *Sheffield* under the impression that it was the *Bismarck*)—it isn't difficult to accept that the whole thing was a tragic error.

But the inherent extreme improbability, despite Simpson's words, of a president already enmired in Vietnam and pushing through one of the most ambitious domestic programs of the postwar period deliberately courting the possibility of a nuclear exchange in a region as volatile as the Middle East puts Hounam's theory on the outer edge of conspiracism. Most other conspiracy theorists do not go so far.

But whatever one's conclusions, what is obvious here is that once again Baker is asserting as fact something that is far more tenuous, to say the very least. It is most certainly not the case that it is "widely accepted that the attack [on the *Liberty*] was ordered by President Lyndon Johnson himself." Subjected to scrutiny by anyone familiar with the examples he is using, Baker's normalization simply evaporates.

Crockford's and the Borgias

Rather delightfully, Baker's list of examples from the history of conspiracy ends with one that has a specific application to the Kelly case, even if it means a decline from grand geopolitics to Trollopian parochial scandal. Baker had noticed, or it had been drawn to his attention, that the Oxfordshire coroner, Nicholas Gardiner, had—fifteen years earlier—presided over another cause célèbre involving suicide.

The end of 1987 saw the publication of the 1988 edition of *Crockford's Clerical Directory*, an annually updated list with brief biographies of all the Anglican clergy in the United Kingdom and Ireland. The appearance of *Crockford's* was much anticipated by the polite prelates of the Church of England largely for its preface, which was rewritten each year by an anonymous contributor and was, by tradition, rather amusing and acerbic. Now, 1987 was a time of considerable anxiety in the Church. The radical Conservatism of Margaret Thatcher was dominant politically, and there was pressure on the liberals in the Church of England, who were perceived as presiding over its decline. As a result, there was more than the usual lay-media interest in the 1988 preface, particularly since it took the form of a distinctly personal attack on the tolerance shown by the Archbishop of Canterbury to the unsuccessful and cliquish liberal elite leading the Church to destruction. All were agog to know who the author was.

On December 7, four days after publication, Canon Gareth Bennett was found dead in his car in his garage in Oxford. A hose attached to the car's exhaust led in through a window. It was then disclosed that Bennett, a conservative and gay Anglo-Catholic, had been—as suspected by many in the Church—the author of the preface. His diary apparently recorded his growing dismay at being involved in such a large media story. The coroner at Canon Bennett's inquest in Oxford, at which a verdict of suicide was recorded, was Nicholas Gardiner.

Baker's deployment of the Bennett case suggests that Gardiner had not done his job properly, and that the whole business was suspicious. "Like David Kelly, his [Bennett's] anonymous actions would infuriate some in positions of power," writes Baker—presumably including in this notional group the then Archbishop of Canterbury, the mild-mannered Robert Runcie. Baker casts doubt on the verdict, citing Bennett's probable moral objections to self-slaughter: "Like Dr. Kelly, he was under some pressure, but those who knew him say suicide was simply not in his make-up, not least for strong religious reasons."[52] Again, there is no source for this assertion, and it conjures up the most extraordinary image, reminiscent of the Borgias, of a middle-aged canon being murdered on the instructions of Church of England liberals. Possibly in on the plot were the Oxfordshire constabulary, as suggested by the case of the cat that did not meow in the night. "Most curious of all is that when the police arrived his cat was found to be dead in the sitting-room." A cat whose food, Baker complains, was not taken away for forensic analysis.[53] In Norman Baker's world, it would be natural to carry out a test to see if anyone might have poisoned a cat before staging a carbon-monoxide suicide. Perhaps it was an attack cat.

If Gardiner was a potential villain, Baker gives a hint that higher officialdom might be capable of much worse. In a prolonged aside, Baker mentions former Labour Cabinet minister and prominent critic of the Iraq War, Robin Cook, and quotes extensively from a *Guardian* article written by Mr. Cook, which was highly critical of the information given to the British public in the run-up to the war. Without giving a date for the article, Baker concludes this section, gratuitously, with: "Mr. Cook died suddenly shortly afterward, on Saturday 6 August 2005, while out walking in the Scottish highlands."[54] "Shortly afterward" was, in fact, nearly a year, the article having appeared in July 2004. But the impression had been given—for those who might wish to be so impressed—that there was perhaps something suspicious about Cook's death—which was diagnosed as a heart attack, and which happened in front of his wife.

Cui Bono?

So, if Kelly didn't kill himself, and if he hadn't died in the way specified at the Hutton Inquiry, how had he been murdered, and why? How many cases, one wonders, are there of people cutting someone else's ulnar artery? And if it was generally known that cutting this artery was rarely fatal, then why—with an infinity of choice in front of you—would you pick that one? Baker doesn't answer this. Instead, he focuses on the vomit. He is interested in the direction of its flow. Maybe it explains why the body was flat on the ground (though, in fact, it wasn't). "If the body had indeed been propped against a tree, it would have been interesting to have had the horizontal direction of the vomit stains explained. No such explanation would, of course, have been necessary if the body were flat on the ground."[55] In other words, killers who were stupid enough not to know that you can't die of a blunt knife across the ulnar artery, and were also sufficiently dim not to press Kelly's fingerprints onto the knife handle, were still sufficiently prescient to consider the exact direction of a vomit trail.

And what about the timing of the police operation, code-named "Mason"? The official start time of this action was given as two-thirty p.m. on the day of Kelly's disappearance. This, of course, preceded the missing-person call by more than nine hours. The police explained to Baker that it was their practice to time the start of an operation to the moment when their interest began, so in this case to round about the time that Kelly left home for the last time. Norman Baker is not satisfied with this. In his mind, there is a more sinister explanation, which "leaves us with the possibility that at least an element within Thames Valley Police had foreknowledge, to at least some degree, of that afternoon's tragic events. If that were the case, then it would of course clearly point to the involvement of another party in Dr. Kelly's death."[56] It is hardly necessary to point out that such an error would mean that this dastardly "element" was among the most stupid groups of plotters in recent history.

Just in case the reader is inclined to think Baker far-fetched, the author dismisses those of his informants who think that the code name "Mason" is itself suspicious. "Wild rumors of a freemasonry angle to the case are almost certainly without foundation,"[57] he opines, thus placing his own theories on the middle of a scale running between the official version and the notions of certifiable paranoids. Baker's by contrast well-founded theory about responsibility is arrived at—as is often the case—courtesy of an anonymous *deus ex machina*. But first the usual suspects have to be dismissed. "I have spoken to a number of individuals in the United States, well connected with the CIA . . . Each separately has come back to me to say that the inside track does indeed report Dr. Kelly as having been murdered, but that the United States was not part of it."[58] It is unfortunate that Baker can't attach even a rough figure to the number of such well-connected informants, let alone a single detail about the nature of any of their connections, just as he can't use even one unattributable quote or let drop even a single name. This is a world in which the plausible fantasist has it all his own way. We may recall that in 1984 "two reliable sources" had given Tam Dalyell MP the entirely false information that Hilda Murrell had been killed during a botched secret-service operation.

But the unnumbered and unnamed CIA-connected folk are none of them so remarkable as the Mr. X who met Baker in London, and who provided the MP with the answer to the mystery. This man told Baker "of a meeting where members of a UK-based Iraqi circle had boasted of people who claimed involvement in Dr. Kelly's death." The motive for the murder, revealed Mr. X, was their anger at what they believed Dr. Kelly had said to Andrew Gilligan—for it was they who had supplied the false information used by the British government in the lead-up to the Iraq invasion. Kelly had "besmirched" them. The source then "told me that the police or security services had got wind of a possible plan to assassinate Dr. Kelly and Operation Mason was originally set up to deal with this threat. But the police were too late."[59] The authorities now had the task of covering the murder up.

Who was this crucial Mr. X? Well, obviously Baker couldn't say. What was his connection with the Iraqis, whose meetings he was familiar with, or with the police, whose motives he was privy to? Presumably, the number of people in this situation was fairly small. Baker wasn't in a position to divulge. However, there was even greater detail available, probably from the same source. "According to information I have been given, the murder itself was carried out by a couple of not very well-paid hired hands. I was told, in fact, that the Iraqi-backed team had given Dr. Kelly an injection in his backside, which perhaps points to succinylcholine or something similar."[60]

Once again, Baker's language is redolent of that of his parliamentary predecessor Tam Dalyell. But the mention of succinylcholine, a muscle relaxant, in the context of disguising a murder suggests either familiarity with the arguments of a certain Michael Shrimpton or the sharing of sources. In February 2004, a few weeks after the first *Guardian* letter signed by the group of doubting doctors, British barrister and self-professed security expert Michael Shrimpton appeared on a U.S. conspiracist radio show. He told its host, Alex Jones, that "based on conversations with sources and with medical experts . . . he [Kelly] was probably murdered by a combination of an injection, not through tablets, but an intravenous injection of dextropropoxyphene and paracetamol, the constituents of co-proxamol, and a muscle relaxant called succinylcholine. Now succinylcholine is a favorite method of assassinating people, it's used by intelligence agencies, particularly the French DGSE."[61]

Shrimpton was also interviewed some time later on the BBC's *Conspiracy Files* program that examined claims about Dr. Kelly's death. A section of the transcript read:

SHRIMPTON: That is the red phone—if that phone goes it could be anyone from the White House to the president's administration in Russia to the CIA to whoever. It's not usual for me to pick up the phone and have Henry Kissinger on the other end but that has happened. He actually has that number but he doesn't have *that* number. That gives me a direct line through to Vice President Dick Cheney's office.

NARRATOR: Michael Shrimpton is also a fan of espionage fiction from Frederick Forsyth to Tom Clancy.

SHRIMPTON: He's one of my favorite authors.

INTERVIEWER: One of Tom Clancy's books, *The Teeth of the Tiger,* concerns an "off the books" team of U.S. government assassins who avoid detection by killing their victims with succinylcholine.

SHRIMPTON: Now yes there is a reference to succinylcholine in this book and I think that follows the assassination of David Kelly. Tom Clancy has very good contacts in the intelligence community. It may be that Tom Clancy picked up a loopback from the Kelly assassination. But if the suggestion is that I got succinylcholine from a Tom Clancy novel then sorry that won't wash.[62]

In fact, *Teeth of the Tiger* was published in 2003, making it more or less impossible for Clancy to have based his plot on any supposed rumors after David Kelly's death, but very easy for Shrimpton to have based his accusations on a newly read Clancy. Interestingly, Shrimpton is not mentioned by name in Baker's book, though he was one of the early supporters of the murder theory.

But whoever Baker's source was, the MP now banked the supposed information and moved on, in characteristic fashion. "The key question," he asks, "is whether the actions of the Iraqi group were self-generated, and subsequently covered up by the government, or whether a tiny cabal within the British establishment commissioned the assassins to undertake this. Perhaps it was somewhere in between, with a nod and a wink being unofficially offered. That would, after all, be very British."[63] Again, the outrageous claim is made to sound almost normal by the last two sentences—as though there is plenty of evidence that such things have occurred before. But turn it around. It would be very British for the authorities to permit or connive in the assassination of a British subject on British soil by representatives of another country. There is not a single case of such a thing happening in modern British history. Of course there isn't.

So strong is Baker's notion of the corruptibility of his fellow Britons that he is prepared to suggest that both Dr. Kelly's wife and the head of the subsequent inquiry might have been persuaded into selling the idea of suicide to the nation. "It is even possible to surmise," he writes, "that perhaps both Lord Hutton and Janice Kelly were told [that there had been a murder], and each was asked to go along with the story for the sake of the country, although there is of course no evidence to this effect."[64] To "surmise" means to infer something from incomplete evidence, and Baker admits that there is none at all. So what he means is that it is possible to speculate, as, of course, it is about anything.

So, where does Norman Baker arrive at the end of all this? It was more likely that there was a Tom Clancy operation involving exiled Iraqis who were never seen, found, or identified (whom one might have expected to be busy just after the liberation of their country) to kill a British subject and government employee who had already spoken to the press and who was at the epicenter of British media attention, and that this operation was covered up by a combination of the Oxfordshire police, the Oxfordshire coroner, those working for the Hutton Inquiry, and—quite possibly—Lord Hutton, Tom Mangold, and Janice Kelly herself, than that a man in a fix was prepared and able to sever his ulnar artery and take twenty-nine co-proxamol tablets.

Even before Baker's book was excerpted and serialized in the mass-circulation *Daily Mail*, one of its most serious columnists, Melanie Phillips, declared herself convinced by what she had heard of his arguments. "Mr. Baker cannot easily be dismissed as a crank," she wrote. "He is an exceptionally tenacious digger into things others prefer to keep hidden."

She, too, had received information from unnamed "people familiar with the shadowy world in which Dr. Kelly moved," and they were convinced it was murder.[65] Her colleague on the *Mail on Sunday*, Peter Oborne, contributed to the blurb on the book's back cover, writing that Baker's "research is very detailed and his conclusions must be taken seriously." In a review in the *Daily Telegraph*, a former MP, Nigel Jones, saluted this "somberly factual book," the antihero of which "is Tony Blair, and the cronies, lickspittles and murderous spooks who throng his corrupt court." Jones was utterly persuaded by Baker and intolerant of his critics. "His own courageous and well-publicized probing into Kelly's death has been dismissed with the usual 'we don't do that kind of thing, old boy.' But, as this disquieting book makes very clear—unfortunately, we do."

This was a reminder, were one needed, that, given the desire to believe, it is easy to confuse detail with thought. In conclusion, it is worth referring to the preface to the English edition of Fritz Tobias's book on the Reichstag fire, in which one great British historian, A. J. P. Taylor, quotes another, Sir Lewis Namier: "There would be little to say on this subject, were it not for the nonsense that has been talked about it."[66]

9. "I WANT MY COUNTRY BACK!"

I do not know whether Vincent Foster was depressed before his death. It is irrelevant anyway. The hard evidence indicates that the crime scene was staged, period. Even if Foster was depressed, somebody still put a gun in his hand, somebody still inflicted a perforating wound on his neck, his body still levitated 700 feet into Fort Marcy Park without leaving soil residue on his shoes, and he still managed to drive to Fort Marcy Park without any car keys.

—AMBROSE EVANS-PRITCHARD, 1997

The Lady in Red

In the summer of 2009, many in the world's media suddenly became aware of a new conspiracist phenomenon. A video shot by a citizen cameraperson sitting approximately halfway back in the auditorium at a town-hall meeting in Georgetown, Delaware, on June 30 was put on YouTube a week or so later, and within days went viral.

The clip begins with the rangy figure of Congressman Mike Castle, Delaware's sole representative in the U.S. House, face to the camera, choosing a questioner from the audience. "This lady in red . . ." he says. From the back it is hard to make out anything about the woman who now stands up, except that she seems to wear glasses and have her hair in what might be called a Sarah Palin semi-bun. The woman in red is brandishing something. She announces, "I have a birth certificate here from the United States of America, saying I am an American citizen, with a seal on it, signed by a doctor, with a hospital administrator's name, my parents, my date of birth, the time, the date. I want to go back to January 20, and I want to know why are you people ignoring his birth certificate." There is a loud cry of "Yeah!!!" and some applause, and a little booing. The woman continues, without specifying whom she is talking about—perhaps because she does not need to. "*He* is *not* an American citizen! He is a citizen of Kenya! My father fought in World War Two with the greatest generation in the Pacific theater for this country, and I don't want this flag to change." She waves a small American flag and shouts, "I want my country back!"[1] And sits back down.

Mr. Castle, a moderate Republican, seemingly taken aback by both the sentiment and the support for it, insists that "if you're referring to the president there, he is a citizen of the United States." Some catcalls follow. Apparently emboldened, the questioner rises and shouts out, "I think we should all stand up and pledge allegiance to the flag!" Several people yell, "Pledge allegiance!" and one loudly opines that Castle "probably doesn't even know it!" Surreally, Castle then leads the people of Georgetown in this enforced act of loyalty, as though there had been a doubt about his patriotism that now needed to be expunged.

The Lady in Red was many people's first Birther. But for the next few weeks the question of whether Barack Obama was an American citizen at birth, and the fact that there was a debate about that question, were hotly discussed on mainstream news channels in the United States, and the peculiarity that a significant number of Americans thought that he wasn't a citizen (and that he was therefore ineligible to be president) was featured widely outside the country. One of the earliest Birthers, the Philadelphia lawyer (and 9/11 Truth activist) Philip J. Berg, observed that until the Delaware eruption, "the coverage has been minuscule" and confined to Internet and marginal radio stations, but that the Georgetown meeting had set off "a vast uptick." On his radio broadcast, the sonorous CNN host Lou Dobbs, in "only asking" mode, repeatedly suggested that Obama set minds at rest by producing his long-form birth certificate. The more pungent right-wing radio host Rush Limbaugh argued that the new president had "yet to prove that he's a citizen."

At the same time, a group of mostly Texan Republican congressmen sponsored a measure, drafted by Bill Posey of Florida, "to amend the Federal Election Campaign Act of 1971 to require the principal campaign committee of a candidate for election to the office of President to include with the committee's statement of organization a copy of the candidate's birth certificate," a requirement that had somehow been regarded as superfluous in the previous 230 years of the republic. By mid-August 2009, a quarter of Americans polled were of the opinion that Barack Obama was not an American citizen by birth, and another 14 percent were unsure, with 10 percent naming Indonesia as his place of birth, 7 percent opting for Kenya, and 6 percent agreeing that it was Hawaii, but a Hawaii that, in their opinion, was not part of the United States in 1961 when Obama was born. Twelve percent, when prompted by the mischievous pollsters, pronounced themselves unsure that Obama wasn't French. There were political, gender, and ethnic disparities. Sixty-two percent of Birthers were Republicans (44 percent of Republicans believed that Obama was not a citizen, compared with 36 percent who thought he was), 57 percent were "conservative," 56 percent were male, and 86 percent were white.[2]

A Question of Certification

Section 1 of Article II of the U.S. Constitution lays down that "no person except a natural born citizen, or a citizen of the United States, at the time of the adoption of this Constitution, shall be eligible to the office of President; neither shall any person be eligible to that office who shall not have attained to the age of thirty five years, and been fourteen Years a resident within the United States." It follows that a diehard Republican, discovering that Barack Obama failed to meet these provisions, might feel like Henry VIII when advised that his marriage with Catherine of Aragon was conveniently illegal, and that he would now be free to discard her in favor of Anne Boleyn. Americans had felt this way before. In the 1880s, Democrats had tried to discredit the Republican president, Chester Arthur, alleging that he had been born half a century earlier in Canada, and had at some time purloined his dead brother's Vermont birth identity.

Obama himself had always said that he was born in Hawaii, on August 4, 1961, by which time (despite subsequent eccentric objections) the state had been in the Union for almost two years. Clearly being over thirty-five and having dwelt in the United States for more than fourteen years, he met the eligibility test. Indeed, at a relatively early stage in the presidential campaign, his election team—unnoticed by most of the world—had released details of his Certification of Live Birth, a computer-generated contemporary document with the Hawaii state seal. Such family as Obama had and all his early friends either attested to his Hawaiian birth or else knew nothing to contradict it. There seemed, then, little ground for doubting his eligibility, unless one believed that some form of conspiracy had taken place to suppress information of his true place of birth—a conspiracy that had lasted (by November 2008) Obama's forty-seven years on the planet.

Yet even by the time of the Georgetown meeting, there had been or were a number of lawsuits in various parts of the United States in which plaintiffs sought judgment against the new president on the basis of his disputed citizenship. In New Jersey, one Charles Kercher had claimed that Congress had failed in its duty to ascertain properly whether or not Obama was qualified; in Pennsylvania, Philip Berg (who spoke at the meeting in London described on pages 229–31) had filed three suits; Alan Keyes, a black Republican presidential primary candidate in 2008, was at the top of a list of Californians who requested that the state's electoral college votes be withheld from Obama until his eligibility had been established in a manner that satisfied them. In Hawaii, an Illinois lawyer filed a suit demanding that the state's euphoniously named governor, Linda Lingle, release further documents establishing Obama's birth in the state; again in California, a dynamic if erratic Moldovan-born immigrant, Orly Taitz, filed on behalf of the independent presidential candidate Ron Paul's running mate, Gail Lightfoot, and separately on behalf of an Army Reserve major, Stefan Cook, who argued that he couldn't be sent by an ineligible president to serve in Afghanistan. And so on in Georgia, Washington state, North Carolina, Ohio, Texas, and more.

Not all Birthers (as people questioning the new president's eligibility quickly became known) adopted the Lady in Red's direct approach to the issue of Obama's birthplace. The advanced Birthers did not even doubt that, when Obama's Kenyan grandmother appeared to agree that he had been born in Africa, this was a case of a fairly obvious linguistic misunderstanding between her and her questioners. The more sophisticated professed not to know or have theories about where else he might have been born, or indeed, not even to doubt his word, but simply—guilelessly—to demand that he furnish further proof that he had been hatched in Honolulu. They demanded that he "produce the birth certificate"—the long-form document referred to in Georgetown, and thus allay doubts. The short-form certification, they argued, would not do, because it was a noncontemporaneous and less detailed document. And what, they asked, could be more reasonable than that? If Mr. Obama himself were only to, say, appear on prime-time TV displaying his long-form certificate with "a seal on it, signed by a doctor, with a hospital administrator's name, my parents, my date of birth, the time," and so on, then all this could be laid to rest!

Billboards and bumper stickers appeared, asking, "Where is the birth certificate?" Conservative news websites of some venerability boiled the issue down to simple transparency. Cliff Kincaid, of Accuracy In Media, announced, on Obama's forty-eighth birthday, that he was releasing a copy of his own birth certificate: "This certified copy of an original long form document is what anyone who wants to be president should be prepared to produce. Why is this a controversy? . . . Whatever happened to the public's right to know?"[3] A day later, Christopher Ruddy, head of the online source NewsMax, asked, "Where was Barack Obama born? It's a fair question. But we still don't know the answer because Obama won't tell us, because he remains the most mysterious man ever to sit in the Oval Office." However mysterious the president was, Ruddy nevertheless wanted to make it clear that he believed that Obama was "born somewhere in the state of Hawaii. Days after his birth, a small legal notice was printed in the local newspaper announcing his birth. And the head of Hawaii's Health Department has stated that he reviewed pertinent documents and that Obama was certainly born in that state. So, those who believe Obama was born outside the United States, such as in Kenya, are simply out to lunch."

So why the doubts? Because, said Ruddy, his "presidential historian" brother Dan had pointed out to him that, aside from the frontier-born Zachary Taylor and Andrew Jackson, no U.S. president had had a "disputed birth-site" (Dan had obviously missed out on the Chester Arthur controversy). Ruddy climaxed thus: "So, let me be clear. The issue over Obama's birth certificate is not about President Obama's citizenship. It is about his honesty and his promise to be the most transparent president ever. Releasing his birth certificate and other personal records that presidents have traditionally released to the public would go a long way toward bolstering those claims. P.S. I am listing below all of our presidents and details of their places of birth."[4]

In this odd way, Ruddy had already pointed out two of the major objections to the Birthers' stance. The first was that all the Hawaiian state officials, elected and appointed, who were asked about the birth certificate gave essentially the same reply. It was the state's practice not to issue the long-form certificate, with all essential details having been transferred to computer files, to be generated on demand as Certifications of Live Birth. Still, they had inspected the original documents and attested that they conformed to the information on the certification.[*] End of story.

---

[*]The *Honolulu Advertiser* of November 1, 2008, quoted the Hawaiian state health director, Dr. Chiyome Fukino, as saying that she had "personally seen and verified that the Hawaii State Department of Health has Sen. Obama's original birth certificate on record in accordance with state policies and procedures." Dr. Fukino added, testily, "This has gotten ridiculous. There are plenty of other, important things to focus on, like the economy, taxes, energy."

The second objection was that, back in August 1961, two Hawaiian newspapers, the *Honolulu Advertiser* and the *Honolulu Star-Bulletin*, ran an identical birth announcement: "Mr. and Mrs. Barack H. Obama, 6085 Kalanianaole Hwy., son, Aug. 4." This announcement, apparently, wasn't generated by the family, but by the state health department. Didn't this leave the disingenuous Mr. Ruddy having to answer this question: Given these facts, why insist on the degrading (and therefore unlikely) spectacle of the country's first black president having to go before the cameras to "prove" his Americanness, when his Hawaiian birth was corroborated by officials and unforgeable contemporary record? There is transparency, and then there is a perverse desire never to be satisfied.

The permanent dissatisfaction was evident in the succeeding blizzard of Birther minutiae that struck the Internet. Obama's teenage mother, Stanley Ann Durham, had registered for a college course in Seattle ten days after the supposed date of birth of her son, and how likely was that? The address in the newspapers was discovered by sleuths to be one where the Obamas had never lived; it had been rented by Barack Obama's maternal grandparents and therefore might have been a fraudulent attempt to provide a Hawaiian address for a baby born elsewhere (the clear problem here being the health-department-generated announcements). As to the question of how the supposed birthplace forgers managed to have such prescience concerning the need, several decades later, to supply the infant with the credentials necessary for a run at the U.S. presidency, Birthers replied that perhaps the original object had simply been to furnish the boy—unhappily born abroad—with American citizenship.

The Farah and Corsi Show

Mainstream journalists in the United States and Europe receive all kinds of e-mails from PR companies and lobbyists promoting products, events, books, even arguments. During the 2008 U.S. presidential campaign, an "M. Sliwa" would send me—and hundreds of other writers—e-mails drawing our attention to various disobliging analyses of Barack Obama. My first, cursory thought was that M. Sliwa was a political lobbyist for someone supporting the Hillary Clinton campaign. When, however, the Democratic primaries were over and the e-mails kept coming, I began to think this was a Republican source. In the summer of 2009, I noticed that M. Sliwa was promoting the Birther cause.

M. Sliwa turned out to be Maria Sliwa, an ex-policewoman and—exotically—sister of the red-bereted New York Guardian Angel subway vigilante Curtis Sliwa. She was running a PR company in New York, serving a number of clients in various walks of life. I wrote to her and asked whether she would be willing to be interviewed on the subject of Birtherism. She replied that the best person to talk to was her client Joseph Farah, founder, editor, and CEO of the Internet news agency WorldNetDaily. Once based in Oregon, WND now had its offices near Washington, D.C., where about twenty employees mostly published medium-length pieces on its highly professional-looking site, WND.com. It also published books and sold related merchandise.

Farah was unwilling to be interviewed in person, but he agreed to discuss Birtherism over the telephone. He was persuasive and affable, with a hint of a laugh in much of what he had to say. The personality on the phone seemed to fit in with his most widely used publicity photograph: a handsome man with tanned skin and a black mustache, displaying a wide smile of very even white teeth.

He had first heard about the birth certificate issue, he told me, during the early part of the election campaign. "Obama is an unusual guy," said Farah. "He lived in Indonesia, his father was a Kenyan, he was born in Hawaii—so there were a number of questions. . . . There were also no records from his university and college career. So what we knew about him was what we got in his autobiography—and that was the official version." Even so, despite what Farah considered Obama's "unusual" background, he did not focus on the question, nor did his agency, until one of its writers, Jerome Corsi, forced him to. "Jerry began talking about some of the unanswered questions, and about how no one knew anything about the birth—no doctors, no nurses, no living person—and it seemed implausible to me. That was late September, October 2008. And we didn't get serious about it till just before the election."

But when Farah got serious, he got serious. "Our focus shifted to activism. I considered this issue was so critical, because the country had taken a major step toward ignoring the constitution." WND began to argue that the electoral college should not formally permit Obama's election until it was "proved" that he was constitutionally eligible. WND was the source of the birth-certificate-seeking billboards and some of the bumper stickers.

Where, I asked, did Farah believe Obama had been born, if not in Hawaii? "I don't know. I'd be very surprised if he was born in Kenya. We don't know if he was born in the U.S., either. But you know, his mother gives birth to him in Hawaii and fourteen days later she's in Seattle and Barack Obama, Senior, is in Honolulu. That's not part of the official story. So you see these holes, and you say, What else is there? And all the other records, school and college, remain sealed."

In Farah's version, Obama becomes a man of almost impenetrable, perhaps dangerous mystery. What in another person's past might seem fairly interesting questions for a committed biographer are translated here into the outward signs of something unhealthy. After all, if Obama is hiding things, then they can't be good.

That there is more to Farah's questioning than mere curiosity is given force when you know more about Jerry Corsi, his associate and employee, and author of "the *New York Times* number-one bestseller," *The Obama Nation*, which could most kindly be described as a critical biography, published in 2008 with the admitted intention of opposing Mr. Obama's candidacy. "*The Obama Nation*," Farah mused, "I gave him the title of the book." Being British and long in vowel, I hadn't noticed the play on words before Farah pronounced the title. I was amazed, and Farah was amused. The title of a book about the U.S. president sounded—on purpose—like "The Abomination." I wondered (though didn't ask) whether Farah was aware of the meaning of the word. *Abomination* doesn't connote something just undesirable or even hateful, but something loathsome or disgusting.

I turned to the book. Jerome Corsi is a soft-spoken, florid, round little man, who insists on being given his full title—Jerome R. Corsi, Ph.D.—a Harvard qualification he wears like a knighthood. He has written many books, five of which have enjoyed the accolade "*New York Times* bestseller"—a more promiscuous category than many book buyers may realize. Two—*The Obama Nation* and the coauthored *Unfit for Command: Swift Boat Veterans Speak Out Against John Kerry*—coincided with presidential election campaigns (2008 and 2004, respectively), and were unflattering about senior Democrats. Most of the others are, in effect, hugely extended paleoconservative opinion pieces, usually warning against some disaster about to befall America as a consequence of its politicians' venality and lack of patriotism. These tomes include *The Late Great USA: The Coming Merger with Mexico and Canada*; *Black Gold Stranglehold: The Myth of Scarcity and the Politics of Oil*; *Atomic Iran: How the Terrorist Regime Bought the Bomb and American Politicians*; and *Minutemen: The Battle to Secure America's Borders*. In his columns for WND, Dr. Corsi opines on how the "wider Panama Canal would aid [the] Chinese," on the global-warming "hoax," and on whether "the dollar's collapse [could] prompt a new currency." (The last question was posed in 2006; the answer appears to have been in the negative.)

The claim for *The Obama Nation*, with its subtitle, *Leftist Politics and the Cult of Personality*, was as a "definitive source for information on defeating Barack Obama—not by invective and general attacks, but by detailed and documented arguments that are well-researched and fact-based." But an early flavor of how such research and how these facts were to be deployed could be gleaned from clues such as the title of Corsi's third chapter: "Black Rage, Drugs and a Communist Mentor."

Corsi builds a tower of insinuation, rather than fact, giving full weight to what other writers might consider incidental, and in so doing sends a series of signals to primitive sensors in the oldest and darkest parts of the white American brain. He makes sure that the reader notes an odd propensity of Obama's white mother for nonwhite "mates," first in the shape of Obama Sr. and then in Lolo Soetoro, young Barack's Indonesian stepfather. Corsi mentions several times that Obama Sr. was a polygamous drunk. He repeatedly invokes signs that Obama sides with his "African blood" as a matter of preference, rather than as someone might who gradually discovers himself to be black. He strenuously overemphasizes the role of Islam in Obama's early life, and then just as deliberately interprets Obama's links to a Kenyan politician as favoring the pro-Islamization of Kenya. There are numerous errors of fact, all of which lead in broadly the same direction. The overall impact is to suggest that Obama is a foreigner who wishes, for atavistic reasons of his own, to undermine the old (white) USA. Obama is an abomination. If Corsi's preoccupations have antecedents, they seem to be in the paranoias of the 1950s, which, as we've seen, fostered McCarthyism and which, at the cultural level, were visible in numerous films about alien infiltration and invasion. Corsi's Obama is a political body-snatcher.

Naturally, in the early twenty-first century, it is unfashionable to wear such prejudices too openly, and fortunately the Internet provides opportunities to express them in more covert fashion. But not, perhaps, as covertly as everybody might like. After the publication of *The Obama Nation*, Corsi himself was the target of scrutiny, and it was discovered that in the recent past, while contributing to the website Free Republic, the doctor had delivered himself of some fruity opinions. "Isn't the Democratic Party," he had asked, "the official SODOMIZER PROTECTION ASSOCIATION of AMERICA?" Of Muslims he wrote: "RAGHEADS are Boy-Bumpers as clearly as they are Women-Haters—it all goes together." "After he married TerRAHsa," he demanded, "didn't John Kerry begin practicing Judiasm [*sic*]? He also has paternal gradparents [*sic*] that were Jewish. What religion is John Kerry?" Kerry became "John F*ing Commie Kerry" in subsequent posts, while Mrs. Clinton was "Hellary," the "fat hog," who couldn't keep "BJ Bill" satisfied. "Not lesbo or anything, is she?" Corsi speculated. There was much more in this vein.

Unfortunately for Corsi, several of his media appearances to promote the Obama book were plagued by the presence of liberal commentators who pointed out what lay behind his claims to dispassion. Corsi's replies were peculiar examples of infantile evasion. "You haven't mentioned all my apologies for those statements," was his standard, slightly plaintive response, rather as a child might crossly insist that he had said he was sorry for hitting his sibling—while fully intending to do it again.[5]

This, then, was Farah's Corsi. But what about Corsi's Farah? It soon became clear to me that the agreeable Farah, with his outwardly professional organization, was something of a shark in guppy's clothing. First there was his tendency toward exaggerated theses based on unreliable evidence. Take this exchange from an interview conducted in the summer of 2005 with Jamie Glazov for the Internet magazine FrontPage, titled "An American Hiroshima?" Farah is arguing that Al Qaeda not only has a nuclear weapon, but has already smuggled it into the United States.

> FARAH: Several reporters and top intelligence analysts, people including me ... have been working quietly and independently for years on this issue of al-Qaida's acquisition and plans for nuclear weapons ... and, based on the evidence, I believe some of that arsenal has already been delivered to this country.
>
> GLAZOV: Could you expand a bit on the sources for this information? How do we know they are reliable?
>
> FARAH: About 90 percent of the information I have gathered on this plan is from publicly sourced documents available to you and anyone else who wants to spend the time looking for them. It's only the analysis and interpretation that requires skilled—and sometimes unnamed—intelligence sources.

In other words, it's all on the Internet, if you know where to look and you're as clever as I am. But it begs the obvious question, which Glazov then asks.

> GLAZOV: Why wouldn't the Bush administration secure our borders? What are the advantages of leaving them unsecured? Is it too politically incorrect to secure them?

FARAH: No, I believe there is another more sinister reason. There is a master plan for global governance being plotted in meetings of groups like the Council on Foreign Relations. You can read its reports. And I believe this open-borders policy is a direct result of those plans, which have been secretly adopted by our highest leaders, including President Bush.[6]

To recapitulate: Farah argues that the Bush administration will not deal with an imminent threat of terrorist nuclear attack in the United States because of a secret scheme for global governance. And Joe Farah can be even madder than that. In a 2003 article for WND, he praises a woman, Clara Harris, who murdered her unfaithful orthodontist husband in front of his teenage daughter by running him over several times in her Mercedes. "If I were on that jury," Farah concluded, "I would find Clara Harris not guilty. After she was sprung, I'd give her a medal. She did the world a favor. She may have acted emotionally. She may be sorry for what she has done. But, frankly, she did the right thing. That creep deserved what he got."[7]

Perhaps more significant, though, was a story run by Farah in February 2008. Under the headline "Sleaze Charge: 'I Took Drugs, Had Homo Sex with Obama,'" it detailed the claims of a Minnesota man, Larry Sinclair, who alleged that in 1999 he had met Obama "in an upscale Chicago lounge." They supposedly got into Sinclair's limousine, where Obama smoked crack cocaine and Sinclair snorted powdered cocaine given to him by the future president. It was also in the limousine, said Sinclair, that the sex took place. The photograph accompanying the story depicted a man of limited physical charms, suggesting either that the drugs were very powerful, or that Sinclair had gone into a decline in the intervening years.[8]

The real significance of the Sinclair story—consisting as it did of an utterly uncorroborated and unlikely series of accusations—was Farah's readiness to run it, and to report it in such a way as to give it credibility. In this the report recalled a series of accusations leveled a decade and a half earlier at the last Democratic president, William Jefferson Clinton, accusations in which a younger Joseph Farah had played a role.

I had heard Farah speak about this period on a far-right radio show, when he had mentioned in passing the toll that his part in the campaign against Clinton had taken on him. In our interview I asked him what he had meant. Back then, he told me, he was operating out of Sacramento, as head of an organization called the Western Journalism Center. The WJC had been active in publicizing a series of scandals purportedly involving Clinton, all of them far more serious than the Lewinsky affair. "The Clinton scandals got rolled up into the one—Lewinsky—that was least significant," Farah maintained. "With the real issues, none were fully answered. Like Vince Foster [the Clinton aide who died of a gunshot wound in July 1993]—to conclude that he committed suicide, that takes faith!"

Having drawn attention to this and a number of other supposed Clinton crimes, Farah believed that he was targeted for harassment by authorities operating at the command of the White House. "Twice my offices were broken into in 1995 [and 1996]. Nothing was stolen. We were in a big complex, with various businesses and several suites, yet only our office was burglarized. Then the IRS came and announced an audit. I asked why. 'It's a political case, and it's a national decision,' I was told. It took nine months. We gave 'em a desk and in the end got a clean bill." But the result was to make Farah feel threatened, and not just financially. "I went down [to Arkansas in the late nineties] to testify at the 'boys on the tracks' case [this case, described later, concerned two boys found dead on railway tracks] and"—he laughed—"I thought my life was at risk. I wrote about it beforehand, I wrote, 'I'm going to Arkansas, and this might be my last article!'"

Going to Arkansas

Farah, the son of Christian Lebanese immigrants, started his political life in the center left. The way I heard him tell it, he was one of those who then swung to the right when Ronald Reagan was president—a "Reagan Democrat." However, it is clear that Farah's journey took him beyond the fiscal conservatism and sunny patriotism that characterized the former California governor to a position of intense hostility to those forces he saw as undermining the moral center of America. When he was editor of the *Sacramento Union* (now defunct, but then described as the "oldest newspaper in the West"; Mark Twain worked for the paper in the mid-1860s), Farah presided over an agenda that was avowedly antiabortion, antifeminist, anti–gay rights, and pro-faith. In 1991, after Farah's stance failed to prevent a slide in circulation—despite his employment of a new front-page columnist, Rush Limbaugh—he left the paper.[9]

Farah's next project, the Western Journalism Center—a hybrid of activist organization, news agency, and publisher, issuing a newsletter, *Dispatches*—was an almost perfect forerunner for the structures that would soon prosper on the nascent Internet. Among the board of advisors were such then mainstream conservative luminaries as Marvin Olasky and Arianna Huffington—whose capacity for political reincarnation has been kabbalistic. Money was raised from a number of right-wing sources, including James Davidson, chairman of the National Taxpayers Union and a coeditor of the *Strategic Investment* newsletter.

But not until after the defeat of George H. W. Bush by Bill Clinton in November 1992, and the miasma of rumors and alleged scandals that rose to surround the new administration, did the WJC begin to achieve significance. Farah's organization funded research, journalism, and advertisements in mainstream newspapers championing work that appeared to accuse President Clinton of involvement not just in minor acts of corruption but in murder as well.

Farah joined a group of media lobbyists agitating for public acceptance that in Bill Clinton, the former governor of Arkansas, the nation had opted for one of the most morally flawed, if not criminal, politicians in the history of the republic. It was in Clinton's Arkansas past, this group believed, that the evidence of the president's unique character defects was to be found—an assertion given wider credibility by the tortuous, complex, and sapping process of the public inquiry into the so-called Whitewater Affair, the supposed cash-and-land scandal whose origins dated back to the late 1970s. It was the investigation of the Whitewater Affair that led, bizarrely, to the celebrated Starr Report on President Clinton's relationship with White House intern Monica Lewinsky nearly twenty years later. In journalistic terms Whitewater was conjured into life on the pages of the *New York Times*, but once there it mutated into an extraordinary series of books, website postings, radio shows, and videos, most of them containing one or more conspiracy theories concerning the Clintons and Arkansas. What eventually took Farah to the southern state was a libel action at the tail end of one of these theories.

The Apotheosis of Conspiracism

Anyone seeking to relive the strangeness of the Clinton-era controversies should begin with a book written by a Cambridge- and Sorbonne-educated Englishman. *The Secret Life of Bill Clinton: The Unreported Stories*, by Ambrose Evans-Pritchard, was published in 1997, at the end of Evans-Pritchard's stint as Washington bureau chief for the venerable and respected British broadsheet the *Sunday Telegraph*. Despite the subtitle, most of the stories in the book had already been reported (if that's the right word), by Evans-Pritchard himself and by others, including Joe Farah, over the previous three or four years. But *The Secret Life* stands out as an almost perfect encapsulation of the most extreme of the theories about the man from Hope, its four-hundred-plus pages documenting a complex series of accusations that together suggested that in November 1992 the American people had placed in the White House a family more devious and more versatile than even the Borgias.

In essence, Evans-Pritchard, who had reported for *The Economist* from Central America, and was later to report from Brussels, had gone to Arkansas in pursuit of a series of rumors about Bill Clinton's past as governor, and discovered there—or so he thought—not just that they were all true, but that there were other, worse things so far only partly disclosed. "Arkansas," he told readers, "was a mini-Colombia within the United States, infested by narco-corruption."[10] With Bill in power, this sickness had infiltrated national government, so that "malfeasance [had] become systemic over the last five years."[11]

The consequence had been a sundering of the ties of respect that held together citizen and state. It was Clinton, rather than the McVeighs and the Idaho militias, who was responsible for the nineties phenomenon of armed far-right groups wandering the American hinterland preparing for the final battle. "It is under Clinton that an armed militia movement involving tens of thousands of people has mushroomed out of the plain, an expression of dissent that is unparalleled since the Southern gun clubs before the Civil War." "The actions and the character of the president," proclaimed Evans-Pritchard, "have engendered the most deadly terrorist movement in the industrialized world." This was an interesting judgment, coming as it did toward the end of the thirty-year-long "troubles" in Northern Ireland—familiar to most British journalists—in which some 3,500 people had died. "To a foreign eye," Evans-Pritchard continued, in one of those unfortunate prophecies that are almost always destined to be betrayed by time, "America looks like a country that is flying out of control."[12]

The book represented an overwrought final testimony to Clintonian corruption, bequeathed by the departing Englishman to those he was leaving behind. "To put it with brutal honesty," he told them, "you can sniff the pungent odors of decay in the American body politic."[13]

An acquaintanceship with Evans-Pritchard's writings would convince most people that he was sincere, that he believed in what he wrote. Even so, from the beginning of *The Secret Life* there is a willingness to bend the truth to meet the thesis. This is evident when the famous public Catholic priest Richard Neuhaus is quoted as commenting on Clinton's mores: "Has it reached the point where conscientious citizens can no longer give moral assent to the existing regime?"[14] What the ungiven context makes clear is that Neuhaus is attacking not Clinton's personal qualities

or villainies, but his and his fellow liberals' political beliefs and in particular their support for abortion rights. Such an analysis was, and is, a
very different matter.

And just as the rather slippery praying-in-aid of the clergyman suggested an agenda, so too did Evans-Pritchard's attitude toward research.
For several years before writing *The Secret Life*, he had been part of a
loose group of like-minded writers and researchers who had grown ever
more convinced of Clinton's master-criminality. One of those who met
Evans-Pritchard at the time was David Brock, the conservative writer who
later recanted his role in pursuing the Clintons. Brock's later confessions
must, of course, be seen in the light of his admission to earlier journalistic wrongdoings, yet they seem plausible when it comes to the *Sunday
Telegraph* man.

"Of all the 'Clinton crazies' I would meet—the term was one that
Ambrose [Evans-Pritchard] and many others openly embraced—Ambrose
was the least cynical of the bunch, and perhaps the craziest. He seemed to
truly credit the seamy gossip that I now knew anyone could hear if they
poked around Arkansas for a few days. Ambrose had no capacity to judge
the credibility of sources; to him, the word of a drug-addled ex-con was as
good as anybody else's, or perhaps better."[15]

This harsh and amusing judgment is borne out in Evans-Pritchard's
book, where time and again he is struck by the inner nobility and true
bravery of anyone, however problematic his background and improbable his story, who implicates the Clintons in crime and sordid behavior.
Evans-Pritchard's credulity, naturally enough, was followed by paranoia.
Brock writes:

"One night . . . I visited Ambrose at his home in the Maryland suburbs to hear about his latest scoop. This one involved Clinton's alleged
abuse of the penal system in Arkansas, where Ambrose said that he
compelled prison warders to make inmates available to him for his sexual gratification. . . . When [I] arrived at the house, a sparsely furnished
suburban rambler, Ambrose drew the shades and asked if [I] had been
followed. The CIA, he was sure, had tapped his phones, and he believed

his house was under surveillance by the Clintons' 'death squads.' A few minutes into the conversation, it was apparent to me that poor Ambrose had lost his grip on reality."[16]

Lies, Spies, and Stings Gone Wrong

The Secret Life begins in Waco, Texas, in April 1993. To most of the watching world, uninitiated in the Clinton felonies, the mishandled storming of the compound of the Branch Davidian sect of David Koresh seemed the outcome of a regrettable mix of cultism, propensity for groups to carry firearms and to use them against the authorities (four Alcohol, Tobacco and Firearms agents had been killed during a raid in February—a rather high number for a peacetime operation), and pressure on the authorities to bring the consequent fifty-one-day siege to an end. Not quite fifteen years earlier in Guyana, supporters of the cult leader Jim Jones had killed an investigating U.S. congressman on a local airstrip, and Jones then organized the mass suicide and murder by poisoning in which more than nine hundred perished. That the government should want to terminate the siege in Waco was understandable. The bloody ending, however, was fraught with contradictory claims about how necessary a final assault really was, and about the circumstances in which seventy-five Davidians met their deaths.

Evans-Pritchard was in little doubt that a crime had been committed by the federal authorities, and that this had been subsequently covered up in their attempts at self-exculpation. To him the events at Waco could be seen as having provoked further armed extremism among other parts of the millenarian American underground. "Every salient fact put forward by the Clinton administration about Waco is a lie," he wrote, adding, in almost religious tones, "There has to be a ritual expurgation of some kind if the open wound of Waco is ever to heal."[17]

Of course, that "ritual expurgation" had in some people's minds already happened, two years before the publication of Evans-Pritchard's book and two years to the day after the end of the Waco siege. Accordingly, the first seven chapters of the book are devoted to the bombing of the Alfred P. Murrah Federal Building on April 19, 1995, and to the propositions that those convicted for the crime, Timothy McVeigh and Terry Nichols, had not acted alone, and that the bombing had been either part of a government sting operation that had gone wrong and then had to be covered up, or a deliberate false-flag atrocity, conducted with the objective of justifying draconian antiterrorist legislation. Readers may now recognize this trope from elsewhere in this book.

Readers may also recognize a familiar tone in the claim made by another writer that "many an 'expert' and many an expert believe that McVeigh neither built nor detonated the bomb that blew up a large part of the Murrah Federal Building on April 19, 1995. . . . Evidence, however, is overwhelming that there was a plot involving militia types and government infiltrators—who knows?—as prime movers to create panic in order to get Clinton to sign that infamous Anti-Terrorism Act."[18]

Writing in the September 2001 edition of *Vanity Fair*—copies of which one may imagine being incinerated in offices and waiting rooms in the Twin Towers—Gore Vidal nodded toward the "Opus Dei conspiracy" in the Justice Department and the "FBI conspiracy" over Waco. He pointed out that "no less than a retired Air Force general has promoted the theory that in addition to Mr. McVeigh's truck bomb, there were bombs inside the building." Vidal also referred to the anger of the mother of two children lost in Oklahoma City when she was told that no Alcohol, Tobacco and Firearms agents had been killed in the explosion. The woman, Edye Smith, was said to have asked: "Did the A.T.F. have a warning sign? I mean, did they think it might be a bad day to go into the office? They had an option not to go to work that day, and my kids didn't get that option." The ATF, noted Vidal, "has a number of explanations. The latest: five employees were in the offices, unhurt." There was also the fact, not mentioned by Vidal, that the ATF offices were in the part of the building least affected by the blast.

The unsatisfactory dearth of ATF fatalities was only one component of Vidal's insinuated argument that Timothy McVeigh was a patsy. Books by men who (long after the article was published) turned out to be mad, newsletters quoting unnamed and untraceable "Pentagon analysts," and anonymous sources "close to" unpublished and unseen reports made up the bulk of the evidence. The rest was Vidal's instinct that McVeigh (whom, Capote style, he saw to his death) had been a rather noble figure—practically Kiplingesque—taking the full rap for an event that should be best and most positively seen as "a wake-up call to a federal government deeply hated, it would seem, by millions." Vidal ended with what might be termed a cry for a better narrative: "Finally, the fact that the McVeigh-Nichols scenario makes no sense at all suggests that yet again, we are confronted with a 'perfect' crime—thus far." The perfect crime being, of course, the work of the successfully hidden hand.

Vidal, like Philip J. Berg, was an equal-opportunity conspiracist, and was comfortable whether accusing FDR, Harry Truman, LBJ, Bill Clinton, or George W. Bush of complex and dastardly secret acts for various nefarious purposes—usually as pretexts for war or domestic crackdowns. Evans-Pritchard, writing four or five years earlier, had no such history, but when it came to Oklahoma he essentially shared Vidal's view. Having spoken to and, almost inevitably, come to admire a number of those dissatisfied with the "official" explanation for the bombing, Evans-Pritchard had immersed himself in militia culture and its strange attendant world of latter-day Nazis, cultists, racists, weaponry, and drugs, to attempt to explain why the trial of McVeigh had been "skillfully managed [by unspecified persons] to ensure that collateral revelations were kept to a minimum."[19] After ninety pages Evans-Pritchard reached the conclusions that a German named Andreas Strassmeir was the key to the affair, and that Strassmeir had been a spy for the German government whose job was to infiltrate a militia community called Elohim City "to find out whether the US neo-Nazi movement had the capability or intent to graduate to weapons of mass destruction." According to Evans-Pritchard, "A high-level counterintelligence operation of this kind would explain why

Elohim City was being protected, even though it was engaged in every weapons violation in the US code, not to mention manifest sedition."[20] As a result of this toleration, a group called the Aryan Republican Army—presumably with the knowledge of the cowardly ATF (whose members seem peculiarly dispensable in modern American culture)—had carried out the bombing. Official persons unknown had organized for these truths to be covered up, to the intense distress of those brave interviewees who had worked with Evans-Pritchard.

The Killing Fields

None of this, however, compared with the obscenity of Clintonian Arkansas as revealed by some of her doughtier citizens to the horrified Englishman. In six chapters these admirable and brave characters dish the dirt on orgies, drug-smuggling, drug-taking, and murders indulged in, covered up, or possibly initiated by Clinton and the Dixie Mafia. Chapter 17 of Evans-Pritchard's book, "Death Squad," concerns the case of the boys on the tracks, two teenagers from Alexander, Arkansas, who were found dead on railway lines in 1987; their deaths, originally ascribed to marijuana-induced misadventure, were later diagnosed as murders. Evans-Pritchard found people to testify that the two had stumbled across a drug shipment organized by a Clinton associate, and had therefore been eliminated. The FBI, he was informed by a "charming, educated" woman with a "strong sense of duty," knew who had done it, but couldn't take it to trial. This was a shame, because "already people associated with the case were beginning to die in what amounted to a reign of terror among young people in Alexander. . . . Keith Coney, who told his mother he knew too much about the railway deaths . . . died in a motor-cycle accident after a high-speed chase. . . . Bonnie Bearden, a friend of the boys, disappeared. His body was never found. Jeff Rhode, another friend, was killed with a gunshot to the head in April 1989. And on it went. The killing fields."[21] As it happens, a successful libel case brought by two police officers accused by various right-wing sources of involvement in the tracks murders became the occasion of Joseph Farah's perilous visit to the South in 1999.

Perhaps the best illustration of the Evans-Pritchard approach to investigative journalism concerned the September 1993 murder of Jerry Parks, a "security executive" from suburban Little Rock, who was shot and killed in his Chevrolet Caprice while returning from a Mexican restaurant he regularly patronized with his wife, Jane. She was not with him at the time, and it wasn't until a little later that she spoke to Evans-Pritchard about her husband's murder.

The reason the *Sunday Telegraph* man was interested was that back in 1992, Parks had had the contract for managing security at Clinton–Gore campaign headquarters in Little Rock. Evans-Pritchard had already met one of Parks's sons, Gary, in a Little Rock hotel, accompanied by the twenty-three-year-old's security detail. Gary informed Evans-Pritchard that his father had maintained a file detailing Clinton's infidelities, based on his own surveillance operations. In 1988, Jerry had taken the teenage Gary with him on "nocturnal missions" to stake out Clinton's trysts. One day Gary had come across some of these files, and sure enough, there were photographs of the priapic governor with various women.

The files had evidently survived for nearly half a decade and a whole presidential campaign when, just two months before Jerry's murder, there had been a "sophisticated" burglary at the Parks residence, and the whole lot had been stolen, never to be seen again.

It is hard, when describing Evans-Pritchard's willingness to believe such a transparent, almost schoolboyish tale, not to be rude. Absolutely none of this story makes sense, and it couldn't—by its very nature—be substantiated.

Or could it? Sometime later Mrs. Parks opened her heart to the "outsider" journalist. The process took no less than three years, during which she elaborated on a story that was far more than sensational, and incrementally recalled "details that had been repressed and buried." Her account, Evans-Pritchard admitted, "confronted me with a journalistic dilemma of the first order. Certain episodes could be corroborated, which established a pattern of veracity, but the most shocking allegations were based on her word alone. I made an intuitive decision to publish. At times the moral imperatives of reportage require one to violate the Columbia School codex."[22] Clearly his bosses shared his intuitions, and agreed on the moral imperative of running truly head-turning, banner-headline stories on the uncorroborated say-so of a woman apparently uncovering repressed memories.

But what a woman. His Jane Parks is "a slender, elegant brunette, with high cheekbones and a Scots-Irish look about her. . . . Tanned and carefully made up, with a soft southern voice, she is undoubtedly an attractive woman." A woman who, it transpired, also turned out to have firsthand knowledge of just what a debauched Lothario Bill Clinton really was. Back in the summer of 1984, she had been the manager of an apartment complex called Vantage Point. While there she was told to take care of Roger Clinton, the ne'er-do-well drug-taking brother of the governor. She put him in a corporate suite, room B107, which had been part of a still larger space, now divided "by a thin partition." The utility of this arrangement became clear when the governor himself came to call on Roger, as he did many times, usually in the middle of the afternoon. Jane, whose office seems to have been housed in the other part of the divided room, "soon learned to distinguish between the voices of the two brothers behind the thin partition." She could, for example, hear them discussing the quality of the marijuana available, with Bill commenting, "This is really good shit." Then this:

"It was just not marijuana either. Two or three times a week the Governor was buoying his spirits with a snort of Kid Brother's Colombian rock. The repartee was coming through the vents. She was as certain as if she had been in the suite herself. Sometimes the two brothers were alone. Sometimes young women were invited to join, and the little party was consummated with raucous orgasms. The bed was pressed up against the partition wall, just a few feet from the desk of Mrs. Parks. On two occasions she heard the Governor copulating on the bed. Who the visitors were, exactly, she did not know. But some of them appeared surprisingly young."[23]

Mrs. Parks's hearing—allowing for the thinness of the partition—seems to have been as good as her capacity to work quietly at her desk and to muffle incoming phone calls. Somehow—perhaps because of the drugs and orgasms—no one ever seemed to suspect that she had her office barely inches away. And her perspicacity wasn't bad, either. She told Evans-Pritchard that she had alerted her husband to the "goings-on at B107" and that Jerry had written it all down, complete with dates, license plates, and photos, which were then consigned to the same files so irrevocably lost nearly nine years later.

Later still, remarried to an attorney, Jane Parks recalled that in July 1993, Jerry had been called by a White House aide and Arkansas friend of the Clintons, Vincent Foster. Now she remembered that Jerry had shouted at Foster, "You're not going to use those files! My name's all over this stuff. You can't give Hillary those files. You can't! Remember what she did, what you told me she did. She's capable of doing anything!" Jane's excellent hearing also picked up what Foster said in reply: "He was going to meet Hillary at 'the flat' and he was going to give her the files."[24] A few hours later Foster was dead, found shot.

As Evans-Pritchard conceded, the telephone timetable outlined by the widow was impossible. He suspected that "Jane Parks has muddled the day." It annoyed him, however, that some people in the press did not think that muddle was involved. He contrasted their attitude with the way in which Vincent Foster's wife, Lisa, was treated when she accepted that her husband's death was a suicide and not, as we shall see, the cunning murder that Evans-Pritchard believed it to be. "Why is it," he demanded, "that every utterance from the lips of one widow—Lisa Foster—is treated with reverence, while the other widow, brushed aside by an arrogant FBI, offers a conflicting version of events that is totally ignored by the American press? Is Lisa Foster an inherently more accurate witness of events than Jane Parks simply because she belongs to a higher social caste? Is that what American justice and journalism has come to?"[25]

This splendid outrage might have had even more force had Evans-Pritchard been able to scan the future. It wasn't just that Jane Parks was subsequently accused by her stepdaughter, on equally thin evidence, of killing her husband. By 2006, Jane Parks was divorced from the attorney and married to a well-known local urologist, Dr. David Millstein. On Saturday, June 18, in the first homicide seen in Mountain Home, Arkansas, in five years, Millstein was stabbed to death at a home that he does not seem to have shared with his wife. To lose one husband to an unknown killer is certainly a rare misfortune. To lose two . . . The odds are against it.

To the Internet keepers of something called the "Clinton Body Count," though, Millstein's murder was simply chalked up as yet another, though very late-era, suspicious death associated with Bill Clinton, along with the boys on the tracks, Vince Foster, Jerry Parks, former Secretary of Commerce Ron Brown and entourage lost in a plane crash over Croatia, the four ATF men killed at Waco, and just about anybody else who met someone whom Bill Clinton had met and who subsequently died.

An interestingly circular form of narrative transmission had developed, in which the fringe would communicate rumors to a journalist like Evans-Pritchard, who would "investigate" and then declare himself satisfied in print that the rumors were true, thus apparently giving intellectual and mainstream support for fringe contentions. Helping this process along were people who straddled the formal and informal news worlds, people like Joe Farah. There are many examples of Farah's own journalistic approach to the Clinton stories, but one of his WND pieces from 1998 illustrates his way of knitting elements together to create an impression, while leaving himself enough room to deny that he was making a concrete accusation. Under the title "Clinton Body Count," he referred to the impeachment process and added that "a growing number of Internet denizens and talk-radio listeners are all but convinced he's much worse than a lying Gigolo." Actually they believed he was a murderer, but Farah wondered whether the list of those suspicious deaths that could be linked to Clinton wasn't too low. "For instance, not one version of the 'body count' lists that I have seen," he wrote, "included the name of Eric L. Henderson. Yet, everything about his remarkable death cries out for examination." This young man had been shot while riding his bicycle in Northeast Washington, D.C., sixteen months earlier, and a juvenile had been convicted of the murder. So perhaps Henderson had died at the hands of a young criminal "or maybe, just maybe, he knew too much." Too much about what? Well, he had been associated with the plane-dead Ron Brown, and Brown, it was rumored, had been about to reveal something unknown about Clinton. On this utterly fatuous basis, Farah concluded, "Is it time to add one more name to the growing and staggering Clinton body count? I don't know, but the fact that such questions are not even raised in polite media company is not a good sign in a supposedly free society."[26]

If you paraphrase this insouciant masterpiece you get the following: I don't know if this outrageous theory of mine for which there is no evidence is true, but the very fact that I have invented it is itself a sign of the terrible times we live in and the terrible president we live under. It is a perfect demonstration of what psychotherapists call "violent innocence."

The Death of Vince Foster

There was plenty of room among those who suspected Bill Clinton of being a criminal to disagree about precisely which charges could be held against his account. But one thing they all tended to agree upon was that there was something very suspicious indeed about the death, on July 20, 1993, of Vincent Foster, deputy legal counsel to the president and former law firm colleague of Hillary Clinton's.

The police did not concur, nor did the FBI, nor did two separate investigations by two independent prosecutors (both Republican), nor did the Republican-chaired Senate Oversight Committee. All these bodies concluded that, on that day, suffering from depression, Mr. Foster had driven to Fort Marcy Park near Washington, D.C., walked to a remote spot near an antique cannon, and placed a revolver in his mouth and taken his own life. This was also the conclusion of the writer Dan Moldea, who alone among the authors of books on the Foster death interviewed all the police and emergency personnel involved.[27]

A torn-up note discovered in Foster's briefcase indicated that he was struggling in his job, felt that he had made mistakes, and thought that he was being pursued by newspaper reporters concerned only with creating scandal and destroying people, not with telling the truth. In his wallet were the names and numbers of three psychiatrists given to him by his sister, in whom he had confided that he was depressed. He had also been sent antidepressants by his own physician in Little Rock, but had not taken them. Photographs shot at the scene showed the gun under his hand, with his thumb trapped by the trigger. The autopsy revealed a wound from his mouth to an exit point in his head. There was no sign of a struggle, there were no other marks on the body, there was no indication of the presence of a second party. In his car an oven mitt was discovered, which forensics established had carried the revolver, and traces of which were found in Foster's pocket. His pager had been switched off. Unsurprisingly, from the very beginning the police believed that they were dealing with a suicide.

Almost from the very beginning too, a number of Clinton critics believed that it was, in reality (though they were reluctant to say so), a murder. Helping them were a series of minor contradictions between the testimonies of incidental witnesses and emergency personnel, the absence of certain crime-scene objects, and a number of incompetencies. The bullet, for example, was never found. No one heard the shot. Some people who saw the body didn't see the gun, or thought they saw a wound in the neck. A roll of film shot by the police at the scene proved useless. Some witnesses said that they didn't see Foster's car in the parking lot, while others said that they saw menacing and unidentified men. There were disputes between the police and the White House counsel about which documents from Foster's office the police could see or impound.

The mainstream press began to suggest, without much evidence, that

Foster's death might have been linked to an effort to cover up information concerning Whitewater—an effort that gave rise to the depression that caused him to take his own life. Some people even raised old rumors that he had been a lover of Hillary Clinton's back in Arkansas.

Leading the case for murder—first in articles, then in books—were a reporter for the *New York Post*, Christopher Ruddy, and Ambrose Evans-Pritchard. The latter devoted nine chapters of *The Secret Life* to the Foster case. His conclusion was unequivocal, if vague. "I do not know whether Vincent Foster was depressed before his death. It is irrelevant anyway. The hard evidence indicates that the crime scene was staged, period. Even if Foster was depressed, somebody still put a gun in his hand, somebody still inflicted a perforating wound on his neck, his body still levitated 700 feet into Fort Marcy Park without leaving soil residue on his shoes, and he still managed to drive to Fort Marcy Park without any car keys."[28]

As Moldea showed in his book, every assertion in this passage is wrong. But it did have the advantage of being bold, implicating, as it did, a large number of people in multiple agencies, in a cover-up of a murder committed somewhere else. Ruddy's *The Strange Death of Vince Foster: An Investigation*, on the other hand, using much the same "fact set" as Evans-Pritchard and strongly suggesting that suicide was impossible, never confronted the obvious implication of this accusation. Ruddy was keen to tell his readers that he was alleging not a conspiracy, but something positively accidental. Terms such as "conspiracy," he wrote, "serve to marginalize legitimate criticisms of the handling of the case. . . . 'Complicity' would be a far more appropriate term. A major cover-up, rather than being an active effort by a tight-knit group of conspirators, may simply be the result of a number of people—acting on their own, for any number of reasons—whose interests would be threatened by the disclosure of some part of the truth. These individuals become 'compliant' with a tendency to conceal information or misdirect investigators." A witness in the Foster case, for example, "might have been asked by someone who told him it would embarrass the administration and Foster's family if it were revealed where Foster really was that afternoon. The staffer tells the Park Police this 'little fib' thinking he is doing a noble service to Foster's family, his superiors or even his country. To others that little fib is one of inestimable importance: it conceals the fact that Foster perhaps did not eat lunch at his office, but somewhere else. It might also explain why Foster's autopsy found a full meal of meat and potatoes in his stomach."[29]

As might the fact, confirmed by Foster's staff, that he had ordered a cheeseburger and french fries for lunch before departing the White House that day. In 1993, one imagines, a burger was made of meat, and french fries from potatoes. In any case, what was the relevance of this unless Ruddy was arguing that Foster had been in some incriminating alternative covered-up place before appearing dead in Fort Marcy Park.

Ruddy's significance lay in the fact that his journalism of insinuation was picked up by other groups and writers in the period after Foster's death, and then disseminated widely enough to noticeably affect public opinion and so keep several unnecessary and expensive investigations in motion. One of these groups was Farah's Western Journalism Center, which would regularly parcel up Ruddy's reportage on Foster and buy expensive full-page ads in papers including the *New York Times* and the *Washington Post* to showcase Ruddy's work. In this way, as Moldea put it later, the Foster affair became the story of "how a simple suicide of a troubled White House official developed—and was manipulated—into a long-running soap opera with historical significance."[30]

The Vast Right-Wing Conspiracy

In late January 1998, as the Lewinsky affair burgeoned, the First Lady, Hillary Clinton, appeared on NBC's *Today* show and told the host, Matt Lauer, that there had been an underhanded campaign to destroy her husband, a campaign that amounted to a "vast right-wing conspiracy." There were two elements of this campaign. The first, she said, involved the charges "accusing my husband of murder, of drug-running." As far as some of the things written and said about him, her attitude was, "You know, we've been there before. We have seen this before." The second element was Kenneth Starr, whom she described as a "politically motivated prosecutor who is allied with the right-wing opponents of my husband, who has literally spent four years looking at every telephone call we've made, every check we've ever written, scratching for dirt, intimidating witnesses, doing everything possible to try to make some kind of accusation against my husband." Starr was part of "an entire operation."[31]

The phrase "vast right-wing conspiracy" was widely ridiculed in the media, some of whose members doubtless felt themselves accused by Mrs. Clinton. But was she right? Certainly many of those on the center-left of American politics thought so. In their 2001 book *The Hunting of the President: The Ten-Year Campaign to Destroy Bill and Hillary Clinton*, journalists Joe Conason and Gene Lyons, both of whom worked for Salon.com, detailed meetings, payments, and inducements involving anti-Clinton forces, including one bank-rolling multimillionaire. In the journalists' view, by the time it became clear how special prosecutor Kenneth Starr's office had behaved during the Lewinsky affair, "there was little argument about the existence of a 'conspiracy' and still less about whether the plotters were 'right-wing.' Only the 'vastness' of their enterprise remained in question."[32]

Broadly the facts were these: A conservative billionaire, Richard Mellon Scaife, grandnephew of the legendary Andrew Mellon and major financial backer of Richard Nixon, had used his money—among other things—to fund a number of bodies, newspapers, magazines, news agencies, and research foundations to attempt to discover and publish material damaging to the Clintons. The group Accuracy In Media, whose Cliff Kincaid we found earlier in this chapter trying to turn up the heat on President Obama over his birth certificate, received nearly $700,000. AIM's then head and founder, Reed Irvine, ran many stories supporting the idea that Vincent Foster had not committed suicide. So too did Joe Farah's Western Journalism Center, which in 1994–1995 benefited from $330,000 in donations from Scaife. When Christopher Ruddy's time at the *New York Post* came to an end, possibly because of his continued fixation on Foster, Scaife employed him on his own paper, the *Pittsburgh Tribune-Review*.

The most controversial Scaife initiative was the so-called Arkansas Project, in which, from 1993 to 1997, $2.4 million of Scaife money—channeled though the charitable foundation linked to the conservative *American Spectator* magazine—was spent on digging up stories in Arkansas, where Scaife and his associates seemed to believe there would be *the* story that would destroy Bill Clinton. The editor of *The American Spectator*, R. Emmett Tyrrell, Jr., subsequently described how the idea for the Arkansas Project emerged, on a fishing trip in Chesapeake Bay in late 1993, with Scaife's right-hand man, Richard M. Larry, a conservative PR man, and a Washington lawyer. The last two had links to people in Arkansas who, for various reasons, loathed Clinton and who were willing to pass on the rumors that percolated the state.[33]

With their eyes on the various political and journalistic prizes that publishing unprecedented scoops on Clinton misdemeanors might bring, those involved set about employing private detectives (one of whom, Rex Armistead, received more than $350,000 for his efforts), chasing down "witnesses," flying indiscreet state troopers to rendezvous in Washington, and generally doing everything they could to attract every gold-digging story manufacturer in Arkansas. The long-term result was disaster for *The American Spectator*, which did not uncover any real scoops, ran at least one story on drug-smuggling that was described by staff as "an embarrassment," lost circulation, and eventually, after running a review hostile to Ruddy's book on Foster, lost Scaife's money, too. By mid-1997, the Arkansas Project was stopped, leaving a residue of Internet stories, pointless congressional inquiries, urban legends, and the impression among many on the right that the supercriminal in the White House had somehow escaped justice.

However dubious the methods of those behind the Arkansas Project, the problem with describing their actions as a "conspiracy" is that they were not carried out in secret. Those funded by Scaife made no effort to hide his largesse, or to deny what it paid for. More problematic was the willingness of Kenneth Starr's prosecutorial team to use one-to-one press briefings to insinuate stories about the Clintons. Dan Moldea gave an example of this in an interview with *Salon* magazine in the spring of 1998. The week after the Lewinksy story broke, while he was researching his Foster book, Moldea spoke to an unnamed source in Starr's office. Moldea offered the opinion that there was nothing substantial in the rumors of an affair between Foster and Hillary Clinton. He went on:

> I was not asking a question; I was making a declaration of fact. His response was, "I can't comment on that." I said, "I didn't ask you a question." He said, "I would be violating a statutory responsibility if I said something about that." I said, "I didn't ask you a question. What are you telling me, here?" He said, "Let us just say that is in play."[34]

This is a dark art at work, but hardly a conspiracy. Almost everything had happened in plain view, even if people dazzled by Clinton rumors couldn't see it.

Wagging the Dog

When it was all over, and Clinton had left the White House and the second Bush had entered it, a few people had a little time to analyze what had happened. Clinton's aide Sidney Blumenthal, himself once a youthful conspiracist, reflected on how the "pseudoscandal" of Whitewater had come to dominate the presidency despite the fact that "there never was anything to it, in the beginning, middle and end." And yet it led to perpetual investigation of the president, numerous stories together hinting at massive personal corruption, and a soured memory of an entire decade. Blumenthal concluded that the origins of the Whitewater pathology lay in Old South opponents of his New South boss, who had been active in campaigns to unseat segregationist Democrats, and that the scandal "was traceable to conflicts in Southern history over race and power."[35]

But to Gene Lyons, who had watched appalled as his state was traduced as a kind of Haiti without the compensating beaches, there were much more mainstream culprits than the manipulative leftovers of bad-old-days Jim Crow politics. He was aghast at "how the right-wing sleaze campaign eventually succeeded in dictating mainstream news coverage." Mainstream media had, in his view, latched on to chronically unreliable sources and, in its story lust, lost sight of any notion of fairness. Lyons cited cases of respected reporters passing on salacious gossip to other journalists that their own editors wouldn't print, and noted a determination to create a story out of Whitewater, which led to a lack of discrimination about the sources and a willingness to run stories that were speculative.

In some cases, well-respected editors or columnists had allowed themselves to engage in or recycle innuendo that strengthened the view that there were conspiracies brewed up at the White House. In the *New York Times*, William Safire wrote a series of pieces in 1993 and 1994 that certainly hinted that all was not what it seemed when it came to Vincent Foster's "apparent suicide." On August 2, 1993, the famous conservative columnist pointed out that "the discoverer of the body remains unknown and no gun license has been found," but that "assuming no crime, the question remains: Was Vincent Foster irrationally morose because of criticism of his office's abuse of the F.B.I. in 'Travelgate'—or was the President's closest legal confidant dreading the exposure of malfeasance yet unknown?"[36] Safire offered no evidence for this speculation.

Ten days later the columnist was asking about the Foster note, and particularly "the missing 28th piece, a triangular piece of the puzzle where the signature would have been" (in fact there is no reason why there should have been a signature on this note, and no reason to believe that there was one), before asking yet again, "Was dread of further scandal a triggering cause of the apparent suicide? Was there anything else Foster was working on, in Arkansas business dealings involving Clinton friends or in intelligence matters, that bears on his state of mind?"[37] Again there was no basis for such a contention. Yet for some reason, when it came to Clinton, such stuff was all right. The crazy tail had managed to wag the sober dog. Arguably, a decade and a half later, as CNN's Lou Dobbs championed the case for President Obama to present his long-form birth certificate to the world to establish that he was born where the *Honolulu Advertiser* in 1961 had said he was born, something similar was happening. The fringe had, temporarily, taken over the show.

Back After a Long Vacation

What is noticeable when comparing the Clinton conspiracies with the Birther movement is how many of the same people and organizations are involved. True, there are some like Philip Berg, the Truther and Birther who discerned conspiracies from all points on the political spectrum. But the Birther charge has been led by Joseph Farah at WND, Christopher Ruddy at NewsMax, and by Accuracy In Media, making use of the Internet and right-wing radio and cable television shows. It is as though they had been on vacation through the eight years of the George W. Bush presidency, only to rediscover, on arriving home, that there was yet another slippery liar in the White House.

It would be easy to dismiss Farah and company as cynical pols, who are interested only in dragging down Democrats. But they seem rather to belong to the old populist tradition in American politics, ever vigilant, almost pathologically sensitive, to the possibility that the true Republic is in danger from those who wish to change and undermine it. In different ways, both Clinton, the flower-power-generation president with the feminist wife, and the cosmopolitan and black Obama have represented unwanted change from their imagined paradisaical United States.

In 1996, a former FBI man in the White House, Gary Aldrich, published a book outlining what a chamber of horrors the place had become under Clinton. Aldrich's work is a classic example of a book that reveals far more about its author than its subject, as the former agent devotes page after page to his horrified reaction to the new generation of staffers. On page 30, Aldrich observes that "there was a unisex quality to the Clinton staff that set it far apart from the [George H. W.] Bush administration. It was the shape of their bodies. In the Clinton administration, the broad-shouldered, pants-wearing women and the pear-shaped, bowling-pin men blurred distinctions between the sexes. I was used to athletic types, physically fit persons who took pride in body image and good health." And later: "Hillary . . . had an affirmative action program that favored tough, minority, and lesbian women, as well as weak, minority, and gay men. . . . If you compared the staffers of the Bush administration with those of the Clinton administration, the difference was shocking. It was Norman Rockwell on the one hand and Berkeley, California, with an Appalachian twist on the other."[38] Aldrich's book sold 150,000 copies, mostly, one suspects, to people who shared his sense of disgust at such gender-bending. To Aldrich, the Clinton White House was truly an abomination.

Evans-Pritchard ended his 1997 book on Clinton with an Aldrichian aesthetic. "The American elite, I am afraid to say," he wasn't afraid to say, "is almost beyond redemption. Moral relativism has set in so deeply that the gilded classes have become incapable of discerning right from wrong."[39]

This is a conservative's lament in a changing world. So it is interesting that the latest poster boy of the conservative media, Glenn Beck, has sold his book *Glenn Beck's Common Sense* on the argument that his fellow countrymen "know that something just doesn't feel right." The something is change, and that is also how Farah thinks of Obama, now that the changers are back in power.

Strange Symmetry: Birthers and Truthers

It occurred to some pollsters and analysts in 2009, as they pondered the figures showing how many Republicans believed that Barack Obama was in fact a secret foreigner, that they had seen these statistics before, but in a different context. In some polls, up to 58 percent of Republicans were skeptical about Obama's right to be president. And in a 2006 Scripps Survey Research Center poll (see page 234), 54 percent of Democrats had agreed with the proposition that people in the federal government had either assisted the 9/11 attacks or taken no action to stop them because they wanted the United States to go to war in the Middle East. In other words, people were quite likely to believe conspiracy theories supposedly involving the other side—when that side was in power—but disinclined to accept those aimed at their own side.

Just as the implications of this were being digested by those who think about such things, one of President Obama's main advisors, the Harvard law professor and author Cass R. Sunstein, produced a book that seemed to speak to this precise condition. *Going to Extremes: How Like Minds Unite and Divide* is a series of observations based on studies carried out by Sunstein and associates on group polarization—the phenomenon by which people become more extreme in the company of the like-minded. Two Colorado groups, for example—one in liberal Boulder and the other in conservative Colorado Springs—were given the same information about certain topics and then asked to discuss them. Among other findings: "Mildly favorable toward affirmative action before discussion, liberals became strongly favorable toward affirmative action after discussion. Firmly negative about affirmative action before discussion, conservatives became even more negative about affirmative action after discussion."[40] Sunstein found that a predisposition in a particular direction would be exaggerated, sometimes substantially, when people were in a group with others who shared the predisposition. And this would be as true for a group of judges as for a group of plumbers. One could add that such groups might easily exist in disembodied form as an Internet forum, the users of and posters to interlinked websites and news sites, the listeners to Web radio and watchers of YouTube. Once you decide what your predisposition is—Birther, Truther, or indeed, skeptic, there are myriad places to have it confirmed and then enhanced.

CONCLUSION: BEDTIME STORY

We're academics and we're rational, and we really believe Congress or someone should investigate this. But there are a lot of crazies out there who purport that UFOs were involved. We don't want to be lumped in with those folks.

— DAVID GABBARD, EAST CAROLINA UNIVERSITY
EDUCATION PROFESSOR AND 9/11 SCHOLAR[1]

Kevin began this book and Jim can end it. Jim is a man I first met when we were both school governors in North London. He has an inquiring mind, an irascible look, and has never encountered a politician he doesn't suspect of lying. And yet his is an interesting sort of skepticism, as demonstrated by our conversation over lunch one day. I was writing chapter 6 of this book and immersed in materials about the Templars and the bloodline of Christ. I told him briefly what I was doing, and he leaned forward and began to speak in what for Jim constituted a confiding tone. "You know," he reminded me, "that I am a skeptic by nature. But I tell you, there's something to all this *Da Vinci Code* business."

The "something" was this. A year earlier, Jim and his wife had visited the Louvre in Paris and had gone to the room where the Poussin painting of the shepherds in Arcadia—the one mentioned in *The Holy Blood and the Holy Grail*—was supposed to hang. But it wasn't there. Intrigued, Jim sought out an attendant and asked where exactly the picture had gone.

The inquiry, for some reason, became an altercation, and as a result of the argument, Jim was asked to leave the Louvre. "I obviously hit a nerve," said Jim, adding reasonably, "You don't get thrown out of a museum just for asking a question!" The conclusion he drew was that the curators had had some kind of secret to hide, and what could that be other than some link to the controversy about the bloodline of Jesus?

I didn't tell Jim that an alternative explanation might well center around a Louvre attendant, whose mood we don't know, finding himself aroused from torpor by an irate Englishman bellowing at him in questionable French about a picture that had already been the subject of several dozen inquires that day, and simply deciding that he'd had enough. In early 2007, six months after our conversation, staff at the Louvre went on strike in protest against the stress brought on by dealing with what they called "aggressive" or even "dangerous" visitors. But this rather less sinister and slightly more comic possibility wasn't likely to appeal to Jim, who seemed happy with his accidental role in discovering the Greatest Conspiracy in History.

RFK Must Die

Such is the pleasure of those who find themselves in on a secret that even the producers of reputable news programs get drawn in. The BBC's TV news flagship, *Newsnight*, is regarded by many of its audience as a model of impartiality and journalistic probity, yet in late November 2006 the program screened a twelve-minute taster documentary made by an Irish filmmaker, Shane O'Sullivan, about the assassination of Robert Kennedy.

The killing of John Kennedy's younger brother at a crucial moment in the 1968 presidential race was always going to be a fodder for conspiracy theories. Conspiracists have been largely thwarted, however, by the open-and-shut nature of the case. The assassin, a Palestinian, Sirhan Sirhan, was seen firing his gun by dozens of people in the Ambassador Hotel that night, before he was overpowered. His gun matched the bullets taken from Kennedy and wounded bystanders, and a search revealed notebooks written before the shooting, in which Sirhan had written over and over again, "RFK must die." Attempts to construct a conspiracy theory from the killing centered, rather desperately, either on the idea that Sirhan was "programmed" by some unknown force to commit the murder or on supposed discrepancies between the number of bullet holes in the pantry area where the shooting took place and the number of shots fired by Sirhan. Doubts were also raised about whether Sirhan ever got close enough to Kennedy to cause the most serious wound (as several eyewitnesses say he certainly did), and about the sighting of a woman in a polka-dot dress who supposedly said, "We killed him."

So far, so (by November 2006) old hat. But O'Sullivan now added something extra to the mix, and it was this novel element that persuaded the editor and senior producers at *Newsnight* to run with his film. As O'Sullivan put it in a newspaper article that appeared on the same day as his program, in the course of researching a fictional screenplay based on the brainwashing theory, he had "uncovered new video and photographic evidence suggesting that three senior CIA operatives were behind the killing."[2] The video was a sequence of high-lit characters, once anonymous but now prominent, moving around the Amabassador Hotel in the moments before and after the shooting, spliced together with a sequence of contemporary interviewees identifying them. It was like something out of a cold-case TV show.

First, O'Sullivan thought he had pictures of a secret-service operative, David Morales: "Fifteen minutes in, there he was, standing at the back of the ballroom, in the moments between the end of Kennedy's speech and the shooting. Thirty minutes later, there he was again, casually floating around the darkened ballroom while an associate with a pencil mustache took notes." But who was the balding man with Morales? Various men who claimed either to have been involved with the CIA or to have been present at the hotel said that it was a Gordon Campbell, who had worked for the CIA in Miami. And if that was so, then who was the third chap talking to Campbell? O'Sullivan thought he knew.

He looked Greek, and I suspected he might be George Joannides, chief of psychological warfare operations at JM-Wave. Joannides was called

out of retirement in 1978 to act as the CIA liaison to the House Select
Committee on Assassinations (HSCA) investigating the death of John
F. Kennedy . . . Ed Lopez, now a respected lawyer at Cornell University,
came into close contact with Joannides when he was a young law student
working for the committee. We visit him and show him the photograph
and he is 99 percent sure it is Joannides. When I tell him where it was taken,
he is not surprised: "If these guys decided you were bad, they acted on it."[3]

O'Sullivan finished his article in the same vein as he finished his film,
with this peroration:

> Given the positive identifications we have gathered on these three, the CIA
> and the Los Angeles Police Department need to explain what they were
> doing there . . . Today would have been Robert Kennedy's 81st birthday.
> The world is crying out for a compassionate leader like him. If dark forces
> were behind his elimination, it needs to be investigated.[4]

After the broadcast of his mini-documentary, O'Sullivan went on to
complete a five-hundred-page book on the killing of RFK, and to put the
finishing touches to a two-and-a-quarter-hour documentary, *RFK Must
Die*. But as he headed back to the cutting room, his entire thesis was
beginning to collapse.

Three other researchers, two American and one British, who had also
been looking at the RFK assassination, began to chase down O'Sullivan's
supposed trio of CIA men. Jefferson Morley and David Talbot—ironically,
pursuing their own conspiracy theory about the Dallas murder—soon discovered that Gordon Campbell, far from being in Los Angeles that night in
1968, had died rather publicly of a heart attack in 1962. The two Americans
communicated this to Shane O'Sullivan, whose response was to suggest
"that the man caught on camera might have expropriated the dead man's
name as an alias, since taking false names was a common practice among
CIA covert operatives."[5]

It got worse. Several people who had known Morales, including his family, were adamant that the man picked out in O'Sullivan's film was not him. O'Sullivan, as he himself recounts in his documentary, now took his identifications to the LAPD. The files showed "Campbell" and the Greek-looking "Joannides" to be Michael Roman and Frank Owens, respectively, both sales managers with the Bulova watch company, which happened to be holding a convention at the Ambassador on that day.

So the "positive identifications" were erroneous, and it seems a fair guess that had *Newsnight* known that there were not three supposedly identifiable CIA agents wandering unaccountably around the Ambassador but two watch salesmen and A. N. Other, they would never have given airtime to O'Sullivan's original movie. This being so, the way the Irishman dealt with this disappointment must be considered a classic of insouciance in adversity.

First, he suggested it didn't really matter. As he told one British conspiracist website (whose members were, at this point, unaware of the collapse of the original theory), "The heart of the film is a thorough reexamination of the other controversies in the case . . . There's rare archive footage from the hotel that night, with more clips of 'Morales' and 'Campbell.'"[6] Second, he implied that the watch convention might have been suspicious. The Bulova company, he told his viewers, had been chaired by former U.S. Army general and Johnson adviser Omar Bradley, and did a significant proportion of its business with the Department of Defense. An anonymous source had told O'Sullivan that Bulova was a "well-known CIA cover." The notion that the CIA sent watch salesmen to superintend its most sensitive assassinations was such a breathtaking example of making the best of a bad job that it led British author Mel Ayton to speculate wryly that perhaps O'Sullivan had made this connection because Bulova used to advertise its Accutron watch in the 1960s spy drama series *The Man From U.N.C.L.E.*[7]

Watching *RFK Must Die* at the Institute of Contemporary Arts in Pall Mall in London, I marveled at O'Sullivan's resilience. When the identifications in his first film collapsed, everything else collapsed, since O'Sullivan had relied on the identifiers for much of his material. But what they said they were so sure of, they were, in fact, utterly mistaken about. Why had this happened? Who knows? Glory, money, stupidity . . .

The True Skeptic

Shane O'Sullivan and my friend Jim are both intelligent, both educated men, and both were holding fast to the idea of their own skepticism while simultaneously creating arguments to suggest that something singularly incredible might actually be true. But far from being skeptics, they were being willfully credulous. True, like many other believers in conspiracy theories, they were selective in their credulity, choosing to dismiss certain theories while endorsing other similarly implausible ones. It is a pattern one notices when reading books with lists of conspiracy theories from which the authors seem to feel obliged, almost arbitrarily, to accept one or two as being true, as though needing some kind of respite from the pure effort of exercising genuine skepticism.

Real skepticism is indeed tiring and in many ways unattractive. "There are more things in heaven and earth, Horatio, Than are dreamed of in our philosophy," Hamlet reminds his friend in words that almost every doubter has had quoted to them at some point in their adult lives. Such an admonition may have been uttered during a discussion of religion, spirituality, New Age philosophy, or alternative therapies, in which the doubter (or real skeptic) has tried to invoke common sense. It always means the same thing: it is the skeptic who has a closed mind, and the believer whose being is open to the world. So the believer in a conspiracy theory or theories becomes, in his own mind, the one in proper communion with the underlying universe, the one who understands the true ordering of things. There are plenty of other ways of enjoying that feeling of transcendence, however, such as embracing esoteric religion or Eastern philosophies. But at certain times and under certain circumstances in the modern, developed, and industrialized world, a large number of people find the story of a conspiracy, no matter how shallowly rooted in fact, almost impossibly seductive. Why?

We should admit here that there is an objection to this entire line of inquiry. After an article I had authored in *The Times*, criticizing 9/11 conspiracists, a British psychoanalyst wrote to me in very civil terms, questioning my own psychological motives. "There is perhaps," he suggested, "an even deeper anxiety that can lead us to dismiss possibilities that imply betrayal by those whom we expect to protect and care for us." And, as an abstract proposition, one can see how this might be true. There are many examples of family members not being able to believe—denying—that a loved father or a respected grandfather was capable of sexual abuse. The reaction of Communists to the Moscow trials was to comfort themselves with the thought that, somehow, the party leadership in Russia must have known what they were doing.

It is when we get down to practicalities that my critic's analysis begins to fray. The evidence that I might be suffering from such a denial lay in my specific rejection of the writings of David Ray Griffin, whose role in the 9/11 Truth movement is discussed in chapter 7 of this book. Griffin's work was, argued the analyst, "carefully and scholarly presented . . . [and] a highly disciplined philosophical analysis of some of the questions that have arisen in relation to official accounts of 9/11."[8] The problem, of course, as we have seen, is that Griffin's account was no such thing, even if it maintained the outward limbs and flourishes of scholarship. Its evasions, half-truths, and bad science suggested a pathology of a kind not displayed by those who pointed out where Griffin parted from scholarship.

So we return to the attractions of conspiracism with the observation that there are some obviously gratifying aspects to creating or consuming theories using its components and techniques. Who, for example, wouldn't want to be on the side of the gifted and insightful? What is less explicable is the drive behind the determination—the need, if you prefer—that something so unlikely as, say, permitting an enemy government to blow up all your battleships should nevertheless be proved to be true. What creates the desire of large numbers of intelligent people to go along with such an idea?

If the preceding chapters have demonstrated anything, it must be that conspiracy theories originate and are largely circulated among the educated and the middle class. The imagined model of an ignorant, priest-ridden peasantry or proletariat, replacing religious and superstitious belief with equally far-fetched notions of how society works, turns out to be completely wrong. It has typically been the professors, the university students, the artists, the managers, the journalists, and the civil servants who have concocted and disseminated the conspiracies.

One thinks here of the Potsdam audience for Professor Hans Kania's lectures on the *Protocols of the Elders of Zion* in 1924, of the readers of the *New York Review of Books* settling down with Professor Richard H. Popkin's theory of the two Oswalds, of the 1940s admirers of the revisionist writings of John T. Flynn and Charles Beard, of Dudley Collard QC and Joseph Davies on their returns from Moscow, of the series editor of BBC's *Chronicle* programs considering making a program about the lost bloodline of the Merovingians, of Tam Dalyell MP and Norman Baker MP, two decades apart, breathlessly retailing stories of anonymous insider tip-offs about murderous British agencies, of comfortable millennial Westerners debating whether they were about to be victims of a state-sponsored coup d'état. In the summer of 2004, the British writer Jonathan Raban, domiciled in the American Northwest, described the mood among his acquaintances before the U.S. presidential election of 2004:

> The backyard barbecue sounds like a convention of spooks . . . A bumper sticker, popular among the sort of people I hang out with, reads: BUSH-CHENEY '04—THE LAST VOTE YOU'LL EVER HAVE TO CAST. That's funny, but it belongs to the genre of humor in which the laugh is likely to die in your throat—and none of the people who sport the sticker on their cars are smiling. They are too busy airing conspiracy theories, which may or may not turn out to be theories.[9]

One hardly needs to add that in November 2006, with no tanks appearing on anyone's lawn, Americans successfully cast their ballots against the ruling Republicans, giving the opposition Democrats a majority in both Houses of Congress. Perhaps by the summer of 2007, the barbecue debaters were back to discussing basketball and celebrity. Even so, Raban was describing a real feeling, and one which, at certain times and in certain ways, has become widespread and politically significant.

History for Losers

There is a more than plausible argument to be made that, very often, conspiracy theories take root among the casualties of political, social, or economic change. More particularly, there is something of a pattern in which overarching theories are formulated by the politically defeated and taken up by the socially defeated, deriving "from the concrete experience of modernity by losers who will not go softly into the night but instead rage against it."[10] These losers left behind by modernity can be identified in the beached remnants of vanished European empires: the doomed bureaucrats, the White Russians, and the patriotic German petit bourgeois. They are the America Firsters, who got the war they didn't want; the Midwest populists watching their small farmers go out of business; the opponents of the New Deal; the McGovern liberals in the era of Richard Nixon; British socialists and pacifists in the decade of Margaret Thatcher; the irreconcilable American right during the Clinton administration; the shattered American left in the time of the second Bush.

If it can be proved that there has been a conspiracy, which has transformed politics and society, then their defeat is not the product of their own inherent weakness or unpopularity, let alone their mistakes; it is due to the almost demonic ruthlessness of their enemy. Richard Hofstadter noted that one of the most important characteristics ascribed to the conspirator (other than his complete lack of moral inhibition) was "his possession of especially effective techniques for fulfilling his desires." Hofstadter saw in this a psychological opportunity for conspiracists "to project and freely express unacceptable aspects of their own minds" while suggesting that this was all the fault of the conspiring "other."[11] Such projections made of the enemy "a perfect model of malice, a kind of amoral superman: sinister, ubiquitous, powerful, cruel, sensual, luxury-loving."[12] This is certainly true of the way in which, at various times, Jews, Communists, Trotskyites, or big corporations have been depicted by theorists.

In its most basic form, this demonic projection consists of the assertion that "they" are capable of almost any act. Writing in the skeptical *New Humanist* magazine in 2005, Derek Kaill asked whether the U.S. government could possibly do such a thing as organize the mass murder of its own citizens, and answered himself, "I think that the flag-waving, war-minded, fundamentalist Christian administration currently in control of the United States would do almost anything to retain and expand their control over the world." Note here how the humanist Kaill adds "Christian fundamentalist" to the list of attributes possessed by the particularly villainous.[13] A few weeks later, in another publication, the Scottish novelist A. L. Kennedy pointed out to those critics of the United States who might dismiss such conspiracism that they were able to accept:

> We and our controlling U.S. interests continue fearlessly to terrorize countries unconnected with the attacks, to place permanent military bases near oil reserves and pipeline routes, to harass and murder Muslims anywhere we can, and to foment terrorist resistance at every opportunity . . . But you'd never want to think that on 9/11/2001 covert U.S. government intervention killed thousands of innocents and handed the country, if not the world, to a commerce-friendly, torture-loving, far-right junta. That would make you a paranoid, depressed conspiracy theorist.[14]

Again, it is impossible not to mark Kennedy's idiosyncratic linking of "commerce-friendly" with "torture-loving," as though shopping was but a prelude to the thumbscrews. Making allowance for the author's use of irony and her specific devils, however, it is possible to recognize the sentiments of Joe McCarthy on the Commie-riddled pinko Establishment that had sold China to the Reds, of John T. Flynn on the amazing villainies of Franklin Roosevelt; and of prosecutor Vyshinsky on the incredible destructiveness of Comrade Pyatakov. In each case, the claim was that the miscreant combined malign intention and a remarkable capacity for deceit with omnipotence in action. Or at least did, until they met their match in the far-sighted exposer of their malevolence.

When the opponent has magic powers, the hero must match these powers or else be inevitably doomed to defeat. If it's the latter, then the forces of good, though overwhelmed, have their excuse: We were robbed. This psychic cop-out has always irritated dissidents who are not conspiracists, with writers such as I. F. Stone and Noam Chomsky in the United States and George Monbiot in the United Kingdom urging fellow radicals not to effectively rule themselves out of the great leftist struggle by following the false trail of the theorists. Conspiracy theories about 9/11 were a "coward's fantasy," wrote Monbiot, "an excuse for inaction used by those who don't have the stomach to engage in real political fights."[15] The response from various corners of the conspiracist world was that Chomsky and Monbiot had become self-appointed "gatekeepers," whose purpose was to police the dissident movement so that it didn't do too much damage to the corrupt Establishment.

The Soul's Version of the Truth

For some more radical students of conspiracism, the possibility that conspiracy theories are history as written by the losers confers a kind of underdog's truth upon them. According to this view, the theory is the fuzzy shadow cast by the hidden bulk of real oppression: it has a kind of reality. The O. J. Simpson case of 1994–1995, in which a black athlete and movie star was acquitted, by a predominantly black jury, of the murders of his white wife and a white man, was seen by many as an appalling case of injustice in which a palpably guilty man was freed because of his color. But there were those who argued that the jury's decision was almost valid, because, in the words of Sam Smith in the *Progressive Review*, "Simpson is carrying the mythic weight of decades of ethnic abuse under the justice system . . . [his] case serves as the mythic translation of stories never allowed to be told."

Smith was writing just two months after Timothy McVeigh, a former soldier with connections to the extreme-right-wing militia movement in the United States, blew up a federal building in Oklahoma City, killing nearly two hundred people. Although McVeigh was a drifter without strong community ties, Smith's article posits an overarching analysis that is applied to both Simpson and McVeigh:

> Like urban blacks considering the justice system, the rural Right has seen things the elite would prefer to ignore. It has observed correctly phenomena indicating loss of sovereignty for themselves, their states and their country. They have seen treaties replaced by fast-track agreements and national powers surrendered to remote and unaccountable trade tribunals . . . Like urban blacks, they have not been paranoid in this observation, merely perceptive.

Seen this way, conspiracist and similar narratives, however crazy they sound, contain real validity, something that the economists and dusty actuaries of politics and the press are unable to comprehend. What is needed, argues Smith, is a more poetical reading of these claims, because "the poet understands that a myth is not a lie but the soul's version of the truth."[16]

A decade on, in the late summer of 2005, Hurricane Katrina struck the American Gulf Coast, resulting in the flooding of the city of New Orleans and the evacuation of 80 percent of its population. Since those worst affected by the disaster were poor, most of the poor were black, and the response of the authorities was considered utterly inadequate, it was wholly understandable that claims of official racism would be made. But for some people what had happened was more sinister than that, and stories began to circulate that some of the flood defenses, or levees, had been destroyed specifically so as to flood black areas.

The following year, the renowned black filmmaker Spike Lee completed a four-hour-long documentary on the disaster, titled *When the Levees Broke*, which dealt with many aspects of the catastrophe, and in which some of the participants repeated their belief in the conspiracy to drown the blacks of New Orleans. Though the film did not specifically support or contest these theories, Lee made plain his own ambivalence in a late-night live TV discussion hosted by Bill Maher.

MAHER: [Black activist] Louis Farrakhan . . . was saying, last Saturday in Washington, that he thinks that the federal government, there was a conspiracy to actually blow up those levees so that they would flood the poor black districts in New Orleans. I have to tell you, I'm not a conspiracy theorist. I don't believe it. But when you see some of the things that have gone on in this country . . .

LEE: Exactly. It's not far-fetched.

MICHEL MARTIN [TV JOURNALIST]: That would require a conspiracy. I mean, look, we can all understand, anybody with any knowledge of history can understand why a lot of people can feel this way, that that's a reasonable theory. But it would also require a conspiracy at three levels of government—the local, the state, and the federal. It would require no white residents—

LEE: Presidents have been assassinated. So why is that so far-fetched?

MARTIN: Because it would require, because it would require no white person in the government to have a moral compass. It would require no black person to have a spine and I think that's a very hard case to make.

LEE: Let me ask you a question: do you think that election in 2000 was fair? You don't think that was rigged? [audience applause]

MARTIN: It's not a question of not being fair, it's a question of—

LEE: If they can rig an election, they can do anything![17]

A number of critics, while praising Spike Lee's film, were disturbed by the conspiracy claims. In the *New York Times,* Nicholas Kulish described the effect as "by turns powerful and frustrating," because "without quite endorsing them," wrote Kulish, "Mr. Lee presents the utterly unfounded charges that the failed levees were blown up to flood poor black neighborhoods."[18] Kulish soon found himself under fire in the letters page. He had missed the point, according to several correspondents, including a professor of African-American studies at Columbia University, which was that Lee offered "alternative perspectives from other residents, journalists, and scholars. That so many black residents believe that the levees were purposely blown up is a result of their historical experience and their continuing sense that their safety and well-being will be sacrificed."[19] In other words, the possible untruth of the allegations was far less important than the bigger truths revealed by them. So, in that sense, arguing about whether there really had been a conspiracy was not just beside the point, but amounted to an attempt to try and deny the larger alternative truth.

This is an approach that dovetails with an intellectual trend, loosely labeled postmodernist or post-structuralist, which has become increasingly attractive to academics and intellectuals in recent years. One aspect of this inclination is a distrust of normative notions of truth. "You show me your reality," it suggests, "I'll show you mine," and the man in Maine with a lobster in his hand will show you his. All accounts of events are essentially stories, and no single account ought to be privileged above another. It is a seductive and not entirely worthless way of looking at the world. Intellectuals like Spike Lee can take this one step further, to suggest that the truth or otherwise of conspiracy theories is less important than their existence, because they are, properly analyzed, an expression of an underlying reality, representing "a not entirely unfounded suspicion that the normal order of things itself amounts to a conspiracy."[20] So they are valid even if they are themselves actually false. They may be, writes Mark Fenster, professor of law at Florida University, "an ideological misrecognition of power relations" but "Just because overarching conspiracy theories are wrong does not mean they are not on to something. Specifically, they ideologically address real structural inequities, and constitute a response to a withering civil society and the concentration of the ownership of the means of production."[21]

This analysis is as sweeping as it is specific. It had its counterpart in the arguments of the American feminist academic Jodi Dean, concerning the widespread suspicion of official science, which was evident in the alien abduction craze of the 1990s. According to Dean, given the "political and politicized position of science today, funded by corporations and by the military, itself discriminatory and elitist, this attitude toward scientific authority makes sense." This idea of an alternative truth was strengthened, in Dean's view, not by the official suppression of information but by its historically unparalleled availability. In the modern world, she argued, "voters, consumers, viewers, and witnesses have no criteria for choosing among policies and verdicts, treatments and claims."[22] As ever, one would be more convinced by Dean's analysis if one thought that there was any real chance of her living her own life according to such relativist precepts. Perhaps one may imagine her standing stock-still for hours in the middle of a supermarket, paralyzed by her own incapacity for making rational judgments between the thousands of goods on display. And perhaps not.

Arguments like those of Dean and some of the crossovers in conspiracist thinking led the British writer Damian Thompson to suggest the existence in modern society of a trend toward what he labeled counterknowledge—knowledge in which the proper use of scientific method in the collection and evaluation of evidence is simply absent. This counterknowledge might be expressed in terms of a belief in bogus therapies, in suffering from nonexistent illnesses, or in embracing unlikely historical theories. "People," he wrote, "who share a muddled, careless, or deceitful attitude toward gathering evidence often find themselves drawn to each other's fantasies. If you believe one wrong or strange thing, you are more likely to believe another."[23] This trend was, in Thompson's view, exacerbated by the moral cowardice of some intellectuals. He recounted a seminar he had attended at Boston University in 1999, at which there was some discussion of the rumor that the American government had devised the

AIDS epidemic as a weapon against black Americans. Thompson asked each panelist whether they believed this theory or not. "One of the speakers, Professor Glenn Loury, currently director of the Institute on Race and Social Division at Boston University," Thompson reported, "explained that he didn't want to be 'disrespectful' to his own African-American community by giving his real opinion."[24]

"Good" and "Bad" Conspiracism

Such relativism is fine (for the relativist) as long as the conspiracist fantasy is concocted by the "right" side and aimed, more or less, at people of whom you disapprove. It becomes much more problematic when the theorist is someone who is seen as being repulsive or dangerous and/or whose targets are people like yourself. Sometimes this difficulty is dealt with by suggesting that the other side's theories are somehow not quite as well grounded and somehow not quite as true. Mark Fenster, the Florida law professor, worries about just this point. It is slightly mystifying to him, he told an interviewer, that there should have been "at least as many wild conspiracy theories" about the Clinton administration as surfaced about his more right-wing successor George W. Bush. But, he reflected, the Bush accusations seemed "more grounded in logic and fact than those about Clinton, which often seemed so utterly beside the point."[25] The question is, of course, whose point? It is also difficult to see why the idea that Bush should have connived at the 9/11 attacks is "more grounded in logic" than the notion that Bill Clinton used murder to cover up a series of financial scandals.

In fact, as we've seen, some of the essential ingredients of conspiracism are common between political factions and over time. Take, for example, brainwashing. Professor Timothy Melley, author of *Empire of Conspiracy*, has shown how "agency panic"—the fear that individuals can be controlled against their wills by omnipotent outside forces—features in work by both left- and right-wing theorists. In 1957, the American journalist Vance Packard published his massive bestseller *The Hidden Persuaders*, which purported to show how advertisers and the media were manipulating the American people into having desires and leading lives that they would otherwise have shunned. The following year, the director of the FBI, J. Edgar Hoover, wrote *Masters of Deceit: The Story of Communism in America and How to Fight It* [*sic*], suggesting that Communists were pulling very much the same kind of trick. Hoover's account, writes Melley, is "remarkably similar to Packard's." But, Melley reminds us, "there is a striking political difference between the two texts, and this difference makes their structural resemblance all the more odd."[26]

Some of the more politically sensitive conspiracists have been keenly aware of the dangers and anxious to distinguish between their own correct conspiracism and the unjustified theories of the other side. Robin Ramsay, British editor of the long-running journal of conspiracy theory, the *Lobster*, considers implausible the idea of a "Left-Right fusion . . . an ideologically neutral conspiracy mindset."[27] In his view, "bad" conspiracism is essentially aimed at scapegoats, such as Jews and Communists, while the target of "good" conspiracism is almost invariably authority: the state itself. "The Right," says Ramsay, "is interested in conspiracies . . . against the state . . . The liberal Left, on the other hand, is chiefly interested in conspiracies committed by the state."[28]

Ramsay's distinction does not survive scrutiny. John T. Flynn's right-wing conspiracism was aimed at the state as represented by the treacherous Roosevelt, and at Owen Lattimore, the supposedly infiltrating pro-Mao Communist. Right-wing U.S. militia movements are both anti-state and anti-minority. Liberal-left defenders of the Soviet Union (and there were many) swallowed the idea of an international gang of infinitely wicked Trotskyites attempting to subvert the world's first socialist state.

What we might call Ramsay's Problem is deliciously evident in his musings on banking and Judaism. The radical leftist is impatient with the anti-Semite's attempt to bring the Jews into the equation, not least because it muddies the waters. "The 'Jewish conspiracy' nonsense," writes Ramsay, "has served for half a century in this country to make people nervous about researching the power of finance capital in this society," presumably lest they be associated with the far right.[29] Ramsay continues, "There are bankers ripping us off, but few of them are Jewish." This is a flimsy objection to someone else's theory. What if many of the bankers— a third, say, or a half—were indeed Jewish? Would that constitute prima facie evidence that, in addition to the bankers being part of a conspiracy, their Judaism was a significant aspect of their quest for money and power? Attitudes may have changed since Ramsay's hopeful distinction was made. Ten years later, substitute "Zionist" or "pro-Israeli" for "Jewish" and you will create a banking conspiracy that almost every modern-day conspiracist can agree upon.

But Ramsay's desire to avoid contamination hints at an important conclusion. You may argue, as some do, that "understanding why normal people believe weird things is harder but ultimately more fruitful than trying to disprove these weird beliefs by dogmatic insistence on the proper events"[30] and this book certainly seeks to understand. But without the "dogmatic insistence," it is hard to see why the beliefs are "weird." Aren't they just alternative narratives, in a world full of blind alleys, spin, and disinformation? The trouble here, of course, is that it means taking the appalling rough with the playful smooth, the professional anti-Semite with the recreational Templarist.

It is worth remembering, too, that almost every conspiracy theory, if believed, has a victim. The Duke of Edinburgh may be rich and grumpy, but that doesn't mean that the repeated charge that he was responsible for ordering the murder of his son's ex-wife is any less painful or damaging. Whether or not the charges are true will matter to him, to the people close to him, and to history itself. The accusations against Leon Trotsky and his followers still reverberated around the global left forty years later.

If all narratives are relative, then we are lost. Widespread anti-Semitic fantasies may have reflected the plight of Germans, may even have been their "soul's version of the truth" in the post-1918 period, but they were still fantasies, and the failure to counter them, or to see the fantasies as themselves creating terrible political realities, proved totally catastrophic. Relativism doesn't care to distinguish between the scholarly and the slapdash, the committed researcher and the careless loudmouth, the scrupulous and the demagogic. For that reason, it is hard to see how an insistence on "proper events" can ever be said to be dogmatic, or a refusal to insist can be anything other than treacherous. Spike Lee is entirely wrong.

Hysteria

This book has, I hope, dogmatically insisted, and now arrives at the point where it seeks finally to account for the phenomenon of conspiracism. The examples used in the book, which were not chosen for their similarities but for their outward differences, suggest that the answer does not lie entirely in power relations, the abundance or scarcity of information, or the experience of disenfranchisement—a word which has become ubiquitous in recent years, and seems now merely to mean not getting your way.

In what sense were or are Connecticut professionals, West Country hippies, Liberal Democrat MPs, the middle-class members of the Campaign for Nuclear Disarmament, BBC TV drama producers, Senator Joe McCarthy, Dan Brown, Dudley Collard QC, Mohamed Al Fayed, and Alfred Rosenberg disenfranchised? In what way does their own experience of powerlessness inform those who believe, no matter what, that the British royal family executes its more awkward members, that Robert Kennedy had a poisoned suppository inserted into Marilyn Monroe before being assassinated by a Manchurian Candidate, or that the Catholic Church has for two millennia been suppressing the truth about the secret bloodline of Christ?

It isn't dispossession or capitalism. State ownership in Russia was no guarantee against the most fabulous of conspiracy theories. As to Mark Fenster's "withering civil society," it must be recognized that conspiracism flourishes in notoriously unwithered civil societies. Arab countries, beloved by many in the West for their unspoiled and therefore more authentic social relations, are rife with popular conspiracism. This isn't to say that such factors are unimportant. We've seen how, at certain times, conspiracy theories become particularly attractive to the losers in any process of political or social change. But from their similarities, it does look as though conspiracy theories somehow fill a need that societies, groups, or individuals feel more or less intensely at different moments.

In Oxford in 1963, days before the assassination of President John F. Kennedy, American historian Richard Hofstadter gave a lecture titled "The Paranoid Style in American Politics." Hofstadter's immediate target was the American right of post-McCarthyites, who seemed still to see a Red under every bed. Hofstadter called their style paranoid because "no other word adequately evokes the qualities of heated exaggeration, suspiciousness, and conspiratorial fantasy."[31] The same psychological property, he argued, was present in Moscow in the 1930s, where the trials demonstrated "a wildly imaginative and devastating exercise in the paranoid style."[32] Overall, Hofstadter concluded, "the feeling of persecution is central."[33]

That conspiracism is, at bottom, a symptom of paranoia subsequently became an anti-conspiracist cliché, and it's easy to see why. In modern society, paranoia seems omnipresent. Most journalists and many writers will have received letters from members of the public, often long and containing diagrams, detailing how this or that agency or relative has been interfering with their brainwaves. It is hard not to be reminded of these communications when reading about the queen's supposed remarks to Princess Diana's butler Paul Burrell to the effect that there were "powers at work in this country about which we have no knowledge" (as if Her Majesty would deliver herself of such an obvious contradiction), or when looking at the reaction to Dr. David Kelly's final e-mails, sent hours before his death, in which he wrote of "many dark actors playing games." Someone is trying to get us.

The idea that supposedly rational arguments about how big bad things happen originate not in the real world but in our internal selves—that they are the outer expression of inner problems—was explored by Elaine Showalter in her 1997 book *Hystories: Hysterical Epidemics and Modern Culture*. Showalter looked at a series of moral and health panics that had erupted at various times in Britain and America, including ritual child abuse, Gulf War syndrome, and CFS (chronic fatigue syndrome). In them, she discerned common patterns".

Skeptical about all these phenomena, Showalter argues that what we are in fact looking at is hysteria, the external manifestation of repressed feelings. "Hysteria has not died," she writes. "It has simply been relabeled for a new era . . . Contemporary hysterical patients blame external sources—a virus, sexual molestation, chemical warfare, satanic conspiracy, alien infiltration—for psychic problems."[34] In the era of mass media and instant communication, these hysterias find traction with other people looking for explanations for their feelings and symptoms and "multiply rapidly and uncontrollably."[35]

One of Showalter's pieces of evidence may cast some light on an underremarked aspect of conspiracism—its gender. She points out that a Harvard Medical School study discovered that 80 percent of chronic fatigue syndrome sufferers were women, as were 90 percent of those who, usually under hypnosis, supposedly recovered hidden memories of sexual abuse, and two-thirds of those reporting alien abduction.[36] This, together with the number of times I have been told "My husband/boyfriend will be very interested in your book" prompts the thought that conspiracy theories may be hysterias for men.

Unsurprisingly, Showalter's analysis was unpopular. In nonclinical usage, "hysteria" connotes a somewhat ridiculous lack of control rather than a genuine psychological condition. Furthermore, to the person who believes that her son's all-too-real autism must be explicable, and that the explanation must be external interference in the shape of a state-sponsored measles jab, Showalter will seem insulting. Such psychologizing didn't find favor among sociologists either. To Peter Knight, Showalter's thesis was something of a conspiracy theory itself. "The figuration of the spread of paranoid thinking as an 'epidemic' or a 'plague,'" he charged, "likewise renders it an inscrutable and virtually unstoppable force that infiltrates innocent minds."[37] This, it seems to me, is a misreading of Showalter's attempt to explain how we create or borrow stories for ourselves. In fact, Showalter was concerned to argue that this impulse to grasp half-baked and damaging but attractive notions of why the world is as it is could be replaced through emotional literacy. "Men and women, therapists and patients," she concluded, "will need courage to face the hidden fantasies, myths, and anxieties that make up the current hysterical crucible; we must look into our own psyches rather than to invisible enemies, devils, and alien invaders for the answers."[38]

About Fashion

In her work on hysteria, Showalter argues that "like all narratives," her mass hysterias have "their own conventions, stereotypes, and structures."[39] The more the specific thesis is talked about, the more people feel that they have had the same experience or are suffering the same symptoms, the more voluminous the literature becomes, the more aggressive in defense of their illness the victims become, and the more the idea is accepted into the mainstream. Eventually, however, the panic dies down, to be replaced fairly soon by another, similar outbreak, though with a completely different focus. The same is true of conspiracy theories. The set of charges and allegations surrounding the 1984 Hilda Murrell death were, as we've seen, highly specific in type to the period between 1980 and 1987. During that time, a large number of theories, or beliefs, or dramas, focused precisely on a supposed matrix composed of the nuclear industry, American and British intelligence, and semi-corrupt politicians. After Mikhail Gorbachev's summit with Ronald Reagan in Iceland in late 1986, the nuclear-matrix conspiracy all but ended.

Based, as they supposedly are, on the uncovering of hidden truths, conspiracy theories should not be subject to fashion, and yet they clearly are. As a result, one suspects that conspiracy theories also have a social function and that they could be classic examples of what the biologist Richard Dawkins has called "memes": ideas that replicate themselves because of the utility of sharing notions but that are genuinely felt. In the immediate aftermath of 9/11, it was extremely rare to find someone outside the Arab press arguing that there had been a cover-up. That had changed by 2006, and what had altered was not, I would argue, the presentation of any new facts but the widespread social acceptability of blaming the U.S. administration.

The Triumph of Narrative

While I was writing this book, I went on a visit to the University of Winchester to give a talk about conspiracism and *The Da Vinci Code*. At dinner, I found myself sitting with a senior member of the drama department. I told him that one of the things I found interesting about conspiracy theories was the need for a narrative that they suggested. "Ah, yes," he said. "You should read Mamet."

This was excellent advice. The American playwright and screenwriter's fourth collection of essays almost starts with the words, "It is in our nature to dramatize." By this, Mamet doesn't mean that we are all a bit histrionic sometimes, but rather that we need to construct, or have constructed, dramas and stories for ourselves. Therapists and psychoanalysts know the truth of this. Their patients, like the rest of us, invariably have a story about inexplicable or mundane aspects of their lives. Our illnesses are due to stress or genetics or that day we went out for a walk and it was cold. Adopted children very often create a backstory of their real parents, and unadopted children have fantasies of their "real" mothers and fathers. As Mamet points out, we will have a story even if it means giving characteristics to the elemental. So "the weather is impersonal, and we both understand it and exploit it as dramatic, i.e., having a plot, in order to understand its meaning for the hero, which is to say, for ourselves."[40]

This is not some kind of occasional preference, done merely to keep ourselves entertained. Mamet observes that just as children use up the last of the day's energy by jumping around, "the adult equivalent, when the sun goes down, is to create or witness drama—which is to say to order the universe into a comprehensible form. Our sundown play/film/gossip is the day's last exercise of that survival mechanism . . . We will have drama in that spot, and if it's not forthcoming we will cobble it together out of nothing."[41]

At first, hearing this may sound like a clever artist's generalization—an observation and nothing more. But in 2006, the British human biologist Lewis Wolpert theorized that the compulsion to create a story, "to have drama in that spot," might actually be biological—that it represented a "cognitive imperative," an innate need to have the world organized cognitively. Wolpert speculated that the requirement to establish causality was a necessity for an animal that made tools in order to survive, and had thus become instinctive. "Once there were causal beliefs for tool use," he argued, "then our ancestors developed causal beliefs about all key events."[42] If we are impelled, therefore, to find causes, it follows that failure to do so created discomfort or anxiety. Consequently, human beings evolved with "a strong tendency to make up a causal story to provide an explanation . . . ignorance about important causes is intolerable."[43] Wolpert's focus was on the universality of religious beliefs, a universality that prevailed even though the beliefs themselves were mutually incompatible. But his idea works rather well with conspiracism: "We construct apparently coherent stories about what happened . . . but where consistency and internal satisfaction have to compete with testing against the real world, we choose consistency."[44]

If Wolpert is right, then a religious conspiracy theorist like David Ray Griffin represents the ultimate in the triumph of narrative. Meanwhile, all of us who argue for a living, including this author, might do well to consider Wolpert's observation of the tendency always to look for confirmation of preexisting stories rather than their falsification.

The Catastrophe of Indifference

So, we need story and may even be programmed to create it. But why are certain types and structures of story more successful, more satisfying than others? One possible answer is that a successful story either represents the way we think things should happen, or is the best explanation we can get of why they didn't. A New York fire chief asked to account for the various theories surrounding the collapse of buildings at the World Trade Center attributed them to the disappointment of people's belief in the omnipotence of the emergency services. "In the movies," he said, "it's always wrapped up in the end." Or, as Norman Cohn puts it when discussing paranoid thought in his history of apocalyptic movements, people cannot accept "the ineluctable limitations and imperfections of human existence, such as transience, dissention, conflict, fallibility whether intellectual or moral."[45]

The paradox is that, seen this way, conspiracy theories are actually reassuring. They suggest that there is an explanation, that human agencies are powerful, and that there is order rather than chaos. This makes redemption possible. "After all," argues Dr. Jeffrey M. Bale, an American academic specializing in the ideology of terrorism, "if evil conspirators are consciously causing undesirable changes, the implication is that others, perhaps through the adoption of similar techniques, may also consciously intervene to protect a threatened way of life or otherwise alter the historical process."[46] There is, however, another possible form of reassurance, of an altogether more personal kind. The classic view of paranoia, the unwarranted belief that one is being persecuted, is that it is a wholly negative state. But what if paranoia is actually the sticking plaster that we fix to a very different kind of wound? That of feeling ourselves to be of no importance whatsoever, and our lives (and especially our deaths) of little real significance except to ourselves.

The London-based American psychoanalyst Stephen Grosz believes this may be the case. He argues, after twenty-five years of practice, that paranoia may often be a defense against indifference, against the far more terrible thought that no one cares about you. The elderly, at a time of their lives when no one very much wonders what they think, often become classically paranoid, believing that someone wishes to rob or hurt them. The lonely person fears that there is a burglar or a murderer in the empty house waiting for them. Indeed, they may often perceive the real symptoms of such threats—the noises, the shadows, the displaced objects. These fears disguise the truly obliterating disaster, the often well-founded fear that no one is thinking about them at all, what Grosz calls "the catastrophe of indifference."[47]

Everyone knows Oscar Wilde's famous dictum "There is only one thing in the world worse than being talked about, and that is not being talked about." Fewer will have heard Susan Sontag's clever development of it: "I envy paranoids. They actually feel people are paying attention to them." If conspiracism is a projection of paranoia, it may exist in order to reassure us that we are not the totally unconsidered objects of a blind process. If Marilyn was murdered, then she did not die, as we most fear and as we most often observe, alone and ingloriously. A catastrophe occurred, but not the greater catastrophe that awaits all of us.

But if conspiracy theories are paradoxically comforting, it doesn't mean that they are not harmful. It is worth quoting at length here the judgment of the historian Stephen E. Ambrose:

> We should care because conspiracy theories about past events usually carry with them a political agenda for today. Erroneous or downright mythical views of the past can have important, even crucial, influence on the present. The coming to power of the Nazis, German rearmament, ultimately World War II might not have happened without widespread German belief in the stab-in-the-back conspiracy. Widespread acceptance by the American people of the "merchants of death" conspiracy thesis about our entry into World War I was a prelude to the ill-fated, nearly disastrous neutrality legislation of the 1930s. The unhappy consequences of McCarthyism would not have come about had the American people rejected his conspiracy thesis about the triumph of Communism in China.[48]

Ambrose could have added many more examples and, facing some dangerous challenges in the early twenty-first century, so could we. I am with John Maynard Keynes, whose view was that "the power of vested interests is vastly exaggerated compared to the gradual encroachment of ideas." I have written this book because I believe that conspiracies aren't powerful. It is instead the idea of conspiracies that has power.

ACKNOWLEDGMENTS

This book has taken a long time to write. When my wife, Sarah Powell, first made a joke about feeling like Dorothea Brooke in *Middlemarch*, I went back to Eliot and discovered that Edward Casaubon's ever-delayed *Key to All Mythologies* was indeed a precursor of this book, at least in its early stages. Casaubon's project, like his soul, "went on fluttering in the swampy ground where it was hatched, thinking of its wings and never flying." Sarah and the girls have had to put up with a lot and for a long time.

So, too, have my patient, ever-encouraging agent, Georgia Garrett, and the ebullient Dan Franklin at Cape, who punished wing-flapping with excellent lunches and then supplied the wonderful Rebecca Carter as editor. I am grateful, I suppose, to Kevin Jarvis for launching me on this journey. Quite how grateful will depend on sales. I am indebted to Chris Brougham, though only he knows why. Francis Wheen consciously supplied me with Dudley Collard and—less deliberately—with an example of how writers can write, and my hugely valued colleague at *The Times*, Danny Finkelstein, read the manuscript and made invaluable suggestions. Eamon O'Connor procured me a priceless DVD.

Finally, I couldn't have coped without the Yankee friends of my middle age, John Lahr and Stephen Grosz, one of whom effortlessly solved an immense problem I was having with structure, thus clearing the way, while the other dipped deep into his own discipline, psychoanalysis, to bring things to a conclusion. Unbelievably, much of this was accomplished whilst eating porridge.

NOTES

Complete publishing information on sources here referred to only in part may be found in the bibliography.

Introduction: Blame Kevin

1. Russ Kick, ed., *Everything You Know Is Wrong: The Disinformation Guide to Secrets and Lies*, 5.
2. James McConnachie and Robin Tudge, *The Rough Guide to Conspiracy Theories*, xi.
3. Richard Hofstadter, *The Paranoid Style in American Politics and other Essays*, 29.
4. *The Skeptic's Dictionary*, http://skepdic.com/occam.html.
5. Skip Willman in Peter Knight, ed., *Conspiracy Nation: The Politics of Paranoia in Post-War America*, 25.
6. Ibid.
7. Lewis Namier, *Avenues of History*, cited in Daniel Pipes, *Conspiracy*, 38.
8. Robin Ramsay, *Conspiracy Theories*, 38.
9. Daniel Pipes, *The Hidden Hand*, 325.
10. *Guardian*, February 4, 1999.
11. David Ray Griffin, *The New Pearl Harbor*, 26.
12. http://smithmag.net/2006/08/10/korey-rowe-the-loose-cannon-of-911.
13. *Morning Star*, March 26, 2005.

1. "The Uncanny Note of Prophecy"

1. Cited in Norman Cohn, *Warrant for Genocide*, 166.
2. State Department Decimal File 861.00/5339.
3. More than a decade later, the issue of the Jewishness of Soviet Communism still preoccupied British diplomats. In the recently published diaries of Reader Bullard, British consul in Saint Petersburg from 1931 to 1934, there is constant mention of the Jewishness of various party and state officials, as well as of the apologists from abroad who defended the Stalin regime. Buller himself was a liberal, but his diary records an article in the *Listener*, of May 2, 1934, in which a Professor Hyman Levy argued that the Soviet system was the opposite of fascism. Buller remarks, "I have ceased to expect a Jew to criticize anything in Soviet Russia. I understand their point of view. The Russian Jew was bottom-dog before the Revolution, and now he is a member of

the ruling class, with the diplomatic service, foreign trade, journalism, and propaganda largely in his hands." Reader Bullard, *Inside Stalin's Russia*, 264.

4. Binjamin W. Segel, *A Lie and a Libel*, 51.
5. Marsden version, 184–85.
6. Richard S. Levy, Introduction to Binjamin W. Segel, *A Lie and A Libel*, 7.
7. Quoted in Cohn, 149.
8. Cited in Cohn, 149.
9. Levy, 120.
10. Cited in Cohn, 168.
11. Marsden subsequently produced his own translation of the *Protocols*. It's the one sitting on my desk as I write this, bought from an American mail-order company. In an anonymous preface, the edition tells readers that Marsden was imprisoned by the Bolsheviks and his health ruined. He came back to Britain but died suddenly after covering the empire tour of the Prince of Wales. "His sudden death," says this edition, "is still a *mystery*." Marsden version, 6.
12. Cohn, 170.
13. Neil Baldwin, *Henry Ford and the Jews*, 49.
14. Ibid., 59.
15. Ibid., 81–85.
16. *Dearborn Independent*, January 22, 1921.
17. Baldwin, 140.
18. Cohn, 284.
19. Marsden version, 293.
20. Stephen A. Bronner, *A Rumor Against the Jews*, 85.
21. Hermann Bernstein, *The Truth About the Protocols of Zion*, 31.
22. Cited in Cohn, 88.
23. Bronner, 91.
24. Levy, 16.
25. Douglas's *Plain English* was full of surprises, some of them hilarious. The anti-Semitic Conservative MP Captain A. H. M. Ramsay—interned during the war against Hitler—records in his book *The Nameless War*, "According to a letter published in *Plain English* on 3rd September, 1921: 'The Learned Elders have been in existence for a much longer period than they have perhaps suspected. My friend, Mr. L. D. van Valckert, of Amsterdam, has recently sent me a letter containing two extracts from the Synagogue at Mulheim. The volume in which they are contained was lost at some period during the Napoleonic Wars, and has recently come into Mr. van Valckert's possession. It is written in German, and contains extracts of letters sent and received by the authorities of the Mulheim Synagogue. The first entry he sends me is of a letter received:

"'*16th June, 1647. From O.C. (i.e., Oliver Cromwell), by Ebenezer Pratt. In return for financial support will advocate admission of Jews to England: This however impossible while Charles living. Charles cannot be executed without trial, adequate grounds for which do not at present exist. Therefore advise that Charles be assassinated, but will have nothing to do with arrangements for procuring an assassin, though willing to help in his escape. In reply was dispatched the following: 12th July, 1647. To O.C. by E. Pratt. Will grant financial aid as soon as Charles removed and Jews admitted. Assassination too dangerous. Charles shall be given opportunity to escape: His recapture will make trial and execution possible. The support will be liberal, but useless to discuss terms until trial commences.'*"

26. Segel, 68.
27. Adolf Hitler, *Mein Kampf*, 307–8.
28. Cohn, 254.
29. Levy, 42.
30. Quoted in Segel, 83.
31. Ibid., 89.
32. Segel, cited Cohn, *Warrant for Genocide*, 151.
33. Levy, 32.
34. Hannah Arendt, *Origins of Totalitarianism*, 357.
35. Levy, 35–36.

2. Dark Miracles

1. Quoted in Leonard Schapiro, *The Communist Party of the Soviet Union*, 384–85.
2. *Report of the Court Proceedings in the Case of the Anti-Soviet Trotskyite Center. Trial*, 22.
3. Ibid., 23.
4. Isaac Deutscher, *The Prophet Unarmed: Trotsky 1921–1929*, 174.
5. Ibid.
6. V. I. Lenin, *Collected Works*, vol. 36, 594–96.
7. J. Arch Getty and Oleg U. Naumov, *The Road to Terror*, 36–37.
8. Trotsky's wife, quoted in Deutscher, 249.
9. Deutscher, 342–43, 352.
10. Getty and Naumov, 43.
11. Trotsky, quoted in Michael Sayers and Albert E. Kahn, *The Great Conspiracy Against Russia*, 75.
12. *Trial Report*, 26.
13. Ibid., 27–28.
14. Ibid., 29.
15. Ibid., 31.
16. Ibid., 36.
17. Ibid., 43.
18. Ibid., 169.
19. Ibid., 47.
20. Ibid., 119.
21. Ibid., 60.
22. Ibid., 62.
23. Ibid., 65.
24. Ibid., 185.
25. *Pravda*, August 21, 1936, quoted in Robert Conquest, *The Great Terror*, 98.
26. *Trial Report*, 539.
27. Ibid., 541.
28. Ibid., 550.
29. Lion Feuchtwanger, *Moscow 1937*, 149.
30. Central Committee, secret resolution, cited in Getty and Naumov, 255.
31. Getty and Naumov, 293–94.
32. Joseph Davies, *Mission to Moscow*, 45.
33. Ibid., 44.
34. Feuchtwanger, 135.

35. Ibid., 147.

36. John D. Littlepage and Demaree Bess, *In Search of Soviet Gold*, 102.

37. Dudley Collard, *Soviet Justice and the Trial of Radek and Others*, 82.

38. Ibid., 93.

39. Ibid., 90.

40. Ibid., 99–100.

41. Ibid., 102.

42. Ibid., 107.

43. Feuchtwanger, 137–38.

44. Ibid., 162.

45. Dmitri Volkogonov, *Trotsky: The Eternal Revolutionary*, 376.

46. Ibid., 388.

47. Trotsky, letter to Smirnov, cited in Getty, 62.

48. *Sotsialistichesky Vestnik*, no. 5 (243), March 14, 1931, 11–12. Cited in University of East Anglia document website: http://www.uea.ac.uk/his/webcours/russia/documents/ambam onch.shtml.

49. Chuyev, cited in Getty and Naumov, 3.

50. Extract of diary published in Veronique Garros, Natalia Korenevskaya, and Thomas Lahusen, eds., *Intimacy and Terror: Soviet Diaries of the 1930s*.

51. Michael Sayers and Albert E. Kahn, *The Great Conspiracy Against Russia*, 79.

52. Collard, 8.

53. Cited in Getty and Naumov, 51.

54. Feuchtwanger, 173–74.

55. Keynes, talk for BBC Radio, 1936.

56. François Furet, *The Passing of an Illusion*, 155.

57. Note of June 28, 1937, published in Joseph E. Davies, *Mission to Moscow*, 161.

58. Cited in Roy Medvedev, "European Writers on Their Meetings with Stalin," *Russian Politics and Law*, vol. 42, no. 5, 161.

59. Feuchtwanger, 128.

60. Service, *Lenin*, 361.

61. Getty and Naumov, 26.

62. Felix Chuyev, *Tak govoril Kaganovich* (Thus Spake Kaganovich), Moscow, 1992, cited at http://www.revolutionarydemocracy.org/rdvln2/chuyev.htm.

63. *Time*, February 8, 1937.

3. Conspiracies to the Left

1. *See It Now*, CBS Television, March 9, 1954.

2. Theodore Roosevelt, speech to the Gridiron Club, Washington, March 17, 1906.

3. Cited in Hugh Brogan, *The Penguin History of the United States*, 439.

4. Ibid., 542.

5. John T. Flynn, *As We Go Marching*, 252–53.

6. Smedley D. Butler, "I Was a Gangster for Capitalism," speech, 1933.

7. Smedley D. Butler, *War Is a Racket*, 23.

8. *Report of the Special Committee on Investigation of the Munitions Industry*, 3–13.

9. G. P. Nye, speech to the Mecca Temple, February 9, 1936.

10. Roosevelt, radio address, December 29, 1940.

11. J. T. Flynn, radio address, March 8, 1941.

12. *War Is a Racket*, 49–50.
13. Ibid., 55.
14. Founding public statement of the America First Committee, September 4, 1940.
15. Lindbergh, speech, Des Moines, Idaho, September 11, 1941.
16. Charles Lindbergh, *The Wartime Journals of Charles Lindbergh*, September 18, 1941.
17. Ibid., October 4, 1941.
18. Ibid., December 8, 1941.
19. John T. Flynn, *The Final Secret of Pearl Harbor*, reproduced at http://geocities.com/Pentagon/6315/flynnfs.html.
20. Ibid.
21. Ibid.
22. Ibid.
23. Gore Vidal, *The Last Empire*, 260.
24. *New York Review of Books*, May 17, 2001.
25. Harry Elmer Barnes, *Pearl Harbor After a Quarter of a Century*, cited in Gordon W. Prange, *At Dawn We Slept*, 841.
26. John Toland, *Infamy: Pearl Harbor and Its Aftermath*, 324.
27. Prange, 843.
28. Stephen E. Ambrose, "Writers on the Grassy Knoll," *New York Times*, February 2, 1992.
29. Robert Stinnett, *Day of Deceit*, 5.
30. Stephen Budiansky, "Closing the Book on Pearl Harbor," *Cryptologia*, vol. 24, issue 2, April 2000, 119–30.
31. Vidal, 265.
32. Adolf Hitler, speech to Reichstag, December 11, 1941.
33. H. E. Barnes, "Revisionism and the Promotion of Peace," reprinted in the *Journal of Historical Review*, Spring 1982.
34. H. E. Barnes, "The Public Stake in Revisionism," *Rampart Journal of Individualist Studies*, Summer 1967.
35. H. E. Barnes, "Zionist Fraud," *American Mercury*, Fall 1968.
36. For what follows, see John E. Moser, "Gigantic Engines of Propaganda: The 1941 Investigation of Hollywood," *The Historian*, Summer 2001.
37. Cited in Eric Bentley, ed., *Thirty Years of Treason. Excerpts from Hearings Before the House Committee on Un-American Activities, 1938–1968*, 24–25.
38. David M. Oshinsky, *A Conspiracy So Immense*, 92.
39. Ibid., 140.
40. Ibid.
41. Cited ibid., 105.
42. Cited ibid., 83.
43. Cited ibid., 107.
44. Ibid., 109.
45. Ibid.
46. Senator Joseph McCarthy, speech to the United States Senate, June 14, 1951.
47. John T. Flynn, *The Decline of the American Republic and How to Rebuild It*.
48. Oshinsky, 507.
49. Richard Hofstadter, *The Paranoid Style in American Politics*, 24.
50. Raymond Williams, *The County and the City*, 9–12.
51. Lawrence Levine, "Frank Capra's America," *The Journal for Multi-Media History*, vol. 2, 1999.

52. Hofstadter, 45.
53. H. E. Barnes, "The Public Stake in Revisionism."

4. Dead Deities

1. Gerald Posner, *Case Closed*, 402.
2. Mark Lane, "Defense Brief for Oswald," *National Guardian*, December 19, 1963.
3. Cited in I. F. Stone, "The Left and the Warren Commission Report," *I. F. Stone's Weekly*, vol. 13, no. 33, October 5, 1964.
4. *Annie Hall*, director Woody Allen, 1977.
5. Bill Hicks, *Rant in E-Minor*, 1997.
6. Todd Gitlin, *The Sixties*, 311.
7. Richard H. Popkin, "The Second Oswald," *New York Review of Books*, July 28, 1966.
8. Ibid.
9. Ibid.
10. Ibid.
11. Ibid.
12. I. F. Stone, "Report."
13. Sid Blumenthal, ed., *Government by Gunplay*, Foreword.
14. Ibid., 265.
15. Oglesby, 189.
16. James Di Eugenio and Lisa Pease, eds., *The Assassinations*, 635.
17. Ibid., 639.
18. Evidence to the Warren Commission, cited in Posner, *Case Closed*, 113.
19. Warren Commission, *Exhibits*, vol. 16, 106–16.
20. Di Eugenio and Pease, 314. The most comprehensive history of the Kennedy assassination, debunking subsequent conspiracy theories, is Vincent Bugliosi's massive 1,600-page *Reclaiming History: The Assassination of President John F. Kennedy* (New York: W. W. Norton, 2007).
21. For a full discussion of this, see Posner, chapters 11, 14, 19 and appendices; Vincent Bugliosi, *Reclaiming History*, 450–512.
22. John K. Lattimer, et al., *Journal of the American College of Surgeons*, May 1994.
23. Peter Knight, *Conspiracy Culture*, 83.
24. Ibid., 87.
25. Irving Howe, "The Fate of the Union: Kennedy and After," *New York Review of Books*, December 26, 1963.
26. Dwight MacDonald, ibid.
27. Andrew O'Hagan, "St. Marilyn," *London Review of Books*, January 6, 1999.
28. Matthew Smith, *Victim*, 186.
29. Sarah Churchwell, *The Many Lives of Marilyn Monroe*, 334.
30. *Los Angeles Times*, August 5, 2005.
31. Anthony Summers, interview with Dan Abrams, MSNBC Television, August 8, 2005.
32. Ibid.
33. Seymour Hersh, *The Dark Side of Camelot*, 104–5.
34. Robert Sam Anson, *Vanity Fair*, November 1997.
35. *New York Times*, September 27, 1997.
36. Smith, Foreword.

37. Churchwell, 328.
38. http://www.larouchepub.com/tv/index.html.
39. *Sunday Express*, June 23, 2002.
40. Gordon Thomas, *Gideon's Spies*, 1.
41. Ibid., 17.
42. "Mugabe 'Paid Israeli Spy to Frame Opposition Leader,'" *Independent*, July 10, 2002.
43. David Cohen, *Diana, Death of a Goddess*, 6.
44. Ibid., 219.
45. Ibid., 230.
46. Ibid., 237.
47. Ibid., 236.
48. http://www.cesnur.org/testi/Grace.htm.
49. *Richard and Judy*, Channel 4, June 15, 2005.
50. Umberto Eco, *Foucault's Pendulum*, 200.
51. *Who Killed Diana?* Sky One television, August 21, 2006.
52. Stephen Glover, "It Is No Longer Possible to Scoff at the Idea that Diana Was Murdered," *Spectator*, October 25, 2003.
53. Colin Randall, *Daily Telegraph* blog, September 21, 2006.
54. *Independent*, December 15, 2006.
55. Stephen Bates, *Guardian*, April 8, 2008.
56. Daniella Relph, February 13, 2008.
57. http://www.scottbaker-inquests.gov.uk.
58. http://www.scottbaker-inquests.gov.uk/hearing_transcripts/230108pm.htm.
59. "Princess DVDiana," *Sunday Mirror*, May 25, 2008.
60. Truman Capote, *In Cold Blood*, 224.
61. Churchwell, 324.
62. Gitlin, 311.

5. A Very British Plot

1. *Guardian*, March 21, 1994.
2. Judith Cook, *Unlawful Killing: The Murder of Hilda Murrell*, 18.
3. Ibid., 19–20.
4. Ibid., 13.
5. "Thatcher Makes Falklands Link Attack on 'Enemy Within,'" *Times*, July 20, 1984.
6. *20/20 Vision*, "MI5's Official Secrets," Channel 4, March 1985.
7. *True Spies 3*, BBC2, September 2002.
8. *True Spies 2*, "Something Better Change," BBC2, September 2002.
9. David McKittrick et al., *Lost Lives*, 973.
10. Cook, 33.
11. Ibid., 10.
12. Ibid., 36.
13. Laurens Otter, cited ibid., 39.
14. Ibid., 45.
15. Andrew Brown, *Guardian*, April 13, 2002.
16. Ibid.
17. This and quotations in the following paragraph: Hansard (transcript of parliamentary debates), December 20, 1984.

18. Paul Keel and Richard Norton-Taylor, *Guardian*, December 21, 1984.
19. Cited in Cook, 112.
20. Ibid., 103.
21. Richard Norton-Taylor, *Guardian*, April 22, 1985.
22. Cook, 69.
23. Ibid., 73.
24. "Death of an English Rose," *World in Action*, Granada television, March 4, 1985.
25. Cook, 183.
26. Ibid., 120.
27. Neil Mackay, "The Hate Machine," *Sunday Herald*, July 2, 2002.
28. http://www.hildamurrell.org/home.htm.

6. Holy Blood, Holy Grail, Holy Shit

1. *Daily Telegraph*, October 3, 2004.
2. *Financial Times*, April 8, 2006.
3. *Observer*, February 26, 2006.
4. For this and what follows, see Michael Baigent, Richard Leigh, and Henry Lincoln, *The Holy Blood and the Holy Grail*, preface.
5. *Time Shift*, "The Da Vinci Code—The Greatest Story Ever Told," BBC4, May 2006.
6. Baigent, et al., *The Holy Blood and the Holy Grail*, preface.
7. Ibid., 12.
8. Ibid., 14.
9. Ibid., 379.
10. Michael Baigent, Richard Leigh, and Henry Lincoln, *The Messianic Legacy*, 311.
11. Henry Lincoln interviewed in *Da Vinci Code Decoded*, DVD, 2004.
12. Richard Barber, *The Holy Grail*, 17.
13. Paul Smith, http://priory-of-sion.com/psp/id174.html.
14. Ibid.
15. Smith, http://priory-of-sion.com/psp/id174.html.
16. Ibid.
17. Ibid.
18. Lincoln, interviewed in *Da Vinci Code Decoded*.
19. *The Real Da Vinci Code*, Channel 4, 2005.
20. Baigent, et al., *The Holy Blood and the Holy Grail*, 469.
21. Baigent, et al., *The Messianic Legacy*, 294.
22. Interview with Jonathan Milne, *New Zealand Herald*, March 12, 2006.
23. Smith, http://priory-of-sion/baigent.html.
24. *Spectator*, March 25, 2006.
25. Lincoln interviewed in *Da Vinci Code Decoded*.
26. Norman Cohn, *Warrant for Genocide*, 34–35.
27. Baigent, et al., *The Holy Blood and the Holy Grail*, 200.
28. Ibid., 199–203.
29. Immanuel Velikovsky, *Worlds in Collision*, viii.
30. Erich von Däniken, *In Search of Ancient Gods*, 197–98.
31. Erich von Däniken, *Chariots of the Gods*, 1.
32. http://www.grahamhancock.com/library/sats/default.htm.

33. Graham Hancock, interviewed on *Horizon*, November 4, 1999.
34. http://www.grahamhancock.com/supernatural.
35. http://luckymojo.com/hancocklecture.html.
36. Hugh J. Schonfield, *The Passover Plot*, 125.
37. Lynn Picknett and Clive Prince, *The Sion Revelation*, 17.
38. Dan Burnstein, *Secrets of the Code*, introduction.
39. Ibid.
40. Umberto Eco, *Foucault's Pendulum*, 261.
41. David Mamet, *Three Uses of the Knife*, 12.

7. A Few Clicks of a Mouse

1. *Washington Post*, September 6, 2006.
2. "Click Here for Conspiracy," *Vanity Fair*, August 2006.
3. Ibid.
4. Ibid.
5. The survey was conducted by telephone between July 6 and 24, 2006, at the Scripps Survey Research Center at the University of Ohio.
6. *The Alex Jones Show*, GCN radio network, March 2006.
7. *Wereldgasten*, VPRO television, December 3, 2006.
8. "Click Here for Conspiracy."
9. Marco Thompson cited on http://www.911myths.com/html.
10. Bill Strauss, et al., http://www.spectrum.ieec.org/mar06/3069.
11. http://www.serendipity.li/wot/operation_pearl.htm.
12. David Ray Griffin, *The New Pearl Harbor*, foreword.
13. Ibid., xxiii.
14. *Washington Post*, September 6, 2006.
15. "Debunking 9/11 Myths: Why Conspiracy Theories Can't Stand Up to the Facts," *Popular Mechanics*, March 2005.
16. Griffin, 27.
17. Ibid., 30–31.
18. Ibid.
19. http://www.aerospaceweb.org/question/conspiracy/q0265.shtml.
20. Griffin, 40.
21. http://www.aerospaceweb.org/question/conspiracy/q0274.shtml.
22. Ibid.
23. Griffin, 28.
24. *New Statesman*, September 11, 2006.
25. *Jim Fetzer Radio Show*, Republic Broadcasting Network, June 29, 2006.
26. *New York Times*, June 22, 2002.
27. http://news.bbc.co.uk/1/hi/world/europe/1907955.stm.
28. http://www.periodico26.cu/english/opinion/ivashov011806.html.
29. Ibid.
30. http://petras.lahaine.org/articulo.php?c=1&p=138/.
31. James Petras and Robin Eastman-Abaya, *The Caricatures in Middle East Politics*, http:/petras.lahaine.org/articulo.php?c=1&note=1&p=9.
32. http://www.rumormillnews.com/cgi-bin/archive.cgi?read=83815.

33. *Le Journal du Dimanche*, February 8, 2004.

34. *Ha'aretz*, January 19, 2006.

35. Ibid.

36. John Lichfield, *Independent on Sunday*, March 26, 2006.

37. http://www.amnistia.net/news/articles/voltaire/voltaire_552.html.

38. http://www.erichufschmid.net/wingTV/BollynPickeringwingTV.html.

39. http://www.erichufschmid.net/Hufschmid-Dylan-Korey-Jason.mp3.

40. *American Free Press*, April 10, 2005.

41. *Der Spiegel*, September 8, 2003.

42. James Hollander, *CounterPunch*, March 11, 2004.

43. *Guardian*, April 6, 2004.

44. *New Statesman*, September 11, 2006.

45. *Guardian*, June 27, 2006.

46. Griffin, 139.

47. Interview with Amy Goodman, *Democracy Now!* WBAI radio, May 26, 2004.

48. Griffin, 127.

49. David Hackett Fischer, *Historians' Fallacies*, 209–11.

50. David Ray Griffin, *The 9/11 Commission Report: Omissions and Distortions*, 189.

51. Noam Chomsky, e-mail, November 17, 2002.

8. Mr. Pooter Forms a Theory

1. Matthew Parris on the BBC *Today* program, June 14, 2002.

2. Peter Oborne, *Daily Mail*, February 16, 2007.

3. http://www.parliament.the-stationery-office.co.uk/pa/cm200607/cmhansrd/cm070115/text/70115w0018.html.

4. http://www.martinfrost.ws/htmlfiles/sept2006/uncovering.html.

5. http://beyondbelief.blogspot.com/.

6. Norman Baker, *The Strange Death of David Kelly*, 196.

7. Ibid., 192.

8. http://www.bahai-library.com/introductory/suicide.html.

9. Baker, 38.

10. Ibid., 36.

11. Ibid., 193.

12. Nadine Melhem, et al., "Familial Pathways to Early-Onset Suicidal Behavior," *American Journal of Psychiatry*, 164, September 2007, 1364–70.

13. Baker, 7.

14. Ibid.

15. Ibid., 197.

16. Ibid.

17. Ibid., 36.

18. Ibid., 38.

19. Ibid., 39.

20. Ibid., 37.

21. http://news.scotsman.com/huttoninquiry/Dr-Kellys-bitter-end.2445290.jp.

22. Baker, 14.

23. Ibid., 19.

24. Ibid., 21.

25. http://news.bbc.co.uk/1/hi/programs/conspiracy_files/6378681.stm.
26. Baker, 368.
27. http://news.bbc.co.uk/nolpda/ifs_news/hi/newsid_6269000 /6269157.stm.
28. *Channel 4 News*, March 9, 2004.
29. http://news.bbc.co.uk/1/hi/programs/conspiracy_files/6378681.stm.
30. Baker, 17.
31. Ibid., 21.
32. Ibid., 22.
33. Ibid., 19.
34. Ibid., 20.
35. Ibid.
36. Ibid.
37. Ibid., 58.
38. Ibid., 27.
39. Ibid., 41.
40. Ibid., 43.
41. Ibid., 46.
42. Ibid., 47.
43. Ibid., 53.
44. Ibid., 66.
45. Ibid., 52.
46. Ibid., 307.
47. Ibid., xiii.
48. Ibid.
49. A. Jay Cristol, *The Liberty Incident*, 2002.
50. According to its synopsis, the book *Who Killed Diana?* (cowritten with Derek McAdam) "casts doubt on the assumption that the driver was three times over the legal limit. It assembles the evidence that Diana and Dodi had become a threat to the British Establishment. It shows who might have intervened in the most brutal fashion, examining their motives and how an assassination could have been carried out."
51. Peter Hounam, *Operation Cyanide*, 3.
52. Baker, 96–97.
53. Ibid., 98.
54. Ibid., 110.
55. Ibid., 60.
56. Ibid., 50.
57. Ibid., 49.
58. Ibid., 302–3.
59. Ibid., 333.
60. Ibid., 345.
61. http://www.prisonplanet.com/022504shrimptontranscript.html.
62. http://news.bbc.co.uk/1/shared/spl/hi/programs/if/transcripts/ david_kelly.txt.
63. Baker, 348.
64. Ibid.
65. Melanie Phillips, "The 'Facts' About David Kelly's Death Just Don't Add Up. This Was Murder," *Daily Mail*, February 28, 2007.
66. Fritz Tobias, *The Reichstag Fire: Legend and Truth*, 16.

9. "I Want My Country Back!"

1. http://www.youtube.com/watch?v=9V1nmn2zRMc&feature=related.
2. www.publicpolicypolling.com.
3. AIM press release, August 4, 2009.
4. http://www.newsmax.com/ruddy/Obama_birth_certificate/2009/08/05/244380.html.
5. A good example of the Corsi defense can be found at http://www.youtube.com/watch?v=n8foOU6n9S4.
6. http://frontpagemag.com/readArticle.aspx?ARTID=7741.
7. http://www.wnd.com/news/article.asp?ARTICLE_ID=30762.
8. http://www.wnd.com/index.php?fa=PAGE.view&pageId=56626.
9. For a sympathetic but revealing portrait of Farah as editor of the *Union*, see Tom Bethell, "Fighting for the Union," *National Review,* September 9, 1991.
10. Ambrose Evans-Pritchard, *The Secret Life of Bill Clinton: The Unreported Stories* (Washington, DC: Regnery, 1997), xii.
11. Ibid.
12. Ibid., xiii–xiv.
13. Ibid., xiii.
14. Ibid.
15. David Brock, *Blinded by the Right: The Conscience of an Ex-Conservative* (New York: Crown, 2002), 204.
16. Ibid., 204–5.
17. Evans-Pritchard, *The Secret Life of Bill Clinton*, xv.
18. Gore Vidal, "The Meaning of Timothy McVeigh," *Vanity Fair*, September 2001.
19. Evans-Pritchard, *The Secret Life of Bill Clinton*, 5.
20. Ibid., 94.
21. Ibid., 268–69.
22. Ibid., 238.
23. Ibid., 243.
24. Ibid., 248.
25. Ibid., 251.
26. WND website, September 24, 1998. http://www.wnd.com/news/article.asp?ARTICLE_ID=14583.
27. Moldea's book, published in 1998, was *A Washington Tragedy: How the Death of Vincent Foster Ignited a Political Firestorm* (Washington, DC: Regnery, 1998).
28. Evans-Pritchard, *The Secret Life of Bill Clinton*, 226.
29. Christopher Ruddy, *The Strange Death of Vince Foster: An Investigation* (New York: Free Press, 1997), 249–50.
30. Moldea, *A Washington Tragedy*, 14.
31. "First Lady Launches Counterattack," *Washington Post*, January 28, 1998.
32. Joe Conason and Gene Lyons, *The Hunting of the President: The Ten-Year Campaign to Destroy Bill and Hillary Clinton* (London: Channel 4 Books, 2001), 371.
33. See the account in "Arkansas Project Led to Turmoil and Rift," *Washington Post*, May 2, 1999.
34. Lori Leibovich, "Why Vincent Foster Can't Rest in Peace, *Salon,* May 28, 1998.
35. Sidney Blumenthal, *The Clinton Wars* (London: Penguin, 2004), 72.
36. "When an Aide Dies Violently," *New York Times*, August 2, 1993.

37. "The 28th Piece," *New York Times, August 12, 1993.*
38. Gary Aldrich, *Unlimited Access: An FBI Agent Inside the Clinton White House* (Washington, DC: Regnery, 1996), 30, 93.
39. Evans-Pritchard, *The Secret Life of Bill Clinton*, 366.
40. Cass R. Sunstein, *Going to Extremes: How Like Minds Unite and Divide* (New York: Oxford University Press, 2009), 7.

Conclusion: Bedtime Story

1. *Guardian*, September 5, 2006.
2. Shane O'Sullivan, "Did the CIA Kill Bobby Kennedy?" *Guardian*, November 20, 2006.
3. Ibid.
4. Ibid.
5. http://www.maryferrell.org/wiki/index.php/Essay-The_BBCs_ Flawed_RFK_Story.
6. http://educationforum.ipbhost.com/index.php?showtopic=13105.
7. Mel Ayton, "Still Guilty After All These Years," http://www.washingtondecoded.com, May 11, 2008.
8. Private letter to author.
9. Jonathan Raban, "Running Scared," *Guardian*, July 21, 2004.
10. Stephen Eric Bronner, *A Rumor About the Jews*, 142.
11. Richard Hofstadter, *The Paranoid Style in American Politics and Other Essays*, 34.
12. Ibid., 31–32.
13. Derek Kaill, "Beyond 9/11," *New Humanist*, April 4, 2005.
14. *Guardian*, May 11, 2005.
15. *Guardian*, February 20, 2007.
16. Sam Smith, "America's Extremist Center," *Progressive Review*, July 1995.
17. *Real Time with Bill Maher*, HBO, October 21, 2006.
18. *New York Times*, August 21, 2006.
19. Letter from Farah Jasmine Griffin, *New York Times*, August 22, 2006.
20. Peter Knight, *Conspiracy Culture*, 3.
21. Mark Fenster, *Conspiracy Theories*, 67–74.
22. Jodi Dean, *Aliens in America: Conspiracy Cultures from Outerspace to Cyberspace*, cited by Frederick C. Crews, "The Mindsnatchers," *New York Review of Books*, June 25, 1998.
23. Damian Thompson, *Counter-Knowledge*, 10–11.
24. Ibid., 23.
25. Mark Fenster, interview with Chip Berlet for *New Internationalist* supplement on Judeophobia, September 2004.
26. Timothy Melley, "Agency Panic and the Culture of Conspiracy," in Peter Knight, ed., *Conspiracy Nation*, 73–74.
27. Robin Ramsay, *Conspiracy Theories*, 92.
28. Ibid., 85.
29. Ibid., 64.
30. Knight, 13.
31. Hofstadter, 3.
32. Ibid., 39.
33. Ibid., 4.
34. Elaine Showalter, *Hystories: Hysterical Epidemics and Modern Culture*, 4.

35. Ibid., 5.
36. Ibid., 10.
37. Knight, 7.
38. Showalter, 207.
39. Ibid., 6.
40. David Mamet, *Three Uses of the Knife*, 1.
41. Ibid., 7.
42. Lewis Wolpert, *Six Impossible Things Before Breakfast: The Evolutionary Origins of Belief*, 27.
43. Ibid., 29.
44. Ibid., 99.
45. Norman Cohn, *The Pursuit of the Millennium*, 309–10.
46. *Lobster*, June 29, 1995.
47. Stephen Grosz, conversations with the author.
48. Stephen E. Ambrose, "Writers on the Grassy Knoll," *New York Times Book Review*, February 2, 1992.

BIBLIOGRAPHY

Ahmed, Nafeez M. *The London Bombings: An Independent Inquiry.* London: Duckworth, 2006.

Aldrich, Gary. *Unlimited Access: An FBI Agent Inside the Clinton White House.* Washington, DC: Regnery, 1998.

Andrews, R. F. *The Truth About Trotsky.* London: Communist Party of Great Britain, 1934.

Baigent, Michael. *The Jesus Papers: Exposing the Greatest Cover-up in History.* London: Harper Element, 2006.

Baigent, Michael, Richard Leigh, and Henry Lincoln. *The Holy Blood and the Holy Grail.* London: Arrow, 1996.

Baigent, Michael, Richard Leigh, and Henry Lincoln. *The Messianic Legacy.* New York: Dell, 1986.

Baker, Norman. *The Strange Death of David Kelly.* London: Methuen, 2007.

Baldwin, Neil. *Henry Ford and the Jews: The Mass Production of Hate.* New York: Public Affairs, 2001.

Barber, Richard. *The Holy Grail, The History of a Legend.* London: Penguin, 2005.

Ben-Itto, Hadassa. *The Lie That Wouldn't Die: The Protocols of the Elders of Zion.* London, and Portland, OR: Valentine Mitchell, 2005.

Bennett, Richard M. *Conspiracy, Plots, Lies and Cover-ups.* London: Virgin Books, 2003.

Bernstein, Carl, and Bob Woodward. *All the President's Men.* London: Quartet, 1974.

Bernstein, Hermann. *The Truth About the Protocols of Zion.* New York: KTAV, 1971.

Blumenthal, Sidney. *The Clinton Wars.* London: Penguin Books, 2003.

Blumenthal, Sid, and Harvey Yazijian, eds. *Government by Gunplay.* New York: Signet, 1976.

Bollas, Christopher. *Hysteria.* London: Routledge, 2000.

Bower, Tom. *Maxwell, the Outsider.* London: Viking, 1992.

Brent, Jonathan, and Vladimir P. Naumov. *Stalin's Last Crime: The Plot Against the Jewish Doctors, 1948–1953.* London: Harper Perennial, 2004.

Bresler, Fenton. *Who Killed John Lennon?* New York: St. Martin's Press, 1989.

Brock, David. *Blinded by the Right: The Conscience of an Ex-Conservative.* New York: Crown, 2002.

Brogan, Hugh. *The Penguin History of the United States of America.* London: Penguin, 1985.

Bronner, Stephen Eric. *A Rumor About the Jews: Reflections on Anti-Semitism and the Protocols of the Learned Elders of Zion.* New York: St. Martin's Press, 2000.

Brown, Madeleine Duncan. *Texas in the Morning: The Love Story of Madeleine Brown and President Lyndon Baines Johnson.* Baltimore: Conservatory Press, 1997.

Bryson, Bill. *Shakespeare.* London: Harper Perennial, 2008.

Budiansky, Stephen. *Battle of Wits: The Complete Story of Code-Breaking in World War II.* New York: Free Press, 2000.

Bugliosi, Vincent. *Reclaiming History: The Assassination of President John F. Kennedy.* New York: W. W. Norton, 2007.

Burman, Edward. *The Templars, Knights of God.* Bath, England: Crucible, 1986.

Burnstein, Dan, ed. *Secrets of the Code: The Unauthorised Guide to the Mysteries Behind the Da Vinci Code.* London: Weidenfeld & Nicolson, 2004.

Butler, Smedley D. *War Is a Racket.* Originally published 1935; repr. Los Angeles: Feral House, 2003.

Campbell, J. R. *Soviet Policy and Its Critics.* London: Left Book Club, 1939.

Carto, Willis A., ed. *Populism vs. Plutocracy: the Universal Struggle.* Washington, DC: Liberty Lobby, 1996.

Churchwell, Sarah. *The Many Lives of Marilyn Monroe.* London: Granta, 2004.

Cohen, David. *Diana, Death of a Goddess.* London: Century, 2004.

Cohn, Norman. *The Pursuit of the Millennium.* London: Paladin, 1970.

Cohn, Norman. *Warrant for Genocide.* London: Serif, 1996.

Collard, Dudley. *Soviet Justice and the Trial of Radek and Others.* London: Left Book Club, 1937.

Conason, Joe, and Gene Lyons. *The Hunting of the President: The Ten-Year Campaign to Destroy Bill and Hillary Clinton.* London: Channel 4 Books, 2001.

Cook, Judith. *Unlawful Killing: The Murder of Hilda Murrell.* London: Bloomsbury, 1994.

Corsi, Jerome R. *The Obama Nation: Leftist Politics and the Cult of Personality.* New York: Threshold, 2008.

Cristol, A. Jay. *The Liberty Incident: The 1967 Israeli Attack on the U.S. Navy Spy Ship.* Washington, DC: Brassey's, 2002.

Dallin, Alexander, and F. I. Firsov, eds. *Dmitrov and Stalin, Letters from the Soviet Archives, 1934–1943.* New Haven: Yale University Press, 2000.

Davies, Joseph E. *Mission to Moscow.* New York: Simon & Schuster, 1941.

Deutscher, Isaac. *The Prophet Armed: Trotsky 1879–1921.* London: Verso, 2003.

Deutscher, Isaac. *The Prophet Outcast: Trotsky 1929–1940.* London: Verso, 2003.

Deutscher, Isaac. *The Prophet Unarmed: Trotsky 1921–1929.* London: Verso, 2003.

Di Eugenio, James, and Lisa Pease. *The Assassinations.* Port Townsend, WA: Feral House, 2003.

Dixon, Norman. *On the Psychology of Military Incompetence.* London: Futura, 1983.

Duranty, Walter. *I Write As I Please.* New York: Simon & Schuster, 1935.

Eco, Umberto. *Foucault's Pendulum.* London: Vintage, 2001.

Evans-Pritchard, Ambrose. *The Secret Life of Bill Clinton: The Unreported Stories.* Washington, DC: Regnery, 1997.

Feuchtwanger, Lion. *Moscow 1937.* London: Left Book Club, 1937.

Fischer, Louis, Harrison Smith, and Robert Haas. *Soviet Journey.* Harrison Smith and Robert Haas, 1935.

Ford, Henry, Sr. *The International Jew: The World's Foremost Problem.* Originally published in *The Dearborn Independent,* 1920–1921, repr. in four vols., Oregon: CPA, n.d.

Foster, William Z. *Questions and Answers on the Piatakov-Radek Trial.* New York: Workers Library, 1937.

Freud, Sigmund, and Joseph Breuer. *Studies in Hysteria*, trans. Nicola Luckhurst. London: Penguin Modern Classics, 2004.

Fried, Albert. *McCarthyism: The Great American Red Scare—a Documentary History*. Oxford: Oxford University Press, 1997.

Furet, François. *The Passing of an Illusion: The Idea of Communism in the Twentieth Century*. Chicago: University of Chicago Press, 1999.

Gardner, Laurence. *Bloodline of the Holy Grail: The Hidden Lineage of Jesus Revealed*. London: Harper Element, 1996.

Getty, J. Arch, and Oleg V. Naumov. *The Road to Terror, Stalin and the Self-Destruction of the Bolsheviks 1932–1939*. New Haven: Yale University Press, 1999.

Gide, André. *Return from the USSR*. New York: Alfred A. Knopf, 1937.

Gregory, Martyn. *Diana: The Last Days*. London: Virgin Books, 2007.

Gregory, Martyn. *The Diana Conspiracy Exposed*. UK: Olmstead, 1999.

Griffin, David R. *Debunking 9/11 Debunking*. UK: Arris, 2007.

Griffin, David R. *The New Pearl Harbor: Disturbing Questions About the Bush Administration and 9/11*. UK: Arris, 2004.

Griffin, David R. *The 9/11 Commission Report: Omissions and Distortions*. UK: Arris, 2005.

Griffin, David R., and Peter D. Scott, eds. *9/11 and American Empire: Intellectuals Speak Out*. UK: Arris, 2007.

Henshall, Ian, and Rowland Morgan. *9.11 Revealed: Challenging the Facts Behind the War on Terror*. London: Robinson, 2005.

Hersh, Seymour. *The Dark Side of Camelot*. London: HarperCollins, 1998.

Hitler, Adolf. *Mein Kampf*. Boston: Houghton Mifflin, 1971.

Hofstadter, Richard. *The Paranoid Style in American Politics and Other Essays*. New York: Alfred A. Knopf, 1965.

Hounam, Peter. *Operation Cyanide: Why the Bombing of the USS* Liberty *Nearly Caused World War III*. London: Vision, 2003.

Hounam, Peter, and Derek McAdam. *Who Killed Diana?* London: Vision, 1998.

Hughes-Wilson, Colonel John. *Military Intelligence Blunders*. London: Robinson, 1999.

Kick, Russ, ed. *Abuse Your Illusions: The Disinformation Guide to Media Mirages and Establishment Lies*. New York: Disinformation Company, 2003.

Kick, Russ, ed. *Everything You Know Is Wrong: The Disinformation Guide to Secrets and Lies*. New York: Disinformation Company, 2002.

Knight, Christopher, and Robert Lomas. *The Hiram Key: Pharoahs, Freemasons and the Discovery of the Secret Scrolls of Jesus*. London: Arrow, 1997.

Knight, Peter. *Conspiracy Culture: From Kennedy to the X-Files*. London: Routledge, 2000.

Knight, Peter, ed. *Conspiracy Nation, the Politics of Paranoia in Post-War America*. New York: New York University Press, 2002.

Koch, Stephen. *Stalin, Willi Münzenberg and the Seduction of the Intellectuals*. London: HarperCollins, 1996.

Kotkin, Stephen. *Magnetic Mountain: Stalinism as a Civilization*. Berkeley: University of California Press, 1995.

Littlepage, John D., and Demaree Bess. *In Search of Soviet Gold*. London: Harrap, 1939.

Mailer, Norman. *The Time of Our Time*. London: Abacus, 1998.

Mamet, David. *Three Uses of the Knife: On the Nature and Purpose of Drama*. London: Methuen, 2002.

McConnachie, James, and Robin Tudge. *The Rough Guide to Conspiracy Theories*. London: Rough Guides, 2005.

McNamara, Robert S., Thomas J. Biersteker, Robert K. Brigham, Herbert Schandler, and James Blight. *Argument Without End, in Search of Answers to the Vietnam Tragedy.* New York: Public Affairs, 1999.

Meyssan, Thierry. *9/11 The Big Lie.* New York: Carnot, 2002.

Moldea, Dan E. *The Killing of Robert F. Kennedy.* New York: W. W. Norton, 1997.

Moldea, Dan E. *A Washington Tragedy: How the Death of Vincent Foster Ignited a Political Firestorm.* Washington, DC: Regnery, 1998.

Morgan, Rowland. *Flight 93 Revealed: What Really Happened on the 9/11 "Let's Roll" Flight?* London: Constable and Robinson, 2006.

Oshinsky, David M. *A Conspiracy So Immense: The World of Joe McCarthy.* New York: Free Press, 1983.

Picknett, Lynn, and Clive Prince. *The Sion Revelation: Inside the Shadowy World of Europe's Secret Masters.* London: Time Warner, 2006.

Picknett, Lynn, and Clive Prince. *The Templar Revelation: Secret Guardians of the True Identity of Christ.* London: Touchstone, 1998.

Pipes, Daniel. *Conspiracy: How the Paranoid Style Flourishes and Where It Comes From.* New York: Free Press, 1997.

Pipes, Daniel. *The Hidden Hand: Middle East Fears of Conspiracy.* New York: St. Martin's Griffin, 1998.

Posner, Gerald. *Case Closed: Lee Harvey Oswald and the Assassination of JFK.* New York: Anchor, 2003.

Posner, Gerald. *Killing the Dream: James Earl Ray and the Assassination of Martin Luther King, Jr.* London: Little, Brown, 1998.

Posner, Gerald. *Why America Slept: The Failure to Prevent 9/11.* London: Random House, 2003.

Prange, Gordon W. *At Dawn We Slept: The Untold Story of Pearl Harbor.* New York: McGraw-Hill, 1981.

The Protocols of the Learned Elders of Zion. Trans. Victor Marsden. Originally published 1934; repr. Escondido, CA: Book Tree, 1999.

Ramsay, Robin. *Conspiracy Theories.* UK: Pocket Essentials, 2000.

Ramsay, Robin. *Who Shot JFK?* UK: Pocket Essentials, 2002.

Ranelagh, John. *The Agency: The Rise and Decline of the CIA.* London: Sceptre, 1987.

Report of the Court Proceedings in the Case of the Anti-Soviet Bloc of Rights and Trotskyites. Verbatim report, People's Commissariat of Justice of the USSR, Moscow, 1938.

Report of the Court Proceedings in the Case of the Anti-Soviet Trotskyite Center. Verbatim report, People's Commissariat of Justice of the USSR, Moscow, 1937.

Report of the Court Proceedings in the Case of the Trotskyite-Zinovievite Terrorist Center. Verbatim report, People's Commissariat of Justice of the USSR, Moscow, 1936.

Ruddy, Christopher. *The Strange Death of Vincent Foster: An Investigation.* New York: The Free Press, 1997.

Sayers, Michael, and Albert E. Kahn. *The Great Conspiracy Against Russia.* New York: Boni and Gaer, 1946.

Schonfield, Dr. Hugh J. *The Passover Plot.* London: Bantam, 1967.

Segel, Binjamin W. *A Lie and a Libel: The History of the Protocols of the Elders of Zion,* trans. and ed. Richard S. Levy. Lincoln, NE: Bison, 1995.

Service, Robert. *Stalin: A Biography.* London: Macmillan, 2004.

Showalter, Elaine *Hystories: Hysterical Epidemics and Modern Culture.* London: Picador, 1997.

Siegelbaum, Lewis, and Andrei Sokolov. *Stalinism as a Way of Life: A Narrative in Documents.* New Haven: Yale University Press, 2000.

Slessor, Tim. *Lying in State: How Whitehall Denies, Dissembles and Deceives.* London: Aurum, 2004.

Smith, Matthew. *Victim: The Secret Tapes of Marilyn Monroe.* London: Arrow, 2004.

Southwell, David, and Sean Twist. *Conspiracy Files.* New York: Gramercy Books, 2004.

Spence, Donald P. *Narrative Truth and Historical Truth: Meaning and Interpretation in Psychoanalysis.* New York: W. W. Norton, 1982.

Stinnett, Robert B. *Day of Deceit, the Truth About FDR and Pearl Harbor.* New York: Touchstone, 2000.

Stoyanov, Yuri. *The Hidden Tradition in Europe: The Secret History of Medieval Christian Heresy.* London: Arkana, 1994.

Strasser, Steven, ed. *The 9/11 Investigations.* New York: Public Affairs, 2004.

Sturdivan, Larry M. *The JFK Myths: A Scientific Investigation of the Kennedy Assassination.* St. Paul: Paragon House, 2005.

Summer, Anthony. *The Kennedy Conspiracy.* London: Time Warner, 1998.

Sunstein, Cass R. *Going to Extremes: How Like Minds Unite and Divide.* New York: Oxford University Press, 2009.

Tanenhaus, Sam. *Whittaker Chambers: A Biography.* New York: Modern Library, 1998.

Thomas, Gordon. *Gideon's Spies: Mossad's Secret Warriors.* London: Pan Books, 2000.

Thomas, Gordon, and Martin Dillon. *The Assassination of Robert Maxwell, Israel's Superspy.* London: Robson, 2002.

Thomas, Keith. *Religion and the Decline of Magic.* London: Penguin, 1973.

Thompson, Damian. *Counter-Knowledge: How We Surrendered to Conspiracy Theories, Quack Medicine, Bogus Science and Fake History.* London: Atlantic, 2008.

Tobias, Fritz. *The Reichstag Fire: Legend and Truth.* London: Secker & Warburg, 1963.

Toland, John. *Infamy: Pearl Harbor and Its Aftermath.* New York: Doubleday, 1982.

Vidal, Gore. *Dreaming War, Blood for Oil and the Cheney-Bush Junta.* UK: Clairview, 2003.

Vidal, Gore. *The Last Empire.* London: Abacus, 2002.

Vidal, Gore. *Perpetual War for Perpetual Peace.* UK: Nation Books, 2002.

Volkogonov, Dmitri. *Stalin: Triumph and Tragedy.* London: Weidenfeld & Nicolson, 1995.

Volkogonov, Dmitri. *Trotsky: The Eternal Revolutionary.* New York: Free Press, 1996.

Waldron, Lamar, and Thom Hartmann. *Ultimate Sacrifice.* London: Constable, 2005.

Webb, Sidney and Beatrice. *Soviet Communism: A New Civilisation.* New York: Charles Scribner's Sons, 1936.

Weinstein, Allen. *Perjury: The Hiss-Chambers Case.* New York: Alfred A. Knopf, 1978.

Wolfe, Donald H. *The Assassination of Marilyn Monroe.* London: Time Warner, 1999.

Wolpert, Lewis. *Six Impossible Things Before Breakfast: The Evolutionary Origins of Belief.* London: Faber & Faber, 2006.

DVDs

Da Vinci Code Uncoded. Disinformation Company, 2004.

Unlocking Da Vinci's Code: Mystery or Conspiracy? HC Ltd, 2004.

The Real Da Vinci Code. Channel 4, 2006.

Confronting the Evidence: A Call to Reopen the 9/11 Investigation. Distributed free, 2005.

INDEX

Page numbers followed by "n" indicate notes.

David Aaronovitch is an award-winning journalist who has worked in radio, television, and for the newspapers in the United Kingdom since the early 1980s. His first book, *Paddling to Jerusalem*, won the Madoc prize for travel literature in 2001. A recipient of the Orwell Prize for political journalism, Aaronovitch writes a regular column for *The Times* (UK). He lives in North London with his wife and three daughters.

David Aaronovitch is an award-winning journalist who has worked in radio, television, and for the newspapers in the United Kingdom since the early 1980s. His first book, *Paddling to Jerusalem,* won the Madoc prize for travel literature in 2001. A recipient of the Orwell Prize for political journalism, Aaronovitch writes a regular column for *The Times* (UK). He lives in North London with his wife and three daughters.